Age Discrimination

Age discrimination is a highly topical issue in all industrialised societies, against a background of concerns about shortening working lives and ageing populations in the future. Based upon detailed research, and adopting an interdisciplinary approach, this unique study traces the history of the age discrimination debate in Britain and the USA since the 1930s. It critically analyses the concepts of ageism in social relations and age discrimination in employment. Case-studies on generational equity and health care rationing by age are followed by an analysis of the British government's initiatives against age discrimination in employment. The book then traces in detail the history of the debate on health status and old age, addressing the question of whether working capacity has improved sufficiently to justify calls to delay retirement and extend working lives. It concludes with a detailed examination of the origins and subsequent working of the USA's 1967 Age Discrimination in Employment Act.

JOHN MACNICOL is Visiting Professor in Social Policy at the London School of Economics. He has published extensively on current social policy and the history of social policy, including *The Politics of Retirement in Britain, 1878–1948* (Cambridge University Press, 1998).

Age Discrimination

An Historical and Contemporary Analysis

John Macnicol

CAMBRIDGE
UNIVERSITY PRESS

CAMBRIDGE UNIVERSITY PRESS
Cambridge, New York, Melbourne, Madrid, Cape Town, Singapore, São Paulo

CAMBRIDGE UNIVERSITY PRESS
The Edinburgh Building, Cambridge CB2 2RU, UK

Published in the United States of America by Cambridge University Press, New York

www.cambridge.org
Information on this title: www.cambridge.org/9780521847773

First published 2006

Printed in the United Kingdom at the University Press, Cambridge

A catalogue record for this book is available from the British Library

ISBN-13 978-0-521-84777-3 hardback
ISBN-10 0-521-84777-X hardback
ISBN-13 978-0-521-61260-9 paperback
ISBN-10 0-521-61260-8 paperback

Contents

Figures

Tables

Acknowledgements

This book began life as a research project funded by a Leverhulme Fellowship. My first and considerable debt of gratitude is therefore to the Leverhulme Trust. I am most grateful to the two referees for the original application, Hilary Land and Alan Deacon, who have always been so generous with their advice and encouragement.

The research would have been impossible without the generosity of numerous academic libraries, and I would particularly like to thank the following: the British Library of Political and Economic Science; the Wellcome Medical Library, London; Age Concern England; New York Public Library; the main library of the University of Southern California, and that of the Andrus Gerontology Center; the American Association for Retired Persons, Washington, DC; the Equal Employment Opportunity Commission, Washington, DC; the National Archives, Kew (formerly the Public Record Office). Transcripts of Crown Copyright material in the National Archives appear by permission of the Controller of Her Majesty's Stationery Office.

Most of the research on the American age discrimination debate was conducted during a two-month research visit to the USA, where I enjoyed a warm welcome and much intellectual stimulation. My special thanks go to many people at the Andrus Gerontology Center, University of Southern California: Vern Bengtson (who acted as my host, and whose kindness, erudition and good humour were much appreciated); Eileen Crimmins (who generously allowed me to attend her graduate classes in ageing, demography and health care, and effortlessly demonstrated to me what really good teaching is like); Linda Hall (who looked after my everyday needs); and others who gave of their time so generously. At the Andrus Center, I was also privileged to be part of a lively and happy academic community, and to meet an impressive cadre of graduate students (among whom I should specially like to thank Joe Angelelli and Maria Schmeekle). Two weeks of my US visit were spent in Washington DC, at the American Association for Retired Persons. There, my main helper was Sara Rix, who has been a good friend and whose erudite advice was much appreciated.

My thanks go to other AARP staff, including Clare Hushbeck, Helen Dennis, Sally Dunaway and Michelle Pollak.

I am grateful to my previous institution (Royal Holloway, University of London) for supporting this research. At my new home (the Department of Social Policy, London School of Economics) I should like to thank those who advised me on difficult problems (in some cases, reading extracts of this book) or helped in other ways: Howard Glennerster, Julian Le Grand, David Piachaud, John Hills, Tania Burchart, Anne West and John Wilkes. I am most grateful to two London School of Economics students, Hester Barsham and Amir Akhrif, for their invaluable help in checking the bibliography.

During the research for this book, I was privileged to spend periods of time as a visiting researcher at the Institute for the Study of Ageing and Later Life, University of Linkoping, Norrkoping, Sweden, enjoying a most stimulating intellectual atmosphere. My thanks go to Elisabet Cedersund, Britt-Marie Oberg, Lars Andersson, Anna Olaison, Bengt Sandin and others.

A large number of people discussed aspects of this book with me, and/or provided invaluable support when the going got tough. Chris Phillipson has been a source of excellent advice, and always so generous with his time. I also owe a great debt of gratitude to Andy Achenbaum. Among the many others, my particular thanks go to Andrew Blaikie, Howard Davies, Keith Frost, Emily Grundy, Kim Harris, Harry Hendrick, Chris Holden, George Lawson, Martin Lyon Levine, John Mattausch, Roger Middleton, Grace Rose, Marc Rosenblum, Adrian Sinfield, David Smith, John Stewart, Jim Tomlinson, Jonathan Wadsworth and John Welshman (who provided me with some very helpful research assistance for a part of chapter 5). Aspects of this work were presented at various seminars and conferences, and I am grateful to the participants for their comments.

Needless to say, these friends and advisers are completely absolved from responsibility for any inaccuracies or speculative ideas that are inevitable if one is trying to pull aside the dead weight of a prevailing political culture and apply rigorous analysis to a very complex topic. Originally intended to be much shorter, this book expanded as the complexities of age discrimination became increasingly apparent. Hopefully readers will find these complexities interesting in the pages that follow.

JOHN MACNICOL

J.Macnicol@lse.ac.uk

Part I

Ageism and Age Discrimination

1   Analysing ageism and age discrimination

Introduction: the importance of age

At every stage in our lives, we are confronted by the inevitability of our own ageing. As we progress through the 'journey of life',[1] we are acutely conscious of the ageing process as it affects our bodies, our attitudes, the environment we create for ourselves and our interactions with other people of different ages.[2] In personal relationships, we tend to choose friends and partners from those proximate in age – most 'lonely hearts' advertisements stipulate age – and the fact is that most people are still fascinated or even horrified by intimate relationships that span wide age-gaps: Joan Collins's marriage in early 2002, to a man thirty-three years her junior, was newsworthy precisely because it broke such unwritten, but powerful, rules.[3] Most of us are intensely aware of the precise social demarcations based upon age, and feel uncomfortable if we stray into an age-inappropriate social setting (a nightclub for the twenty-somethings on the one hand, a summer evening game of bowls on the other). Our everyday social judgements are frequently age-based, even if we consciously deny it: for example, most of us, on meeting a new person, will try to guess their age and will make assumptions about them as a result.

Explaining the collective behaviour and social characteristics of a population sub-group by reference to its average age is still relatively uncommon, perhaps because social scientists are wary of age stereotyping, demographic determinism and gerontophobia: the idea that ageing societies are inevitably societies in decline – with diminishing stocks of collective energy, enterprise and innovation – has a long and undistinguished pedigree, going back at least to the 1930s.[4] A basic truism in gerontology is that

---

[1] Thomas R. Cole, *The Journey of Life: a Cultural History of Aging in America* (1992).
[2] There is, of course, a debate in gerontology over how far the 'inner self' remains young as the body ages.
[3] It also contravened the gender double standards, in that the Michael Douglas/Catherine Zeta Jones marriage aroused less comment.
[4] John Macnicol, *The Politics of Retirement in Britain 1878–1948* (1998), pp. 259–64.

age per se is meaningless: it is always mediated through social processes and cultural attitudes.

Yet the average age of a population *does* in part determine its social characteristics. One effective counter to the apocalyptic, pessimistic jeremiads associated with population ageing is to point out that a youthful population carries considerable social costs: youth correlates with high levels of crime, single parenthood, unemployment, suicides, homicides, drug abuse, traumatic deaths of all kinds, motor vehicle accidents, high health and education expenditure, and so on.[5] Elizabethan England suffered considerable problems of vagrancy, crime and social disorder because it had a relatively youthful age structure. Likewise, it has been suggested that the social problems of northern urban ghettos in the United States of America are exacerbated by their relatively large proportions of young people, caused by high birth rates and continued in-migration. Differences of income between age-groups in the USA are greater than those between ethnic groups, and the average age of ethnic groups in part explains their varying educational, occupational and economic levels.[6] As William Julius Wilson has observed, 'the higher the median age of a group, the greater its representation in higher income categories and professional positions'.[7] In most Western societies, recorded crime shows a pronounced age and gender bias, with young males around the age of twenty having high rates of offending; the rate of offending then falls rapidly, until by the age of thirty British men are nearly four times less likely to commit a crime.[8] Some speculative work has also been conducted on the possible link between the age of political leaders and the style, and effectiveness, of their leadership.[9] Clearly, the analysis of society 'according to age' is still in its infancy, but it could be an interesting field of study.

Age distinctions, age stratifications, age judgements and 'age-appropriate behaviours' are subtly woven into our patterns of thinking, as a way of making sense of the world. When we are children, for example, we are always reminded of age divisions and their importance in the hierarchies of power that surround us. We long to be older, and frequently feel ourselves to be the 'wrong' age. Likewise, as adults we judge our own achievements by reference to some notion of 'normal' stages of life. Commonly-used

---

[5] For an interesting exploration, see Fred C. Pampel and John B. Williamson, 'Age Patterns of Suicide and Homicide Mortality Rates in High-Income Nations', *Social Forces*, vol. 80, no. 1, Sept. 2001, pp. 251–82.

[6] Thomas Sowell, *Markets and Minorities* (1981), pp. 10–13.

[7] William Julius Wilson, *The Truly Disadvantaged: the Inner City, the Underclass and Public Policy* (1987), pp. 36–9.

[8] Office for National Statistics, *Social Focus on Men* (2001), p. 78.

[9] Angus McIntyre (ed.), *Aging and Political Leadership* (1988).

phrases, such as 'act your age', 'at my time of life', 'when I was young', 'I'm too old for that' or 'twenty things to do before you are thirty', testify to this. It is a regrettable but undeniable fact that most people like to be told that they look younger than they really are, and the goal of staying 'forever youthful' has become something of a fetish in modern societies: the popularity of Botox, Viagra, facelifts, anti-ageing potions and other modern elixirs of youth testify to that. In the last few years, social gerontologists have moved away from the idea of the 'lifecycle' (a series of discrete stages), preferring the term 'lifecourse' (denoting ageing as a continuous process). The latter is held to be less ageist, in that it does not impose rigid norms and expectations, and hence prejudicial stereotypes, via discrete categories like 'childhood', 'youth', 'adolescence', 'middle age', and so on.[10] Yet it is possible to argue that the notion of a lifecycle did not grow up as a repressive concept: it may instead be part of the process of convenient labelling, whereby we construct markers of time and view the ageing of ourselves and others as a series of recognisable 'stages'. Interestingly, Thomas Cole has criticised the way that, since the 1960s, the attack upon ageism has become something of an 'enlightened prejudice', resting upon assumptions that have been insufficiently explored. Gently defending the use of 'stages' of life, he argues that 'Stereotypes are a universal means of coping with anxieties created by our inability to control the world ... Stereotypes are embedded in larger archetypes, ideals, or myths that societies use to infuse experience with shared meaning and coherence.'[11]

Social gerontologists often distinguish between different meanings of age – for example, chronological, social and physiological age. Of these, social age is the most intriguing, since it refers to socially ascribed age norms, age-appropriate behaviours and age as a social construct.[12] The idea of social age has been very well explored by the distinguished social gerontologist Bernice Neugarten, who has confronted some of gerontology's central dilemmas. Neugarten argues that, in all societies, age 'is one of the bases for the ascription of status and one of the underlying dimensions by which social interaction is regulated': we all construct norms and expectations, based upon 'social clocks', regarding such landmarks as the 'right' time to marry, have children, start working, retire, and so on, which are manifested in everyday linguistic expression. (Of course, the time

---

[10] For a succinct exploration, see John Vincent, *Inequality and Old Age* (1995), esp. ch. 3.
[11] Cole, *Journey*, pp. 228, 230.
[12] For a useful exploration, see Jay Ginn and Sara Arber, '"Only Connect": Gender Relations and Ageing', in Sara Arber and Jay Ginn (eds.), *Connecting Gender and Ageing. A Sociological Approach* (1995).

shown by such 'clocks' will vary generation by generation: for example, average ages of marriage have risen in the Western world over the past fifty years.) In all societies, observes Neugarten, rights, rewards and responsibilities are differentially distributed by age, and she perceptively concludes that 'all societies rationalise the passage of life time, divide life time into socially relevant units, and thus transform biological time into social time'.[13]

Yet age is also a powerful discriminator in modern societies. Along with class, gender and race, age is one of the four key components of structured inequality, and no serious social analysis can be adequate unless it takes all four components into account. Of these, age is arguably the most virulent, since it is the least acknowledged and most likely to be accepted as 'normal' or 'inevitable'. It is significant that, in Britain, legislation to prevent discrimination on grounds of gender, race and disability is well established, but it has taken a recent European Union Council Directive (November 2000) to force the British government to act in the case of age. However, it may be that age discrimination is the most complex and difficult of all the discriminations that affect modern societies, and therefore is very problematic to define, quantify and counter. These difficulties will be explored in the pages that follow.

Defining ageism and age discrimination

As an analytical starting-point, it is useful to make a distinction between ageism (in social relations and attitudes) and age discrimination (in employment) – although the two are often used interchangeably. Like all discriminations, ageism can essentially be thought of as the application of assumed age-based group characteristics to an individual, regardless of that individual's actual personal characteristics. By contrast, age discrimination in employment refers to the use of crude 'age proxies' in personnel decisions relating to hiring, firing, promotion, re-training and, most notably, mandatory retirement. In practice, of course, ageism and age discrimination may be closely intertwined: for example, the negative prejudices of employers (deriving, say, from a fear of their own ageing and decrepitude) may profoundly influence their personnel policies towards their older employees.

---

[13] Bernice L. Neugarten, Joan W. Moore and John C. Lowe, 'Age Norms, Age Constraints, and Adult Socialisation', and Bernice L. Neugarten, 'Age Distinctions and Their Social Functions', in Dail A. Neugarten (ed.), *The Meanings of Age: Selected Papers of Bernice L. Neugarten* (1996), pp. 24–5, 59–60.

According to the *Oxford English Dictionary*, the original meaning of the verb 'to discriminate' was a neutral one – 'to divide, separate, distinguish' and 'to make or constitute a difference in or between; to distinguish, differentiate'. The idea of negative discrimination ('to discriminate against' or 'to make an adverse distinction with regard to') appears to have entered popular usage towards the end of the nineteenth century, especially with regard to race.[14] By the mid twentieth century, discrimination was being defined as the 'unequal treatment of equals'.[15]

There has been a debate over age discrimination in employment since at least the 1920s and 1930s in both Britain and the USA; but the concept of ageism in social relations and attitudes has more recent origins. The actual term 'ageism' seems to have been first coined by the eminent American gerontologist Robert Butler in 1969, while he was chair of the District of Columbia Advisory Committee on Aging and was involved in setting up public housing for older people. First in a report in the *Washington Post* of 7 March,[16] and then in an article in *The Gerontologist* later in 1969, Butler described the irrational hostility displayed by a group of middle-aged, middle-class white citizens against a proposal to build special housing for older, poor black people: it was the 'complex interweaving of class, color and age discrimination' that he found so striking, and he acknowledged that ageism could operate against any age-group.[17] Developing his classic definition, Butler concluded that ageism was 'a process of systematic stereotyping and discrimination against people because they are old, just as racism and sexism accomplish this for skin color and gender. Older people are characterised as senile, rigid in thought and manner, and old-fashioned in morality and skills.' He argued that ageism derives partly from ignorance – stereotyping and myths surrounding old age are explicable 'by a lack of knowledge and insufficient contact with a wide variety of older people' – and partly from 'a deep and profound dread of growing old'. But he maintained that ageism by the young and middle-aged against the old often serves a rational purpose, in that it favours the former and excludes the latter in the sharing-out of societal resources. Ageism thus manifests itself in

stereotypes and myths, outright disdain and dislike, or simply subtle avoidance of contact; discriminatory practices in housing, employment and services of all kinds;

---

[14] 'Discriminate' and 'Discrimination', *Oxford English Dictionary* (1989 edn), pp. 757–8.
[15] Frank H. Hankins, 'Social Discrimination', in Edwin R. A. Seligman and Alvin Johnson (eds.), *Encyclopaedia of the Social Sciences, Vol. 14* (1934), p. 131.
[16] 'Ageism', *Oxford English Dictionary* (1989 edn), p. 247.
[17] Robert N. Butler, 'Age-Ism: Another Form of Bigotry', *The Gerontologist*, vol. 9, no. 4, pt. 1, Winter 1969, pp. 243–6.

epithets, cartoons and jokes. At times ageism becomes an expedient method by which society promotes viewpoints about the aged in order to relieve itself from the responsibility toward them, and at other times ageism serves a highly personal objective, protecting younger (usually middle-aged) individuals – often at high emotional cost – from thinking about things they fear (aging, illness and death).[18]

Such closure by the non-old against the old, it is argued, must ultimately be irrational since we will all become old one day – if lucky enough. Our ageism thus over-rides our long-term rational self-interest,[19] and can be seen as a kind of 'self-hatred' or 'cognitive dissonance'[20] whereby, puzzlingly, we view the old as 'somehow different from our present and future selves and therefore not subject to the same desires, concerns or fears'.[21] As Catherine Itzin observes: 'Ageism is a system in which nobody can be seen to benefit because everyone is, or once was, a child, and everyone (who survives) will eventually be an old person. And yet the system – in which adults have rights and privileges which are denied to young people and old people – continues to the detriment of everyone.'[22]

Ageism usually involves the ascription of negative qualities to one particular age-group. As Thomas McGowan puts it, it constitutes 'a social psychological process by which personal attributes are ignored and individuals are labeled according to negative stereotypes based on group affiliation. In American society elders are stereotyped as rigid, physically unattractive, senile, unproductive, sickly, cranky, impoverished and sexless.'[23] When directed against the old, it can be disguised by patronising, false praise via 'a paternalistic breed of prejudice' whereby old people are 'pitied but not respected'.[24] Thus Erdman Palmore warns us against lapsing into 'pseudopositive' attitudes towards older people, characterised by insincere admiration: describing an old person as 'beautiful', for example,

[18] Robert N. Butler, 'Ageism', in George L. Maddox (ed.), *The Encyclopedia of Aging* (1995 edn), p. 35. See also, Robert N. Butler, *Why Survive? Being Old in America* (1975).

[19] Andrew Blaikie and John Macnicol, 'Ageing and Social Policy: a Twentieth Century Dilemma', in Anthony M. Warnes (ed.), *Human Ageing and Later Life: Multidisciplinary Perspectives* (1989), p. 79; Todd D. Nelson, 'Preface', in Nelson (ed.), *Ageism. Stereotyping and Prejudice Against Older Persons* (2002), p. x.

[20] Molly Andrews, 'The Seductiveness of Agelessness', *Ageing and Society*, vol. 19, pt. 3, May 1999, pp. 302–3.

[21] John Hendricks and C. Davis Hendricks, 'Ageism and Common Stereotypes', in Vida Carver and Penny Liddiard (eds.), *An Ageing Population. A Reader and Sourcebook* (1978), p. 60.

[22] Catherine Itzin, 'Ageism Awareness Training: a Model for Group Work', in Chris Phillipson, Miriam Bernard and Patricia Strang (eds.), *Dependency and Interdependency in Old Age: Theoretical Perspectives and Policy Alternatives* (1986), pp. 114–15.

[23] Thomas G. McGowan, 'Ageism and Discrimination', in James E. Birren (ed.), *Encyclopedia of Gerontology. Age, Aging, and the Aged, Vol. I* (1996), p. 71.

[24] Amy J.C. Cuddy and Susan T. Fiske, 'Doddering But Dear: Process, Content, and Function in Stereotyping of Older Persons', in Nelson, *Ageism*, p. 17.

can only be on the basis of a different standard of beauty from that applied to the young.[25]

Ageism is embedded in patterns of thinking (thus frequently manifesting itself in covert and subtle ways) and in unspoken assumptions, enduring myths, stereotypes, popular imagery and iconography, and societal acceptance of age-based decline as inevitable. This is 'implicit ageism' – feelings towards old people 'that exist and operate without conscious awareness, intention or control'.[26] It operates on both an interpersonal (micro) level (through internalised attitudes), and an institutional (macro) level (in legal, medical, welfare, educational, political and other systems).[27] The latter form of discrimination, it is argued, cannot be easily demonstrated, since it is often accompanied by strenuous denials of any intent to discriminate. Thus Eric Midwinter sees ageism as endemic in all social relations: there is, he argues, a bias against older people as consumers in fashion and design, in marketing strategies (which constantly perpetuate 'negative' images of ageing), in civic life (via age barriers to jury service, for example) and in politics and the media.[28] Likewise, Bill Bytheway has offered an entertaining and stimulating analysis of the virulence of negative images of ageing: 'humorous' ageist birthday cards; sexual innuendos of impotence or, paradoxically, excessive libido; the 'double standard of ageing' or 'double jeopardy' by gender; and so on.[29]

The origins of ageism

Where does ageism originate? A variety of answers have been offered, placed somewhere on a spectrum. At one end are psychological explanations: ageism derives from deep-rooted, irrational, subconscious fears of our own ageing, and our apprehension at the prospect of impending physical and mental decay. It has been suggested that, as death is increasingly postponed to later ages in modern societies, so old people have become ever more visible reminders of our own mortality: they represent 'the face of the future'.[30] Hence Butler declares that 'Age-ism reflects a deep seated uneasiness on the part of the young and middle-aged – a

---

[25] Erdman B. Palmore, *Ageism. Negative and Positive* (1990), pp. 34–5.

[26] Becca R. Levy and Mahzarin R. Banaji, 'Implicit Ageism', in Nelson, *Ageism*, p. 51.

[27] Itzin, 'Ageism Awareness', p. 114; McGowan, 'Ageism and Discrimination', p. 71.

[28] Eric Midwinter, *Citizenship: From Ageism to Participation* (1992).

[29] Bill Bytheway, *Ageism* (1995).

[30] Jeff Greenberg, Jeff Schimel and Andy Martens, 'Ageism: Denying the Face of the Future', in Nelson, *Ageism*, pp. 29–30.

personal revulsion to and distaste for growing old, disease and disability; and fear of powerlessness, "uselessness", and death.'[31]

Such a definition raises the question of whether these deep-rooted fears can be eradicated by reason alone. Steve Scrutton doubts this: 'Ageism surrounds us, but it passes largely unnoticed and unchallenged. Moreover, just like racism and sexism, it is so engrained within the structure of social life that it is unlikely to be challenged effectively by rational argument or appeals to the more philanthropic side of human nature.'[32] Others, however, believe that education, persuasion (perhaps involving 'ageism awareness' training)[33] and even resistance can achieve much. As Alex Comfort comments,

Ageism is the notion that people cease to be people, cease to be the same people or become people of a distinct and inferior kind, by virtue of having lived a specified number of years ... Like racism, which it resembles, ageism is based upon fear, folklore and the hang-ups of a few unlovable people who propagate these. Like racism, it needs to be met by information, contradiction and, when necessary, confrontation. And the people who are being victimised have to stand up for themselves in order to put it down.[34]

In similar vein is Robert Butler's call to arms:

It is increasingly within our power to intervene directly in the processes of aging, with prevention, treatment and rehabilitation. It is also within our power to intervene in social, cultural, economic and personal environments, influencing individual lives as well as those of older persons *en masse*. If, however, we fail to alter present negative imagery, stereotypes, myths and distortions concerning aging and the aged in society, our ability to exercise these new possibilities will remain sharply curtailed. Fortunately, we can treat the disease I call 'ageism' – those negative attitudes and practices that lead to discrimination against the aged.[35]

At the other end of the spectrum are broadly economic explanations: modern capitalist economies have marginalised older people into enforced retirement and idleness, involving a lowering of economic and social status.[36] From this has arisen the blanket assumption that the average male worker becomes unproductive around the age of 65. Such age

---

[31] Butler, 'Age-Ism', p. 243.
[32] Steve Scrutton, 'Ageism: the Foundations of Age Discrimination', in Evelyn McEwen (ed.), *Age: the Unrecognised Discrimination* (1990), p. 25.
[33] For an interesting account, see Itzin, 'Ageism Awareness', pp. 114–26.
[34] Alex Comfort, *A Good Age* (1976), p. 35.
[35] Robert N. Butler, 'Dispelling Ageism: the Cross-Cutting Intervention', *Annals of the American Academy of Political and Social Science*, vol. 503, May 1989, p. 143.
[36] See, for example: William Graebner, *A History of Retirement. The Meaning and Function of an American Institution, 1885–1978* (1980); Judith C. Hushbeck, *Old and Obsolete. Age Discrimination and the American Worker, 1860–1920* (1989).

proxies can be viewed as discriminatory, in that they lump together a wide range of abilities. This, it is argued, was always manifestly unfair, in that heterogeneity in health status, cognitive ability and working capacity increases as one moves up the age range; and it becomes even more unfair as each cohort of old people are – presumably – healthier than their predecessors. However, age proxies can also be seen as cheap, convenient and quick methods of decision-making, based upon judgements about working capacity which are fundamentally correct in the aggregate, even if their use may involve individual cases of injustice. Much depends upon the broad accuracy of the age proxy.[37] What appears to be age discrimination in employment may therefore be essentially rational decision-making in matters of personnel management. Ageism thus has complex origins – as Andrew Blaikie observes, 'the reasons behind discrimination are frequently economic, but the capacity to maintain oppression is primarily psychological'[38] – and manifests itself in diverse, often contradictory ways.

The ageism debate

Many who are involved with social gerontology argue that ageism is rampant in modern Western societies. Certainly, there is powerful anecdotal and impressionistic evidence of this. Old people are subject to the kind of casual, gratuitous ageism that is deeply woven into our culture and is manifest in linguistic expression – contemptuous epithets like 'wrinkly', 'old codger', 'old git', 'grannie', 'old biddy', 'mutton dressed as lamb', and so on. Even 'pensioner' is often used as a term of abuse in Britain: as Eric Midwinter drily comments, it has that dire sense 'of withdrawal, of taking a back seat, of being the pit-pony turned out to pasture for a brief, valedictory spell'.[39] With some honourable exceptions, many newspapers persist in putting a person's age in brackets after their name, as if this offered an instant 'explanation' of their behaviour. The perniciousness of latent ageism has been exposed by researchers who, disguising themselves as an old person, have encountered hostility, prejudice, contempt and patronising sympathy.[40] In short, we live in a culture that worships youth and beauty; so many prevailing images depict old age as a time of decrepitude and social marginality. 'Youthism' dominates.

---

[37] Neugarten, 'Age Distinctions', p. 66.
[38] Andrew Blaikie, *Ageing and Popular Culture* (1999), p. 17.
[39] Eric Midwinter, *The British Gas Report on Attitudes to Ageing 1991* (1991), p. 12.
[40] For example, Sheila Green, 'A Two-Faced Society', *Nursing Times*, vol. 87, no. 33, 14 Aug. 1991, pp. 26–9.

In human terms, age discrimination appears all too evident to those who have suffered it. The unemployed 'fifty-somethings', spending their days at home completing job applications in an exercise they know will be futile, can testify eloquently and bitterly to the difficulties faced by older job-seekers. Whether or not their plight arises principally from age discrimination – an issue to be explored later in this book – there is no doubt that they *feel* substantially discriminated against on grounds of age. Despite the efforts of old age activists to construct models of 'positive' or 'successful' ageing, replicated at populist level by brave slogans like 'fifty is the new forty', 'you are only as old as you feel' or the delightfully whimsical 'age doesn't matter unless you're a cheese', most older citizens are painfully aware of the subtle cruelties of ageism. In the last ten years in Britain, the press has been full of stories of workers thrown on the employment scrap-heap at a time of life when they feel themselves to be in their prime. One example will suffice:

I am fifty, a graduate with a postgraduate qualification. I've worked all my life and earned a reasonable salary, but I was made redundant in 1993 and now find myself in dire poverty and debt. The only reason I can think of is ageism. I've had periods of signing on and doing voluntary work and part-time teaching. I have been told by my local Employment Service that my job search strategy and CV are 'exemplary'. But it's been five years now and I feel powerless and angry, and as if I am in a downward spiral. This is manifesting itself in increasing dependence on prescription drugs and alcohol, loss of confidence, a three-stone increase in weight and poor self-image. The thought of carrying on like this until I'm sixty is humiliating, depressing and frightening. I am also terrified at the prospect of having no pension apart from a state pension.[41]

Pressure groups such as Age Concern or Help the Aged (via its Third Age Employment Network) are inundated with complaints from those who believe themselves to be victims of ageism at work, and during its 'Age Discrimination Week' in early February 1998 Age Concern even set up a special hotline for such complaints. Other areas of everyday life are also affected: after the age of 65, obtaining a mortgage or financial credit can be more difficult, and travel or private medical insurance premiums are often higher.[42] In 1999, Age Concern found that one in twenty people aged 65+ had been refused treatment by the National Health Service (NHS), despite such treatment being a right.[43]

'Age is an increasingly unreliable sign of someone's needs and ambitions', declares a recent government publication, going on to add that 'the blurring of the various stages in our lifecycle means that older people are as

---

[41] 'Private Lives', *Guardian*, 23 Nov. 1998.
[42] 'Job to Combat an Age Old Problem', *Guardian*, 31 Jan. 1998.
[43] Age Concern, *Turning Your Back on Us. Older People and the NHS* (1999), p. 7.

varied as any other age-group in society'.[44] Although there is undeniably some physical and mental decline with the ageing process, the extent of this decline varies greatly between individuals; variations in performance and ability between age-groups are less than those within age-groups. In the final analysis, the perception of decline depends upon contextual factors, both economic and social. For example, if older people expect to perform less well in intelligence tests, because they have internalised prevailing societal attitudes, then they will tend to perform less well – a 'self-fulfilling prophecy' effect. Likewise, the cognitive decline of a resident in an old people's home may be greatly exacerbated by the unstimulating environment within which they feel themselves trapped. It has always been the case that heterogeneity in health status, physical mobility, artistic creativity, cognitive ability and employment skills increases with age: a random sample of twenty-year-olds will all be able to run 200 metres, probably within quite a limited time; but a random sample of seventy-year-olds will encompass a wide spectrum of abilities, ranging from those who can run that distance in an impressive time, to others who are unable to run it at all. One example cited by the clinician James F. Fries is that of a middle-aged runner who completes a marathon in three-and-a-half hours (in the ninety-ninth percentile for that age-group); not until the age of 73 would that time set an age-based world record. Fries argues that, between the ages of 30 and 70, the age-related decrement in maximal performance is only 1 per cent per annum, and concludes that 'Variation between healthy persons of the same age is far greater than the variation due to age; age is a relatively unimportant variable, and training in marathon running is clearly more important.'[45] Improving rates of survival will make this heterogeneity even more pronounced in tomorrow's older population. If working lives continue to shrink and chronological lives lengthen, the retired population will span thirty-five or more years and will become increasingly diverse.[46] The use of crude age proxies to measure individual ability will become even more unjust and economically irrational. In the future, the issue of 'biological age versus chronological age' will become ever more pressing.

Those who campaign against age discrimination argue that many role models of 'positive' or 'successful' ageing exist. There have been innumerable famous figures who have achieved eminence in old age, or have continued functioning past notional 'retirement age' and well into later

---

[44] Office for National Statistics, *Social Focus on Older People* (1999), p. 7.

[45] James F. Fries, 'Aging, Natural Death and the Compression of Morbidity', *New England Journal of Medicine*, vol. 303, no. 3, 17 July 1980, p. 134. Obviously, Fries's comment here does not apply to very extreme physical exertion, like boxing or soccer.

[46] For a useful discussion, see Frank Laczko and Chris Phillipson, *Changing Work and Retirement. Social Policy and the Older Worker* (1991).

life, with no diminution of their creative powers – 'heroes of ageing', as Mike Featherstone has called them[47] (though there are probably more 'heroines of ageing'). Indeed, some have only found their true avocation in old age. Michelangelo was still drawing designs for St Peter's in Rome in his eighty-ninth year; Benjamin Franklin helped draft the Declaration of Independence at the age of 70; Thomas Edison was patenting inventions at age 81; Winston Churchill became Prime Minister for the first time, experiencing his own personal 'finest hour', at the age of 65; Gladstone became Prime Minister for the fourth time at the age of 82; Daniel Defoe's best work (including *Robinson Crusoe*) was written from his late fifties onwards; George Bernard Shaw produced his first play when he was aged 36, and his last when in his eighties; Pablo Casals was still playing the cello at 90, as was the jazz trumpeter Doc Cheatham; Titian was painting in his ninety-ninth year, when he was cut short by the plague; the astronaut John Glenn orbited the earth aged 77; the Frenchwoman Jeanne Calment aroused much public comment by living until the age of 122. Recently, a women aged 60 had a baby by embryo implant, and Mario Curnis reached the summit of Mount Everest at the age of 66.[48] The list is endless, and is not confined to the exalted: there are 'local heroes and heroines of ageing' all around us in our everyday lives. In 1999 the 87-year-old Jenny Wood Allen ran the London marathon for her thirteenth time: when she started long-distance running at the age of 71 (having been relatively inactive for thirty years), her friends predicted an early death.[49] In January 2002, John Marr, aged 62, was selected to play in goal for Scotland in the World Lacrosse Championships. If survival rates continue to improve, these heroic figures will become more common. Rather than being rare exemplars of what might be possible, they will be the norm. They represent the joyous half of the enduring dualism in images of ageing: activity, achievement and admiration on the one hand; decay, decrepitude and denial on the other.[50]

'Optimistic' projections of future trends in health status in old age suggest that disability-free, high-quality life can be extended up to the age of eighty-five and beyond. The 'use-it-or-lose-it' school of thought argues, with heady optimism, that much of the seemingly inevitable physical and mental decline associated with ageing can be altered by human

---

[47] Mike Featherstone, 'Post-Bodies, Aging and Virtual Reality', in Mike Featherstone and Andrew Wernick (eds.), *Images of Aging: Cultural Representations of Later Life* (1995), p. 227.

[48] For one discussion of achievement in old age – a favourite topic among gerontologists – see Lucille B. Bearon, 'Famous Aged', in Erdman B. Palmore (ed.), *Handbook on the Aged in the United States* (1984), pp. 17–30.

[49] 'Staying Power', *Guardian*, 13 April 1999.   [50] Cole, *Journey*, p. 230.

agency. Hence three medical demographers assert that 'There is good reason to argue ... that chronological age in itself, although once a useful proxy indicator of characteristics and functioning, is becoming an increasingly imperfect measure that can trap us in dysfunctional metaphors and stereotypes'.[51] Likewise, from two sociologists of ageing comes the statement that 'It is no longer possible to make adequate generalisations about the ageing process that are grounded on biological assumptions about the ages of life.'[52]

The aim of many gerontologists is thus to achieve the 'democratisation of old age' by adding years to life and, more importantly, life to years. Molecular biologists even believe that a human lifespan of several hundred years (with little physical ageing) is possible, if only cell deterioration can be arrested. Research in industrial gerontology and psychology has shown that older people *can* adapt to new technology in the workplace, that continual improvements have taken place in their health status, that technological innovations have made work 'lighter' and less physically demanding, and that a pronounced 'cohort effect' is steadily improving the education and skills levels of successive waves of retirees. All of these factors make the denial of work to older people, enforced by a fixed age of retirement, even more morally objectionable than ever. Older people should be able to lead active, independent and economically productive lives well past what used to be considered 'normal' retirement ages – in Britain, 65 for men and 60 for women. These retirement ages were always arbitrary, dating back to the nineteenth century, and they are looking increasingly anachronistic, so the argument goes. Instead, they should be abolished, and employers should obey 'good practice' in relation to age diversity, implemented via a package of policies: the removal of age limits in job advertisements; recruitment on grounds of ability, not age; performance appraisal (or 'individualised testing') for job competence, conducted at regular intervals, to assess 'work fitness'; strategies to target older workers; a clear 'age neutral' equal opportunities policy; effective re-training programmes for jobless older workers; preretirement preparation; and, most of all, the abolition of mandatory retirement, and its substitution by 'flexible' or 'phased' retirement that would give older workers more choice.[53]

[51] Richard M. Suzman, Kenneth G. Manton and David P. Willis, 'Introducing the Oldest Old', in Richard M. Suzman, David P. Willis and Kenneth G. Manton (eds.), *The Oldest Old* (1992), p. 12.

[52] Mike Featherstone and Mike Hepworth, 'Ageing, the Lifecourse and the Sociology of Embodiment', in Graham Scambler and Paul Higgs (eds.), *Modernity, Medicine and Health: Medical Sociology Towards 2000* (1998), p. 161.

[53] See, for example, J. Kodz, B. Kersley and P. Bates, *The Fifties Revival* (1999), pp. x–xi.

The social justice case

The 'social justice' case against ageism can be traced back to Enlightenment ideas about natural rights. A 'rights-based' view would contend that it is contrary to notions of natural justice to apply certain assumed group characteristics to individuals solely on the grounds of their age. As Palmore puts it, 'The democratic ideal is that each person should be judged on the basis of individual merit rather than on the basis of group characteristics such as race, sex and age.'[54] The persuasive argument is that the twentieth century has seen the gradual, if imperfect, equalisation of rights by gender and race, yet age equality has still to be addressed.[55]

Indeed, some might argue that, historically, old people's rights have diminished. A recurring theme in social gerontology is that the transition to modernity has brought with it a degradation in the status of old age: whereas in preindustrial societies, old people were venerated for their scarcity, judgement, authority and experience, it is argued, now they are economically, socially and culturally marginalised. For example, the spread of information systems – from the written word to electronic data storage – is said to have robbed older people of their prestigious position as living repositories of knowledge and wisdom. Over the past century-and-a-half, the 'bureaucratisation of society' has brought about the increasing application of age classifications and stratifications.[56] Arguably, 'age consciousness' has become heightened and, as a result, age discrimination has increased.[57] Although this view has been much criticised, in that it mythologises a past 'golden age of senescence', it does nevertheless underline the paradox, noted by Butler, that ageism appears to have intensified as old people have become an increasing proportion of the population in Western societies.[58] Since the early 1990s, there has been a crescendo of protest against age discrimination in Britain. A growing number of individuals and organisations – from right across the political spectrum – have 'discovered' that, as a leading employers' pressure group declares, 'ageism is deeply entrenched in society and the workplace'.[59] Another theme to be explored in this book is why this 'discovery' has taken place only recently.

---

[54] Palmore, *Ageism*, p. 7.
[55] John Macnicol, 'Analysing Age Discrimination', in Britt-Marie Oberg, Anna-Lisa Narvanen, Elisabet Nasman and Erik Olsson (eds.), *Changing Worlds and the Ageing Subject. Dimensions in the Study of Ageing and Later Life* (2004), p. 23.
[56] Carole Haber, *Beyond Sixty-Five: the Dilemma of Old Age in America's Past* (1983), p. 127.
[57] McGowan, 'Ageism and Discrimination', pp. 71–5.
[58] Butler, 'Dispelling Ageism', p. 143.
[59] Employers Forum on Age, *Why Is Age Important?* (2002); www.efa.org.uk.

The social justice case has been articulated in both Britain and the USA by old age pressure groups (notably, Age Concern and the American Association of Retired Persons) who have for years fought a long-running battle against ageism in social attitudes and inter-personal relationships, as well as age discrimination in employment. Central to their view is the contention that age discrimination amounts to a fundamental denial of the right to work in the case of a substantial proportion of citizens. Campaigners like Eric Midwinter have long suggested remedial action via legislation, a code of practice covering areas such as the banning of age specifications in job advertisements, alternatives to crude age-based criteria in the assessment of job competence (for example, by objective testing), campaigns to re-educate public opinion, and adequate represen-tation of older people on public bodies (possibly via targets).[60] Other organisations, like the Third Age Employment Network, assist unem-ployed older people to obtain jobs. In academic gerontology, the campaign against ageism has also been central to the 'critical gerontology' that has emerged since the 1970s.[61]

Anti-ageism activists hold up as an ideal the possibility of an 'age neutral' or 'age irrelevant' society – much like a 'gender blind' or 'race blind' one – in which individuals would be judged by ability and content of character rather than by chronological age. This view also implies that a dynamic, modern society with liberal values embodying respect for the rights of the individual can only flourish if artificial restrictions and prejudices – based upon irrational, 'false' stereotypes – are removed. However, there is also a more troubling impetus, which will be discussed in future pages. The transition to modernity may have been accompanied by an increasingly robust notion of human rights, but it has also seen the growth of competitive individualism. The emergence of a new 'disorgan-ised' or 'postindustrial' capitalism in the last thirty years, based upon 'flexible accumulation', has created a need for workers who are selected, using highly refined testing procedures, on the basis of ability rather than by crude age proxies (which may not correlate with ability). The current nostrums about 'active' ageing in part reflect this new economic agenda.

Difficulties of proof

There are a number of serious difficulties inherent in both ageism and age discrimination, which make remedial action difficult. The first of these has

---

[60] Midwinter, *Citizenship*, esp. pp. 25–8.
[61] See, for example, Meredith Minkler and Carroll Estes (eds.), *Critical Gerontology. Perspectives from Political and Moral Economy* (1999).

been alluded to already: age distinctions are so firmly embedded in society, and so intertwined with deeply ingrained conceptions of 'natural' age stratifications, career patterns, promotion criteria and expectations of a slow 'winding down' in employment when in late middle age, that age discrimination is notoriously difficult to identify precisely, detect, and hence 'prove'. This is particularly true in the case of age discrimination at the hiring stage (probably the most common form), since job applicants are not privy to secret personnel decisions.

Other than in a few occupations – those which depend upon extreme physical ability, like sport, or upon concepts of youthful beauty, like modelling, or are exceptionally high-stress, like some Stock Market trading – age gradations are inevitably part of seniority systems in firms and organisations. Increasing age and experience tend to be rewarded by promotion and higher salaries: employees gradually filter up the ladder of seniority. Most of the distribution of rewards is thus *in favour* of older employees – until, it is argued, they become too expensive to employ, or are perceived to be, in the aggregate, too old to continue in work, or need to be retired in order to remove blockages to promotion and free up space for new employees. Conversely, those who fail to be promoted as they grow older may feel discriminated against on grounds of age, whereas they may simply be less job-competent or ambitious. A further difficulty is that of the 'cohort effect': each generation is better educated and (presumably) healthier than the one that precedes it. Hence the problems of older workers may be primarily due to their lack of current, up-to-date employment skills (notably the ability to operate new technology) relative to the demands of new jobs – a 'skills mismatch'.[62] Again, there may be a 'spatial mismatch' (new jobs are in geographical areas or labour market sectors which unemployed older people tend not to occupy), or a 'gender mismatch' (older unemployed men are judged unsuitable for new feminised jobs). The age profile of a firm is likely to be attributable to factors other than discrimination per se: for example, newly established enterprises tend to have youthful age structures. The balance of cultural and economic barriers is subtle. If age discrimination were the major explanation, then older women would have experienced it also; yet their economic activity rates have risen. We might therefore ask – somewhat impishly – whether the 'problem' is really one of sex discrimination.

How widespread is age discrimination in employment? Answering this question is highly problematic for, as two US authorities comment,

---

[62] Richard Disney, 'Why Have Older Men Stopped Working?', in Paul Gregg and Jonathan Wadsworth (eds.), *The State of Working Britain* (1999), pp. 72–3.

'Anecdotal evidence that older workers experience discrimination because of their age is easy to find ... However, there is little empirical research documenting the prevalence or impact of age discrimination in the labor market.'[63] As a recent British government publication also emphasises, age discrimination in employment 'is a complex issue', for which 'there is no simple solution'. Even now, 'we do not have a clear picture of how widespread the problem is'.[64] In a House of Commons debate of 6 February 1998, David Winnick MP declared that 'many people experience discrimination on the ground of age alone',[65] and in Parliamentary debates there has been no shortage of impressionistic, anecdotal evidence. Opinion surveys in Britain have substantiated this, but have offered very different estimates, depending on the kind of questions asked, the methodological rigour of the research, the sample selection, and so on. A survey of 1,140 personnel managers in 1992 found that nearly 80 per cent considered age discrimination to be a problem, and 'there was a strong desire for some form of government action, either a voluntary code or new legislation'.[66] Another by Labour Research in the mid-1990s found that over 40 per cent of job advertisements specifically excluded those aged in their forties,[67] and in 1995 the then Minister of State at the Department of Education and Employment (DfEE), Ann Widdecombe, stated that roughly 40 per cent of employers openly admitted practising some form of age discrimination.[68] A Eurobarometer survey in the early 1990s found that 82.4 per cent of British citizens surveyed considered that older workers were discriminated against in recruitment, and 77.7 per cent were discriminated against in promotion. Interestingly, this survey also showed little public support for the view that older people should give up work to make way for younger people.[69] Age Concern's late-1990s finding was that 25 per cent of individuals had encountered age discrimination in the workplace (half of them because they were too young).[70] Other surveys have revealed 70 to 80 per cent of respondents believing that age discrimination exists, or attesting that

---

[63] Richard W. Johnson and David Neumark, 'Age Discrimination, Job Separations, and Employment Status of Older Workers. Evidence from Self-Reports', *Journal of Human Resources*, vol. XXXII, no. 4, Fall 1997, pp. 779–80.

[64] Department for Education and Employment, *Action on Age: Report of the Consultation on Age Discrimination in Employment* (1998), pp. 2, 6, 12.

[65] *H of C Deb.*, 6s, vol. 305, 6 Feb. 1998, col. 1405.

[66] Peter Warr and Janet Pennington, 'Views About Age Discrimination and Older Workers', in Institute of Personnel Management, *Age and Employment. Policies, Attitudes and Practices* (1993), p. 77.

[67] *H of C Deb.*, 6s, vol. 271, 9 Feb. 1996, col. 557.

[68] *H of C Deb.*, 6s, vol. 260, 23 May 1995, col. 816.

[69] Commission of the European Communities, *Age and Attitudes. Main Results from a Eurobarometer Survey* (1993), pp. 22, 26.

[70] Age Concern, *Age Discrimination. Make It a Thing of the Past* (1998), p. 5.

they have had personal experience of it.[71] However, one by the Chartered Institute of Personnel and Development, published in 2001, found that only 12 per cent of those surveyed who were in paid work stated that they had been discouraged from applying for a job in the previous year because the recruitment advertisement stipulated either an age limit or an age range.[72] The same body published a further survey in 2003, in which 40 per cent of respondents of all ages reported that they had felt discriminated against at work; 35 per cent of these felt discriminated against on grounds of age. Therefore, only 14 per cent felt that they had experienced age discrimination in the workplace.[73] An even lower incidence was revealed by the government's Family and Working Lives Survey, conducted in 1994–5 for the Department for Education and Employment (DfEE): only some 5 per cent of those aged between 45 and 69 believed that they had ever been discriminated against on grounds of age when making job applications. However, the hazards of interpreting such opinion surveys were revealed by the fact that a far higher proportion believed that age discrimination was widespread: half of those aged 50–69 agreed strongly with the statement 'even if an older person studies to get qualifications, employers will usually choose a younger person'.[74] A major problem with all such surveys is that many ordinary citizens – understandably unversed in the complexities of long-run labour market change – may fall into the trap of assuming that the problems of older workers amount to clear evidence of discrimination.

It is instructive to examine briefly the experience of the USA, where many research projects have been conducted – with considerable methodological rigour – into the effect of age discrimination and mandatory retirement on older workers' employment prospects. Most verdicts downplay the role of age discrimination per se, relative to other factors – such as lack of firm-specific skills, declining labour market demand, spatial mismatch, and so forth.[75] Methodologically, it is very difficult to separate out discrimination from these contextual factors. However, Johnson and Neumark, having controlled for them, found that self-reported age discrimination in employment (related to a current employer) had affected

[71] '139 MPs Oppose Blair Stand Against Ageism Law', *Guardian*, 3 Feb. 1998.

[72] Chartered Institute of Personnel and Development, *Age Discrimination at Work* (2001), p. 11.

[73] Chartered Institute of Personnel and Development, *Age, Pensions and Retirement* (2003).

[74] Office for National Statistics, *Social Focus on Older People*, pp. 31, 34.

[75] See, for example, David Shapiro and Steven H. Sandell, 'The Reduced Pay of Older Job Losers: Age Discrimination and Other Explanations', in Stephen H. Sandell (ed.), *The Problem Isn't Age. Work and Older Americans* (1987), esp. pp. 43–9; Sandell, 'The Labor Force by the Year 2000 and Employment Policy for Older Workers', in Robert Morris and Scott A. Bass (eds.), *Retirement Reconsidered. Economic and Social Roles for Older People* (1988), pp. 107–15.

only 3 per cent of a sample of workers between 1966 and 1980.[76] Likewise, mandatory retirement tends to be viewed as a relatively insignificant causal factor. Two contemporary calculations suggest that, in the late 1960s and early 1970s, only about 8–10 per cent of the American workforce were affected by mandatory retirement provisions that had forced them to retire unwillingly at a set age; of these, many were not physically capable of continuing in work, reducing the proportion who were work-fit but unwilling retirees to a mere 5–7 per cent.[77] Reinforcing this is Herbert Parnes's 1988 estimate that compulsory retirement had probably accounted for only 7 per cent of labour force exits in the previous two decades, and that therefore its complete elimination in the USA would probably make little difference.[78]

Obtaining convincing proof is particularly problematic where the discrimination is 'statistical', 'institutional' or 'indirect' (probably the most common type).[79] Direct age discrimination is openly stated, and obvious to all (such as age limits in job advertisements). Indirect discrimination is that which is apparently neutral and therefore not openly admitted, or not necessarily age-specific, but which has an adverse impact upon older people.[80] In practice, distinguishing between direct and indirect discrimination is extremely difficult; the US experience tells us that it would give rise to much legal controversy. In the case of indirect discrimination, outcome matters more than intent: a 'facially neutral' policy can have an adverse impact on a particular group, even if no intent to discriminate exists. Evidence thus tends to be circumstantial: for example, the absence of a lift in a building may be primarily an economy measure, but it will discriminate against disabled people. One problem is that age-based niche marketing can come very close to indirect discrimination: for example, the interior decor and background music in a pub is often precisely designed to attract a particular age-group. In a case of sex or race discrimination, 'statistical' discrimination could be proved if a firm had never hired a woman or a member of an ethnic minority; but this might not be applicable in an age discrimination case. Throughout history, older workers have tended to be concentrated in long-established, declining industries with relatively labour-intensive modes of production; these industries tend to

[76] Johnson and Neumark, 'Age Discrimination', pp. 780–811.
[77] Martin Lyon Levine, *Age Discrimination and the Mandatory Retirement Controversy* (1988), pp. 27–8.
[78] Herbert S. Parnes, 'The Retirement Decision', in Michael E. Borus, Herbert S. Parnes, Steven H. Sandell and Bert Seidman (eds.), *The Older Worker* (1988), pp. 133, 142.
[79] Elizabeth Drury, *Age Discrimination Against Older Workers in the European Community* (1993), p. 13.
[80] See, for example, European Union, *Council Directive 2000/78/EC of 27 November 2000*, article 2, clause 2 (a) and (b).

modernise by dispensing with older workers and replacing them by labour-saving technology. By contrast, new industries have much more 'youthful' age profiles. The average age of a workforce is thus the result of many factors other than discrimination – raising the question of whether a truly 'age balanced' workforce can ever be achieved.

Empirical surveys have thus thrown up somewhat contradictory verdicts on the extent of age discrimination in employment. We cannot therefore be sure of its 'true' extent, which may be greater, or smaller, than what is revealed by surveys. Of course, even if it is a less-than-accurate explanatory term, 'age discrimination' may still be a useful catch-all, heuristic device. But the lesson is that an attack on age discrimination, beneficial though it may be in other areas of life, will not be enough to ameliorate what two recent commentators have called 'the late-career vulnerability of older employees'.[81]

A final difficulty is that rigorous performance appraisal for job competence (replacing mandatory retirement) could be subtly designed to discriminate against older employees (although if an analysis of such testing proved that older employees were more likely to be dismissed, adverse impact would be demonstrated). Unscrupulous employers might use such testing to get rid of 'troublesome' employees. Again, 'hard' legislation, with tough penalties, might only serve to drive discriminatory practices deeper, into the realm of whispered conversations and shared assumptions between senior managers, and make it even more difficult to detect. Personnel officers would become even more careful about what they said, or committed to print. Legislation may reveal the true extent of latent discrimination, or it may make people too 'discrimination conscious', even seeing it when it is not there. The USA has had legislation prohibiting age discrimination in employment since 1967, yet public opinion surveys conducted there in 1971 and 1981 both found that eight out of ten Americans believed that 'most employers discriminate against older people and make it difficult for them to find work'.[82] Unsurprisingly, age discrimination litigation has become a legal minefield in the USA, with employers becoming increasingly adept at avoiding charges. The 'smoking gun' of proof can be extremely difficult to detect.

Public interest defences

In any age discrimination legislation, important exceptions, or defences, have to be written in. One of these is the 'public interest' or 'public safety'

---

[81] Samuel Issacharoff and Erica Worth Harris, 'Is Age Discrimination Really Age Discrimination?: the ADEA's Unnatural Solution', *New York University Law Review*, vol. 72, no. 4, Oct. 1997, p. 782.

[82] Palmore, *Ageism*, p. 27.

defence. We want policemen on the beat to be athletic enough to chase after criminals, especially young male criminals; this means either compulsory retirement (or re-deployment) after the age of fifty, or stringent annual tests of fitness and speed. Most airline passengers would probably prefer pilots to be compulsorily retired at a fixed age, such as 60; yet extrapolating the age-adjusted average risk of a heart attack from life tables, and applying that to a fit and healthy civilian airline pilot aged 63, could be considered discrimination.[83] Much depends upon the accuracy of medical examinations: is the predictive ability of medical science now so good that we can stake the lives of airline passengers on it? Life insurance and motor insurance premiums are adjusted according to age – to the disadvantage of young male drivers who wish to own fast cars: this has a rational economic basis, in that it reflects the proven degree of accident risk by age.

Many other apparent manifestations of 'age discrimination' are subtly woven into everyday life, institutionalised, and widely accepted as sensible age proxies. Examples include: minimum ages for alcohol consumption, consensual sexual intercourse, voting, jury service, running for certain public offices, car driving, entry to and exit from school and attending 'adult' films; 'age-appropriate' school curricula; juvenile justice systems; age-concentrated screening for certain diseases (such as breast cancer).[84] At just what point does this process of categorisation become discriminatory? Recently, the European Union considered a cut in the maximum legal blood alcohol limit of 75 per cent for teenage drivers, based upon the clear evidence of alcohol consumption levels and road traffic accident rates.[85] Would such a negative discrimination be permissible in an 'age-neutral' society? Or would it be one of a very large number of public safety exemptions backed up by empirical evidence of age-based road traffic accident risk? Some examples of 'age discrimination' may seem trivial, such as the tendency of British newsagents (as an anti-shoplifting measure) to admit no more than two schoolchildren into the shop at any one time. Others, such as age-based entitlements (say, in social security) or the targeting of particular consumer age-groups (such as Saga Holidays or Club 18–30 in Britain), or the use of terms like 'junior', 'young' or 'recent graduate', are more problematic. The question is whether all such

[83] Ibid., p. 6.
[84] Peter Schuck, 'The Graying of Civil Rights Law', *The Public Interest*, no. 60, Summer 1990, p. 82; Andrew Remenyi, *Safeguarding the Employability of Older Workers: Issues and Perspectives* (1994), p. 11.
[85] 'Teen Drivers Face Half Pint Limit', *Guardian*, 2 Jan. 2001.

examples, great and small, could or should be outlawed in order to achieve a truly 'age-neutral' society.

Age discrimination versus race or sex discrimination

As has been shown, many campaigners consider age discrimination to be just as virulent and corrosive as race or sex discrimination.[86] Others disagree, suggesting instead that it is fundamentally different. The arguments on both sides are powerful.[87] Those who view age discrimination as qualitatively distinct point out that it has no obviously tragic historical legacy like slavery, in respect of which philosophical justifications of recompense, or 'corrective justice',[88] can be constructed: the twentieth-century debate on age discrimination is not exactly littered with murders, lynchings, 'freedom rides' or marches on Washington.[89] Instead, there is only a complex and subtle process of long-run technological change displacing older workers.[90] Hence the US Supreme Court ruled in 1976 that, unlike race or sex discrimination, older people had not suffered a history of 'purposeful unequal treatment'.[91] This view, of course, ignores the fact that the past sufferings of old people – in overcrowded Poor Law infirmaries, demeaning casual jobs, stoical domestic poverty, and so on – have merely been kept hidden from public gaze.

When the whole issue of civil rights was under discussion in the USA in the 1960s, it was generally contended that discrimination on grounds of race, sex or religion were all substantially different from age discrimination, since the former were pure 'bigotry' that arose from feelings about a person unrelated to that person's ability to perform a specific job;[92] by contrast, working capacity *does* gradually decline with age, even if the

---

[86] See, for example, Midwinter, *Citizenship*, p. vii.

[87] See, for example: Julia Johnson and Bill Bytheway, 'Ageism: Concept and Definition', in Julia Johnson and Robert Slater (eds.), *Ageing and Later Life* (1993), pp. 200–5; Erdman B. Palmore and Kenneth Manton, 'Ageism Compared to Racism and Sexism', *Journal of Gerontology*, vol. 28, no. 3, 1973, pp. 363–9.

[88] Albert G. Mosley and Nicholas Capaldi, *Affirmative Action. Social Justice or Unfair Preference?* (1996), pp. 24–6.

[89] Lawrence M. Friedman, *Your Time Will Come: The Law of Age Discrimination and Mandatory Retirement* (1984), p. 55.

[90] Hushbeck, *Old and Obsolete*, p. 6.

[91] *Massachusetts Board of Retirement* v. *Murgia*, quoted in Howard Eglit, 'Old Age and the Constitution', *Chicago-Kent Law Review*, vol. 57, no. 4, 1981, p. 884.

[92] See, for example, oral evidence by Representative James A. Burke, *Age Discrimination in Employment. Hearings Before the General Subcommittee on Labor of the Committee on Education and Labor. House of Representatives, August 1, 2, 3, 15, 16 and 17 1967* (1967), p. 449.

ability differentials between individuals widen and the requirements of each job vary greatly.

Perhaps the most telling argument is that belonging to a particular race or sex is akin to joining one specific 'club' at the moment of conception, whereas old age is a universal 'club' most of us will join one day.[93] As Butler has put it, 'we don't all grow white or black, but we all grow old'.[94] Hence in some of the legal debates surrounding age discrimination legislation in the USA, age has been judged to be a 'relative characteristic', whereas race and sex are 'immutable characteristics'. For example, one US legal judgement argued that

Age discrimination is qualitatively different from race or sex discrimination in employment, because the basis of the discrimination is not a discrete and immutable characteristic of an employee which separates the member of the protected group indelibly from persons outside the protected group. Rather, age is a continuum along which distinctions between employees are often subtle and relative ones.[95]

On the other hand, many would see 'race' and 'gender' as socially constructed (hence worthy of inverted commas), and thus relative; and age can be seen as immutable, since we only age in one direction. A further complication is that age acts as an accelerator of class, gender and ethnic disadvantage: as Susan Sontag has pointed out, in a celebrated essay, older women experience the 'double standard of ageing' or 'double jeopardy' by age and gender. Prevailing images of beauty and desirability tend to be those of young women; society is more tolerant of ageing in men, who are 'allowed' to age, where women are not. For women, argues Sontag, 'aging means a humiliating process of gradual sexual disqualification'.[96] Given that, in Britain, women are a majority of those aged 65+ (and nearly two-thirds of those aged 75+) ageism is seamlessly joined to sexism.[97] Furthermore, ethnic elders (the majority of whom will be women) may suffer a 'triple jeopardy' of race, sex and age discrimination:[98] in the USA, it is well established that ethnic minority older women may encounter 'multiple discrimination' or 'compounded discrimination'. Some social scientists have even tried to measure age inequality, as against gender

---

[93] Rose Gilroy, *Good Practice in Equal Opportunities* (1993), p. 33.

[94] Butler, 'Age-Ism', p. 246.

[95] Quoted in Daniel P. O'Meara, *Protecting the Growing Number of Older Workers: the Age Discrimination in Employment Act* (1989), p. 94.

[96] Susan Sontag, 'The Double Standard of Aging', in Carver and Liddiard, *An Ageing Population*, pp. 72–80.

[97] For an exploration, see Arber and Ginn, *Connecting Gender*.

[98] Shah Ebrahim, 'Ethnic Elders', *British Medical Journal*, vol. 313, 7 Sept. 1996, pp. 610–13. For a useful discussion, see Ken Blakemore and Margaret Boneham, *Age, Race and Ethnicity. A Comparative Approach* (1994), ch. 4.

and race inequality.[99] Clearly, the inter-relationships between sex, race and age discrimination can be debated endlessly. However, endless debate does not produce good, workable legislation.

Age conflicts, positive and negative discrimination and the dilemmas of 'agelessness'

Age conflicts have always existed and can operate both ways – young against old, and old against young.[100] Most of us can recall as children being tyrannised in an ageist and vindictive manner by adult authority figures, such as ticket inspectors or park keepers. Many who campaign against ageism are quite consistent in opposing discrimination at any age. As Eric Midwinter argues, 'Put plainly, if we are to castigate society for insisting on an end to employment at 65, we should be as wary of an obligation to start school at 5 and raise an eyebrow over the decision to grant the vote at 18.'[101] Likewise, Age Concern has consistently stressed that it is opposed to age discrimination against any age-group, since ageism

occurs when someone makes or sees a distinction because of another person's age and uses this as a basis for prejudice against and unfair treatment of that person. It is something that can affect everyone, regardless of their age. It is just as easy to discriminate against someone because they are too young as it is to say they are too old: both are equally pernicious.[102]

However, if age discrimination can occur at any point in the lifecourse, should the 'protected group' be extended so wide as to include everybody? Legally, this would create difficulties, since proving discrimination requires the identification of perpetrator and victim. Clearly, it is much easier to identify the 'protected group' in cases of race and gender discrimination.

Should positive discrimination in favour of older people be banned in a truly 'age-neutral' society? There are, of course, numerous instances in Britain – bus passes, subsidised public transport, free medical prescriptions and eye tests, additional tax relief (via the 'age allowance'), special insurance policies, reduced admission to events and exhibitions, discounts in shops, concessionary offers that target the 'grey market', and so on. The British welfare state is a complex balance of positive and negative age

[99] See, for example, Palmore and Manton, 'Ageism'.
[100] Nancy Foner, *Ages in Conflict: a Cross-Cultural Perspective on Inequality between Old and Young* (1984).
[101] Eric Midwinter, *Ageism, Discrimination and Citizenship* (1991), p. 1.
[102] Age Concern, *Age Discrimination*, p. 4.

discriminations. On the one hand, it is, like all modern welfare states, essentially a welfare state for old people,[103] since they are its largest single group of clients. The proportion of NHS expenditure allocated to people aged 65+ has steadily risen since 1948, and one estimate is that roughly 80 per cent of an individual's lifetime health care costs are consumed during their first six years and their last three.[104] People aged 65+ constitute 16 per cent of the British population, yet occupy two-thirds of hospital acute beds and absorb 25 to 30 per cent of NHS expenditure on pharmaceuticals.[105] On the other hand, there are areas (such as age-based health care rationing) where substantial negative discrimination has operated.

Positive discrimination in helping older people get jobs might end up as negative age discrimination against the young:[106] much depends upon whether modern labour markets are capable of continual expansion, and can absorb both age-groups. Again, negative stereotypes of older workers (that they are slower to learn, cantankerous, inflexible and overpaid) could be replaced by equally inaccurate positive ones (that they are ever-reliable, courteous, show deference and are unlikely to go on strike). Interestingly, Eric Midwinter is quite consistent in opposing positive discrimination measures in favour of older citizens – or, at the very least, regarding them in principle as highly suspect: they would certainly cause an outcry if applied to ethnic minority groups. He recognises that many old age activists have turned a 'Nelson's eye' to such positive discriminations: a truly 'age-neutral' society should be one in which all age-based categorisations and allocation procedures have been abolished.[107] However, the practicality of this is questionable: as John Vincent whimsically comments, 'a genuine defeat of ageism would involve having choices about what age you wish to be!'[108]

A long-standing conundrum in social gerontology is the question of whether such positive discrimination subtly reinforces the social and cultural ghettoisation of older people. Defining old age as a discrete and deserving stage of life, and campaigning for more resources to be allocated to it, presents problems for old age advocacy groups: as Carroll Estes famously observed, 'the aging enterprise' advocates 'age-segmented' policies that 'single out, stigmatise and isolate the aged from the rest of society'.[109] Gerontology itself can be seen as 'essentially ageist',[110] just as

---

[103] John Myles, *Old Age in the Welfare State: the Political Economy of Public Pensions* (1984), p. 2.
[104] Office for National Statistics, *Social Focus on Older People*, p. 77.
[105] Janice Robinson, 'Age Equality in Health and Social Care', in Sandra Fredman and Sarah Spencer (eds.), *Age as an Equality Issue* (2003), p. 100.
[106] DfEE, *Action on Age*, p. 8.   [107] Midwinter, *Ageism, Discrimination*, pp. 3–4.
[108] Vincent, *Inequality*, p. 82.   [109] Carroll L. Estes, *The Aging Enterprise* (1979), p. 2.
[110] Bytheway, *Ageism*, p. 97.

geriatric medicine can be seen either as a valuable recognition of the particular health needs of older people, or as a contribution to the 'medicalisation', and thus marginalisation, of old age.[111] One response of such advocacy groups is to fashion 'positive' images of old age, and re-educate public opinion accordingly as a response to what they see as the dominance of negative and corrosive ageism. 'Positive', 'successful' or 'active' ageing agendas have become very popular of late. Superficially, the idea of us taking control of our lives, making every effort to remain happy, active and healthy into late old age, and thereby countering negative stereotypes of ageing, is very appealing. However, the whole idea of 'successful ageing' has been criticised: as a kind of postmodern Social Darwinism in which we look to ourselves and not the state for help; as presupposing a norm of decrepitude, which needs to be countered by a 'denial of ageing';[112] as prescribing a kind of authoritarian, 'lifestyle fascism'; as utterly impractical, it being impossible to expect an entire population to live lives of such dull moral rectitude; and as pointless, if in fact genetic or early nutritional factors are all-important in determining our health, and thus quality of life, in old age. In attempting to balance out these positive and negative discriminations, one is in danger of tumbling into arguments of infinite regress.

Related to the above conundrum is the idea of 'agelessness'. The attack on ageism has been accompanied by an intriguing debate (conducted both within the confines of social gerontology and in wider public discussion) on the merits of an 'ageless' society. For example, in their study of early retirees – the interesting and provocatively entitled *Life After Work. The Arrival of the Ageless Society* (1991) – Michael Young and Tom Schuller argued that 'age has become one of the organising principles of modern society and as such has been carried so far as to inflict serious psychological injury on millions of people'.[113] Likewise, Bill Bytheway has suggested that we should dispense with age as a categorisation,[114] and Tom Kirkwood concluded his 2001 Reith Lectures with the challenge that we should 'put an end to age as something that we let get in the way of celebrating all individuals on this earth as true equals'.[115] However, the

---

[111] For explorations, see: Margot Jefferys, 'Is There a Need for Geriatric Medicine? Does it do More Harm than Good?', in Peter Kaim-Caudle, Jane Keithley and Audrey Mullender (eds.), *Aspects of Ageing* (1993), pp. 106–11; Stephen Katz, *Disciplining Old Age. The Formation of Gerontological Knowledge* (1996).

[112] Mike Featherstone and Mike Hepworth, 'Images of Positive Aging: a Case Study of *Retirement Choice* Magazine', in Featherstone and Wernick, *Images*, pp. 29–48; Scrutton, 'Ageism', pp. 23–4; Vincent, *Inequality*, p. 92.

[113] Michael Young and Tom Schuller, *Life After Work. The Arrival of the Ageless Society* (1991), p. 170.

[114] Bytheway, *Ageism*, ch. 9.

[115] Tom Kirkwood, 'New Directions', Reith Lecture 5, 2001, www.bbc.co.uk.

seductive goal of an 'ageless' society has engendered no little controversy, particularly over whether its implication that we should remain 'forever youthful' is in fact a 'denial of ageing', and thus subtly ageist.[116] As is shown throughout this book, it is also being used as a justification for raising state pension ages, lengthening the working life and generally eroding the welfare rights of older people.

Rational versus irrational discrimination

Much of the discussion preceding the USA's 1967 Age Discrimination in Employment Act was predicated upon the assumption that age discrimination was essentially irrational, based upon 'false stereotypes' or 'prejudiced views' towards older people, and thus damaging to employers' real interests and the overall economic prosperity of the nation. The same is true of the current debate in Britain. As one recent British government publication puts it, 'Any employer that allows stereotypical prejudices to cloud their or their employees' approach to staff recruitment and development will run the risk of alienating an increasingly large proportion of the labour market', emphasising that the government consultations with employers included 'tackling stereotypical views about the abilities of older workers'.[117] Likewise, the verdict of Richard Worsley (then Director of the Carnegie Third Age Programme, now Director of the Tomorrow Project and a leading participant in the British age discrimination debate) is that age discrimination in employment 'does not generally occur as a result of deliberate malice or prejudice, but rather as a result of a quite complex set of different attitudes which combine to form an often unconscious but nevertheless potent exclusion of older people from opportunities in employment'. These 'attitudes' include stereotypical or unwarranted assumptions about diminished working capacity, loss of skill, decline in physical and cognitive ability, and so on.[118]

However, matters are rather more complex than this. As William Graebner comments, critically, 'According to the liberal view, any form of age discrimination is bad, its elimination is good, and the journey from one to the other is only a matter of time and knowledge.'[119] Graebner's critique of the liberal fallacy – that persuasion is all that is needed – is

---

[116] Andrews, 'The Seductiveness', pp. 301–18; H. B. Gibson, 'It Keeps Us Young', Bill Bytheway, 'Youthfulness and Agelessness: a Comment', Molly Andrews, 'Ageful and Proud', *Ageing and Society*, vol. 20, pt. 6, Nov. 2000, pp. 773–9, 781–9, 791–5.

[117] DfEE, *Action on Age*, p. 15.

[118] Richard Worsley, *Age and Employment. Why Employers Should Think Again About Older Workers* (1996), p. 80; Richard Worsley, 'Left Out of Things for Ages', *Guardian*, 2 Mar. 1996.

[119] Graebner, *History of Retirement*, p. 247.

telling. We need to ask why, in our apparently 'enlightened' modern societies, such irrational discrimination still exists. It is just as plausible to argue that age discrimination in employment is essentially 'rational', based upon the use of crude age proxies which are correct in the aggregate (even if there are individual cases of injustice), or are cheaper or more convenient to use than individualised testing for job competence. By contrast, race and gender discrimination can be seen as more irrational (for example, the visual image of a black person or a woman does not necessarily denote job competence). Critics of the 'irrationality' model argue that discrimination is incompatible with the rational economic self-interest of employers: if they discriminate consistently, their businesses will suffer. As John Straka argues, it is 'not at all clear that erroneous group generalisations can survive market competition'.[120] Such a view receives strongest support from free-market economists. Hence Richard Epstein has argued that 'The firm that passes over superior older workers in favor of inferior younger ones will find itself at a cost disadvantage that it cannot recoup in the market.' The decision to hire or not hire an older worker is thus dependent not only on what they can do at that age but also on what they can do in the years that follow.[121]

Why, therefore, would an employer have a 'taste for discrimination'? An oft-cited view is that true discrimination in employment means a personnel decision that is made on criteria other than those that are job-related. As Richard Disney puts it, 'To the economist, discrimination arises when an employer selects between two workers, identical in terms of productive characteristics, on grounds that are irrelevant to their productivity, such as their gender or the colour of their skin.'[122] But this only takes us so far. Employers may have a 'taste for discrimination' or a 'prejudice' and be willing to incur some cost in order to indulge it: it is perfectly possible to envisage a situation where a prejudiced employer may consider a small drop in profits a price worth paying in order to keep his or her workforce exclusive members of a 'club' based upon race, gender, age or whatever. The intensity of that prejudice may be measured by the price the employer is willing to pay.[123] The employer may also operate by short-term

---

[120] John W. Straka, *The Demand for Older Workers: the Neglected Side of a Labor Market* (1991), pp. 14–15.

[121] Richard A. Epstein, *Forbidden Grounds. The Case Against Employment Discrimination Laws* (1992), pp. 445, 452. For a similar critique, see Richard A. Posner, *Aging and Old Age* (1995), esp. ch. 13.

[122] Disney, 'Why Have Older Men', p. 75.

[123] Gary S. Becker, *The Economics of Discrimination* (1957), p. 6; Gary S. Becker, 'Discrimination, Economic', in David L. Sills (ed.), *International Encyclopedia of the Social Sciences Vol. 4* (1968), p. 209.

rationality (preferring the immediate satisfaction of keeping the 'club' exclusive) without realising that this will be damaging to his or her long-term economic interests. Much hinges upon the assumption that employers always act rationally, and can perceive their own real interests.

In one of the best and most thoughtful analyses of the issues, the American legal academic Martin Lyon Levine has constructed a typology of rationality/irrationality models. Levine suggests that the term 'systemic rationality' can be applied to the process whereby mandatory retirement is functional to labour turn-over, employee rotation, workforce morale, and so on, by ensuring that promotion channels do not become blocked. 'Substantive rationality' encapsulates the view of employers that productivity declines *do* on average occur with advancing age, and that age is therefore an accurate proxy for employment-relevant characteristics: mandatory retirement may be imposed, for example, when an employee's remuneration becomes too high in relation to their productivity (an unfavourable 'compensation–productivity ratio'). 'Process rationality' applies to the situation where it is easier, cheaper and more convenient to use mandatory retirement rather than individual performance appraisal: as Levine puts it, 'individual case-by-case evaluation is costly; there are information costs, transaction costs, psychic costs, and union objections'.

However, employers may act according to one of these models of rationality, believing themselves to be operating in their true economic self-interest, yet they may be committing 'cognitive error'. In using 'judgemental heuristics' (existing knowledge and experience regarding the common characteristics of older people), they may, for example, operationalise the reasonable, but mistaken, view that older employees have higher rates of industrial accidents. They may also suffer from 'structural lag', holding erroneous views on the health and productivity of older workers (based, say, on outdated empirical evidence). Reflecting his training as a psychotherapist, Levine suggests that, in examining apparently irrational 'negative stereotypes' about older workers, it is necessary to probe deep into the multiple layers of an employer's consciousness and unravel 'the relative causal importance of conscious factual beliefs, conscious evaluative attitudes, and unconscious mental function'. It is also necessary to distinguish between a 'generalisation' (the ascription of assumed group characteristics to an individual), a 'stereotype' (essentially, a false generalisation), and a 'prejudice' (antipathy, hatred, fear or similar negative attitudes towards an individual because of their membership of a group).[124]

---

[124] Levine, *Age Discrimination*, esp. pp. 71, 130–1, 140, 149–56, 162. Levine's excellent study deserves to be read in its entirety.

Levine's sensitive exploration of these issues is an invaluable reminder that the distinction between 'rational' or 'justified' discrimination and 'irrational' or 'unjustified' discrimination is complex and nuanced. Precisely defining 'justified' (job-related) discrimination raises the question of whether one should take account of background cultural and attitudinal factors. For example, a firm may have an all-white workforce whose collective attitudes are racist. The hiring of a black person on strictly rational, job-related criteria may cause resentment, conflict and perhaps even a strike, with a consequent drop in productivity. Should this economic argument be used to justify discrimination against job applicants who are black? The liberal, civil rights response would be that the firm must go through a period of catharsis in order to change the racist attitudes of the workforce (and the local culture). (This was the argument used in the late-1950s civil rights agitation in the USA, regarding school desegregation in the South.) In the case of age, a retail outlet may cater to customers in a particular age-group (for example, a record shop selling pop music CDs largely to young people), and this will affect the age-profile of its staff. Anti-ageism campaigners would argue that these cultural barriers should be overcome by selecting employees on the basis of ability, and not age. If doing so damaged the firm's profits, however, the original (ageist) personnel policy could be judged productivity-related, and hence 'justified'. Again, if the economic activity rates of older males fall further in the future, they may be regarded as a group whose seriously disadvantaged labour market position can only be rectified by positive action – enforced, say, by employment quotas. They would then have to be hired on social, rather than job-related, criteria. Finally, the view that 'job-related' discrimination is justified would seem to indicate that, ultimately, action against age discrimination in employment is more concerned with economic productivity than with social justice towards older people.

Age discrimination and the employment problems of older workers

Mandatory retirement has often been viewed as a striking example of age discrimination in employment. After all, what could be more unjust than denying the right to work to the 92 per cent of British men aged 65+ who are jobless? It is an argument that assumes greater force as older people (presumably) become ever-healthier and as changing labour market conditions – notably, growing job insecurity and impermanence – increasingly undercut the contention that older workers are not worth re-training because they only have a brief working future. According to the US Bureau of Labor Statistics, the median job tenure for a US employee in 1996 was only 3.8 years (though this must include many temporary, low-grade 'McJobs').[125] Conversely, a young employee is now more likely than ever to leave and take a new job shortly after an employer has gone to much trouble and expense in re-training him or her.

Many anti-ageism campaigners take the view that mandatory retirement is, in Laurence Friedman's words, '*the* form of age discrimination par excellence'.[126] Hence Alan Walker suggests that 'retirement is both the leading form of age discrimination and the driving force behind the wider development of ageism in modern societies ... retirement may be seen as an age discriminatory social process designed to exclude older people *en masse* from the workforce';[127] and for Elizabeth Drury, 'the imposition of a specific age for retirement constitutes age discrimination, since it denies free choice for those who wish or need to continue working'.[128] In a number of publications, Philip Taylor and Alan Walker have also analysed the age discrimination that appears to be manifested in the high rates of unemployment among older workers, the treatment meted out to them at Job Centres, the lack of re-training programmes, early retirement policies, and so on. Taylor and Walker conclude that 'ageism is a fault line running throughout the labour market, causing gross injustices in the distribution of secure employment and the economic waste of scarce human capital'.[129] For example, the Carnegie Inquiry into the Third Age found that nine out of ten employees aged 50+ received no training at all from their employer; and a more recent survey revealed that, whereas 23 per cent of employees aged under 25 benefited from job-related training programmes, the corresponding proportion for those between 55 and state pension age was a derisory 7 per cent.[130] Anecdotal examples of work-fit individuals having to give up their jobs on a certain (arbitrary) birthday are numerous. One such was widely reported in November 2001: the world's leading heart surgeon, Professor Sir Magdi Yacoub, was forced to cease operating on attaining the age of 66 (though he was allowed to continue doing research).[131]

---

[125] *Developments in Aging: 1996. Volume 1. Report of the Special Committee on Aging. United States Senate* (1997), p. 77.
[126] Laurence M. Friedman, 'Age Discrimination Law: Some Remarks on the American Experience', in Sandra Fredman and Sarah Spencer (eds.), *Age as an Equality Issue* (2003), p. 192.
[127] Alan Walker, 'The Benefits of Old Age? Age Discrimination and Social Security', in McEwen, *Age*, p. 59.
[128] Drury, *Age Discrimination*, p. 48.
[129] Philip Taylor and Alan Walker, *Too Old at 50? Age Discrimination in the Labour Market* (1991), p. i.
[130] Kerry Platman, *The Glass Precipice. Employability for a Mixed Age Workforce* (1999), p. 15.
[131] 'NHS Says Sir Magdi is Too Old to Operate', *Evening Standard*, 20 Nov. 2001.

Before it was abolished for virtually all occupations, mandatory retirement at age 65 in the USA was frequently criticised as institutionalised ageism. For instance, Erdman Palmore viewed it as 'a major example' of discrimination against older people, since their value as workers does not necessarily decline at that age,[132] and Arthur Flemming (a past US Commissioner on Aging) maintained in 1982 that mandatory retirement was 'in direct conflict with our Judeo-Christian concept of the dignity and worth of each individual', and 'simply a lazy person's device for dealing with what sometimes is a difficult personnel problem ... The calendar makes the decision for you.'[133]

But is age discrimination really the cause of mandatory retirement and the wider labour market problems of older workers? This question has been raised earlier in this chapter, and it recurs throughout this book. The tendency in many current British discussions is to imply that this is so. For example, Malcolm Sargeant sees age discrimination as manifested 'in all stages of the employment process, beginning with attempts to enter the workforce and ending with measures designed to encourage early exit from it'.[134] Patrick Grattan likewise argues that the fall in older men's economic activity rates 'has been driven by the changes in the economy', but these changes, by encouraging early exit policies, have 'led to a set of assumptions and stereotypes which have become widely entrenched'. People in the second half of their working lives thus 'face stereotypes about declining capability' that are unjustified.[135] This is also a commonly held view among politicians. For example, in a House of Commons debate in November 2001, Paul Burstow MP claimed that the increasing level of older men's economic inactivity since the early 1970s has been 'the result of ageist assumptions that lead employers to cast their older staff on to the scrap heap'.[136] Often the 'evidence' provided is just a presentation of the empirical data on older workers' low economic activity rates, accompanied by some very general (and superficial) allegations of age discrimination, with no causal link established. However, there is something distinctly odd about the argument that policies of the 1970s and 1980s which were based upon an essentially *rational* argument – that available jobs ought to be redistributed to younger workers with family responsibilities – should have

[132] Palmore, *Ageism*, p. 5.
[133] *Hearing Before the Subcommittee on Employment Opportunities of the Committee on Education and Labor, House of Representatives, To Amend the Age Discrimination in Employment Act of 1967, 9 September 1982* (1982), pp. 14–15.
[134] Malcolm Sargeant, *Age Discrimination in Employment* (1999), p. 3.
[135] Patrick Grattan, 'Age Discrimination in Employment', in Help the Aged, *Age Discrimination in Public Policy. A Review of Evidence* (2002), pp. 33–5.
[136] *H of C Deb.*, 6s, vol. 375, 23 Nov. 2001, cols. 593–4.

subsequently caused *irrational* 'myths and misconceptions' to become widespread. It may be that, in the 1980s, British employers were so tempted by their pension fund surpluses that they followed short-term rationality in using these funds to induce their older employees to leave; by the 1990s, it could be argued, it had become evident that downsizing by the use of age proxies was contrary to those employers' long-term rational self-interest. But this is a partial, inadequate explanation.

In fact, if we consider the economic and labour market background in the long term, an interesting picture emerges. Essentially, what we can see in Britain and the USA since the 1920s are periodic swings between two opposed labour market strategies. On the one hand, during times of structural stability, when the emphasis has been on economic growth via an expansion of labour supply – the 1950s and the 1990s – older workers have been persuaded to delay retirement, with fears being expressed about the economic losses caused by early exit. 'Obligation' has meant working. Yet at times of major economic restructuring and technological innovation – the 1930s, 1970s and 1980s – the requirement has been that older workers retire from work earlier, making way for younger colleagues who are perceived as possessing more up-to-date skills (and may be more 'deserving', since they tend to have young families). 'Obligation' has meant *not* working. These shifts of emphasis are not explicable in terms of irrational age discrimination: they are much more to do with changing economic and labour market conditions. As William Graebner has perceptively observed, mandatory retirement served a useful economic purpose for most of the twentieth century as a regulator of labour supply; but from the 1970s onwards, with the new emerging labour markets, it began to be seen as counterproductive and there began to be growing calls for its abolition.[137] A crucial question posed throughout this book is: what has determined the *timing* of the recent revival of interest in age discrimination? If the answer suggests that extending working lives may not be in the best interests of older people, then action against age discrimination should be scrutinised carefully and critically.

Certainly, many historical examples of apparent age discrimination can be found. The twentieth-century history of retirement is littered with accusations of unjust treatment of older workers who have often been subject to the blanket judgement that they are industrially obsolete or 'surplus to requirements', particularly in times of recession or economic restructuring. For example, in 1930s Britain many trades unionists and pensioner groups protested that discrimination against older workers in

---

[137] Graebner, *History of Retirement*, p. 250.

the high-unemployment economically depressed areas was rife – notably, in the practice of imposing wage cuts on men aged 65+ equal to the amount of the old age pension (which then carried no retirement condition). Two additional factors contributed to an emergent ageism in public discourses at this time: first, concerns over the low birth rate (which had fallen since the 1870s) gave rise to fears that the resultant ageing population would inexorably increase the burden of public expenditure in the future and lead to a loss of 'enterprise' in political and economic life; second, since older workers were concentrated in the recession-hit industries, some commentators blamed them for being a major contributory factor to the recession.[138]

As will be shown in a future chapter, a common argument in 1950s Britain was that compulsory retirement ages were unjust, economically irrational and damaging to the physical and psychological well-being of men, who found the abrupt transition from the orderly world of the factory to enforced idleness too much to cope with. Social surveys in the 1950s revealed considerable apprehension on the part of older working-class men regarding their impending retirement. (Many men of this era appeared to have been 'killed by retirement'.)[139] Some researchers even investigated how far age discrimination was to blame. There was also a lively debate in America in the 1930s, 1940s and 1950s, with many deploring what they saw as a 'widespread discrimination against older workers in industry'.[140] In 1951, Wilbur J. Cohen even went as far as to argue that 'the arbitrary concept that chronological age is the determinant of retirement or nonemployability is one of the most disastrous and fallacious ideas that we have had in our employment practices in this country'.[141] Britain and America were not alone: in 1938, the International Labour Office published a report on discrimination against older workers in several countries.[142]

However, there has also been a long debate on whether the labour market problems of older workers are really the result of 'discrimination' in the accepted sense of the term, or of other factors – notably their concentration in long-established industrial sectors (which tend to

[138] Macnicol, *Politics of Retirement*, pp. 229–31, 254–64; John Benson, *Prime Time. A History of the Middle Aged in Twentieth-century Britain* (1997), pp. 65–8, 80–91.
[139] Nesta Roberts, *Our Future Selves* (1970), p. 93.
[140] Michael T. Wermel and Selma Gelbaum, 'Work and Retirement in Old Age', *American Journal of Sociology*, vol. 51, no. 1, July 1945, p. 20.
[141] Wilbur J. Cohen, 'Economics, Employment and Welfare', in Nathan W. Shock (ed.), *Problems of Aging* (1951), p. 92.
[142] International Labour Office, *Report of the Office on the Question of Discrimination Against Elderly Workers* (1938).

experience greatest labour force shake-out in times of recession and restructuring), their displacement by new technology, or their lack of skills relevant to the new expanding industries. For example, as far back as 1938 two American researchers examined several large manufacturing enterprises in New England, to ascertain whether employers had inaccurate, and therefore prejudicial, views on older workers' productivity, rates of industrial accidents, skills, sickness absenteeism and so on. They concluded that employers 'generally had a high regard' for their older employees, and 'no prejudice' could be detected; many executives did not consider that productivity declines with age were serious. However, at the same time, employers were disinclined to take on an older worker who was unemployed.[143] Again, in the mid-1940s this issue engendered a controversy in the pages of the *American Journal of Sociology*. Otto Pollak argued that the incidence of true discrimination against older workers, if it existed at all, was 'very small indeed', and that their labour market disadvantages were actually attributable to factors such as higher employment costs, deficient skills and education levels, a perceived greater risk of industrial accidents and a lack of geographical mobility. Stanley Lebergott disagreed, maintaining that unemployment at higher ages was a qualitatively greater problem than it was for younger workers, since as workers aged it became increasingly difficult for them to find new jobs.[144] Social scientists have been debating these issues ever since.

Has age discrimination really been the principal factor, or even a major contributory factor, in the spread of mass retirement since the late nineteenth century? In order to answer this question, we need briefly to consider the prevailing explanations that are the subject of no little controversy. The debate is exceedingly complex, and fraught with methodological difficulties: what follows can only be a very brief summary. Defining retirement was always problematic, but has become even more so with the emergence of more complex work-histories (and hence pathways into retirement), alterations in lifecourse patterns, the changing labour market status of women and falling retirement ages.[145] It could include the following: complete withdrawal from the workforce; a significant

---

[143] Dwight L. Palmer and John A. Brownell, 'Influence of Age on Employment Opportunities', *Monthly Labor Review*, vol. 48, no. 4, April 1939, pp. 765–80.

[144] Otto Pollak, 'Discrimination Against Older Workers in Industry', *American Journal of Sociology*, vol. 50, no. 2, Sept. 1944, pp. 99–106; Stanley Lebergott, 'Comment on "Discrimination Against Older Workers in Industry"', and 'Rejoinder', *American Journal of Sociology*, vol. 51, no. 4, Jan. 1946, pp. 322–4 and 324–5, respectively.

[145] For useful discussions, see: Chris Phillipson, *Transitions from Work to Retirement. Developing a New Social Contract* (2002); Donald Hirsch, *Crossroads After 50. Improving Choices in Work and Retirement* (2003).

reduction in hours of work; a subjective self-definition by the retiree; leaving the main employer, and taking a less demanding 'bridge' job, thus to achieve 'phased' retirement; receiving an employer-provided pension; state pension or social security receipt.[146] None of this, of course, applies to those older women who have had little or no previous labour market participation (much more common in the past). The 'old age experience' of such women was primarily shaped by their role in the extended family. If the category 'retired' was applied to them, it was only by proxy (through their husbands), or by other markers of time (such as dependent children leaving home).[147] In the past, standard models of retirement behaviour thus tended to be highly masculinist.[148] Indeed, aggregate explanations of retirement ignore the complexities of the 'retirement experience', which is differentiated according to factors of class, gender, race, age, marital status, health status and many sociological imponderables (such as the ability to form and retain supportive friendships in old age, or the existence of absorbing hobbies). Nor do they answer a question that has become more and more pertinent with falling average ages of retirement: what determines the precise timing of an individual's labour force exit?

Retirement has always existed. However, before the twentieth century, it was generally confined to a small, wealthy elite who were able to withdraw voluntarily from active life and be financially self-sufficient. It therefore had 'somewhat of an honorific connotation', as F. le Gros Clark elegantly put it.[149] Until the twentieth century, occupational pension schemes were few in number. For the majority of the population – engaged predominantly in agricultural labour – formal paid work was reduced in intensity in old age, until physical incapacity forced a complete cessation of employment. This older form of retirement was essentially 'infirmity' retirement, whereas the unfolding of the twentieth century has been accompanied by the emergence of 'jobless' retirement.[150]

Broadly speaking, historical accounts of the spread of retirement can be divided into those that emphasise a decline in the *supply of* older workers, and those that emphasise a decline in the *demand for* the labour

---

[146] Parnes, 'Retirement Decision', p. 119; Richard Disney, Emily Grundy and Paul Johnson (eds.), *The Dynamics of Retirement: Analyses of the Retirement Surveys* (1997).

[147] An ingenious definition suggested by Clark Tibbitts, 'Retirement Problems in American Society', *American Journal of Sociology*, vol. LIX, no. 4, Jan. 1954, p. 302.

[148] Shelly Lundberg, 'Family Bargaining and Retirement Behavior', in Henry J. Aaron (ed.), *Behavioral Dimensions of Retirement Economics* (1999), pp. 253–72.

[149] F. le Gros Clark, *Work, Age and Leisure. Causes and Consequences of the Shortened Working Life* (1966), p. 21.

[150] Macnicol, *Politics of Retirement*, ch. 2.

of older workers. This rather stark polarisation is heuristic – supply and demand are, of course, interactive – and no serious study has ever suggested one to the exclusion of the other: all have offered a combination of the two, but with important differences of emphasis. However, the distinction remains a useful analytical starting-point. Is retirement a consumer durable that we have 'invented' – or has it been forced upon us as modern capitalist economies have steadily dispensed with the labour of older men?[151]

'Supply-side' explanations include a number of models of 'retirement behaviour' which see human agency as crucial. One early example was disengagement theory, which was very influential in the 1950s and 1960s. Based upon a detailed survey in Kansas, it implied that older people gradually withdrew from active life, reducing their interactions with others; as part of this disengagement process, older men would discard the role of worker.[152] The period since the 1970s has seen the ascendancy of broadly 'supply-side' explanations,[153] with economists offering a variety of rational choice models that purport to explain an individual's 'retirement decision' by reference to the effect of economic incentives. For example, Gary Burtless has argued that 'rising lifetime wages, wealth, social security, and pension benefits have made retirement an attainable goal for most workers'.[154] Supply-side explanations would also include the contention that cultural factors have exerted an important influence, and that the twentieth century has seen the growth of a 'retirement tradition', a 'retirement expectation', or an 'early exit culture' in popular attitudes.[155] This basically liberal explanation would view the 'democratisation of retirement' as an enormous gain; whereas in

---

[151] John Macnicol, 'Retirement', in Joel Mokyr (ed.), *Oxford Encyclopedia of Economic History, Vol. 4* (2003), pp. 371–5.

[152] Elaine Cumming and William E. Henry, *Growing Old. The Process of Disengagement* (1961), esp. pp. 14–15, 76. For contrasting verdicts, see: George Maddox, 'Aging Differently', *The Gerontologist*, vol. 27, no. 5, 1987, p. 559; Peter Coleman, 'Psychological Ageing', in John Bond, Peter Coleman and Sheila Peace (eds.), *Ageing in Society. An Introduction to Social Gerontology* (1993), pp. 84–5.

[153] This is demonstrated in Michael Leonesio's useful summary: Michael V. Leonesio, 'The Economics of Retirement: a Nontechnical Guide', *Social Security Bulletin*, vol. 59, no. 4, Winter 1996, pp. 29–50.

[154] Gary Burtless, 'Occupational Effects on the Health and Work Capacity of Older Men', in Burtless (ed.), *Work, Health and Income Among the Elderly* (1987), p. 104. See also: Stephen H. Sandell, 'Introduction', in Sandell, *The Problem*, p. 8; Leslie Hannah, *Inventing Retirement: the Development of Occupational Pensions in Britain* (1986), p. 124.

[155] Sarah Harper and Pat Thane, 'The Consolidation of "Old Age" as a Phase of Life, 1945–1965', in Margot Jefferys (ed.), *Growing Old in the Twentieth Century* (1989), pp. 43–61; Pat Thane, *Old Age in English History. Past Experiences, Present Issues* (2000), pp. 404–6; Jessica Bone and Samantha Mercer, *Flexible Retirement* (2000), p. 5.

the past, retirement was confined to a small wealthy minority, now all can enjoy it.

Supply-side explanations presuppose a tidy world of pure rationality, with no uncertainty.[156] Econometric modelling of human behaviour is predicated upon the assumption that consumers possess perfect knowledge, can make 'intertemporal lifecycle choices' in their own best interests and can operationalise their 'tastes and preferences', trading off the pros and cons of a wide range of variables – income, savings, working, job satisfaction, leisure, hobbies, family obligations, health status, life expectancy, social security benefits, occupational pensions, income taxes, and so on – against each other. The central tenet is that, as a worker ages, eventually the subjective value of leisure exceeds the value of the remuneration provided by his or her employer.[157] Such econometric modelling suggests that a worker will make the precise and well-informed choice to retire 'when the disutility of working another year just begins to outweigh the extra utility obtained by the additional consumption provided by another year of preretirement savings'.[158]

Central to many 'supply-side' explanations is the contention that 'normal', age-60/65 retirement is attributable to the incentive effect of the state pension, and early retirement to other social security benefits (particularly disability benefits).[159] For Haber and Gratton, federal social security has been 'the decisive catalyst of change' in triggering modern mass retirement,[160] and Richard Posner's confident declaration (alas, vitiated by the empirical evidence) is that 'with the enactment of the Social Security Act in 1935, the labour force participation rate of elderly Americans started to plunge'.[161] Others have emphasised the effect of increasing prosperity, particularly rising levels of accumulated personal savings.[162] Finally, the most convincing causal factor on the 'supply-side' is that workers, by the

---

[156] Peter A. Diamond and Jerry A. Hausman, 'The Retirement and Unemployment Behavior of Older Men', in Henry J. Aaron and Gary Burtless (eds.), *Retirement and Economic Behavior* (1984), p. 97.

[157] Leonesio, 'The Economics', p. 30.

[158] Gary Burtless and Robert A. Moffitt, 'The Effect of Social Security Benefits on the Labour Supply of the Aged', in Aaron and Burtless, *Retirement*, p. 139.

[159] See, for example: Michael J. Boskin, 'Social Security and Retirement Decisions', *Economic Inquiry*, vol. XV, no. 1, Jan. 1977, pp. 1–25; David A. Wise, 'Retirement Against the Demographic Trend: More Older People Living Longer, Working Less, and Saving Less', *Demography*, vol. 34, no. 1, Feb. 1997, pp. 83–95.

[160] Carole Haber and Brian Gratton, *Old Age and the Search for Security. An American Social History* (1994), p. 88.

[161] Posner, *Aging*, p. 40. Posner's book is, nevertheless, a most interesting and thought-provoking study.

[162] Dora L. Costa, *The Evolution of Retirement. An American Economic History, 1880–1990* (1998), esp. pp. 14–21.

time they are middle-aged, have accumulated industry-specific skills that cannot easily be transferred to a new employer.[163] Once made unemployed, they may perceive themselves to be lacking the relevant abilities, educational levels and adaptability to compete effectively in the labour market – the so-called 'cohort effect' – and may therefore leave work before retirement age, or may become so discouraged by their apparent labour market obsolescence that they give up looking for work – especially in today's more stressful labour market.[164] For such workers, the disutility of work may rise sharply at later ages.

By contrast, 'demand-side' explanations of retirement argue that the evolution of capitalist economies has slowly marginalised older workers. Beginning in the last quarter of the nineteenth century, significant changes took place in the structure of industrialised economies, characterised by the formation of larger units of production (notably, the joint stock company) with more 'scientific' management techniques and an increased emphasis on the productivity of individual workers; mandatory retirement was an important method of dispensing with the labour of older workers who were perceived to be 'past their best' in a more technology-intensive mode of production.[165] To this was added the decline in agriculture, which has always employed high proportions of old people. From that point on, the evolution of an increasingly technological capitalism in the twentieth century steadily displaced older workers from the labour force. The economic depression and industrial restructuring of the 1930s probably hastened the labour market exit of older male workers, and the 'second industrial revolution' that has occurred since the 1970s has adversely affected the employment prospects of men aged in their fifties and early sixties, while opening up more jobs for women.

The long-term historical evidence points to 'demand-side' explanations as being much more convincing, for several reasons. The overwhelming weight of contemporary testimony in Britain and the USA from the 1890s onwards indicates a growing concern from a wide spectrum of political opinion that capitalism appeared to be entering a significant, new phase and was dispensing with the labour of older males; this gave rise to an intriguing debate on the 'worn-out' older worker.[166] It is unlikely that state pensions have had much effect: in Britain, modern mass retirement began

[163] Kenneth A. Crouch, 'Late Life Job Displacement', *The Gerontologist*, vol. 38, no. 1, 1998, p. 9.
[164] Sean Rickard, *A Profits Warning. Macroeconomic Costs of Ageism* (n.d. c. 2000), p. 10.
[165] Macnicol, *Politics of Retirement*, esp. ch. 2. For the USA, see: Graebner, *History of Retirement*; Hushbeck, *Old and Obsolete*.
[166] Macnicol, *Politics of Retirement*, pp. 48–59.

to spread from the 1880s onwards – some three decades before the first state pension payments were made; the doubling in the value of the state pension in 1919 did not accelerate the trend to retirement; the second significant rise in value (in 1946), plus the introduction of the retirement condition, likewise had little effect; and in the three decades after the lowering of their pensionable age to 60 in 1940, the economic activity rates of women aged 60–4 actually rose (from 14.1 per cent in 1951 to 28.8 per cent in 1971). The US historical evidence on the 'pension as incentive' argument is also unconvincing. The first federal social security pension payments were made in 1940 – by which time fully 58 per cent of the total decline in labour force participation rates of men aged 65+ between 1880 and 1990 had already taken place.[167] In the first ten years of its existence, social security had no measurable effect on the economic activity rates of American men aged 65+: these remained virtually unchanged between 1940 and 1950, owing to the postwar economic boom, assisted by the Korean War.

Rational choice models also do not fit very easily with the evidence that there is widespread public ignorance of pension systems in Britain,[168] that older Americans display considerable fiscal *un*preparedness for retirement,[169] that there are marked falls in income and even food consumption experienced by many early retirees,[170] that the greatest risk of labour market displacement is experienced by those with the lowest socio-economic status (and therefore the lowest post-retirement incomes),[171] and that no more than one-third of recent early retirements in Britain can be said to be caused by 'voluntary' factors, such as early exit incentives.[172] Significantly, those who remain in work past the age of 65 tend to be those with the most control over their workplace situation: for example, in the spring of 2003, fully 40.5 per cent of British men aged 65+ who were still in employment were self-employed.[173]

---

[167] Costa, *Evolution*, p. 20.
[168] *Simplicity, Security and Choice: Working and Saving for Retirement*, Cm. 5677, Dec. 2002, p. 36.
[169] Annamari Lusardi, 'Information, Expectations and Savings for Retirement', in Aaron, *Behavioral Dimensions*, pp. 81–115.
[170] Jerry A. Hausman and Lynn Pacquette, 'Involuntary Early Retirement and Consumption', in Burtless, *Work*, pp. 151–75.
[171] Crouch, 'Late Life', pp. 7–17.
[172] Cabinet Office. Performance and Innovation Unit, *Winning the Generation Game. Improving Opportunities for People Aged 50–65 in Work and Community Activity* (2000), p. 22.
[173] Department for Work and Pensions, *Older Workers: Statistical Information Booklet. Spring 2003* (2003), p. 5. See also, Stephen McKay and Sue Middleton, *Characteristics of Older Workers* (1998), ch. 4.

Increased wealth-holding is also unconvincing. In Britain in 2001/2, 28 per cent of single pensioners, and 17 per cent of pensioner couples, had no savings at all; at the top end, savings of £20,000 and over were held by only about 30 per cent of pensioner couples and 16 per cent of single pensioners.[174] Finally, while it is undeniable that a 'retirement expectation' has now become embedded in public consciousness, it is necessary to explain how and why this 'expectation' arose: an 'expectation' does not appear, fully formed, from nowhere. In fact, it represents a slow attitudinal adjustment to the long-run labour market displacement of older workers.

Supply-side explanations are, therefore, of only limited value. Their plausibility is confined to that minority of (middle-class) retirees who are beneficiaries of final salary pension schemes. The long-term historical evidence convincingly suggests that declining sectoral labour market demand has been the over-arching context within which citizens have 'chosen' from a very restricted range of options, the degree of choice varying by socio-economic status. Whichever model one prefers, 'age discrimination' does not fit easily as an explanation. It may indeed be an important contributory factor, but it is misleading to interpret the history of retirement as the history of systematic and growing age discrimination.

The pros and cons of mandatory retirement

This brings one to the vexed issue of mandatory retirement. The 'social justice' arguments against it have already been outlined; but the arguments in its favour are also powerful. These opposed arguments have long been known.[175] The most convincing in favour is the 'lifeboat principle' that tends to prevail during high-unemployment recessions, and was accepted by British employers and trades unionists in the 1930s, 1970s, and 1980s: mandatory retirement enables there to take place a just sharing-out of jobs (assuming that there is a fixed number of jobs in a nation's economy at any one time) between old and young workers. The latter, having families to keep, are considered more deserving.[176] Mandatory retirement also removes blockages to promotion and assists the upward career path of employees within a firm. It thus creates a predictable career pattern, allowing employers to plan ahead, to devise pension schemes, and to get

---

[174] Office for National Statistics, *Social Trends No. 34 2004 Edition* (2004), p. 90.

[175] See, for example: Stanley C. Hope, 'Should There Be a Fixed Retirement Age? Some Managers Say Yes', *Annals of the American Academy of Political and Social Science*, vol. 279, Jan. 1952, pp. 72–3; Acton Society Trust, *Retirement. A Study of Current Attitudes and Practices* (1960), pp. 40–1; Erdman B. Palmore, 'Compulsory Versus Flexible Retirement: Issues and Facts', *The Gerontologist*, vol. 12, no. 4, Winter 1972, pp. 343–8.

[176] Friedman, *Your Time*, p. 79.

rid of older workers when they become too costly to employ in relation to their actual productivity.[177] For example, it has been claimed that the abolition of mandatory retirement for tenured academics in the USA may have worsened the academic job prospects of minorities and women, who will now find it even more difficult to obtain a post in universities.[178] If the working life was extended, workers could only continue in employment when aged in their seventies and eighties if lighter and less demanding jobs were reserved for them, in a special, protected labour market niche. This has often been suggested, but has foundered upon the inherent impracticalities.[179] No British or American government has ever contemplated such interference in the labour market.

If, in the aggregate, physical and mental ability does decline with age, there may be a kind of justice (albeit a rough justice) in treating all workers aged 65 the same way and 'throwing out the good with the bad', without individual stigmatisation or victimisation.[180] For example, a piece of research conducted in the 1950s into male employees' attitudes to retirement in a British firm with a fixed retirement age policy found that 'the firm's policy of retirement was accepted by the majority of them as inevitable in view of the nature of the work ... Many of them also expressed approval of a retirement policy which treated all employees alike, from directors downwards.'[181] Mandatory retirement can therefore be a 'face-saving' reason for employment termination in the case of an older worker no longer capable of performing his or her job adequately; the alternative might be a humiliating enforced retirement targeted only at the individual. As already noted, rigorous individual performance appraisal at work could be expensive, cumbersome, controversial and discriminatory in a different way. Both employers and employees might well dislike it. Finally, on a philosophical and existential level there is the argument that we ought to accept what Sartre called the 'necessity of our contingency' – the inevitability of ageing and death.[182]

Much of the anti-ageism literature argues that mandatory retirement should be replaced by more flexible arrangements (such as a 'decade of retirement', 'phased retirement' or 'flexible retirement') that would give individuals more choice over when they retired, enabling them to

---

[177] Edward P. Lazear, 'Why Is There Mandatory Retirement?', *Journal of Political Economy*, vol. 87, no. 6, Dec. 1979, pp. 1261–84.

[178] *Developments in Aging: 1996*, p. 81.

[179] See, for example, Acton Society Trust, *Retirement*, p. 41.

[180] Issacharoff and Harris, 'Is Age Discrimination?', pp. 790–1, 820.

[181] Margaret Pearson, 'The Transition from Work to Retirement (2)', *Occupational Psychology*, vol. 31, no. 3, July 1957, p. 146.

[182] Quoted in Simone de Beauvoir, *Old Age* (translated by Patrick O'Brien, 1972), p. 539.

'downshift' to lighter or more part-time work (perhaps underpinned by an early retirement pension) and thus avoid the abrupt and traumatic move over the 'cliff edge' from full-time work to total retirement.[183] Employers would thereby also be able to retain good employees. A more enlightened approach to retirement, permitting individuals greater choice, would undoubtedly be a welcome development. However, if, as argued above, retirement has spread primarily through declining sectoral labour market demand, the 'choices' open to individuals are in practice very limited. As will be shown in future chapters, 'flexible' or 'phased' retirement has been advocated for at least the last fifty years, and yet has never become widespread in advanced industrial economies. This would seem to indicate that it may be very difficult to implement. Finally, as already argued in this chapter, mandatory retirement may be something of a red herring: it affected relatively few workers in the USA in the 1960s, and because of falling retirement ages in Britain over the past decades its abolition would now make relatively little difference.[184]

Conclusion

The aim of this book is to explore some of the dilemmas and contradictions inherent in age discrimination. In doing so, it recognises that the study of ageing is riddled with dilemmas and contradictions. It therefore tries to examine what Eric Midwinter has called 'the ambivalence of ageism, that continually changing balance of admiration and contempt for older people, [which] is a constant in human societies, historically and geographically'.[185] Modern societies are highly age-stratified and age-conscious. As such, they display complex and shifting attitudes towards their older citizens, who present us with a constant reminder of the inevitability of our own ageing. We all have ambivalent feelings towards older people, which we need to confront.[186] Gerontology is also a field of study that arouses considerable passions, and one in which opposing sides often misinterpret each other. Many who work with older people argue that one cannot be neutral about ageism. Thus, attempting to construct a balanced assessment of all the issues raises what Michael Katz, in a different context, has called 'the tension between activism and scholarship'.[187]

---

[183] Bone and Mercer, *Flexible Retirement*.
[184] Pamela Meadows, *Retirement Ages in the UK: a Review of the Literature* (2003), p. 25.
[185] Midwinter, *Citizenship*, p. vii.
[186] Alison Norman, *Aspects of Ageism: a Discussion Paper* (1987), pp. 3–5.
[187] Michael B. Katz, *Improving Poor People. The Welfare State, the 'Underclass' and Urban Schools as History* (1995), p. 3.

The idea of 'gerontology' as a discrete field of study may however be eroded in the future if older workers are re-enlisted back into the labour market and state pension ages rise. We may then see 'the end of old age' or 'the end of gerontology'. It is interesting that the emergence of the newer 'lifecourse perspective' in gerontology (which partly subverts the notion of old age as a discrete stage) has coincided with powerful economic imperatives to encourage, or force, older workers back into the labour market – a less attractive vision of the 'ageless' society. If this trend continues, the controversies within social gerontology will appear very much twentieth-century concerns. It is a moot point whether moving away from age-based social programmes, and towards a needs-driven, age-neutral approach, would really be in the best interests of old people themselves.[188] Even though age-based programmes carry with them a set of assumptions about old age, they nevertheless protect older people.

The key question is a very difficult one: how far are unequal outcomes by age the product of age discrimination, and how far are they the result of other factors? In other words, *in what circumstances* does age discrimination operate? Or, as Levine succinctly puts it, in the very opening sentence of his study, 'Is "age discrimination" really "discrimination"?'[189] A point often made is that those countries with even quite strong legislation against age discrimination in employment have experienced falls in the economic activity rates of older men similar to Britain's,[190] that this has been primarily caused by declining labour market demand[191] (which has, in response, created an 'early exit culture'), and that the chances of significantly reversing this trend are not good.[192] If this view is correct, then interesting questions arise: What is the point of action against age discrimination? Is it primarily motivated by labour-supply concerns, particularly with regard to the supply of cheap, docile employees? Does it divert attention from the recent failings of the private pensions industry and the fall in the relative value of the state pension since 1980? Is it a sign that we are moving towards a more ruthlessly competitive, Social Darwinist society, in which increasingly sophisticated methods will be used to distinguish between the 'work relevant' and the 'work redundant'? Will twenty-first-century labour markets be like nineteenth-century

---

[188] This issue is explored in Bernice L. Neugarten, 'The End of Gerontology?', in Neugarten, *The Meanings*, pp. 402–3. See also, Bernice L. Neugarten (ed.), *Age or Need? Public Policies for Older People* (1982).

[189] Levine, *Age Discrimination*, p. 1.

[190] See, for example, Richard Spring, *H of C Deb.*, 6s, vol. 271, 9 Feb. 1996, col. 600.

[191] Philip Taylor and Alan Walker, 'The Employment of Older Workers in Five European Countries', in Institute of Personnel Management, *Age*, p. 5.

[192] Drury, *Age Discrimination*, p. 15; Phillipson, *Transitions*, pp. 12–14.

industrial labour markets, with a large, hypercasualised sector of low-skilled, low-paid jobs, and with poorer old people having to continue working until prevented from doing so by chronic infirmity – the 'work till you drop' scenario? Exactly what lies behind the euphemistic use of slogans such as 'ability, not age' and concepts such as labour market 'flexibility'? Questions like these need to be asked as a counter to the heady optimism of the British government's present initiatives. A disturbing feature of the recent age discrimination debate is that little thought seems to have been given to the rights of those 'incompetent' workers, regardless of their age, who would be rendered jobless by the abandonment of age proxies and their replacement by more individualised performance appraisal for job competence. Arguably, they would be victims of a different but equally ruthless kind of discrimination.

The renewed interest in age discrimination can be seen as a movement for social justice – a long-delayed attempt to gain for those discriminated against on grounds of age what has already been won for those discriminated against on grounds of gender, race or disability. But it can also be seen as an attack on the welfare rights of older people. It is precisely this collision between the 'social justice' and the 'labour supply' arguments that makes the present age discrimination debate so intriguing. Opposed arguments are often inextricably bound together, sometimes even being uttered in the same breath. For example, the 1996 report of the *Retirement Income Inquiry* called for 'vigorous action by all concerned to combat unjustified age discrimination in all aspects of employment', yet also for an ending of final salary pension schemes (with their replacement by personal, money-purchase pensions).[193] Again, in a recent government-sponsored publication we find the optimistic declaration that 'age should become irrelevant in the labour market. Individuals' value to employers should be based on their skills and competencies, not on their chronological age' immediately followed by the stern exhortation that 'retirement should be based upon people's capacity to look after themselves financially'[194] (which would mean, for a majority of the population, the inability ever to retire). As both Britain and America move through the early years of a new century, the revival of interest in age discrimination is surely a sign that the 'old age agenda' is profoundly changing. It remains to be seen whether or not these changes will be in the best interests of older people.

---

[193] *Pensions: 2000 and Beyond, Vol. I: The Report of the Retirement Income Inquiry* (1996), pp. 36, 45.
[194] Foresight: Ageing Population Panel, *The Age Shift* (2000), p. 22.

2   Justice between generations

Introduction

Central to the whole age discrimination debate is the question of the 'just' allocation of resources between generations and age-groups. If substantial negative discrimination against old people exists, it follows that it must be possible to detect many examples of positive discrimination in favour of the middle-aged and young. There will be, at any one time, an unequal distribution of resources and opportunities by age.

However, such a view needs careful examination. Two immediate points must be made. The first has been mentioned in the previous chapter: social policy is, at any one time, an intriguingly complex amalgam of both positive and negative discriminations towards particular age-groups. One example will suffice. Throughout history, welfare discourses and policies have been most punitive against those who possess the greatest future labour market value, with the most demonised groups being young, allegedly workshy males and young, 'reproductively deviant' females. The notionally moral categories of 'deserving' and 'undeserving' have always reflected labour market value. Such was the case under the Elizabethan Poor Law, and little has changed today:[1] for example, modern 'underclass' discourses have tended to focus on the working-aged, specifically excluding older people.[2] Yet this classification of the retired as axiomatically 'deserving' has been accompanied by explicit human capital reasoning that they are not worthy of public investment, since their life expectancy is short. Such reasoning has always permeated discussions of state pensions and retirement. For example, the 1954 Phillips Committee Report included several passages portraying retired people as a passive 'burden' on the rest of society. When the old gave up work, the Report maintained, 'they become

---

[1] John Macnicol, 'Is There an Underclass? The Lessons from America', in Michael White (ed.), *Unemployment and Public Policy in the Changing Labour Market* (1994), p. 25.

[2] See, for example, Charles Murray, *Losing Ground: American Social Policy, 1950–1980* (1984), pp. 13, 59.

dependent, directly or indirectly, on the labour of other people'. The 'burden' of old age involved 'the transfer to the elderly of income currently derived from the exertions of others', via the tax and national insurance systems.[3]

The second point to note is that it is misleading to take an instantaneous, cross-sectional view of a population's age structure, comparing the claims of one particular age-group against another at one point in time. If, instead, a longitudinal perspective is adopted, a different picture emerges, based upon the truism that we all grow old, but we cannot change our sex or race. The old are yesterday's young, and – assuming a world of stability – will have received more resources at an earlier stage in their lives.

Can a 'just' sharing-out of resources ever be achieved between different generations and cohorts? The problem is that a longitudinal, lifespan perspective uncovers a subtle mixture of negative and positive age discriminations experienced by individuals as they move through the lifecourse. Further complexity is introduced by the intersecting variables of class, race and gender. For example, the chances of survival to state pension age, and the length of life thereafter, are determined by both socio-economic status and gender. Some 'winners' enjoy a lengthy retirement, and thus receive much more in accumulated pension income than those 'losers' who die before retirement age. This chapter will examine this positive/negative balance with regard to the debates on intergenerational equity and age-based health care rationing.

Generational equity

The generational equity debate has a very long history. Tribal societies often displayed considerable intergenerational tensions in allocating land and resources,[4] and many examples can be found in anthropological literature (such as food-sharing practices).[5] The problem of generational equity can also be traced back to Thomas Hobbes and other 'social contract' theorists (and possibly even to the Biblical injunction to 'honour thy father and thy

---

[3] *Report of the Committee on the Economic and Financial Problems of the Provision for Old Age*, Cmd. 9333, 1954, pp. 27, 33.

[4] Nancy Foner, *Ages in Conflict: a Cross-Cultural Perspective on Inequality between Old and Young* (1984); Richard Wall, 'Intergenerational Relationships Past and Present', in Alan Walker (ed.), *The New Generational Contract: Intergenerational Relations, Old Age and Welfare* (1996), pp. 37–55.

[5] John B. Williamson and Diane M. Watts-Roy, 'Framing the Generational Equity Debate', in John B. Williamson, Diane M. Watts-Roy and Eric R. Kingson (eds.), *The Generational Equity Debate* (1999), pp. 4–5.

mother').[6] It was given a remarkably complex and nuanced exploration by the social theorist Karl Mannheim, in his classic essay on 'The Problem of Generations' (1927).[7] More recent discussions of it are to be found in sources as disparate as Cumming and Henry's classic text on disengagement theory (where it was termed 'intergenerational tension')[8] and the work of the moral philosophers John Rawls and Bruce Ackerman.[9]

It has also figured strongly in policy debates. For example, in Britain concern over an ageing population in the 1920s and 1930s gave rise to some debate on how much each generation should pay for another's pension costs. The strategy of job redistribution from older workers to young unemployed, which was much discussed in the 1930s and the 1970s, was also based upon a crude and implicit notion of intergenerational justice. In the USA, the brief success of the late-1930s Townsend Movement seems to have elicited a degree of concern about the potential power of the emerging 'grey lobby', and its ability to destabilise American politics. For example, in 1940 Ewan Clague (Commissioner of Labor Statistics at the Department of Labor, and a prolific writer on old age) warned that old age pressure groups would grow in influence in the future: this would be 'one of the most important political considerations that will face this country in the next forty years'; unless the new social security system could be developed sufficiently to placate them, he argued, 'they could easily wreck our economic system by their demands'.[10] Likewise, Nathan Shock feared that the Townsend Movement's emphasis on stimulating demand, rather than increasing investment, could 'endanger the total economy';[11] and the gerontologist Robert Havighurst observed in 1949 that, if older people in America combined together to form one coherent political movement, they would be able to exert enormous influence over governments.[12] Abraham Holtzman, evaluating the status of old age politics in 1954, concluded that it had been accommodated within existing political institutions – but he warned that, if such special interest politics

[6] Vern Bengtson, 'Will "Generational Accounting" Doom the Welfare State?', *The Gerontologist*, vol. 33, no. 6, 1993, p. 812.

[7] Karl Mannheim, 'The Problem of Generations', in Mannheim, *Essays on the Sociology of Knowledge. Collected Works Volume Five* (ed. Paul Kecskemeti) (1957 edn), pp. 276–320.

[8] Elaine Cumming and William E. Henry, *Growing Old. The Process of Disengagement* (1961), p. 219.

[9] John Rawls, *A Theory of Justice* (1999 edn), pp. 251–8; Bruce A. Ackerman, *Social Justice in the Liberal State* (1980).

[10] Ewan Clague, 'The Aging Population and Programs of Security', *Milbank Memorial Fund Quarterly*, vol. 18, no. 4, 1940, pp. 347–8.

[11] Nathan W. Shock, *Trends in Gerontology* (1951), pp. 35–6.

[12] Robert J. Havighurst, 'Old Age – an American Problem', *Journal of Gerontology*, vol. 4, no. 4, Oct. 1949, pp. 298–304.

developed, America could face a war between old and young.[13] It was even suggested that in future there might be a movement to disenfranchise older voters in order to protect the interests of other age-groups.[14]

The generational equity debate that has taken place in both Britain and the USA over the past twenty years is thus a revival of interest, rather than something entirely new. It seems to have originated in the USA in the early 1980s, based upon allegations that too great a proportion of social security resources was going to retirees, and insufficient to children and the working-aged. The somewhat elliptical logic behind this was that America had been 'too successful' in reducing old age poverty: the official poverty rate for US citizens aged 65+fell by two-thirds between 1959 and 1990; however, poverty rates for children and single mother-headed families did not drop as fast, leading to concerns about the health and life chances of future generations of adults. By the 1980s, the phrase 'the feminisation of poverty' was being widely used in the USA to denote the increasing concentration of poverty in households headed by a single mother. (The fact that a pronounced 'feminisation of poverty' occurs in old age aroused little comment.) It was argued that pensions and other social security payments to retired people should, as an act of generational justice, be cut. (Curiously, those who articulated such concerns tended to argue that welfare support for single mothers should also be cut.) Clearly, the generational equity debate was part of a much wider attack on all welfare benefits in the 1980s.

Some thoughtful, if ultimately unconvincing, analyses of generational inequity were produced,[15] but most populist commentary was sensationalist in tone. In its most extreme form – a *reductio ad absurdum* of an exclusively 'human agency' view of social change – the argument held that a selfish 'welfare generation' had somehow managed to manipulate the public policy agenda on its own behalf and had secured increases in state pensions and other social security benefits to coincide with its own retirement. These increases could not be afforded in the long term, and at some point a 'war between the generations' would break out, as the young realised that they would be saddled with crippling levels of taxation to pay for the pensions of their parents' generation.

The question of intergenerational justice quickly entered the realm of public discussion and was seized upon by a press eager to find simplistic explanations for America's social and economic problems in the 1980s. At

---

[13] Abraham Holtzman, 'Analysis of Old Age Politics in the United States', *Journal of Gerontology*, vol. 9, no. 1, Jan. 1954, pp. 56–66.

[14] Paul H. Landis, 'Emerging Problems of the Aged', *Social Forces*, vol. 20, no. 4, May 1942, p. 476.

[15] For example, David Thomson, *Selfish Generations? How Welfare States Grow Old* (1991).

the populist level, this debate was not conducted with great intellectual rigour: very quickly, the 'greedy geezers' were being blamed for almost every ill that beset the American economy – from stagnating industrial wages to the low level of aggregate savings.[16] A typical quote was that from Henry Fairlie, in the *New Republic* of 28 March 1988:

Thirty percent of the annual federal budget now goes to expenditures on people over the age of 65. Forty years from now, if the present array of programs and benefits is maintained, almost two-thirds of the budget will go to supporting and cossetting the old. Something is wrong with a society that is willing to drain itself to foster such an unproductive section of its population, one that does not even promise (as children do) one day to be productive.[17]

In similar vein was Lester Thurow's apocalyptic warning that a 'new class of people' was being created – economically inactive, elderly voters 'who require expensive social services such as health care'. These were 'bringing down the welfare state, destroying government finances, and threatening the investments that all societies need to make a successful future'.[18] This rather facile analysis was cleverly orchestrated in the USA by several pressure groups, notably Americans for Generational Equity (founded in 1984, with considerable corporate sponsorship) and the Concord Coalition. In Britain, the generational equity debate did not have quite the same populist impact, but it did influence some academics. For example, in 1989 three commentators argued that it was 'necessary to lower the overall income expectations of the aged, or to change patterns of work' (by stemming the trend to early retirement), and to replace the universal state pension with a means-tested one.[19]

On a more thoughtful level, however, the debate certainly raised some interesting issues and challenges for social gerontology. The whole question of how norms of obligation, reciprocity and expectation between generations are negotiated, at both the micro-social level of the family and the macro-social level of society at large, was well worth scrutiny, as was the issue (never fully explored) of whether ordinary citizens had internalised the idea of an implicit 'intergenerational welfare contract'. Notable among the

---

[16] See, for example, Phillip Longman, *Born to Pay. The New Politics of Aging in America* (1987).

[17] Quoted in Robert N. Butler, 'Dispelling Ageism: the Cross Cutting Intervention', *Annals of the American Academy of Political and Social Science*, vol. 503, May 1989, p. 141.

[18] Lester C. Thurow, 'Generational Equity and the Birth of a Revolutionary Class', in Williamson, Watts-Roy and Kingson, *Generational Equity Debate*, p. 59.

[19] Paul Johnson, Christoph Conrad and David Thomson, 'Introduction', in Johnson, Conrad and Thomson (eds.), *Workers Versus Pensioners. Intergenerational Justice in an Ageing World* (1989), pp. 9, 14. For a critique, see John Macnicol, 'Ageing and Justice', *Labour History Review*, vol. 55, no. 1, Spring 1990, pp. 75–80.

more perceptive recent analyses is Peter Laslett and James Fishkin's argument that much discussion of concepts like justice, fairness, obligation, equality, and so on by existing political theorists assumes fixed populations over short time periods: if obligations to future generations are considered (for example, in the protection of the environment), these issues become much more complex.[20] The debate also has some relevance to the question of whether reparations should be paid to certain groups (for example, Maoris in New Zealand, or Native Indians in the USA) as recompense for past injustices against them.[21] But in the final analysis, the argument that there had been a shift in the balance of public expenditure in favour of a selfish 'welfare generation' remained unconvincing.

A number of telling criticisms were made. There was the central question of whether a 'generation' – often defined as a twenty-five-year birth cohort – could be said to hold monolithic attitudes, given the enormous diversity that exists within any population sub-group. Some shared characteristics can be identified among the 'baby boomers', but these tend to be very general.[22] Inequalities of gender, race and class were rarely examined. (Mannheim had argued that a true generation had to possess 'similarity of location', in terms of shared experiences; mere chronological contemporaneity was not enough.)[23] Some participants in the debate used the term 'generation' as a temporal unit when clearly what they meant was a smaller 'age-group' or 'birth cohort'. Others seemed to be referring to the whole body of pensioners or retirees: given that de facto retirement can now last up to forty years, this definition was unhelpfully broad. In modes of dress, speech, leisure pursuits, consumer behaviour, and so on, the over-sixties behave somewhat differently from their younger fellow-citizens, but they are emphatically influenced by the same wider social trends (for example, the trend towards more casual clothing). They are not hermetically sealed off from the rest of society, occupying some cultural time-warp based upon the prevailing values and attitudes when they themselves were young: for example, in their senior years they marry, get divorced, have live-in partners, and even father children out of wedlock[24] – just like the rest of society. Again, there was much imprecise labelling of a 'baby boom'

---

[20] Peter Laslett and James S. Fishkin, 'Introduction: Processional Justice', in Laslett and Fishkin (eds.), *Justice between Age-Groups and Generations* (1992), p. 1.

[21] Peter Laslett, 'Is There a Generational Contract?', in Laslett and Fishkin, *Justice*, p. 39.

[22] Jane Falkingham, 'Who Are the Baby Boomers? A Demographic Profile', in Maria Evandrou (ed.), *Baby Boomers. Ageing in the 21st Century* (1997), pp. 15–40.

[23] Mannheim, 'The Problem', esp. pp. 282, 290–1, 297.

[24] Thus between 1981 and 1997, the number of out-of-wedlock live births fathered by men aged 50+ in Britain nearly trebled, from 630 to 1,769. Office for National Statistics, *Social Focus on Older People* (1999), p. 14.

generation (those born from the mid-1940s to the mid-1960s), followed by a 'baby bust' generation, and then an 'echo' generation. If, as postmodern theorists of the lifecourse argue, age distinctions are becoming more blurred, it must follow that identifying one particular 'generation' will become increasingly difficult.

At the macro-level of society at large, there is abundant survey-based evidence of strong intergenerational ties and frequent contact between old and young: this has been well chronicled for Europe (using the results of Eurobarometer surveys).[25] Sociologists of the family have convincingly argued that, at the micro-level of the family or the small community, there are many examples of intergenerational reciprocity:[26] for example, as family members age, they take on the roles relinquished by recently deceased older relatives. Again, grandparents perform many important caring tasks for their grandchildren (particularly as more and more parents work in the labour market). Indeed, the large amount of work performed by retirees in the informal economy refutes the idea of the old as passive 'consumers' of wealth.

It would appear that the general public in Britain *do* believe in honouring the intergenerational contract where public expenditure resource allocation is concerned. For example, a survey conducted in Britain in 1993 found only 2 per cent of respondents in favour of lowering the level of the state pension, and 94 per cent against; 67 per cent were against raising the legal retirement age for both men and women, and only 21 per cent in favour; and 47 per cent were in favour of raising National Insurance contributions for all in work, with 37 per cent against.[27] Another survey found that only 9.3 per cent of British respondents judged the state pension to be 'completely adequate', with 38.6 per cent judging it to be 'just about adequate', 28.4 per cent 'somewhat adequate' and 22.8 per cent 'very inadequate'.[28] Again, the 1996 British Social Attitudes survey found that 80 per cent of people aged under forty thought that a married couple living on the state pension would be either 'really poor' or 'hard up'.[29] It would seem, therefore, that only a very small minority of British citizens consider the state pension to be over-generous. It is worth bearing in mind that the level of public expenditure on state pensions in Britain as a share of Gross

[25] Alan Walker and Tony Maltby, *Ageing Europe* (1997), ch. 3.

[26] Dorothy Jerrome, 'Ties That Bind', in Walker, *New Generational Contract*, pp. 81–99.

[27] Central Statistical Office, *Social Trends No. 26 1996 Edition* (1996), p. 155.

[28] Commission of the European Communities, *Age and Attitudes. Main Results from the Eurobarometer Survey* (1993), p. 18.

[29] Office for National Statistics, *Social Focus on Older People*, pp. 55–6. See also Ruth Hancock, Claire Jarvis and Ganka Mueller, *The Outlook for Incomes in Retirement. Social Trends and Attitudes* (1995), p. 9.

Domestic Product is one of the lowest in the Organisation for Economic Co-operation and Development (OECD) countries,[30] and that the value of the basic state pension in relation to average earnings has fallen steadily since 1980. If there is a selfish 'welfare generation', it has been singularly inept at winning more resources for itself.

The 'selfish welfare generation' thesis tended to focus almost exclusively on social security, health care and pension costs. However, as John Hills has observed, 'intergenerational equity is not just about the welfare state'.[31] A more accurate process of generational accounting would need to encompass *all* social costs, and perhaps even include experiential factors. Examining the totality of each age cohort's gains and losses would involve massively complex calculations of all experiences, both negative and positive, across the completed lifecourse.[32] In recent history, these would include: the recession of the 1930s, with its high levels of unemployment; the traumatic effects of the Second World War (involving the incalculable loss of loved ones); the full-employment 1950s and 1960s; inflation in the 1970s and the re-appearance of economic recession in the 1980s; the relative level (and hence affordability) of property prices; inventions that improve (or, conversely, diminish) the quality of life; new medical technologies that lower mortality and lead to better management of morbidity; the conquest of old epidemics (such as tuberculosis), and the emergence of new ones (such as AIDS or CJD); changes in real wages and incomes; taxation levels; and so on. In short, it would be a well-nigh impossible exercise. Again, focusing on social security and health care costs ignores other items in social accounting that make the *young* very costly (as discussed in the previous chapter). We can conclude, therefore, that a proper cost–benefit analysis of different generations would need to consider many more factors than have been discussed by those who warn of impending generational conflict.

Even if generational injustice could be proved, it would be difficult to obtain recompense for past wrongs. As George Sher has observed,

There are surely some persons alive today who would be better off if the Spanish Inquisition had not taken place, or if the Jews had not originally been expelled from the land of Canaan. To discover who these persons are and how much better off they would be, however, we would have to draw on far more genealogical, causal

---

[30] Alan Walker, 'Intergenerational Relations and the Provision of Welfare', in Walker, *New Generational Contract*, p. 17.

[31] John Hills, 'Does Britain Have a Welfare Generation?', in Walker, *New Generational Conflict*, p. 79.

[32] For an interesting example of this approach, see Françoise Cribier, 'Changes in Life Course and Retirement in Recent Years: the Example of Two Cohorts of Parisians', in Johnson, Conrad and Thomson, *Workers Versus Pensioners*, pp. 181–201.

and counterfactual knowledge than anyone can reasonably be expected to possess.[33]

Those who argued that generational inequity was a serious and growing problem were not very forthcoming with practical policy suggestions. In many ways, their aim seemed primarily to establish a pessimistic agenda, whereby public expenditure would be blamed for economic underperformance. But some proposals were suggested: that 'generational accounting' be applied to all public policies, to ensure an equal distribution of resources to each generation;[34] that state pensions be privatised as much as possible, and certainly moved more towards a 'fully funded' basis rather than pay-as-you-go; that state pension ages be raised; and that more early retired older people be encouraged, or forced, back into the labour market.

By the early twenty-first century, the generational equity debate had considerably diminished in intensity. The legacy it had bequeathed was not particularly edifying, and it is ironic that in the 1980s the debate was over 'too much' positive discrimination in favour of older people, yet since then the debate has focused on precisely the opposite. However, the generational equity debate had at least demonstrated that the issue of justice between age-groups is worth exploring, providing that it is undertaken intelligently. Its most constructive legacy for the age discrimination debate has been to remind us that a cross-sectional, instantaneous view of justice between the generations is of limited value. Instead, a longitudinal perspective should be adopted, and from this we can see that each individual experiences a mixture of positive and negative discriminations over the course of a lifetime.

Health care rationing by age

One area that well illustrates the complexity of intergenerational justice is that of age-based health care rationing in the British National Health Service (NHS). It is a debate that arouses strong feelings on both sides, and raises many contentious issues, both moral and medical. Ageism in health care is often seen as 'a reflection of ageist attitudes that exist in the wider society, where youth is given priority over age'.[35] Conversely, it has

---

[33] George Sher, 'Ancient Wrongs and Modern Rights', in Laslett and Fishkin, *Justice*, p. 49.

[34] Laurence J. Kotlikoff, *Generational Accounting. Knowing Who Pays, and When, for What We Spend* (1992); Jagadeesh Gokhale and Laurence J. Kotlikoff, 'Generational Justice and Generational Accounting', in Williamson, Watts-Roy and Kingson, *Generational Equity Debate*, pp. 75–86; Roberto Cardarelli, James Sefton and Laurence J. Kotlikoff, 'Generational Accounting in the UK', *Economic Journal*, vol. 110, no. 467, Nov. 2000, pp. F547–74.

[35] Ann Bowling, 'Ageism in Cardiology', *British Medical Journal*, vol. 319, 20 Nov. 1999, p. 1353.

been argued that the reverse is also true: the medicalised model of ageing has helped perpetuate a negative perception of older people.[36] The relationship is thus interactive and complex.

When Britain's NHS was founded in 1948, the assumption was that it would be available to all, regardless of 'financial means, age, sex, employment or vocation, area of residence or insurance qualification'[37] – which was merely a statement of how resources were *not* to be rationed. However, this commitment marked such a welcome change from the pre-NHS system that its implications were never explored. Being the first tax-funded, universal state medical service among the Western democracies, the NHS was breaking new ground. Its early planners could do little more than nationalise most of the existing health services, and wait and see what the new system cost. As is well known, in the early 1950s a level of NHS funding just under 4 per cent of Gross National Product became fixed as the rather artificial baseline from which future judgements were made. This figure was not justified by any assessment of the population's health care needs, and health spending in the 1950s was kept artificially low by a number of factors – notably a lack of new hospital building.[38] From its inception, the NHS had to survive in the rough-and-tumble of politics; the result was that resources were always constrained. Gradually, various informal rationing devices appeared, notably the use of waiting time.

By the 1970s, the debate on rationing and resource allocation in the NHS was intensifying, against a background of increasing public expenditure limits. But while resource allocation by region began to be explored (notably, with the work of the Resource Allocation Working Party in 1975–6), and while increasing attention was paid to unequal health outcomes by factors such as gender, class and race, age remained something of a lacuna. Since the 1980s, however, there has been a growing discussion of rationing by age and of ageism in the NHS. The burgeoning interest in age discrimination in employment, and the concomitant increasing activity by pressure groups such as Age Concern, has been one reason: such groups have repeatedly raised the issue. Another has been the long-running debate over whether the NHS is 'under-funded' or 'over-funded': should public spending on health care be increased, or should the aim be to achieve

---

[36] See, for example, Alan Walker, 'Older People and Health Services. The Challenge of Empowerment', in Michael Purdy and David Banks (eds.), *Health and Exclusion. Policy and Practice in Health Provision* (1999), pp. 158–78.

[37] 1946 National Health Service Act, quoted in Trevor A. Sheldon and Alan Maynard, 'Is Rationing Inevitable?', in British Medical Journal, *Rationing In Action* (1993), p. 5.

[38] Charles Webster, *The Health Services Since the War, Vol. I. Problems of Health Care. The National Health Service Before 1957* (1988), ch. 5.

greater value for money within existing resource constraints? In addition, the spread of new medical technology has raised public expectations, resulting in a more ruthless scrutiny of what the NHS can and cannot do. The 1990s witnessed a series of high-profile cases (such as that of 'Child B') where treatment was denied on the basis of explicit rationing criteria – most often, high expense of treatment or uncertainty of outcome, but on some occasions extending to the patient's lifestyle (for example, refusal to perform cardiac surgery unless the patient ceased smoking). Finally, the launching of such 'patient empowerment' initiatives as the Patients' Charter in 1991 and the NHS Direct service at the end of the 1990s meant both that the public would become more demanding, and that the efficacy of particular medical interventions would be more closely scrutinised. The cumulative effect has been that the question of the 'right' to health care has become much more contentious.

All health care systems operate rationing procedures, but arguably in a free-at-time-of-use, tax-funded system like the NHS the problem assumes greater importance because of the democratic assumption that health care should be equally available to all citizens. There is always a tension between official reassurances that access to comprehensive health care is a 'right' bestowed upon all citizens, and the realisation that advances in medical technology, rising consumer expectations and a general growth in health awareness may be widening the gap between what the NHS can do and what it is expected to do. In the last ten years, there have been suggestions that this gap has become so wide that the NHS should concentrate on a strictly defined 'core' of business, and leave the rest to the private sector.

The debate on rationing by age has thus emerged as part of a wider debate between, on the one hand, those who wish the NHS to evolve more explicit and transparent rationing procedures, based upon morally acceptable principles, consultation with the public (as in the 'Oregon experiment' in the USA) and more 'evidence-based' criteria of efficacy, and, on the other, those who believe that, in a complex and multi-layered organisation like the NHS, only rough guidelines can be drawn up: day-to-day clinical decisions should thus be left to the discretion of doctors, who operate in complex situations of considerable stress. The debate ranges deep and wide, from abstract principles of moral philosophy (whose application to 'real world' medical situations may be impractical) to the evaluation of treatment outcomes (which may be impossible to measure, owing to the large number of variables involved).[39]

---

[39] For an excellent discussion, see John Butler, *The Ethics of Health Care Rationing* (1999).

Age as a rationing criterion

On the face of it, there is compelling evidence to support the accusation that ageism has been rampant in the NHS. In any tax-funded, state medical service, overt rationing applies, firstly, at the formal level, via specific policy directives or limitations on treatment. (Private health care systems usually ration by the price mechanism.) In the NHS, some of these top-down directives – such as refusal to undertake tattoo reversal, or placing a limit on the number of IVF treatments a woman can have – are relatively uncontentious. Others, such as 'postcode' rationing, merely send a message to governments that more resources should be directed to certain regions. However, those that deny or limit treatment to patients above a certain age have been highly controversial, and have aroused the wrath of old age pressure groups, geriatricians, and so on. Thus, as far back as 1989, Age Concern was protesting that 'there is widespread belief that people over a certain age do not have equal access to health care', pointing out that the NHS then only provided routine breast cancer screening to women aged 50–64, despite the fact that 63 per cent of breast cancer deaths occurred in women aged 65+.[40] (Women aged 65+ could obtain screening on request, but only some 2 per cent did so.)[41] Renal dialysis is another example. In the UK in the mid-1980s, only 8 per cent of patients receiving dialysis were aged 65+, compared with roughly 25 per cent in Germany, France and Italy – despite better survival rates among those aged 65+, compared with those aged 55–64.[42] Two-thirds of heart attack patients treated in NHS hospitals are aged 65+; people aged 65+ are, on average, seven times more likely to have a heart attack than those under 65, and have a much higher risk of dying after a heart attack; their chances of survival can be greatly improved by high-quality care and the provision of thrombolytic drugs in specialist coronary care units. Yet a survey in 1992 found that one-fifth of such units operated an age-related admissions policy (commencing at age 65) – despite the fact that thrombolytic therapy in acute myocardial infarction can have better results in older patients than in younger.[43] Likewise, the standard of care offered to

---

[40] Age Concern memorandum, *Age Discrimination Affecting Older People* (1989); Jane Titley, *Health Care Rights for Older People. The Ageism Issue* (1997), p. 4.

[41] Graham C. Sutton, 'Will You Still Need Me, Will You Still Screen Me, When I'm Past 64?', *British Medical Journal*, vol. 315, 25 October 1997, p. 1032.

[42] John Grimley Evans, 'This Patient or That Patient?', in British Medical Journal, *Rationing*, p. 120.

[43] N. J. Dudley and E. Burns, 'The Influence of Age on Policies for Admission and Thrombolysis in Coronary Care Units in the United Kingdom', *Age and Ageing*, vol. 21, 1992, pp. 95–8; Titley, *Health Care Rights*, pp. 3–4; John Grimley Evans, 'A Rejoinder to Alan Williams', in Bill New (ed.), *Rationing: Talk and Action in Health Care* (1997), p. 13; Age Concern, *Equal Access to Cardiac Rehabilitation* (1998).

cancer patients varies not only by region but also by age, with older people on average being offered treatment of lower quality and dubious efficacy. Many other examples can be unearthed, such as the tendency, in discussions on inequalities in health status, to focus on the problem of premature mortality (before the age of 65), while ignoring the health status of the 65+ population,[44] or the exclusion of those aged 75+ from recent government targets for reducing death rates from heart disease, cancers and strokes,[45] or the tendency to marginalise older people from clinical research.[46]

However, there also occurs covert rationing at the informal level, via what have been called 'primary inhibitors' (for example, the gatekeeping actions of general practitioners, or even their receptionists) and 'secondary inhibitors' (delay, denial and dilution of demand – most notably, in the form of waiting time to see a consultant).[47] This discretionary rationing, operating at the micro-level in day-to-day contact between doctors and patients, is the most difficult to detect. In all probability, it is also the most common form of rationing, although one can never truly 'prove' this. As John Butler puts it, such micro-rationing is 'largely hidden and unaccountable, exercised beneath the cloak of clinical discretion, the skirts of which "society" has not until recently been inclined to lift very far'.[48] It is here that age is frequently used to deny treatment to patients. Now prohibited, the instruction 'do not resuscitate' (DNR) or 'not for resuscitation' (NFR) used to be attached to the medical records of some older patients who were hospitalised with serious illnesses, without consulting their close relatives.[49] Age Concern has collected many harrowing examples of the kind of institutionalised, attitudinal ageism that encourages doctors to hasten the death of older patients by ignoring their symptoms and even withdrawing treatment. These are undoubtedly the tip of a large ageist iceberg.[50]

The pros and cons of age-based health care rationing

The arguments for and against the fairness of age-based rationing in health care are intriguing, and illustrate in microcosm the wider dilemmas

---

[44] John Grimley Evans, 'Challenge of Aging', in Richard Smith (ed.), *Health of the Nation: the BMJ View* (1991), p. 35.

[45] *Saving Lives: Our Healthier Nation*, Cm. 4386, July 1999, p. viii.

[46] G. Bugeja, A. Kumar and Arup K. Banerjee, 'Exclusion of Elderly People from Clinical Research: a Descriptive Study of Published Reports', *British Medical Journal*, vol. 315, 25 Oct. 1997, p. 1059.

[47] John Butler, *Ethics*, p. 27.

[48] Ibid., p. 35.

[49] Emilie Roberts, 'Age Discrimination in Health', in Help the Aged, *Age Discrimination in Public Policy. A Review of Evidence* (2002), pp. 50–1.

[50] Age Concern, *Turning Your Back on Us. Older People and the NHS* (1999).

inherent in age discrimination. The first argument in favour is related to the use of age proxies generally: faced with situations of complexity and uncertainty, such rationing permits the hard-pressed doctor to make quick decisions based upon a rule-of-thumb triage. As three authors put it, age 'provides an automatic pilot for doctors, so simplifying the perplexities, and avoiding the agonies, of choosing between different lives'.[51] Age may well be a useful, if approximate, indicator of capacity to benefit from treatment, even though – as with every use of age proxies – this will be more accurate at group, rather than individual, level. It can be claimed that such rationing is not, therefore, based upon age per se, but on other 'relevant' criteria, such as higher levels of risk (for example, caused by comorbidities). It is thus not ageist. Hence the declaration by the Secretary of State for Health in 1994 that 'The NHS provides services for everybody, on the basis of their clinical need and regardless of their ability to pay. There are no exceptions to this rule, whatever the age of the patient'[52] can be consistent with age-based rationing, since it can be argued that age is an accurate proxy for clinical need.

There is a second argument backed by both economic and philosophical justifications. Even if more national resources were devoted to the NHS, there is no guarantee that older citizens would benefit. Much of the difference in health care expenditure levels between countries is explained by higher levels of surgical intervention, an over-abundance of expensive technology and higher salary costs, rather than extent of coverage. For example, the American health care system is, per capita, the most expensive in the world, yet up to one-fifth of Americans are uncovered or undercovered by health insurance. Recent OECD rankings of health care in different countries demonstrate that there is not necessarily a correlation between resource input and aggregate population health (say, as measured by life expectancy at birth).[53] Faced with this inevitable tendency of demand to outstrip supply, it is argued, resources should be distributed according to the utilitarian principle of the greatest good: what sharing-out of scarce resources will produce the maximum overall benefit to the population as a whole? Should health care resources be directed at the young, who have more useful years of life ahead of them – particularly when the NHS, like all modern health care systems, devotes a disproportionate level of resources to older people? Any tax-funded, universal health

---

[51] Rudolf Klein, Patricia Day and Sharon Redmayne, *Managing Scarcity. Priority Setting and Rationing in the National Health Service* (1996), p. 87.

[52] Cited in Bill New and Julian Le Grand, *Rationing in the NHS. Principles and Pragmatism* (1996), p. 19.

[53] Organisation for Economic Co-operation and Development, *Health at a Glance 2003* (2003), www.oecd.org.

care system must deploy cost–benefit analyses in order to target resources effectively. Such analyses must inevitably place age limits on treatment: thus it used to be argued that extending routine breast cancer screening to all women aged 65+ would save more statistical lives, but at an unacceptably high cost.[54] In a situation of finite resources, other patients would be deprived of care.[55] Giving equal treatment to all may engender public support (as in wartime food rationing), but it may not produce the best outcome for society as a whole.

The rather commonsense philosophical justification for this is often termed, in a cricketing metaphor, the 'good innings' argument: the old are less deserving than the young, because they are at the end of their lives and have presumably enjoyed many healthy years. It is akin to the classic argument in favour of mandatory retirement, or firm downsizing by age: if a finite number of jobs are to be shared out, utilitarian principles would award these to the young. Older citizens must accept that they possess a lesser claim to resources. Many people might support such a version of intergenerational justice – although a recent survey of seventy-five senior NHS managers found only one who thought that young people had a greater claim on finite health care resources.[56] As Alan Williams puts it:

In each of our lives there has to come a time when we accept the inevitability of death, and when we also accept that a reasonable limit has to be set on the demands we can properly make on our fellow citizens in order to keep us going a bit longer.[57]

Beneath this commonsense view, of course, lies the frankly human capital consideration that young people have more economic value than do old. Such 'social triage' thinking has always dominated status definitions of old age and is objected to strenuously by old age pressure groups.

A more sophisticated elaboration has been offered by the philosopher Norman Daniels, in his 'prudential lifespan account'. Daniels's arguments are complex and nuanced, and can only be summarised briefly here. (He is at pains to point out that he is emphatically *not* justifying age discrimination: instead, he is merely exploring the philosophical case for and against age-based health care rationing.) Daniels suggests that many of the objections to age-based rationing are predicated upon a 'synchronic' or 'time-slice' view of society that pits the moral claims of different age-groups

[54] Chris Heginbotham, 'Why Rationing is Inevitable in the NHS', in New, *Rationing*, pp. 49–50.
[55] Alan Williams, 'Intergenerational Equity: an Exploration of the "Fair Innings" Argument', *Health Economics*, vol. 6, no. 2, Mar.–Apr. 1997, p. 121.
[56] Emilie Roberts, Janice Robinson and Linda Seymour, *Old Habits Die Hard. Tackling Age Discrimination in Health and Social Care* (2002), pp. 9–10.
[57] Alan Williams, 'Rationing Health Care by Age: the Case For', in New, *Rationing*, p. 109.

against each other at any one time. If, instead, we take a 'diachronic' (or lifespan) perspective, the old become the same persons as the young at a later stage in their lives:

If we treat the young one way and the old another, then over time each person is treated both ways. The advantages (or disadvantages) of *consistent* differential treatment by age will equalise over time.

Thus an old person may receive fewer health care resources when old, but this will be balanced by their having received more when young.[58]

There are several problems with this argument. First, it is extremely unlikely that the structure, and level of availability, of a health care system would remain fixed over an individual's lifespan: a working-class woman born in 1910 would have had poor access to health care when young (before the NHS), yet would still be faced with age-based rationing when old. Technological innovation, increasing overall resource input, and many other developments in medicine render such a lifespan comparison completely unworkable. Daniels's assumption that 'policy is stable over time and that all people go through the whole age range'[59] is unrealistic: we cannot in practice compare complete lives. Second, it may have some plausibility when applied at the level of group rights, but collapses when applied at a sub-group or an individual level. There are substantial inequalities of socio-economic status, gender and race in patterns of morbidity and mortality, and in access to health care and other public resources: lower social classes have a markedly worse chance of surviving to retirement; their need for health care is always greater; women use more health care resources than men; and so on. Again, at the individual level, someone who needed no health care until the age of seventy might then have an unassailable moral right to a very large amount, and vice versa.[60] (We must remember that it is at the individual level that the arguments against the use of age proxies is strongest.) Third, Daniels's argument could be used to justify both negative and positive discrimination at any stage in the lifecourse.

A second and slightly more convincing point made by Daniels is that allocating more health care resources to the young might improve their chances of survival to old age, and thus, on utilitarian criteria, benefit

[58] Norman Daniels, 'Justice and Transfers Between Generations', in Johnson, Conrad and Thomson, *Workers Versus Pensioners*, pp. 57–79, 61 (quote). See also Daniels, *Just Health Care* (1985), pp. 91–2; Daniels, 'Justice Between Age-Groups: Am I My Parents' Keeper?', *Milbank Memorial Fund Quarterly/Health and Society*, vol. 61, no. 3, 1983, pp. 489–522; Daniels, *Am I My Parents' Keeper? An Essay on Justice between the Young and the Old* (1988).

[59] Daniels, 'Justice and Transfers', p. 61.

[60] Dennis McKerlie, 'Equality Between Age-Groups', *Philosophy and Public Affairs*, vol. 21, no. 3, Summer 1992, p. 281.

everyone. Again, this is open to a large number of practical objections, notably that it assumes that health care plays a major role in determining survival (compared with factors such as socio-economic status, nutrition, lifestyle and genetics), and that there would not merely be more 'impaired survivors' in old age.

Finally, it can be argued that all explicit, open and transparent rationing devices used in the NHS – in the pursuit of clinical effectiveness, 'evidence-based' medicine and value for money – will inevitably discriminate against older people, since they are bound to be based upon cost–benefit calculations of the value of life. For example, using Quality Adjusted Life Years (QALYs) involves calculating the additional years of life that can be expected to result from a particular medical intervention, weighted by measures of disability and distress, and relating this to the cost of such intervention. In one sense, QALYs can be viewed as egalitarian, since they do not decide deservingness on grounds of race, class, intelligence, civic worth, and so on; but they inevitably discriminate against the old, who have fewest years left to live. Only if QALY weightings were adjusted by age would age bias be eliminated.[61]

By contrast, those who oppose age-based rationing argue that the 'finite resources/infinite demand' equation is an abstraction: it bears little relation to the social realities of ordinary people (the vast majority of whom do not present trivial medical demands), and could only be verified once Britain's health care resources had been increased (say by another 2–3 per cent of GDP). The use of age proxies, it is argued, is fundamentally unfair and should be replaced by individualised assessment based upon clinical need, and not age, gender, race, class, region, deservingness, and so on. Rationing by age is condemned on both medical and moral grounds: as John Grimley Evans puts it, it is based upon 'poor science and woolly ethics'.[62] He concludes that 'We have grown so inured to using a patient's age as an excuse for laziness in investigating him or her properly that we have failed to build into our scientific paradigms proper identification of the true physiological determinants of outcome.'[63]

---

[61] For a succinct discussion, see John McKie, Jeff Richardson, Peter Singer and Helga Kuhse, *The Allocation of Health Care Resources. An Ethical Evaluation of the 'QALY' Approach* (1998), p. 47. For the general issues, see: Andrew Edgar, Sam Salek, Darren Shickle and David Cohen, *The Ethical QALY. Ethical Issues in Healthcare Resource Allocations* (1988); Alan Williams, 'Economics, QALYs and Medical Ethics: a Health Economist's Perspective', in Souzy Dracopoulou (ed.), *Ethics and Values in Health Care Management* (1998), pp. 29–37.

[62] Grimley Evans, 'This Patient', pp. 120–1.

[63] John Grimley Evans, 'Age Discrimination: Implications of the Ageing Process', in Sandra Fredman and Sarah Spencer (eds.), *Age as an Equality Issue* (2003), p. 20.

The medical indictment is based upon several arguments. The first is one that is often used against age proxies generally: there is considerable heterogeneity in health status among older adults, and this is increasing as survival rates improve. Basing access to medical treatment upon generalised arguments about the over-65s *as a group* is thus manifestly unfair. Second, many clinicians argue that recovery rates for older patients can be better than those for younger. But even if the recovery rates for older patients can be shown to be worse, there is still a medical case for allocating more resources to them to tackle those conditions (such as myocardial infarction, or breast cancer) which have a higher incidence among older patients.[64] Third, it is argued that more prevention might reduce age differentials in outcomes, rendering age-based rationing even more clinically dubious. With every such reduction, the arguments for age-based rationing would be weakened. The training of medical students should thus impart an understanding of the needs of older patients and more sensitive clinical skills.[65]

The ethical case against age-based rationing can be quickly summarised. First, there is the argument that patients should have individual rights to treatment: the essence of good clinical practice is to assess each patient's symptoms and prognosis individually. Second, it is obvious that 65 is an arbitrary cutoff age, with no medical significance, having gradually emerged over time as the state pension eligibility age in many advanced welfare states. The third argument is a powerful one: it would be morally and politically unacceptable to withhold treatment from a patient on grounds of ethnicity, gender or class, simply because, on average, the group they belonged to had a poorer-than-average health outcome.[66] Why should age be any different? Finally, there is the interesting argument that age-based rationing may set up a 'self-fulfilling prophecy' effect. John Grimley Evans calls this 'aggravated ageing': 'Because you expect old people to do badly you do not notice that they are doing worse than they need because you are treating them badly.'[67]

The campaign against ageism in the NHS, spearheaded by organisations like Age Concern and Help the Aged, has produced some results. The *NHS Plan* of July 2000 included a chapter – albeit a rather generally worded one – on the health and social care needs of older people, declaring that ageism would not be tolerated in the NHS and promising the 'elimination of any

[64] Klein, Day and Redmayne, *Managing Scarcity*, p. 88.
[65] Shah Ebrahim, 'Demographic Shifts and Medical Training', *British Medical Journal*, vol. 319, 20 Nov. 1999, pp. 1358–60.
[66] Grimley Evans, 'The Case Against', in New, *Rationing*, p. 116.
[67] Grimley Evans, 'This Patient', p. 120.

arbitrary policies based on age alone'.[68] A year later the *National Service Framework for Older People* promised to 'root out' ageism in health care and provide NHS services 'on the basis of clinical need alone'.[69] Breast cancer screening is being extended to women aged 65–70; explicit upper age limits in cardiac units are now said to be 'almost unknown';[70] and there is a commitment to increase the number of cataract operations, hip replacements and coronary resuscitations, as well as to extend more health promotion to older people. Interestingly, general practitioners are now also encouraged to take the symptoms of young adults more seriously, instead of dismissing them as products of lifestyle excess. The question that remains is whether age discrimination should be made illegal in the distribution of goods and services, including health care. If this were done, it would impose on the NHS the obligation to demonstrate (for example, by age analysis of hospital referrals, admissions, treatments, after-care and so on) that no discrimination was being perpetrated; this would be contentious and very expensive.[71]

The arguments for and against age-based health care rationing are illustrative, in microcosm, of the bigger arguments over age discrimination. It is clear that, in the hard world of limited resources and stressful, 'real world' clinical situations, age has been widely used as a convenient proxy for treatment outcomes. There are philosophical and practical arguments for this: indeed, all cost–benefit analyses based on rule-of-thumb utilitarian principles will tend to discriminate against older patients, who have fewer prospective 'life years'. However, such generalised decisions are undoubtedly morally unjust and medically illogical at the individual level – and are becoming increasingly so, as health status heterogeneity among older adults increases. Some age-based rationing has taken place by official directive, but most has operated at the informal level, buried deep in the shared assumptions of doctors and negative attitudes of staff – making it difficult to stamp out.[72] Since the late 1990s, there have been governmental directives aimed at eradicating explicitly ageist policies; however, it is likely that much institutional ageism remains alive and well in the NHS.

[68] *The NHS Plan. A Plan for Investment. A Plan for Reform*, Cm. 4818-I, July 2000, ch. 15 and p. 124 (quote).
[69] Department of Health, *National Service Framework for Older People* (2001), pp. 12, 16–17.
[70] Ibid., p. 16.
[71] Sarah Spencer and Sandra Fredman, *Age Equality Comes of Age. Delivering Change for Older People* (2003), p. 85; Janice Robinson, 'Age Equality in Health and Social Care', in Fredman and Spencer, *Age as an Equality Issue*, pp. 112–13.
[72] Age Concern, *Health and Care. Interim Report* (1998), p. 56.

Conclusion

At every stage of the lifecourse, there is over- and under-distribution of resources, and a balance of positive and negative discriminations. On the one hand, modern health care systems have increasingly become health care systems for older people; on the other, they operate formal and informal procedures of age-based rationing that discriminate against older people. Any careful examination of this balance of positive and negative discriminations must be a very difficult exercise. It is well-nigh impossible to compare completed lives: doing so would involve controlling for an enormous number of variables. And even if one could, 'corrective justice' would come too late. Norman Daniels's 'prudential lifespan account' is an interesting attempt, but faces several insuperable obstacles. The most important of these is that societies are constantly evolving, and thus the experience of being aged in one's twenties (including the level of public resources received) fifty years ago was quite different from being that age now. Again, the substantial inequalities of class, gender and race within notionally monolithic age-groups render such aggregate comparisons virtually meaningless. The question of 'justice between generations' has produced some interesting and thoughtful work – often more at the level of philosophical abstraction than 'real world' applicability – but it has only served to highlight the difficulties involved in tackling age discrimination.

Part II

The Current Revival of Interest in Britain

3 New Labour and age discrimination

Introduction

Age discrimination has once again become a topic of public debate in Britain. The period since the late 1980s has witnessed the emergence of a 'new retirement agenda', the essential component parts of which are the renewed concerns over a future ageing population, the ticking 'timebomb' of state pension funding, the growth of male 'early' retirement, and an overall redefinition of old age.[1] Intriguingly, these economic concerns have been paralleled by an emerging postmodern sociology of old age which suggests that the lifecourse is becoming more 'blurred', that society will become more 'ageless' and that 'positive ageing' or 'active ageing' will increasingly be a social aim. Pathways into retirement are becoming increasingly complex, diverse and multi-layered, and retirement itself may be becoming 'deinstitutionalised'. Rightly, Chris Phillipson has observed that these combined tendencies constitute 'a historic turning-point in the debate about the character and significance of ageing populations'.[2] Central to this new agenda is the question of whether older people should remain in paid employment for longer. If so, those 'age discriminatory' barriers to their economic activity should be identified and removed.

The policy background

Since the early 1990s, British governments have become increasingly concerned about the problems of older workers. During John Major's Conservative administrations (1990–7) there was growing activity within the Department of Employment (later Department for Education and

---

[1] John Macnicol, 'The New Retirement Agenda', *Work, Employment and Society*, vol. 13, no. 2, June 1999, pp. 403–5.
[2] Chris Phillipson, *Reconstructing Old Age: New Agendas in Social Theory and Practice* (1998), p. 3.

Employment).[3] In 1993 a campaign was launched to educate employers in the value of older workers, via the booklet *Getting On*. The leading ministerial figure was Ann Widdecombe, Minister of State at the Department, but she was only continuing (albeit with greater energy) efforts made by her predecessors, Robert Jackson and Michael Forsyth. An 'older workers' roadshow' toured various cities in an attempt to persuade employers that an 'age diverse' workforce was economically desirable. In 1995, a second publication, *Too Old, Who Says?*, also targeted employers, followed by *Age Works* in 1996. Job Centres were discouraged from displaying job notices that specified age limits, seminars were held, and research was conducted into age discrimination legislation in twenty countries to gauge its effectiveness. The emphasis throughout was on persuasion and education, in the face of strong employer opposition to any legislative compulsion.[4] However, support for a voluntary code of practice came from bodies such as the Confederation of British Industry, the Institute of Personnel Management, Age Concern and (after its formation in 1996) the Employers Forum on Age (EFA). The Conservative government was anxious to support employers, and stressed both the economic advantages that they would gain by employing older workers and the 'social justice' case of ameliorating unemployment in the upper age ranges. The 1990s also saw several firms – particularly those in the retail trade – specifically recruiting older workers, with apparently beneficial results. Finally, various old age pressure groups (notably Age Concern) continually stressed the social justice case against all forms of age discrimination, running several imaginative campaigns to improve public awareness.

While all of this was going on, the Labour Party in opposition was also taking up the issue, and for a time appeared to be strongly supportive of an age discrimination in employment Act. Thus in the House of Commons on 9 February 1996, Ian McCartney MP (Shadow Employment Minister) declared that, having had 'extensive consultation' over the past year with relevant organisations and industry, an incoming Labour government would introduce 'comprehensive legislation to make age discrimination in employment illegal'.[5] The Labour front bench gave its support to a private member's Bill introduced by the back bench Labour MP, David Winnick. Sponsored by Age Concern, the Bill would merely have made

---

[3] Some earlier policies (such as the abolition of the earnings rule for receipt of the state pension by Nigel Lawson, when Chancellor of the Exchequer in 1989) can be seen as attempting to raise the employment rates of older people.

[4] For example, statement by Cheryl Gillan (Parliamentary Under-Secretary of State for Education and Employment), *H of C Deb.*, 6s, vol. 271, 9 Feb. 1996, col. 611.

[5] *H of C Deb.*, 6s, vol. 271, 9 Feb. 1996, cols. 618–19.

illegal any upper age limits in job advertisements. (There had been growing support for this in the 1990s, as an initial step.) Winnick admitted that it was deliberately a 'limited and modest' measure, but he hoped that it would begin to 'undermine the type of blatant discrimination that continues to exist' and lead on to a wider attack on ageist attitudes. The Bill was supported by a Conservative, Peter Brooke, and received all-party backing. Discussion ranged over the evidence of such discrimination, whether a voluntary code of practice for employers would be better, and the likely effectiveness of legislation (since countries with even stronger laws had also experienced falling economic activity rates among older males).[6] Winnick's initiative was hardly an isolated case: between May 1983 and May 2001, fourteen private member's Bills on age discrimination in employment were presented to Parliament.

In the year leading up to the May 1997 general election, an increasing number of articles appeared in the press, reflecting this growing interest in political circles.[7] By now, however, Labour's interest had cooled. Determined to offer a 'low tax' agenda to the electorate, the Party re-examined its spending commitments and placed them under strict fiscal limits. Plans for age discrimination legislation were jettisoned in the 'bonfire of commitments' ordered by Tony Blair, and Labour's general election manifesto only included a promise to value the contribution of older people to society, with a declaration that they should not be discriminated against on grounds of age.[8] Labour's landslide election victory of 1 May 1997 was accompanied by much rhetoric on the virtues of youth, modernisation, 'cool Britannia' and the like – not perhaps the best way to woo the grey lobby. Once in office, Labour proceeded cautiously: it began a long process of consultation with interested parties, and became increasingly aware of the complex issues raised by age discrimination.

By this stage, it had become obvious that action against age discrimination was going to be placed firmly in the context of the government's overall macro-economic strategy of securing economic growth through an expansion of labour supply. The 'problem' was going to be addressed by encouraging (or, if necessary, forcing) the economically inactive and long-term unemployed aged 50+ back into work, rather than by legislating against employers. Thus the only promise made by Andrew Smith (Minister for Employment, Welfare to Work and Equal Opportunities) was that the new government was 'consulting widely' and was taking every

---

[6] Ibid., cols. 556–619.
[7] For example: 'Warning! Ageism at Work', *Guardian*, 2 Mar. 1996; 'On Yer Bike, You Ageists', *Guardian*, 26 Oct. 1996.
[8] Labour Party, *New Labour. Because Britain Deserves Better* (1997), pp. 26–7.

opportunity to explain to employers 'the benefits of a diverse workforce'.[9]
In February 1998, another private member's Bill outlawing age limits in
job advertisements was presented to the Commons by Linda Perham MP,
supported by 139 other MPs (109 of them Labour).[10] The response by the
Blair government was to announce in August 1998 that a voluntary code of
practice would be drawn up in consultation with interested parties. Smith
expressed the view that any such code could become a 'soft law' (changing
employment practice over time by establishing a 'standard of reasonable
behaviour', but without actual legal penalties).[11] Smith declared that the
government had not ruled out the possibility of future legislation, but old
age pressure groups and the Trades Union Congress were unimpressed.
A coalition of such groups, Equal Rights on Age, was formed in late 1998 to
campaign for more effective legislation.[12] Others, too, were sceptical that a
code would do much to counter the long-run social and economic forces
(for example, new electronic technologies) that were causing workers to
'burn out' at earlier ages.[13]

The Blair government certainly did intensify the anti-age discrimination
activities of the Department for Education and Employment (DfEE). A
Ministerial Group was set up to develop a 'Strategy for Older People',
covering a number of areas and manifesting the Blairite commitment to
'joined-up government'. In August 1998 *Action on Age* was published by
the DfEE. It unveiled the interim conclusions from the consultation process: legislation was ruled out for the immediate future; the complexities
and difficulties inherent in age discrimination were repeatedly emphasised,
as were the economic advantages of an 'age-diverse' workforce, selected
and retained on the basis of ability rather than mere age; and action on age
discrimination was placed firmly in the context of the government's New
Deal programme.[14] This was followed in November by a consultation
document on the proposed new code,[15] and a report by the Department
of Social Security, *Building a Better Britain for Older People*. The latter

---

[9] *H of C Deb.*, 6s, vol. 294, 22 May 1997, cols. 825–6, and vol. 301, 24 Nov. 1997, cols. 363–5.
[10] *H of C Deb.*, 6s, vol. 305, 6 Feb. 1998, cols. 1396–1419.
[11] 'Code to Counter Ageism at Work', *Guardian*, 14 Aug. 1998; 'Age Code Fails to Satisfy
     Campaigners', *Guardian*, 17 Nov. 1998. Other measures announced by the government
     included extending student loans to those aged 50+ and removing upper age limits from
     vacancies at Job Centres.
[12] 'Greys Attack Ageist Firms', *Guardian*, 3 Dec. 1998.
[13] See, for example, Christopher Hudson, 'It Will Take More Than This to Fortify the Over
     Forties', *Evening Standard*, 16 Nov. 1998.
[14] Department for Education and Employment, *Action on Age: Report of the Consultation on
     Age Discrimination in Employment* (1998).
[15] Department for Education and Employment, *Advantage – Consultation on a Code of
     Practice for Age Diversity in Employment* (1998).

outlined a 'positive ageing' agenda, emphasising that 'we can prolong our active and independent lives' through healthy living, good diet and exercise: it discussed ways of improving life for older citizens in the areas of health, income, travel and employment; and the economic contribution made by older people as volunteers and helpers was emphasised.[16] From several Cabinet ministers came repeated messages that 'grey is good' and that 'ability, not age' should be the criterion in good employment practice.[17] Laudable though these sentiments may have been, they were often at the level of studious generality, not to say banality: the 'solution' was often identified as little more than a much-needed 'cultural change' in attitudes towards older workers. It was evident that, on this sensitive issue, Labour ministers were being very cautious about what they said.

Throughout 1999 the upbeat tone continued: in February, the DfEE claimed that 96 per cent of those consulted on *Action on Age* were pleased that age discrimination was being tackled, and the March Budget measures extending the New Deal to those aged over 25 were welcomed.[18] Finally, in June 1999 the *Code of Practice* was published.[19] Employers who signed up to it had to undertake to remove age limits in job advertisements and to staff interview panels with employees of varying ages. Further guidelines on the elimination of ageism in training, promotion and redundancy policies were to be forthcoming, as was a significant extension of the New Deal to those aged 50+. Many campaigners for age discrimination legislation were disappointed, believing that the *Code* would make little real difference: it would be observed only by those employers who were recruiting older workers anyway. This seemed borne out by the results of a survey conducted by the EFA of 430 employers, and published in September 1999: 30 per cent of employers surveyed showed no knowledge of the government's new *Code*, and only one in twenty were 'fully aware' of it. The *Code* appeared to have made little impact on employer practice with regard to older workers: fewer than one in ten employers intended to make any changes in the way they recruited and trained their workers, and 68 per cent said that the *Code* would make no difference to the way they ran their businesses. For the government, Andrew Smith put a more optimistic gloss on things, concluding that to have 70 per cent of employers aware of the *Code* just twelve weeks after its publication was an impressive achievement. But two years later, there still appeared to be poor employer

---

[16] Department of Social Security, *Building a Better Britain for Older People* (1998).
[17] For example, 'Darling's New Dictum: Grey is Good', *Daily Telegraph*, 13 May 2000.
[18] *DfEE press releases*, 23 Feb. and 9 Mar. 1999.
[19] Department for Education and Employment, *Age Diversity in Employment: a Code of Practice* (1999).

awareness of the *Code*.[20] An even more pessimistic verdict came from a survey of 800 companies in the year 2000: it showed that only 1 per cent had introduced changes in employment practices as a direct result of the *Code*, and only 4 per cent thought that future change was likely.[21]

From 1999 onwards, there was concerted governmental action to supplement the *Code*. Most notably, the 'Better Government for Older People' initiative (run from the Cabinet Office, but with the involvement of leading organisations like Help the Aged, Age Concern and the Carnegie UK Trust) covered twenty-eight pilot projects in localities aimed at improving health and social services for older people. The Inter-Ministerial Committee on Ageing, the Older People's Advisory Group, the Cabinet Office Performance and Innovation Unit and the Social Exclusion Unit were also formulating policies on ageing. Again, in early 2000 the DfEE launched a media campaign (including striking posters) aimed at re-educating public opinion; pressure began to be applied on the European Union to get it to drop its practice of attaching age limits to EU job advertisements; and the Employment Service ushered in a new policy of not generally accepting job vacancies with upper age limits. Another interesting development was the establishment of the government's *age positive* website, disseminating information, advice and updates on recent policy.

A major event was the publication of the Cabinet Office Performance and Innovation Unit Report *Winning the Generation Game*, in April 2000. This offered a wide-ranging survey of the problems of older workers (including a welcome recognition of the informal economic contribution made by retired people). It analysed the growth in economic inactivity among people aged 50–64, and acknowledged the uncomfortable reality that no more than one-third of the increase in worklessness among that age-group could be attributed to fully voluntary early retirement; two-thirds must have been caused by economic restructuring and the shedding of older workers. Unsurprisingly, it found that the majority of early retirees suffered very low incomes.[22]

The final road to actual legislation was taken in November 2000, when the European Council of Ministers agreed a European Employment Directive on Equal Treatment (2000/78/EC), under which all fifteen EU member states undertook to introduce legislation prohibiting direct and

---

[20] *EFA press release*, 7 Sept. 1999; *DfEE press release*, 6 Sept. 1999; *EFA Newsline*, 13, Autumn 1999, p. 2, and 20, Autumn 2001, p. 2.

[21] Cited in Sandra Fredman, 'The Age of Equality', in Sandra Fredman and Sarah Spencer (eds.), *Age as an Equality Issue* (2003), p. 67.

[22] Cabinet Office. Performance and Innovation Unit, *Winning the Generation Game. Improving Opportunities for People Aged 50–65 in Work and Community Activity* (2000).

indirect discrimination at work on the grounds of age, sexual orientation, religion and disability. The Directive reflects the agreed EU strategy of achieving economic growth by raising employment rates and increasing the supply of labour across all member states via workfarist policies. It originated partly in the 1999 Amsterdam Treaty's provisions regarding 'equal treatment' with regard to gender, race, religion and belief, disability, sexual orientation and age, and partly in the European Council's March 2000 Lisbon Agreement to aim for an overall EU employment rate of nearly 70 per cent by 2010. Accordingly, the Directive seeks to achieve 'the social and economic integration of elderly and disabled people ... as a means of developing a co-ordinated European strategy for employment to promote a skilled, trained and adaptable workforce'. Central to this strategy are policies to support older workers, 'in order to increase their participation in the labour force'. Improving the *quality* of labour supply is also an aim: the Directive explicitly states that, with the exception of disabled workers (who, presumably, may benefit from employment quotas), its provisions will not cover workers who are 'not competent'.[23]

The age discrimination legislation must be introduced by December 2006 at the latest, and the British government has indicated that it will be in place 'well before' then.[24] Consultation on many aspects of the new anti-discrimination policies has taken place from 2002 onwards under the *Towards Equality and Diversity* initiative.[25] The precise details of each EU state's legislation can be different, depending upon its particular circumstances. Significantly, both direct and indirect discrimination will be covered, as well as workplace harassment and victimisation. (The Directive optimistically suggests that indirect discrimination may be established 'by any means including on the basis of statistical evidence'.) The legislation must cover discrimination at any age. It is likely that a mandatory retirement 'default age' will initially be set; but this may prove impossible to hold. (At the time of writing, this precise age is the subject of controversy.) Differences of treatment on grounds of age will not constitute discrimination if they can be 'objectively and reasonably justified by a legitimate policy aim' or if they are 'a genuine and determining occupational requirement'. In other words, a large number of exceptions will probably be permitted where age is a bona fide occupational qualification.

---

[23] European Union, *Council Directive 2000/78/EC of 27 November 2000*, preamble, clauses 6, 7, 8, 17.

[24] Statement by Alan Johnson (Minister for Employment and the Regions), *H of C Deb.*, 6s, vol. 375, 23 Nov. 2001, col. 623.

[25] Department of Trade and Industry, *Equality and Diversity: the Way Ahead* (2002).

Public safety defences (for example, in the armed forces, police, prison and emergency services) will be permitted. To the disappointment of many campaigners, goods and services will not be covered. There are many difficult problems to be overcome, particularly with regard to instances of indirect discrimination – for example, whether redundancy payments, being based on length of service, amount to differential treatment by age, how occupational pensions will be affected, what to do about job advertisements with wording like 'experience necessary' and to what extent terms like 'young person' will be illegal. It is likely that one single Commission for Equality and Human Rights will deal with all issues of discrimination. Claims will be brought at an employment tribunal, and no limits will be placed on compensation. At the time of writing, the British government is consulting with interested parties and drafting the legislation. The future of mandatory retirement in Britain is thus uncertain.[26]

Why a resurgence of interest?

Why has age discrimination become a topical issue in Britain once again? As is shown elsewhere in this book, the debate on age discrimination in employment has a long history: it was particularly intense in the 1930s and the 1950s. There was also a tantalisingly brief discussion in the early 1970s. Against a background of industrial restructuring and workforce downsizing (especially in coal mining areas) the Labour MP for Blythe, Edward Milne, attempted on several occasions to introduce a Bill in the House of Commons to outlaw age discrimination against workers aged 45+. On 5 May 1971, Milne introduced an 'Age Level of Employment Bill', declaring that 'There are many thousands, not yet old, not yet voluntarily retired, who find themselves jobless because of arbitrary age discrimination.'[27] Milne made further attempts in 1973, to no avail.[28] There was some discussion in Britain of the possibility of revising the Disabled Persons (Employment) Acts of 1944 and 1958 to include age: employers would be legally obliged to employ a fixed percentage of disabled, and older, persons in their workforces. However, experts conceded that the economic restructuring that was taking place in Britain, and displacing older workers, could not be easily explained by the simple concept of 'age discrimination'. Writing in *New Society*, the industrial psychologist Robert Slater argued that employers did not necessarily use age per se as grounds for redundancy;

---

[26] European Union, *Council Directive*; Employers Forum on Age, *EFA Newsline*, 21, Spring 2001, p. 1; *Rude Shock* (2001); *Age Discrimination Legislation* (2002); *Speak Up* (2003).

[27] *H of C Deb.*, 5s, vol. 816, 5 May 1971, cols. 1377–8.

[28] For example, *H of C Deb.*, 5s, vol. 856, 16 May 1973, cols. 1513–15.

it was more the case (as in the 1930s) that those industries that were restructuring and making workers redundant were those that contained disproportionate numbers of older men.[29]

Age discrimination in employment has therefore been discussed for decades, not only in Britain but in many industrialised nations. Some have introduced quite comprehensive legislation against it – most notably, Spain, Canada, Sweden, New Zealand, Finland, Australia and the United States of America; in others, there is partial protection. The USA has had, at federal level, legislation since 1967 – the Age Discrimination in Employment Act (ADEA) (with subsequent amendments). We must therefore ask the questions: What has determined the *timing* of the current resurgence of interest in Britain? Why did America – a country with so little employment protection in other areas – prove to be so innovative here? And why in this respect is Britain a 'welfare laggard' compared with the USA?

The conventional explanation for this curious example of American exceptionalism is straightforward. It is that the 1967 ADEA came about because it was attached to the coat-tails of race and sex discrimination legislation. In other words, the civil rights movement was the great engine that drove the whole package of rights-based measures. Many of the procedural and interpretative problems involved in the ADEA spring from the fact that it is a legislative hybrid – part employment protection (dating back to the 1938 Fair Labor Standards Act), and part Title VII of the 1964 Civil Rights Act. By contrast, in Britain, the 'grey lobby' was less well developed and powerful, and (Northern Ireland apart) there was nothing like the same level of civil rights agitation in the 1960s.

The 1965 Redundancy Payments Act

However, this is only part of the answer. In order to arrive at a better explanation, it is necessary to consider the broader economic and labour market background. If one searches for a legislative equivalent to the ADEA in Britain in the mid-1960s, the most likely candidate is the 1965 Redundancy Payments Act.[30] The Act had both economic and social purposes. Its economic purpose was to facilitate industrial restructuring and technological modernisation by making it easier to dismiss workers; in other words, 'to increase labour mobility by making redundancy more

---

[29] Robert Slater, 'Age Discrimination', *New Society*, 10 May 1973, pp. 301–2.
[30] For the background, see Paul Bridgen, 'The State, Redundancy Pay, and Economic Policy-Making in the Early 1960s', *Twentieth Century British History*, vol. 11, no. 3, 2000, pp. 233–58.

acceptable to workers and their organisations'.[31] In the early 1960s there had been growing concern that over-manning and restrictive practices were hindering the forward development of British industry, and that better methods should be introduced to enable employers to shed surplus labour. The Ministry of Labour conducted a survey of existing redundancy schemes, published as *Security and Change* (1961), and an interdepartmental committee (the Dunnett Committee) reported in May 1963. The 1964 Labour government's 'National Plan' aimed at a 25 per cent increase in total industrial output between 1964 and 1970, by improving per capita productivity, enlarging the size of the labour force, speeding up technological innovation and facilitating labour mobility.[32]

Other measures in the 1960s – the 1963 Contracts of Employment Act, the 1964 Industrial Training Act, and the introduction of earnings-related supplements in unemployment benefit in 1966 – also had the aim of creating 'a favourable climate within industry' whereby workers would be more willing to accept technological changes and consequent labour turn-over.[33] At the same time, the Redundancy Payments Act also had secondary, social aims (which probably assumed greater importance in the public perception of it, and in the support for it from the Trades Union Congress), whereby 'property rights' were vested in a job and length of service would thus determine redundancy compensation.[34]

The economic changes of the 1960s are highly significant, because they were the overture to the massive industrial restructuring that took place from the mid-1970s onwards. The Redundancy Payments Act introduced a state-enforced minimum level of compensation for dismissed workers, and, while welcomed by those older workers who were contemplating early retirement anyway, was primarily designed to break the opposition of organised labour to the human consequences of industrial restructuring: as the Minister of Labour (Ray Gunter) commented in April 1965, during the passage of the Act in the House of Commons, the new redundancy payments were part of the government's 'general programme to push forward the modernisation of British industry as fast as possible, and to enlist the co-operation of workers as well as management in the process'.

---

[31] Memo, 'Treatment of Redundancy' (1971), Public Record Office PRO LAB 108/3.

[32] *The Outline Plan. Memorandum by the First Secretary of State and Secretary of State for Economic Affairs*, C. (65) 53, 30 March 1965, PRO CAB 129/121; *The National Plan. Memorandum by the First Secretary of State and Secretary of State for Economic Affairs*, C. (65) 116, 29 July 1965, PRO CAB 129/122; *The National Plan*, Cmnd. 2764, 1965.

[33] N. D. Ellis and W. E. J. McCarthy, 'Part One: Introduction and Interpretation', in S. R. Parker, C. G. Thomas, N. D. Ellis and W. E. J. McCarthy, *Effects of the Redundancy Payments Act. A Survey Carried Out in 1969 for the Department of Employment* (1971), p. 3.

[34] 'Treatment of Redundancy'.

He added that the Act had 'an important and necessary part to play in allaying fears of redundancy and resistance to new methods and economic change'. It would, therefore, 'create the conditions in which those employers who are now carrying surplus labour can face up to the job of getting their basic labour requirements on to a more realistic basis'.[35]

The 1971 official report on the working of the Act likewise concluded that it had 'made it easier for many employers to discharge workers, largely because it enabled them to dismiss men with an easier conscience, and reduced costs and argument'.[36] (The number of working days lost through strikes over redundancy declined immediately after the Act was introduced.)[37] The labour-supply and human capital motives behind the Act were clear: its aim was to create 'an effective manpower policy', based upon 'criteria of efficiency about whom to retain and whom to dismiss'.[38] The overt aim of the Act may not, therefore, have been to target older workers; but it certainly had that effect. Evidence of its operation suggested that it made employers more inclined to dismiss older workers, or for older workers to volunteer to leave before conventional retirement age when a firm was faced with the need for workforce reductions.[39] Older workers who agreed to be made redundant received a larger lump sum pay-off than their younger colleagues (though the cost to the employer was the same in each case).[40] Redundancies following the Act were also most likely to occur in those industries – such as shipbuilding and construction – that had high proportions of older employees.[41]

The 1965 Act was followed by a twenty-five-year period in which governments, employers and trades unionists shared the view that modernisation of the British economy necessitated the exit of older workers via early retirement schemes. Geopolitical events made this imperative: the 1973 Yom Kippur War was quickly followed by the OPEC-led oil price rise which sent shock waves rippling through all Western industrialised economies, revealing their incipient faults. The British economy underwent a huge transformation and restructuring, amounting to a virtual 'second industrial revolution'. The trickle of older workers eased out by the 1965 Act now became a torrent. As they had done in the 1930s, trades unionists argued that available jobs should be redistributed to younger workers with

---

[35] *H of C Deb.*, 5s, vol. 711, 26 April 1965, cols. 33, 36, 43–4.
[36] S. R. Parker and C. G. Thomas, 'Part Two: the Findings of the Survey', in Parker, Thomas, Ellis and McCarthy, *Effects*, p. 29. Significantly, employees dismissed for misconduct were ineligible for redundancy payments.
[37] Memo by E. G. Whybrew, 'Redundancy Payments Act and Industrial Disputes', 25 Aug. 1970, PRO LAB 108/3.
[38] Ellis and McCarthy, 'Part One', p. 10.   [39] Ibid., pp. 11, 30, 95.
[40] P. L. P. Davies to E. Betterton, 14 Mar. 1967, and other material in PRO LAB 8/3290.
[41] Memo, 'Review of Redundancy Payments Scheme' (1972), PRO LAB 108/11.

families to support. The most notable policy expression of this consensus was the Job Release Scheme of 1977–88, which has been called 'the most explicit policy of generational substitution yet seen on the statute book'.[42] Under it, older workers were permitted to retire early, on condition that their jobs were filled by unemployed school leavers.[43] From 1983, unemployed men aged 60+ were not required to seek work, possibly encouraging them to see themselves as 'retired' at that age.

This economic restructuring was greatly speeded up in the 1980s, when the 'Thatcher experiment' effected a massive shift from manufacturing to new service- and information-based enterprises, marked by greater job insecurity and more youthful workforces. Added to this was the long-run growth in part-time jobs (most of them occupied by women), and the fact that the large birth cohorts of the 'baby boom' generation were entering the labour force, putting pressure on available vacancies. Between 1979 and 1983, registered unemployment rose from *c.* 1,100,000 to *c.* 3,100,000; and between 1980 and 1983, over 2,000,000 British workers were made redundant, three-quarters of whom were in manufacturing.[44] Between 1979 and 1999, manufacturing's share of total employment in Britain fell from 26 per cent to 17 per cent.[45] As always, older workers suffered disproportionately in this de-industrialisation: from the early 1970s, their economic activity rates fell catastrophically.[46]

We can conclude, therefore, that in the USA the economic restructuring that began in the mid-1960s was assisted by labour market policies that tried to retain the most efficient workers *regardless of their age*, whereas the British approach was to rely on crude age proxies, whereby old age was automatically (and inevitably unfairly) equated with industrial obsolescence. Both economies were modernising, and shedding surplus labour in the process. Ironically, though, the American approach had only limited success: the economic activity rates of older men in the USA also fell from the 1970s onwards. If, therefore, the broader economic and labour market

---

[42] Philip Taylor and Alan Walker, 'Intergenerational Relations in the Labour Market: the Attitudes of Employers and Older Workers', in Alan Walker (ed.), *The New Generational Contract: Intergenerational Relations, Old Age and Welfare* (1996), p. 162.

[43] Frank Laczko and Chris Phillipson, *Changing Work and Retirement. Social Policy and the Older Worker* (1991), p. 49.

[44] Ron Martin, 'Industrial Restructuring, Labour Shake-out and the Geography of Recession', in Mike Danson (ed.), *Redundancy and Recession. Restructuring the Regions?* (1986), p. 1.

[45] Cabinet Office, *Winning the Generation Game*, p. 34.

[46] For a comprehensive account, see Frank Laczko and Chris Phillipson, 'Great Britain: the Contradictions of Early Exit', in Martin Kohli, Martin Rein, Anne-Marie Guillemard and Herman van Gunsteren (eds.), *Time for Retirement. Comparative Studies of Early Exit from the Labor Force* (1991).

considerations must be borne in mind when considering the timing of developments in Britain and the USA, why has a debate emerged in Britain only recently? The revival of interest in Britain has been driven by several obvious, immediate concerns. Yet each of these concerns is contestable, being open to interpretation in a variety of ways. The prevailing interpretation has been fashioned by contextual factors – social, economic and political.

Male early retirement

The first and most obvious reason is that labour market restructuring since the early 1970s has led to the growth of 'early' retirements among men aged in their late fifties and early sixties. Economic activity and employment rates among men aged 50–64 fell from the early 1970s to the mid-1990s; since then, they have risen slightly and there is currently much debate about whether this slight improvement will be sustained.

At every stage in the twentieth century, older workers have been concentrated in long-established industries which have tended to rely upon more labour-intensive and outmoded production methods. In times of recession and economic restructuring, these industries go into decline, and shed labour. As was discovered in the 1930s, it is very difficult to re-employ older men who are workless through industrial re-structuring because of the pronounced skills, spatial and sectoral mismatches that inevitably arise: new jobs require different skills from those possessed by older workers, or they are located in different regions, or they are in emerging sectors of the economy more suitable to younger workers (and, more recently, women workers). Unlike younger unemployed, who will tend to return to work when a recession ends and unemployment falls, older 'discouraged' workers judge it to be pointless to look for work, and give up doing so: tellingly, a person made redundant after the age of fifty is, on average, eight times less likely to return to work than a person made redundant under that age.[47] A fall in unemployment improves their chances only slightly, since the growth of new jobs does not occur in regions or labour market sectors previously occupied by them. Such was the pattern in the 1930s, and it has occurred again since the early 1970s.

However, this second wave of de-industrialisation will not be followed by a re-stimulation of manufacturing industry, as happened during the Second World War and for the twenty-five years following. This postwar manufacturing boom boosted the employment rates of older men and

---

[47] Patrick Grattan, *Work After 60 – Choice or Necessity, Burden or Benefit?* (2003), p. 3.

tended to disguise the seriousness of the problem. In retrospect, we can see that the boom may have been but a temporary phase in the long-run de-industrialisation of older males that began as far back as the 1880s.

Ignoring the 1945–70 period, one can see that joblessness has slowly spread down the age structure, due primarily to industrial restructuring driven by technological changes and competition from newly industrialised countries – to which employers have responded with the increased use of 'early exit' incentives. The proportion of males aged 65+ defined in each census as 'economically active' has fallen steadily each decade (although at varying rates), from 73.4 per cent in 1881 to 7.5 per cent in 2001. The trend to male early retirement has in some ways shadowed that of conventional 'age-65' male retirement, but has been even more sensitive to labour market conditions. Just detectable as commencing in the 1880s, it continued during the economic restructuring of the inter-war years but was temporarily halted in the 1950s with relative economic stability. Thus the economic activity rates of men aged 60–4 were 88.7 per cent in 1921, 87.2 per cent in 1931, 87.7 per cent in 1951, and actually rose slightly to 91.0 per cent in 1961 (no census was held in 1941). The 1954 Phillips Committee Report noted, with some relief, that economic growth appeared to have 'arrested and perhaps even reversed' this trend.[48] But it was not to be. Essentially, the average age of male retirement has steadily fallen over the past fifty years: in the early 1950s, roughly six out of ten British men continued to work on past the state pensionable age of 65 (albeit not for very long), mainly for reasons of financial hardship; by the late 1990s, six out of ten British men had retired by the age of 64.[49]

Between 1951 and 1971, the economic activity rates of men aged 55–9 remained fairly constant: they rose slightly between 1951 and 1961 (from 95.0 per cent to 97.1 per cent), but then declined by 1971 (to 95.3 per cent). By 1994, however, this rate had fallen to 76.1 per cent. For men aged 60–4, the 1971 level of 86.6 per cent had fallen to 51.2 per cent by 1994.[50] By the late 1990s, nearly one-third of men aged 50–64 had no paid work, and most of these, it was alleged, had given up looking for a job. Had the employment rates of men aged 50+ not fallen since 1979, fully 800,000 more of them would have been in work in 1998. One pessimistic estimate is that as many as

[48] *Report of the Committee on the Economic and Financial Problems of the Provision for Old Age*, Cmd. 9333, 1954, p. 24.

[49] *National Advisory Committee on the Employment of Older Men and Women. Second Report*, Cmd. 9628, 1955, p. 10; Office for National Statistics, *Social Focus on Older People* (1999), pp. 25–6.

[50] Alan Walker and Tony Maltby, *Ageing Europe* (1997), p. 76; Clive Collis and Tony Mallier, 'Third Age Male Activity Rates in Britain and its Regions', *Regional Studies*, vol. 3, no. 8, Dec. 1996, p. 804.

one in fifteen men aged 45–9 may never work again.[51] As would be expected, economic activity rates fall with rising age: by the age of 60, only 58 per cent of men are employed, and only 34 per cent of those aged 64.[52]

Although concerns were beginning to be expressed about lengthening chronological life but shortening working life some fifty years ago, it is clear that a major social change has occurred since the 1970s. As Laczko and Phillipson observed in 1991, we have entered 'a new period in the history of retirement. An intermediary phase has emerged between the end of employment and receipt of a state pension.'[53] There has been much comment on the fact that the working lives of successive generations of men born since the First World War appear to have been shortening, consequent upon leaving school later and retiring earlier.[54] 'Retirement age' never really coincided with 'state pension age', but now a widening gap is opening up between the two in all industrialised societies as the average age of retirement has steadily fallen over the past decades.[55] In some quarters, there is considerable pessimism over the prospects of 'the detached male workforce' of all ages, who have become marginal to the labour market, being re-absorbed into jobs.[56] Future employment growth in Britain is likely to be in service-based enterprises, self-employment and feminised jobs, and not in those sectors with high proportions of older, economically inactive men. For the foreseeable future, therefore, employment prospects for older workers may not be good.[57]

The gender differences are striking. Women aged 55–9 experienced *increasing* economic activity rates from the Second World War to the mid-1990s – from 29.1 per cent in 1951, to 50.9 per cent in 1971 and 55.7 per cent in 1994; for those aged 60–4 there was a sharp rise between 1951 and 1971 – from 14.1 per cent to 28.8 per cent – and then only a slight fall, to 25.6 per cent in 1994. Clearly, there has operated a complex, symbiotic interaction between the growth of feminised jobs (most of them part-time) and the increasing desire on the part of women to gain more economic independence by entering the labour market. In total, fully 2,617,000 people in Britain aged between 50 and state pension age (1,412,000 men and 1,205,000 women) were jobless in the spring of

[51] Nigel Campbell, *The Decline of Employment Among Older People in Britain* (1999), p. 44.
[52] Office for National Statistics, *Social Focus on Older People*, pp. 25–6.
[53] Laczko and Phillipson, *Changing Work*, p. 5.
[54] Ruth Hancock, Claire Jarvis and Ganka Mueller, *The Outlook for Incomes in Retirement. Social Trends and Attitudes* (1995), p. 36; Ruth Hancock, 'Financial Resources in Later Life', in Maria Evandrou (ed.), *Baby Boomers: Ageing in the 21st Century* (1997), pp. 64–9.
[55] For useful surveys, see Walker and Maltby, *Ageing Europe*; Kohli, Rein, Guillemard and van Gunsteren, *Time for Retirement*.
[56] Christina Beatty and Stephen Fothergill, *The Detached Male Workforce* (1999), p. 46.
[57] Collis and Mallier, 'Third Age', p. 807.

United Kingdom
Percentages

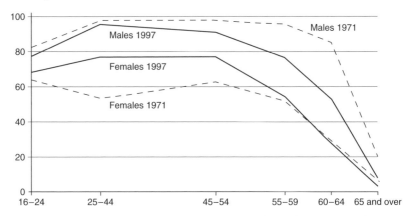

Figure 3.1. Economic activity rates: by gender and age, 1971 and 1997.
Economic activity rate = the percentage of the population that is in the
labour force. The definition of the labour force changed in 1984 when the
former Great Britain civilian labour force definition was replaced by
the ILO definition which excludes members of the armed forces.
Source: Office for National Statistics, *Social Trends No. 29 1999 Edition*
(1999), p. 71. © Crown copyright 1999.

2003.[58] However, the long-run rise in the economic activity rates of older
women indicates that the 'problem' is not one of age discrimination per se.
Were it so, older women's economic activity rates would also have fallen.

A more accurate way of describing the labour market changes of recent
decades is that there has been essentially a 'redistribution of work': from
older men and (to a lesser extent) younger, unskilled men, to women of all
ages; from full-time jobs to part-time; from heavy industry to service
enterprises; and from certain regions to others.

The conventional wisdom that working lives are shortening needs to be
analysed with some caution, though. First, it depends upon a definition of
'work' that excludes full-time education. However, as more people attend
full-time education, and at later ages, it can increasingly be seen as integral
to the labour market – and thus a form of 'economic activity'. Second, it
focuses predominantly upon men, whereas women's employment levels
have been rising (albeit much of this in part-time jobs). Third, it is possible
to argue that improving life expectancy at birth and falling adult mortality

---

[58] Department for Work and Pensions, *Older Workers: Statistical Information Booklet.
Spring 2003* (2003), p. 5.

(in other words, better survival to old age but only small gains in life expectancy at age 65), plus more women working, are going to *increase* the total 'years of work' contributed by a baby born now, compared with one born in, say, 1920. (Such a calculation has been made for the USA by Robert Kahn.)[59] Finally, it is curious that this pessimism about an alleged shortening of working lives co-exists alongside governmental triumphalism over ever-expanding labour markets.

An irreversible shift?

The key question is: will the economic activity rates of older men remain low for the foreseeable future – or will they rise significantly, as some argue?[60] In order to address this question, one must draw the distinction between 'employment', 'unemployment' and 'economic inactivity'. Registered unemployment among men aged 50–64 has tended to fluctuate in parallel with that among younger age-groups. Thus the improving economic conditions in the 1990s brought about a reduction in unemployment among older men: whereas in the spring of 1993 some 9 per cent of men aged 50–64 were unemployed, by the spring of 2003 only 4 per cent were.[61] However, once they are unemployed, workers aged 50+ tend to be out of work longer than their younger counterparts: just over one-fifth of those unemployed aged 50+ had been claiming unemployment-related benefits for more than two years in 1988–98, compared with only one-tenth of those aged under 50. In the spring of 2003, 38.5 per cent of unemployed men aged 50–64 had been unemployed for a year or more, whereas the corresponding figure for men aged 25–49 was 30.2 per cent.[62] Moreover, as workers approach pension age, their unemployment spells become, on average, progressively longer. Older people who are longer-term unemployed eventually give up seeking work and become economically inactive 'discouraged workers', often moving onto disability benefits: in 1987, 8 per cent of those aged 55–64 were in receipt of such benefits, but by 1998 this had risen to 12 per cent.

---

[59] Robert L. Kahn, 'Productive Behavior Through the Life Course', in The Aging Society Project, *Human Resource Implications of an Aging Work Force* (1984), p. 91. Of course, it is reasonable to argue that this calculation should be based upon life expectancy at, say, age 16 (the 'normal' start of working life), which would yield different results.

[60] See, for example, Michael Moynagh and Richard Worsley, *The Opportunity of a Lifetime: Reshaping Retirement* (2004), pp. 13–14, 17. The effect of raising women's state pension age is likewise uncertain.

[61] Office for National Statistics, *Social Focus on Older People*, p. 27; Department for Work and Pensions, *Older Workers*, p. 5.

[62] Department for Work and Pensions, *Older Workers*, p. 5. For the late 1990s, see Debbie Hatch, 'Destination of Claimant Count Departures: How the Over-50s Compare', *Labour Market Trends*, vol. 107, no. 4, April 1999, p. 170.

Table 3.1. *Employment and economic activity rates by age; men and women.*

		Employment rate (percentages)	Economic activity rate (percentages)
Men aged 65+:	Spring 1995:	8.0	8.2
	Spring 2003:	8.7	8.9
Women aged 60+:	Spring 1995:	7.7	7.9
	Spring 2003:	9.0	9.2
Men aged 50–64:	Spring 1995:	65.0	71.5
	Spring 2003:	72.0	74.9
Women aged 50–9:	Spring 1995:	60.3	63.2
	Spring 2003:	67.1	68.7

Source: 'Labour Market Data', *Labour Market Trends*, vol. 112, no. 1, Jan. 2004, pp. S26, S52.

In contrast to registered unemployment, economic inactivity is much less sensitive to fluctuations in aggregate labour market demand. There is only a little movement each month from economic inactivity to unemployment.[63] Thus whereas registered unemployment fell among men aged 50–64 between 1988 and 1998, in each of those years their level of economic inactivity was roughly constant.[64] The highest point in the economic inactivity rates of men aged 50–64 was 1995, at 28.5 per cent.[65] Since then, improving economic conditions and a tighter labour market have increased the total *employment* rate for men aged 50–64. However, the hard core of 'discouraged workers' remains only slightly affected: by spring 2003, the economic inactivity rate of men aged 50–64 had fallen by only three percentage points, to 25.1 per cent.[66]

The contrasting picture since 1995 can be illustrated as in Table 3.1.

Concern has been expressed that de facto ages of retirement will continue to fall in future, as an 'early exit culture' becomes embedded in public expectations. Surveys in the 1990s appeared to show that younger and younger age-groups anticipate progressively earlier retirement. Working people aged 45–9 expected to retire at nearly 61, while those aged 30–4 expected to retire at age 59.[67] An EFA survey of 2001 likewise revealed that

---

[63] Sean Rickard, *A Profits Warning. Macroeconomic Costs of Ageism* (n.d. *c*. 2000), pp. 12–13.

[64] Office for National Statistics, *Social Focus on Older People*, pp. 25–30.

[65] Catherine Barham, 'Patterns of Economic Inactivity Among Older Men', *Labour Market Trends*, vol. 110, no. 6, June 2002, p. 303.

[66] Department for Work and Pensions, *Older Workers*, p. 5.

[67] Stephen McKay and Sue Middleton, *Characteristics of Older Workers* (1998), Table 6.1; Stephen McKay, 'Older Workers in the Labour Market', *Labour Market Trends*, vol. 106, no. 7, July 1998, p. 369.

74 per cent of respondents said that they would like to retire by the age of 60 (though many were worried that they would not be able to afford to).[68]

This may reveal a major, and irreversible, shift in popular expectations. On the other hand, it may indicate that fantasising about early retirement is now a prophylactic against higher levels of workplace stress and 'burn-out'. As Patrick Grattan rightly argues, the desire for early retirement revealed by public opinion surveys is more likely to be a desire for change to a better work–life balance rather than for abundant leisure.[69] There may also be an analogy with the way that people's definitions of 'old age' rise as they themselves age:[70] as the financier Bernard Baruch quipped, 'old age is always fifteen years older than I am'. The economic activity rates of older British men may fall again in the future; on the other hand, current projections suggest only a slight decline until the second decade of the twenty-first century.[71] In the USA, a buoyant economy has recently increased labour market demand for older workers, encouraging older Americans to remain in work, and projections suggest that their economic activity rates will rise in future.[72] An interesting suggestion made by Beatty and Fothergill (regarding claims to incapacity benefit) is that, once the present generation of manufacturing-based early retirees has moved into conventional retirement, or died off, future generations of men (with different labour market backgrounds and lower expectations) may be more willing to take the low-paid, hypercasualised, insecure jobs that postindustrial labour markets offer to entry-level, unskilled job-seekers – work in call centres, fast-food outlets, low-grade service enterprises, the retail trade, and so on.[73] Reports in Britain in 2003–4 also suggested that the erosion of private pension values (owing to falls in the stock market) and fears over the future of the state pension were forcing older people to remain in work longer: this is backed up by empirical evidence of more working past state pension age.[74]

[68] *EFA Newsline*, 20, Autumn 2001, p. 3. See also Hancock, Jarvis and Mueller, *The Outlook*, p. 36.
[69] Grattan, *Work After 60*, pp. 4–5.
[70] Age Concern, *Reflecting Our Age: Images, Language and Older People* (1993), p. 1.
[71] Bob Armitage and Mark Scott, 'British Labour Force Projections: 1998–2011', *Labour Market Trends*, vol. 106, no. 6, June 1998, pp. 284–5.
[72] US Census Bureau, *Statistical Abstract of the United States: 2001* (2001), p. 367; Joseph F. Quinn, 'Retirement Patterns and Bridge Jobs in the 1990s', *Employee Benefit Research Institute Issue Brief*, no. 206, Feb. 1999, pp. 1–22; Mitra Toossi, 'A Century of Change: the US Labor Force, 1950–2050', *Monthly Labor Review*, vol. 125, no. 5, May 2002, pp. 15–28.
[73] Christina Beatty and Stephen Fothergill, *Incapacity Benefit and Unemployment* (1999), p. 45.
[74] 'Return of the Wrinklies', *The Economist*, 16 January 2004.

Of course, the increasing use by the British government of the 'employment rate' tends to paint an over-rosy picture, thanks to the fall in unemployment since the early 1990s. Thus the Blair government applauds the fact that, since 1997, the employment rates of older people have risen faster than those for the working age population as a whole.[75] This cheerful optimism cannot, however, hide the fact that a future economic recession may reverse this slight upward movement and that demographic trends (see below) will mean that the labour market will have to absorb more older workers. If employment rates do not rise significantly, 1 million more people aged 50+ will not be in work in 2020, simply because of the ageing of the workforce.[76] The irony is that the recent falls in older men's economic activity rates took place at a time when the proportion of people aged 50+ in Britain actually declined slightly.

The impact of male early retirement

The 'disappearance of work' for older men has given rise to several concerns. First is the impact of joblessness upon individuals. The effect of early retirement varies, most often according to one's economic status, but it always involves a considerable (and often painful) re-negotiation of social roles. The early retired are a very diverse group.[77] At the top are the better-off professionals on final-salary occupational pensions (perhaps supplemented by income from part-time consultancy work, a 'bridge' job, investments, and so on). Although often presented as 'typical', these are the minority; even then, most of such 'affluent' early retirees have occupational pensions of less than £10,000 per annum. At the bottom are the redundant manual workers solely reliant upon income support or disability benefits, who form the forgotten majority.[78] Early retirement has hit hardest at those in low-paid, industrial jobs, which tend to be located in particular geographical regions – Wales, the North and North-West of England, Yorkshire and Humberside, Scotland.[79] In such areas, a traditional, masculinist 'culture of work' predominates. Attachment to a job has been a major source of personal identity. Robbed of this identity, an older man may encounter considerable psychological problems. He may, for example, experience a dramatic reconfiguration of domestic and gender roles, with his wife and daughter(s) becoming the family breadwinners. A major problem is that the new, low-waged 'flexible' employment is not

[75] 'Facts and Figures' (2002), www.agepositive.gov.uk.
[76] Barham, 'Patterns of Economic Inactivity', p. 302.
[77] Cabinet Office, *Winning the Generation Game*, p. 20, attempts a five-fold typology.
[78] Grattan, *Work After 60*, p. 6.   [79] Collis and Mallier, 'Third Age', p. 806.

attractive to men who have spent a lifetime working in demanding and responsible jobs in manufacturing, and are now long-term unemployed. Put simply, a redundant ex-steelworker is not willing to wear a 'heritage theme' uniform and serve fast-food for the minimum wage. A co-ordinator of Newcastle's Centre Against Unemployment highlighted the problem of older men having to adjust to workless life: 'At one time everyone worked in a large, unionised workplace, where you had a decent rate of pay and some money to spend. Now, you have to be prepared to work unsociable hours, with no job security.'[80] For many such men, therefore, the long period of joblessness and retirement after full-time, industrial work is amounting to a major 'crisis of masculinity' at the upper age ranges. In recent years, there have been many stories in the British press about a 'lost generation' of such older men. Poverty, social exclusion and the disruption of social networks are the usual consequences of economic inactivity. Almost half of non-workers aged 50–64 depend upon social security benefits for most of their income. Some may be surviving via undisclosed work in the informal economy – more research is needed on this – but most suffer a marked drop in income.[81]

Their health status may also be being affected adversely. Half of those not working and aged 50–64 are on sickness or disability benefits.[82] A survey conducted in 1995–6 found that 41 per cent of economically inactive British men suffered from self-reported ill-health (compared with only 12 per cent of those in employment); they also had higher levels of GP consultations.[83] As Candy Atherton MP declared in a House of Commons debate in November 2001,

The cost of getting old is becoming a significant barrier to social inclusion and good health. A man in his 50s who is unemployed is twice as likely to suffer from respiratory illness or depression. Around half of all those claiming incapacity benefit are over 50. For some, this is a matter of life and death.[84]

Again, a 2003 study published by the Department for Work and Pensions found that men who worked past state pension age tended to report better health than those who did not.[85] Of course, such evidence illustrates the

---

[80] 'Men Over 50 Give Up on Jobs', *Guardian*, 11 June 1999.
[81] Rob Macmillan, 'Getting By', in Pete Alcock, Christina Beatty, Stephen Fothergill, Rob Macmillan and Sue Yeandle, *Work to Welfare. How Men Become Detached from the Labour Market* (2003).
[82] Cabinet Office, *Winning the Generation Game*, pp. 19–21; Catherine Barham, 'Economic Inactivity and the Labour Market', *Labour Market Trends*, vol. 110, no. 2, Feb. 2002, p. 72.
[83] Office for National Statistics, *Social Focus on the Unemployed* (1998), pp. 56–7.
[84] *H of C Deb.*, 6s, vol. 375, 23 Nov. 2001, col. 572.
[85] Stephen McKay and Deborah Smeaton, *Research Summary. Working After State Pension Age: Quantitative Analysis* (2003), www.agepositive.gov.uk.

problem of social selection: since ill-health is a frequently cited reason for economic inactivity, it follows that the economically inactive will be a less healthy sub-set of their age-group. Ill-health tends to cause early retirement, rather than the other way round. Nevertheless, it is clear that jobless older people suffer poor health.

Fiscal concerns

There are also rather more hard-nosed economic concerns relating to public finance and income redistribution. The spread of male early retirement has added a burden of de facto unemployed at the top end of the age structure, most of whom will not return to full-time employment. This has increased benefit expenditure, raising the question of whether such early retirees should be allowed to remain on benefit indefinitely. As David Willetts has put it: 'The shift onto benefits earlier, together with increased life expectancy, means that we are rapidly moving to a position where men can look to at least twenty years on benefits at the end of their lives when for much of that time they are perfectly capable of working.'[86] Early retirees will also accumulate less in the way of any occupational pension rights to carry them through their extended retirement. Thus Nigel Campbell observes, 'as a matter of arithmetic, it is harder to have a pension system which is both adequate and affordable if people spend less time in work, whatever definitions of adequacy and affordability are used'.[87] Added to this is the concern over the lost economic contribution (via wealth-creation and tax revenue) from early retirees no longer in work. *Winning the Generation Game* estimates this at £16 billion per annum in lost Gross Domestic Product, plus between £3 billion and £5 billion in additional benefit expenditure, and the EFA puts the figure even higher at £31 billion.[88] From the point of view of employers, early retirement based upon crude 'age proxies' may lead to the loss of valuable human capital, especially in the light of a possible future 'skills shortage' and a decline in the proportion of workers who are young: one recent survey suggested that 68 per cent of employers experience difficulty recruiting skilled staff.[89] Workers who leave early may also represent a poor return on a firm's investment in training, promotion and manpower policies.

---

[86] David Willetts, *The Age of Entitlement* (1993), p. 32.

[87] N. Campbell, *The Decline*, pp. 4–5.

[88] Cabinet Office, *Winning the Generation Game*, p. 30; Employers Forum on Age, *A Summary of the Debate* (2002), www.efa.org.uk.

[89] Employers Forum on Age, *About EFA – Useful Facts and Figures* (2002), www.efa.org.uk. See also Mari Lind Frogner, 'Skills Shortages', *Labour Market Trends*, vol. 110, no. 1, Jan. 2002, pp. 17–26.

Table 3.2. *Number per 100 people of working age.*

	Child	Old age	Overall
1994	34	30	64
2021	28	30	58
2041	28	43	72
2061	29	44	73

Source: Tim Harris, 'Projections: a Look Into the Future', in Office for National Statistics, *Social Trends No. 27 1997 Edition* (1997), p. 17.

Demographic trends and the labour force

Related to these concerns is the problem of an ageing population. Essentially, past fertility rates will create a rise in the proportion of older people in the British population after the second decade of the twenty-first century, as the 'baby boom' generation passes into retirement age. Whereas in 1991 16 per cent of the British population was aged 65+, this is projected to increase to 21 per cent by 2031 (a growth of roughly 30 per cent), and by 2013 the number of people aged 65+ will exceed the number aged under 16. Official projections show a steadily worsening 'dependency ratio' in the medium term (Table 3.2).

Put another way, in 1953 there were 4.6 people of working age for every pensioner; by 2040, there will be only 2.4, even with the equalisation of male and female pensionable ages.[90] Future demographic trends will, of course, exacerbate the problem of low economic activity rates among older men. Population projections suggest that the total number of British citizens aged 50+ will rise from 19,000,000 to 25,000,000 over the next twenty years. Britain's workforce is forecast to become older between 1997 and 2011, with a projected increase of 1,400,000 workers aged 35–54 and 1,000,000 aged 55+, while those aged under 35 will decrease by 700,000.[91] This has heightened concerns over the implications of lengthening chronological lives but shortening working lives, and has greatly fuelled the age discrimination debate. As Andrew Smith (then Minister for Employment, Welfare to Work, and Equal Opportunities) declared, in *Action on Age*, 'we need the contributions which older people can make to wealth creation in order to support an ageing population'.[92]

---

[90] *New Ambitions for Our Country: a New Contract for Welfare*, Cm. 3805, 1998, p. 14.
[91] Armitage and Scott, 'British Labour Force', pp. 282–5.
[92] Foreword by Andrew Smith, in DfEE, *Action on Age*, p. 2.

Several cautionary points need to be made, however. It is easy to become over-alarmist, and lapse into crude demographic determinism – 'demography as destiny' or 'apocalyptic demography', as it is often called. Scare-mongering is regularly used by powerful vested interests (such as the private pensions industry) to further their cause. The use of crude age-based dependency ratios has been subject to intelligent and well-informed scepticism – notably that the combined neontic (youth) and gerontic (old age) dependency ratios are at the moment no worse than in the past, that much depends upon future fertility trends, and that further reductions in unemployment and increases in female economic activity would enlarge the proportion of tax-paying 'producers' to fund pensions.[93] The age distribution of Britain's twenty-first-century population will also depend upon unpredictable factors, such as future immigration trends. We should bear in mind that population projections in the past have been notoriously inaccurate: for example, the 'population panic' of the late 1930s was immediately followed by a sharp rise in the birth rate. The 'crisis' is also a relatively short-term one, commencing after the second decade of the twenty-first century, when the 'baby boomers' move into retirement, and then diminishing once they begin to die out and the smaller birth cohorts (born in the 1970s) move into retirement age. Even then, the 2002 Green Paper on pensions provided reassuring estimates that the cost of state pensions will remain at about 5 per cent of GDP up to the year 2051 (though this depends upon the state pension remaining low in value).[94] It is also worth remembering that previous forty-year periods have seen faster increases in the proportion of the population aged 65+. For example, between 1911 and 1951 the proportionate rise was of the order of 100 per cent; yet an economic cataclysm did not happen. Finally, an intriguing contradiction is that these age-based essentialist arguments about the inevitable 'burden' of an ageing population are often articulated by those who maintain that age is irrelevant.[95]

New Labour and age discrimination

The final, and essential, ingredient in the age discrimination debate in Britain is the response by the Blair government to the broader economic and labour market background. The last thirty years have witnessed

[93] Jane Falkingham, 'Dependency and Ageing in Britain: A Re-Examination of the Evidence', *Journal of Social Policy*, vol. 18, pt. 2, April 1989, pp. 211–33.

[94] *Simplicity, Security and Choice: Working and Saving for Retirement*, Cm. 5677, 2002, Annex 3.

[95] For a critique of the current demographic scare-mongering, see Phil Mullan, *The Imaginary Time Bomb. Why an Ageing Population Is Not a Social Problem* (2002).

substantial changes in the operation of capitalist economies, and attendant shifts in labour market demand. Global competitiveness in the face of the challenge of Far Eastern economies, and changes in economic activity from heavy industry to new service enterprises, have increasingly segmented labour markets into a highly paid, technology-intensive core of relatively secure jobs on the one hand, and, on the other, a large, 'hypercasualised' periphery of insecure, low-paid and/or part-time jobs.[96] Although the British labour force continues to expand – an 'achievement' for which governments regularly take credit – most of this expansion has been via part-time jobs and there has been little, if any, aggregate employment growth (as discussed later in this chapter). The same proportionate volume of work is being shared out among a growing number of citizens, and ideologies of self-support through paid employment have, as a result, become hegemonic. For both the British and US governments, the way forward is to accept the inevitability of globalisation, deregulation and market forces, and expand the supply of cheap, 'flexible' labour via 'welfare to work' policies which will move more working-aged people off benefits and into work. In Britain, the old, Beveridge welfare state is gradually being replaced by a new 'workfare state' – the 1998 Green Paper on welfare reform declared that 'the government's aim is to rebuild the welfare state around work'[97] – and by the creation of an 'active society'.

The concept of the 'active society' is not necessarily new – for example, a section of the 1965 *National Plan* was entitled 'An Active Labour Market Policy'[98] – but it began to be explicitly discussed in several countries in the 1990s and was strongly pushed by the Organisation for Economic Co-operation and Development (OECD) and the European Union.[99] It has a liberal side, particularly in its stated aim of re-integrating back into society, by making them more economically self-sufficient, all those (lone parents, disabled people, the long-term unemployed, the early retired) who have become marginalised from the labour market, and hence 'socially excluded'; but it also has an authoritarian, deeply illiberal side, in its implicit threats of compulsion against those benefit claimants who may not wish to enter low-paid, menial jobs.

For Tony Blair, therefore, the New Deal is designed not only to raise the incomes of those previously out of work, but, crucially, to 'improve the supply of labour available to employers' and 'to decrease the costs of labour

---

[96] For an analysis, see Bill Jordan, *A Theory of Poverty and Social Exclusion* (1996).
[97] *New Ambitions*, p. 23.   [98] *The National Plan*, p. 10.
[99] For a useful discussion, see William Walters, 'The "Active Society": New Designs for Social Policy', *Policy and Politics*, vol. 25, no. 3, July 1997, pp. 221–34.

to the employer'.[100] Raising the aggregate employment rate will, it is argued, drive down wages, increase profits and create steady economic growth without the 'boom and bust' of previous eras. In David Blunkett's words, under this strategy 'firms have more potential recruits to choose from, wage pressure is diminished and non-inflationary growth is promoted'.[101] Older economically inactive citizens must be part of this strategy. Implicit in this supply-side approach is the aim of improving not only the quantity of labour supply, but also its *quality*. The long-term aim must be to distinguish between 'productive' and 'unproductive' older workers, regardless of age, via a regime of individual performance appraisal. Labour's action on age discrimination is therefore strongly motivated by its wider macro-economic strategy.

The 'lump of labour' critique

New Labour's economic and social policies borrow much from American free-market liberals of the 1980s – for example, the proposition that the alleged 'perverse incentives' offered by welfare benefits destroy the inclination to work and restrict the supply of labour – but they purport to place an emphasis on 'social justice' and 'opportunity'. The resulting compromise is said to be 'a new supply-side agenda for the left', yet in essence it is redolent of the same nineteenth-century classical economics that inspired the 1834 Poor Law Amendment Act's attempt to abolish all outdoor relief, thereby expanding the labour force and driving down wages. As one contemporary supply-side enthusiast put it,

> He begs a job – he will not take a denial – he discovers that every one wants something to be done. He desires to make up this man's hedges, to clear out another man's ditches, to grub stumps out of hedgerows for a third; nothing can escape his eye, and he is ready to turn his hand to anything.[102]

In its modern version, the supply-side view argues that contemporary labour markets are capable of significant expansion, such as to produce non-inflationary growth – providing certain conditions are met (such as restricting the right to welfare benefits, and a fall in wages). There is almost the implication that, if enough motivated, skilled and 'flexible' workers seek jobs, jobs will open up. This is in contrast to the more demand-side view that, at any one time, there is a fixed number of jobs available – the 'lump of labour' theory, which is said to have dominated macro-employment

---

[100] Tony Blair and Gerhard Schroder, 'Europe: the Third Way/Die Neue Mitte', appendix in Bodo Hombach, *The Politics of the New Centre* (2000), p. 168.

[101] Quoted in Chris Holden, 'Decommodification and the Workfare State', *Political Studies Review*, vol. 1, no. 3, Sept. 2003, p. 311.

[102] *The Poor Law Report of 1834* (ed. S. G. and E. O. A. Checkland, 1973), p. 358.

policy in the 1970s and 1980s, leading to unsustainable levels of early retirement and skills losses, on the basis that the young unemployed can only ever move into 'dead men's shoes'.

The classic critique of the 'lump of labour' theory came from the US economist Paul Samuelson. Samuelson argued that, if the correct monetary, fiscal and pricing policies were being implemented by a government, recessions could be avoided, and there could be jobs for all. Far from being a cardinal principle of economics, this critique merited only a brief entry in the first (1948) edition of Samuelson's textbook. Even after the full-employment prosperity of the 1950s appeared to have vindicated it, it was still only expanded into a two-page entry ten years later.[103] More recently, the critique has figured prominently in the work of Professor Richard Layard, whose thinking on unemployment, and welfare-to-work solutions to it, has been highly influential on the Blair government. Long-term unemployment was seen by Layard as the great economic and social failure of the Thatcher and Major years: between 1979 and 1986, he pointed out, the proportion of unemployed who had been out of work for over a year rose from *c.* 20 per cent to *c.* 40 per cent. An 'active' manpower policy would, he argued, re-motivate and re-skill those 'discouraged workers' and draw them back into employment, reducing poverty and social exclusion, making the labour force more 'flexible' and able to respond quickly to global economic changes, and thereby contributing to overall economic growth. The model often cited approvingly by Layard and the Blair government is that of Sweden, which has achieved, seemingly via its 'active labour market' policies, a high proportion of older people aged 55–64 who are economically active (68.1 per cent, as opposed to Britain's 51.7 per cent).[104] Policies to encourage early retirement in the 1970s and 1980s came in for particularly strong criticism in Layard's analysis: they were said to have restricted labour supply, increased inflationary pressures, removed valuable skilled workers, and so on. 'Early retirement is not an effective means of reducing unemployment,' argued Layard; it is merely 'an excellent way of making a country poorer'.[105] The 'lump of labour' critique tends to receive unquestioning support by many participants in the current age discrimination debate.[106]

---

[103] Paul Samuelson, *Economics. An Introductory Analysis* (1958 edn), pp. 551–2.
[104] Cabinet Office, *Winning the Generation Game*, p. 18.
[105] Richard Layard, Stephen Nickell and Richard Jackman, *The Unemployment Crisis* (1994), pp. 59, 91–3, 107 (quote); Richard Layard, *What Labour Can Do* (1997), pp. 75–6; Stephen Nickell, 'Unemployment in Britain', in Paul Gregg and Jonathan Wadsworth (eds.), *The State of Working Britain* (1999), p. 26.
[106] See, for example, Sarah Spencer and Sandra Fredman, *Age Equality Comes of Age. Delivering Change for Older People* (2003), pp. 37–8; Fredman, 'The Age of Equality', p. 47.

The idea of an expandable labour market has acquired canonical status in certain quarters (notably, the Treasury). Thus Nigel Campbell, a Treasury civil servant, criticises the 'lump of labour fallacy' and maintains that 'aggregate employment is driven by the number of people competing (effectively) for jobs'.[107] Likewise, *Winning the Generation Game* argues that the total volume of employment can expand if, in conditions of labour market flexibility, more competition for jobs causes wages to fall.[108]

However, this critique is open to considerable debate. An economy is always dynamic, so there is constant change in the level and distribution of employment. The 'lump of labour' is therefore something of a hypothetical abstraction: since new jobs are always opening up in some sectors, and old ones closing in others, it can be neither proved nor disproved. Again, Layard's supply-side critique assumes complete, unfettered free movement of labour and capital, as well as wage elasticity. (Here the national minimum wage, introduced by the Labour government, must be something of a contradictory obstacle.) A further problem is that economic inactivity in Britain today is a product of *both* supply- and demand-side factors. The former will predominate in more prosperous regions (for example, the South-East of England) and new sectors of growth, the latter in de-industrialised, economically depressed areas (notably South Wales) and 'old' sectors (such as manufacturing). However, it is in these latter areas and sectors that the problem of older men's economic inactivity is most acute. Older people's joblessness is highly regionalised, being concentrated in those regions of Britain that experienced the greatest de-industrialisation in the late 1970s and 1980s. Thus, whereas in spring 2002 the employment rate among men aged 50–64 was 78 per cent in the South-East of England, it was only 63 per cent in Wales, 64 per cent in Scotland and 64 per cent in the North-West. So great is the 'job shortfall' for older men in these industrially blighted areas that a regional economic policy to stimulate labour market demand is what is needed, rather than workfarist policies to improve labour supply.[109] Supply-side strategies are, therefore, 'fundamentally ill conceived' when dealing with the problem of economically inactive older men.[110]

Interestingly, it can also be argued that, within these dynamics of change, the total volume of work in the British economy – in full-time

[107] N. Campbell, *The Decline*, p. 5.
[108] Cabinet Office, *Winning the Generation Game*, pp. 39–40.
[109] Christina Beatty and Stephen Fothergill, 'Moving People Into Jobs. Jobcentre Plus, New Deal and the Job Shortfall for the Over 50s' (unpublished paper, Centre for Regional Economic and Social Research, Sheffield Hallam University, 2004), p. 20.
[110] Pete Alcock, Christina Beatty, Stephen Fothergill, Rob Macmillan and Sue Yeandle, 'New Roles, New Deal', in Alcock *et al.*, *Work to Welfare*, pp. 260–1.

equivalents and proportionate to the total population – *has* remained roughly constant (or has even contracted slightly) since the early 1950s. In 1951, the UK labour market contained a total of 22,600,000 employees, employers or self-employed. Of these, 831,000 were part-time (officially defined as fewer than thirty hours per week) and 475,000 were 'out of employment' (sick or unemployed).[111] Giving each part-time job a 50 per cent full-time equivalent, and deducting those out of employment, the 1951 figure is deflated to 21,700,000 full-time equivalent jobs. By 2002, the UK labour force had expanded to a total of 27,700,000 people in employment (plus another 1,500,000 who were out of employment). Of these, however, a massive 6,200,000 were part-time (or 3,100,000 full-time equivalents).[112] Accordingly, the 2002 total must be reduced to 24,600,000 full-time equivalents. The expansion of employment between 1951 and 2002 was therefore of the order of 2,900,000 full-time equivalents, or 13 per cent. By contrast, population growth between 1951 and 2002 was of the order of 17 per cent. On the face of it, therefore, not only was there no expansion of employment between 1951 and 2002, proportionate to total population, but there was in fact a slight *contraction*. Yet massive economic growth was achieved.

Of course, an accurate temporal comparison would involve a much more complex exercise. It would need to control for the size of the 'working-aged' population in each year, to take account of changing average 'actual weekly hours of work'[113] (though the fact that these have fallen would substantiate the argument made here), and to construct a more accurate measure of 'full-time equivalents': a crude allocation of 50 per cent for each part-time job is unsatisfactory, since by 2002 the British labour market contained an enormous variety of hours of work (for example, 3,200,000 women in the labour force worked fewer than twenty hours per week).[114]

Nevertheless, this illustrative comparison between 1951 and 2002 supports the economic historian Roger Middleton's contention that 'at the aggregate level ... there has been almost no employment growth in the British economy for nearly forty years'.[115] The highest total *employment* rate, for example, was achieved in 1974.[116] As noted earlier in this

[111] Central Statistical Office, *Social Trends No. 1 1970* (1970), p. 68.
[112] Office for National Statistics, *Social Trends No. 33 2003 Edition* (2003), p. 79.
[113] For a discussion of this difficult problem, see Duncan Gallie, 'The Labour Force', in A. H. Halsey and Josephine Webb (eds.), *Twentieth-Century British Social Trends* (2000), pp. 305–6.
[114] Office for National Statistics, *Social Trends No. 33*, p. 88.
[115] Roger Middleton, *The British Economy Since 1945. Engaging with the Debate* (2000), p. 55.
[116] Office for National Statistics, *Social Trends No. 33*, p. 78.

chapter, what has taken place in recent decades has been essentially a redistribution of a fixed volume of work. The critique of the 'lump of labour' theory articulated by Layard, Campbell and others may be a supply-side article of faith, but it is not empirically self-evident. If the total proportionate volume of work in the British economy has not expanded in the last fifty years, there must be grounds for scepticism that it can be expanded significantly in the future. Therefore a central assumption behind the current action against age discrimination in employment is questionable.

Another curious piece of supply-side reasoning concerns female economic activity rates. Campbell makes the observation that older women 'have not shared in the substantial general increase in female employment', in that women aged 55–60 have not increased their economic activity rates as much as have women as a whole,[117] and Richard Worsley has argued: 'As the growth in women's employment has shown, we are not in the business of sharing out a fixed volume of work – what economists call the "lump of labour fallacy".'[118] However, using the expansion of women's employment as an example of what could be achieved is fallacious: modern labour markets are highly patterned by cross-cutting divisions of skill, age, region and gender, and each sector can grow or decline independently of others. As has already been argued, at the aggregate level the disappearance of work for older males is a long-run phenomenon, stretching back over 100 years. It represents the slow contraction of that labour market niche occupied by them, and it is by no means certain that a new niche will open up in the future.

Campaigns to educate employers and the general public may help to dispel some of those cultural obstacles to the re-employment of older men, but their effect can only be limited if they are based upon the assumption that the root of the problem is employers' 'irrational' prejudices against older workers. Most participants in the current age discrimination debate admit, in their more candid moments, that reversing or arresting this trend will not be easy: as Richard Spring MP remarked, in a Commons debate on age discrimination in employment, 'the macro-economic background is the crucial determinant of employment opportunities at any age-group'.[119] In effect, the Blair government is engaged in a gigantic experiment in supply-side economics, which has benefited from generally favourable economic conditions in Britain (and across the industrialised world); it

[117] N. Campbell, *The Decline*, p. 1.
[118] Richard Worsley, *Age and Employment. Why Employers Should Think Again About Older Workers* (1996), p. 16.
[119] *H of C Deb.*, 6s, vol. 271, 9 Feb. 1996, col. 597.

may be revealed as misguided if the British economy takes a downturn, and unemployment rises. The question 'where are the jobs?' will then be even more telling.

Sociological justifications

These economic justifications have been accompanied by sociological arguments based upon the notion that we are moving into an era of 'reflexivity' and greater 'self actualisation': as Walters comments, the idea of the active society 'links social policy reform to a particular type of politics of the self'.[120] The most cogent expression of this is to be found in the writings of Anthony Giddens, whose version of the 'active society' has been very influential on Tony Blair. For Giddens, the inevitability of globalisation has been a major factor in creating the 'new individualism' of modern social democracies: citizens must exert greater control over their own futures via 'risk-management'. 'With expanding individualism should come an extension of individual obligations', argues Giddens. The new 'active society' therefore carries with it a set of 'obligations', particularly with regard to welfare benefits, whose existence Giddens robustly criticises for creating 'moral hazard'. He argues that welfare benefits should be time-limited, and should carry a strict work requirement. The concepts of 'retirement' and 'pensioner' come in for scathing criticism, being con-structs of the 'old' welfare state: both are 'as clear a case of welfare dependency as one can find'. Fixed ages of retirement should thus be abolished, and old age, like any other age, should not be seen as 'a time of rights without responsibilities'.[121] This reasoning is uncannily similar to that of the late-nineteenth-century Charity Organisation Society, in its opposition to proposals for state pensions: for example, in 1896 Thomas Mackay contended that there was no logical reason why the age of 65 should mark 'the estate of life to which state subsidy should be given'.[122]

New Labour's motivation

The Blair government's action against age discrimination in employment is thus inextricably linked to its New Deal programme and the whole package of supply-side measures designed to 'achieve high and stable levels of employment, through a combination of stable macro-economic policies and welfare

---

[120] Walters, '"Active Society"', p. 224.
[121] Anthony Giddens, *The Third Way: the Renewal of Social Democracy* (1998), esp. pp. 33, 65, 70, 114–21.
[122] Thomas Mackay, *Methods of Social Reform* (1896), p. 193.

reform to tackle long-term unemployment and benefit dependency'.[123] 'In a modern, competitive market', declared Andrew Smith in 1999,

> organisations need to ensure that they find the best person for the job. They are less likely to do that if they limit their choices by imposing unnecessary and irrelevant restrictions on who they can recruit, train and promote. If the economy is to thrive and businesses to flourish, we have to make the best use of the skills and abilities of everyone in the labour market – older and younger people. That means not using age unnecessarily as a job criterion.[124]

Since a modern economy needs a workforce with the right skills and attitudes, selection on the basis of age 'will often rule out the best candidate for the job'.[125] It follows, conversely, that redundancies should be based on 'objective, job related criteria to ensure that skills needed to help the business are retained. Using age as the sole criterion when selecting people for redundancy can lead to the unnecessary loss of skills and abilities which are essential to the organisation.'[126] In launching the *Code* on 14 June 1999, Smith stated that employing people of all ages would 'boost the economy and encourage firms to flourish, by using the skills and abilities of employees regardless of age'.[127]

Repeatedly, Smith emphasised the complementarity between the government's welfare-to-work measures and its action on age discrimination.[128] Departmental co-ordination, via 'joined-up government', is essential if the 'coherent strategy' to expand labour supply is to work: underpinning this strategy is the New Deal programme and all other measures designed 'to address barriers, such as age discrimination in employment, which can prevent people from working'.[129] And in the authoritarian tone that has engendered some unease on the part of Labour's traditional supporters, *Action on Age* announces at the outset: 'The government wants all people who are able to work, regardless of their age, to be able to contribute to the continued growth and development of the economy, as well as their own careers.'[130] Thus Margaret Hodge (then Parliamentary Under-Secretary at the DfEE) gave the keynote speech to the 1999 Employers Forum on Age (EFA) annual conference and, according to a report of the conference, 'firmly positioned the age discrimination *Code* as part of the government's suite of initiatives – including the New Deal for the over-50s – designed to enable currently under- or unemployed groups to use their skills and experience in the labour market'.

[123] DfEE, *Action on Age*, p. 21.   [124] Foreword by Smith, in DfEE, *Code of Practice*.
[125] Statement by Smith, *H of C Deb.*, 6s, vol. 305, 6 Feb. 1998, col. 1416.
[126] DfEE, *Action on Age*, p. 20.   [127] *DfEE press release*, 14 June 1999.
[128] See, for example, *DfEE press release*, 9 Mar. 1999.
[129] DfEE, *Action on Age*, p. 11.   [130] Ibid., p. 2.

She highlighted the government's commitment to tackling what she described as 'benefits dependency and economic inactivity', adding, somewhat ominously, that 'we need to identify which levers will ensure that older people can participate fully in the labour market'.[131]

In the Blair government's definition of the 'problem' of declining economic activity among older men there is a marked tension between 'supply-side' and 'demand-side' analyses. However, 'supply-side' analyses are preferred: joblessness is seen as arising from personal deficiencies – lack of education and skills, low motivation, a desire to stay on benefit – all adding up to poor 'employability'. For example, having stated that it is very difficult to say with certainty why people aged 50+ experience difficulties finding work, *Action on Age* then merely cites one research study, commissioned by the DfEE, that analysed the problem in terms of the 'characteristics' of older job-seekers (such as their methods of job search).[132] Again, *Winning the Generation Game* was forced to concede that no more than one-third of the recent fall in older men's economic activity rates could be attributed to personal choice, but then suggested that supply-side solutions were the answer:

Economic restructuring and the creation of leaner firms over the past twenty years have done much to trigger the decline in job prospects of older people. But a more competitive economy does not, over the long term, make inevitable a shortening of working lives, at a time when people live longer and remain fitter than ever before.

'The problem' was that older people were hindered from continuing to make a contribution as they grew older by the 'false prejudices' of employers and society, by the 'perverse incentives' in occupational pension schemes that encouraged early exit, by policies in the benefits and employment services, by obsolete skills, or by barriers to volunteering.[133] Clearly, a demand-side explanation does not fit easily with the nostrums of the 'active society', and makes the problem appear much less easy to solve.

Another important feature of current governmental policies to combat age discrimination is that they reflect the desire of employers (particularly in sectors such as retail and service industries) for a more 'flexible' workforce that will adapt quickly and willingly to changes in conditions of employment and remuneration. Action on age should be part of a wider personnel and equal opportunities strategy to create such a workforce, with selection being on grounds of 'merit' and skill, since 'the business with the most skilled, flexible and committed workforce has a more competitive

---

[131] Employers Forum on Age, *EFA Newsline*, 12, Summer 1999, p. 2, www.efa.org.uk.
[132] DfEE, *Action on Age*, pp. 6–7.
[133] Cabinet Office, *Winning the Generation Game*, pp. 5–6.

edge'.[134] These economic advantages have been stressed throughout: for example, in the February 1996 Commons debate Ian McCartney MP promised that legislation against age discrimination introduced by a future Labour government would be part of a package of measures 'to bring about flexible working practices', as 'investment in human capital' and a 'useful tool for management'.[135] The actual workplace reality of 'flexibility' is usually left unexplored.

In their public utterances, New Labour ministers have always been careful to emphasise that they are opposed to 'unjustified' or 'unfair and short-sighted' age discrimination.[136] 'Justified' age discrimination has not been spelled out, but presumably it will be defined as job-related (i.e. productivity-related), and will be covered by the large number of exceptions that the forthcoming legislation will permit. In other words, if an older worker were dismissed because his or her productivity had declined with age, this would be 'justified' age discrimination – or no discrimination at all. There is, of course, an alternative strategy for dealing with discrimination, but this merits little mention – that of positive action. In the case of older workers, this could involve specifying age-based quotas or targets that employers would be obliged to fill. A certain proportion of a firm's workforce would have to consist of older workers of sub-optimal productivity; this would be a counter to the employment discrimination they face. However, age-based targets are never mentioned. There has been exhortation to employers to achieve 'a balanced age profile across the workforce', but no specific guidance on exactly what this 'balance' should be.[137] In any case, it would be strange for this to be a realistic aim, since every firm's age profile is different, and is generally caused by factors other than age discrimination.

The 'irrationality' model of discrimination dominates New Labour's approach. Repeatedly, the problem is seen as one of 'tackling stereotypical views' or 'challenging attitudes and stereotypes' about the job competence of older workers, and persuading employers not to base personnel decisions on 'preconceived ideas about age, rather than on skills and abilities'.[138] As Alan Johnson (then Minister for Employment and the Regions) said in November 2001, 'A large part of the problem is the tendency to think of age in terms of outdated and inaccurate stereotypes. Unlike in other areas of discrimination, differential treatment based on age

---

[134] DfEE, *Code of Practice*, p. 9.   [135] *H of C Deb.*, 6s, vol. 271, 9 Feb. 1996, col. 618.
[136] Statement by Andrew Smith, *H of C Deb.*, 6s, vol. 305, 6 Feb. 1998, cols. 1416–17; DfEE, *Code of Practice*, p. 6.
[137] 'Business – Redundancy', www.agepositive.gov.org.
[138] *Action on Age*, pp. 4, 16; *DfEE press release*, 14 June 1999; 'Minister's Message', www.agepositive.gov.org.

is often not based on hostility or ill feeling, but misconceptions about older workers abound, and the outcome for the victims is just as bad.'[139] The possibility that the use of age proxies could have a rational basis tends to remain uninvestigated. Nor is there any explanation of why employers should have behaved 'irrationally' for decades – only now needing to be enlightened by persuasion.

Labour ministers have likewise been markedly reluctant to advocate performance appraisal for all older workers: employers are generally opposed to this. There have been many vague exhortations, such as the suggestion that 'Performance against agreed measures should be reviewed regularly. Reviews give managers and job holders the chance to identify areas of strength and areas for improvement. An effective and objective evaluation of performance should inform decisions on promotion or career advancement.'[140] However, this is no more than the kind of good personnel practice that many firms have operated for years. It does not confront the many difficulties inherent in the whole idea of individual performance appraisal.

Practical measures

So much for the ideological underpinnings. In practice, Labour's 'New Deal' programme has so far been more carrot than stick. Originally beginning with the 18–25 age-group, it has – significantly – been extended to older workers. From June 1998, all those unemployed for two or more years and aged 25+ had to have mandatory interviews with an 'adviser' on job search; employers received £75 per week for twenty-six weeks for employing them. In his budget of March 1999, Chancellor Gordon Brown specifically addressed the problem of the workless over-fifties by announcing the 'New Deal 50plus'. A one-year £60 per week tax credit was offered to anyone aged 50+ who returned to full-time work after six months or more on benefits (£40 if they work part-time). Together with the new minimum wage of £3.60 per hour (£5.05 per hour from October 2005), this was intended to guarantee a minimum full-time income of £175 per week, or £9,000 per annum (later raised). In addition, these longer-term unemployed were offered the assistance of a 'personal adviser' to help them find a job, and a £750 (later, up to £1,500) grant to help with training, if they found work. Interestingly, there was no upper age limit on the New

---

[139] *H of C Deb.*, 6s, vol. 375, 23 Nov. 2001, col. 622.

[140] Department for Education and Employment, *Age Diversity in Employment. Guidance and Case Studies* (1999), p. 14. For similar very general advice, see *Being Positive About Age Diversity at Work. A Practical Guide for Business* (2002), www.agepositive.gov.uk.

Deal 50plus. All this was available from April 2000. It remains to be seen
whether in future such measures will be strengthened with an element of
compulsion, via an obligation to work. If so, the economically inactive
aged 50+ could find themselves discovering exactly what 'flexibility' in
working practices actually means. On the other hand, these and other
measures (such as the Working Families' Tax Credit, or the December
2003 Pre-Budget's announcement that flexible retirement is to be encouraged by changes in occupational pension regulations) could herald the
growth of generous in-work benefits, which would make work so attractive
to those who wanted to re-enter the labour market that compulsion would
not be needed. The 'active society' would then come about because people
wished it to.

The motives of employers

Since the early 1990s, British employers have displayed increasing interest
in combating age discrimination in employment and taking positive action
to employ older workers. A notable step in this direction has been the
increasing willingness of certain supermarket chains to create a special
labour market niche for older workers, who they judge to be particularly
valuable employees. The DIY retail chain B&Q opened a store in
Macclesfield in 1989, staffed by employees aged 50+, followed by branches
in Exmouth and Cardiff; the employment of more older workers in all
its branches became company policy in the 1990s. Other firms, notably
W H Smith, the Nationwide Building Society, John Laing, Marks and
Spencer, Bovis, the Midland Bank, the TSB Group and Tesco, have
followed suit. The Nationwide Building Society is one of several firms
which have pioneered phased retirement, permitting employees to work
part-time until well past notional retirement age.[141] Some, like Marks and
Spencer, have even removed mandatory retirement ages.[142]

   These sporadic developments are symptomatic of a growing desire on
the part of employers to achieve a more 'mixed-age', 'age-diverse' or 'age-
balanced' workforce. In addition, employers have watched recent political
developments with keen interest, and wish to exert some control over
policy outcomes – particularly the forthcoming legislation. Hence an
important pressure group, the Employers Forum on Age, was founded
in 1996. Chaired by Howard Davies (then Chair of the Financial Services
Authority, now Director of the London School of Economics), the EFA
has enrolled over 160 businesses, representing some 3,000,000 employees

---

[141] Jane Pickard, 'Grey Areas', *People Management*, vol. 5, no. 15, 29 July 1999, p. 37.
[142] *EFA Newsline*, 20, Autumn 2001, p. 3, www.efa.org.uk.

(over 14 per cent of the total UK workforce). Founder members of the EFA included such leading UK companies as B&Q, the Bank of England, the BBC, British Airways, British Telecom, Cadbury Schweppes, HSBC, Littlewoods, Manpower, Marks and Spencer, the Nationwide Building Society, the Post Office, Sainsbury's, Unigate and W H Smith. Support was also forthcoming from the CBI and the TUC. The EFA runs conferences, seminars and other public debates, acts as a pressure group (for example, it served on the working party that helped develop the *Code of Practice*), and attempts to persuade British employers that their long-term economic interests will be served by removing age barriers to employment. The EFA's core aims are: to support member organisations in managing the skills and age mix of their workforces in order to obtain maximum business benefit; to remove barriers to achieving an age-balanced workforce by influencing key decision makers, notably in government, education, training, recruitment and the trade union movement; and to inform all employers of the benefits of a mixed-age workforce.[143] It has also campaigned (apparently, with some success) for an alteration of Inland Revenue regulations so that 'flexible' or 'phased' retirement would be possible: employees would be able to work part-time for lower remuneration while claiming an occupational pension.[144] Presumably this would make good business sense, as only valued employees would be retained in this way.

The EFA tends towards an 'irrationality' model of age discrimination, believing that it can be dispelled by effecting a 'cultural change' on the part of employers. It seeks to 'explode the common myths about workers of different ages' by attacking 'fictional stereotypes' (for example, that older workers have higher rates of absenteeism, deficient technical skills, higher employment costs and general rigidity of thinking – or, conversely, that younger workers are poor attenders, undisciplined and inexperienced).[145] Repeatedly, the EFA proclaims the message that such irrational discrimination is both foolish, since it is based upon false stereotypes, and economically wasteful. British employers originally favoured only a code of practice, and are now watching the approach of the EU-inspired legislation with some apprehension – no doubt fearing the legal hornet's nest that might be opened. The EFA has rather dramatically estimated that employers could be exposed to claims of £193,000,000 in the first year after such

---

[143] Employers Forum on Age, *What Is the EFA?* (1999), p. 1, *All You Need to Know About the EFA* (2004), www.efa.org.uk.

[144] Jessica Bone and Samantha Mercer, *Flexible Retirement* (2000); *EFA Newsline*, 17, Autumn 2000, p. 2.

[145] EFA, *What Is the EFA?*, pp. 1–2.

legislation, and £73 billion as an eventual total.[146] It is doing its best to influence the shape of such legislation, and to warn British employers that they need to be prepared for it: in September 2003, the EFA found that only 9 per cent of employers were fully aware of the government's plans.[147] If, in the future, mandatory retirement is all but abolished, employers will have to refine their individualised testing procedures (via 'performance management'), in order to 'manage the exit of older workers who are underperforming when they would previously have been "retired"'.[148]

Why are many British employers now showing a desire to employ older workers? Intriguingly, their motives are somewhat different from those of the old age pressure groups, even if there has been practical co-operation between the two. (For example, Age Concern helped found the EFA.) Social justice arguments regarding older people's right to work do not figure prominently. Instead, as would be expected, British employers' interest is based upon hard-nosed economic realism. As Richard Ottaway MP accurately observed, employers 'are not doing society a service by taking on older workers: they are making a sound business decision by doing so, and their businesses are becoming fitter and more profitable for it'.[149]

At the macro-economic level, employers have become increasingly concerned over the wider fiscal implications of an ageing population and male early retirement for public expenditure levels and rates of taxation: as the EFA warns, 'It is becoming increasingly urgent that employers work in partnership with the government and individuals to address the economic unsustainability of an increasing ageing population that is retiring younger and younger.'[150] Another employer motivation has been growing concern over the cost of implementing redundancy or final-salary, defined-benefit early retirement pension schemes: changing these to defined-contribution schemes would reduce employers' costs. Action against age discrimination would be the 'sweetener' that made such drastic steps possible. The two are often juxtaposed in discussions of age discrimination: for example, as far back as 1993 David Willetts was urging both a voluntary code of practice against age discrimination in employment and the ending of 'generous' final-salary pension schemes.[151]

Employers appear to share New Labour's view that the expansion of labour supply and the concomitant reduction of wage costs is the way to

[146] Based upon a reported 14 per cent of employees testifying that they had experienced age discrimination in employment. *EFA press release*, 3 April 2003.
[147] *EFA press release*, 3 Sept. 2003.
[148] Employers Forum on Age, *Working Age*, 1, 2004, www.efa.org.uk.
[149] *H of C Deb.*, 6s, vol. 260, 23 May 1995, cols. 814–15.
[150] EFA, *What Is the EFA?*, p. 4.   [151] Willetts, *The Age*, pp. 33–6.

economic growth. As three commentators have put it, employers 'would like to have as much labour as they need, at times when they need it and with the right skills and experiences ... a more imaginative use of older people can help these aims',[152] and an EFA publication argues that 'At the macro-economic level, age discrimination increases the propensity towards wage inflation as the available pool of younger workers dwindles.'[153] A central concern of employers is that, at a time of rapid labour market change, industrial restructuring and workforce streamlining, it is economically irrational to shed labour on grounds of age, since age does not necessarily correlate with job competence. Better criteria are needed, based upon ability rather than age: 'performance management' should replace mandatory retirement.[154] Martin Lyon Levine has summarised this argument succinctly: 'Age-based generalisation is thus a poor method of selecting out weak workers and will simultaneously result in discarding some of the best workers; this method thus suffers from both underprediction and overprediction.'[155] Past policies of basing redundancies upon crude age proxies are said to have caused many businesses to lose their best workers;[156] economic recessions have not had the desired purgative effect precisely because they have led to the exit of older workers rather than inefficient workers.[157] If older workers leave employment prematurely, they may not have given sufficient return on the investment (in terms of training, salary increments, and so on) that the company has made in them; retaining older workers will also maintain 'corporate memory' and ensure greater workforce continuity.[158] Instead of using crude age proxies, so the argument goes, employers should deploy sophisticated performance appraisal of job competence in order to decide who to retain and who to fire. Encouraging (or forcing) productive employees to continue working later in life would be a much more effective way of retaining only the 'work-relevant' and discarding the 'work-redundant'. As Cheryl Gillan (Parliamentary Under-Secretary of State for Education and Employment in the Conservative government) put it in the February 1996 Commons debate, employers can become more competitive in world markets if they ensure that their employees are 'selected, developed,

---

[152] Bernard Casey, Hilary Metcalf and Jane Lakey, 'Human Resource Strategies and the Third Age: Policies and Practices in the UK', in Institute of Personnel Management, *Age and Employment. Policies, Attitudes and Practices* (1993), p. 66.

[153] Rickard, *Profits Warning*, p. 10.   [154] *EFA press release*, 17 Oct. 2003.

[155] Martin Lyon Levine, *Age Discrimination and the Mandatory Retirement Controversy* (1988), p. 120.

[156] 'Introduction', in Institute of Personnel Management, *Age*, p. 1.

[157] Willetts, *The Age*, p. 32.

[158] Employers Forum on Age, *The Business Benefits* (1999), p. 1, www.efa.org.uk.

promoted and retained on the basis of merit'; this could be achieved by dropping age barriers in job advertisements, recruiting on ability rather than age, positively welcoming older job applicants, introducing 'flexible' working practices and investing in workers via more training schemes.[159] Implicit in this argument is the contention that more ruthless measures of job competence should be devised, and these should be used in deciding where redundancies should fall.

Adopting a more 'age neutral' perspective on personnel decisions would enable employers to place employees in more suitable jobs, according to their actual employment characteristics. The perceived principal positive qualities of older workers include experience, loyalty, reliability, the possession of interpersonal skills, confidence, ability to work as part of a team, and so on; on the negative side are lack of adaptability to new technology, loss of health and vitality, higher rates of industrial accidents, lower productivity, unwillingness to learn new skills, general rigidity of thought and behaviour, and unreceptivity to retraining.[160] It is clear, however, that some employers feel that these alleged negative qualities can be overcome by placing older workers in less demanding, low-skilled, poorly paid jobs. Thus an Institute of Personnel Management survey of 1,140 personnel managers in 1992 found that older workers were judged particularly suitable for 'rather low-level' jobs, 'of a kind sometimes described as "within the secondary labour market"'.

Although there is an emphasis on maturity, reliability and special knowledge, almost one-fifth of these jobs are seen as poor-quality, unattractive jobs which younger people would not find acceptable. Older people may be more willing than younger ones to accept such work because of the limited job opportunities otherwise available to them.[161]

Most of the recent 'success stories' regarding the employment of older workers in Britain refer to menial jobs – stacking shelves in supermarkets, delivering pizzas, working on a checkout till – where only low-level skills are required. For example, by 1998 Domino's Pizzas had one-fifth of its workers aged 55+, and planned to increase that proportion: older staff were said to 'chat more easily to customers on the doorstep' and were 'very efficient and scrupulously fair when they handle cash'.[162]

---

[159] *H of C Deb.*, 6s, vol. 271, 9 Feb. 1996, col. 611.
[160] Peter Warr and Janet Pennington, 'Views About Age Discrimination and Older Workers', in Institute of Personnel Managers, *Age*, pp. 75–106; David A. Peterson and Sally Coberly, 'The Older Worker: Myths and Realities', in Robert Morris and Scott A. Bass (eds.), *Retirement Reconsidered. Economic and Social Roles for Older People* (1988), pp. 118–19.
[161] Warr and Pennington, 'Views', p. 85.
[162] 'Older Workers Mean Happier Customers', *Guardian*, 17 Nov. 1998.

One reason, therefore, for the new interest shown by employers in age discrimination is that older workers possess employee characteristics that are highly suited to the casualised, 'flexible' periphery of the new postindustrial labour markets. They may replicate the demographic and social profile of their customers: for example, in a 'DIY' supermarket like B&Q their greater experience of household repairs will be useful, and the type of customer who frequents such stores (more middle-aged, more likely to be property-owners, and with higher disposable incomes) will appreciate this. Other 'desirable' characteristics of older workers include: their lower rates of absenteeism; better interpersonal skills in dealing with enquiries from the general public; the kind of 'maturity' that enables them to conform to the demands of monotonous, casual work; decreased likelihood of having dependants (thus not needing a 'male breadwinner family wage', and perhaps objecting less to working evening and weekend shifts); and the fact that they are less likely to be members of trade unions.[163] As David Willetts puts it, rather starkly, the advantages to B&Q of employing older workers were 'more politeness to customers, less time off sick and less pilfering'.[164] Richard Worsley identifies two reasons that have impelled employers in the retail trades to recruit more older workers: 'the greater willingness of older workers to fit in with the flexible working patterns, often on a part-time basis, required by retailers to cover evenings and weekends' and 'the cost-effectiveness of part-time working'. Successful businesses will in the future be 'leaner and fitter' as well as 'distinctive and outstanding in their markets' – and older workers can assist these ends.[165] Hence the retail chain W H Smith calculated that, through employing older workers, it would achieve a 1 per cent reduction in employee turnover and thus save £800,000 per annum, and the Nationwide Building Society 'saved £7,000,000 through age diversity policies which reduced staff turnover'.[166] B&Q likewise found that, after employing older people in its Macclesfield store, staff turnover was down by 65 per cent, absenteeism down by 39 per cent, and profits up by 16 per cent.[167]

Similar developments have taken place in the USA, where, since the 1980s, several companies have made it their policy to recruit older workers to fill their emerging 'flexible' jobs. As in Britain, this has occurred 'as a result of direct business needs'.[168] One such initiative was undertaken by

---

[163] Worsley, *Age and Employment*, p. 30.   [164] Willetts, *The Age*, p. 32.

[165] Worsley, *Age and Employment*, pp. 28, 134.

[166] Richard Worsley, 'The Generation Game', *The Bookseller*, 8 Mar. 1996, p. 37; Employers Forum on Age, *A Summary*.

[167] 'Greys Attack Ageist Firms'.

[168] Frances R. Rothstein, 'Older Worker Employment Opportunities in the Private Sector', in Morris and Bass, *Retirement Reconsidered*, p. 154.

the fast-food chain McDonald's, with its 'McMasters' initiative to hire employees aged 40+. As one commentator puts it, in deadpan style,

Pat Brophy, head of special employment at McDonald's, told a 1985 National Alliance of Business forum that assembling the company's new line of prepared salads requires the care and attention to detail that often characterise older workers; she also cited older women's success as hostesses for birthday parties, a role in which they drew upon their years as homemakers and mothers.[169]

It has also been quite frankly argued that employing older workers will enhance the 'legitimacy' of employers: being seen to be 'generous' to older workers is good industrial relations practice, in terms of workforce morale and the public's perception of that employer.[170] The 'nice stories' of what private enterprise has done with a small number of disabled or older workers, providing they involve no major financial liability to a company, make 'very good public relations material', as one commentator perceptively observes.[171]

It is worth pausing for a moment to reflect upon what exactly is meant by the 'flexible' working practices that will be facilitated by employing more older workers. 'Flexibility' in this context means a willingness to accept low-skilled jobs at low levels of pay, to work evenings, weekends and unsocial hours, and in general to adapt uncomplainingly to sudden changes in working conditions and remuneration (including, presumably, the abrupt termination of a job). For the EFA, therefore, 'good practice' in recruitment is summed up by the following example, which it cites approvingly. A retail and wholesale firm of delicatessen foods moved its warehouse to a high-unemployment economically depressed area in 1994, and immediately began to suffer very high staff turnover. At this point, the warehouse staff were aged between 17 and 21, with the majority being 18 or 19. Recruited largely from the ranks of the young unemployed, the staff tended to stay for only two to three months and then return to claiming benefits. The work was intrinsically unattractive: it was 'low skilled, with low pay, and offered little in the first few months in terms of knowledge or skills acquisition'. The firm therefore deliberately began to recruit from the ranks of the long-term unemployed (out of work for a year or more) aged 25+, using the auspices of the local government Training Employment Grant scheme which subsidised the wage costs of employers who took on such long-term unemployed for a period of six months. During that initial six-month period, trainees were carefully evaluated for their attendance

---

[169] Ibid., p. 155.   [170] Worsley, *Age and Employment*, pp. 20–1.
[171] E. Douglas Kuhns, 'Employment Opportunities for Older Workers (and Others): A Labor View of Short- and Long-Term Prospects', in Morris and Bass, *Retirement Reconsidered*, p. 169.

and job competence. If satisfactory, they moved on to permanent jobs in the warehouse and received further training (still partly government-subsidised). By this means, the employer had found a cheap and effective method of recruiting and retaining motivated and reliable employees, and discarding those who were not prepared to tolerate the low-skilled, poorly paid jobs on offer. The fact that this new employment regime was highly age discriminatory (selecting only workers aged 25+) passed without comment.[172]

Conclusion

It is clear, therefore, that the social, political and economic imperatives behind the emerging British debate on age discrimination are quite complex. A great many interest groups are participating in the debate, each with its own agenda. There is thus an intriguing amalgam of contradictory motives. Powerful 'social justice' arguments relating to active ageing, the combating of ageist attitudes, and the right to work are counterbalanced by, and often intermixed with, hard-nosed economic arguments about the need to increase the supply of labour and deploy more effective methods for evaluating the productivity of individual employees. Social policy has always been concerned with much more than just the meeting of needs: historically, it has also been about the regulation of labour supply. But we seem to have entered an era in which labour supply arguments are becoming more central than ever, and are fashioning a 'new social policy agenda' in general, and a 'new retirement agenda' in particular.

The current British debate on age discrimination in employment can be thought of as spanning an interpretative spectrum. At one end, action against age discrimination (whether voluntary or legislative) can be seen as offering a much-needed enhancement of the rights of older workers generally, and as part of a wide-ranging employment protection package that would include a number of measures. There would be extensive re-training and re-employment programmes for those aged 50+ who found themselves long-term unemployed, as exist in certain foreign countries (for example, Australia). A radical 'tax and spend' social agenda could subsidise older workers' jobs with generous in-work benefits, underpinned by a robustly enforced minimum wage (to prevent employers from imposing wage cuts). Inland Revenue rules on occupational pensions could be altered to permit semi-retirement at any age above 50 (subsidised by a part-pension)

---

[172] Employers Forum on Age, *Case Studies of the Moment* (1999), pp. 1–2, www.efa.org.uk.

combined with part-time working, lower remuneration and more time for leisure and voluntary work. (A move in this direction was announced in the Chancellor of the Exchequer's Pre-Budget of December 2003.) Other types of 'phased retirement' or 'flexible retirement' could be explored (for example, involving job-sharing), and tax credits could be introduced for those older workers who moved from full-time to part-time work.[173] A radical (but expensive) way of 'making work pay' would be to reduce income tax rates and raise tax thresholds for all aged 50+ – particularly those in low-paid work.[174] The laudable aim of improving lifelong learning and volunteering could be realised with more government help. This version of the 'active society' would be one in which all groups presently marginal to the labour market – single mothers on benefit, disabled people who wish to work, the early retired, the long-term unemployed – would be encouraged (but not forced) back into employment by policies tailor-made to their individual needs. Other fiscal and employment policies would assist those in more secure employment (who are more able to exercise choice) to fulfil the ideal of 'liquid lives' and a more 'fluid' retirement (for example, by moving to less stressful work when aged in their fifties).[175] Strategies to 'make work pay' at later ages would have to counteract the higher levels of workplace stress and 'burn-out' felt by many workers today. Such policies would be very expensive, and might well raise the question of whether jobs should be provided by the state (something which New Labour has strenuously resisted). More radical would be employment quotas for older people: if one aim is to achieve a truly 'age-diverse' workforce in all firms, these would have to be introduced. Most radical of all would be state pensions, a citizen's income or a 'social wage'[176] for all aged 50+, with no retirement condition. This may seem impossibly utopian (a hundred years ago, state pensions at the age of 65 were also seen by many as impossibly utopian), but it would be a logical response to globalisation's effect on the British labour market. Giddens's contention that 'retirement' and 'pensioner' are constructs of the 'old' welfare state can be turned on its head and presented as a rationale for paying pensions at *younger* ages instead of withdrawing benefit support to older people. The bold supporting argument would be that, on a cost–benefit analysis, public funding spent in this way would create economically independent citizens who, in the long run, would cost

---

[173] For several suggestions of this kind, see Donald Hirsch, *Crossroads After 50. Improving Choices in Work and Retirement* (2003), pp. 31–2 and ch. 8.

[174] As suggested by Andrew Rosindell MP, *H of C Deb.*, 6s, vol. 375, 23 Nov. 2001, col. 582.

[175] Moynagh and Worsley, *Opportunity*, pp. 32–3.

[176] Interestingly discussed in Michael Young and Tom Schuller, *Life After Work. The Arrival of the Ageless Society* (1991), pp. 167–8.

less in terms of social security support. It would be a true realisation of the 'active society' at its best.

Yet there is another version of the 'active society' which seems less sympathetic to the real needs of older citizens and more determined by the new global capitalism and its attendant competitive individualism. In reality, the appealing nostrums of 'lifecourse planning', 'liquid lives', 'portfolio careers' and 'choice' in retirement are highly middle-class, and therefore irrelevant to the majority of the population whose options are severely constrained by low incomes and lack of resources. As Kirk Mann rightly observes, 'Amid the chatter of reflexivity, diversity, identity and consumerism it can be hard to hear the voice of the poorest.'[177] This version of the 'active society' lurks beneath, and is legitimated by, the appealing aim of combating discrimination – something which no reasonable person can possibly disagree with. (For example, in March 2004 David Winnick MP declared that only someone who was 'psychotic' would question anti-discrimination laws.)[178] In this 'active society', welfare benefits would be strictly time-limited. Thereafter, draconian and compulsory workfarist policies would be applied to the economically inactive, including the early retired. The state pension age would be raised beyond what is already proposed (the equalisation of men and women's ages at 65 by 2020): an eligibility age of 68 or 70 has been suggested by bodies such as the Confederation of British Industry or the Adam Smith Institute.[179] The state National Insurance pension might even be replaced by means-tested income support (carrying a strong work obligation). As has been shown, the EU Directive's emphasis on the need for more 'participation' by older people in social and economic life appears to be shaped by these imperatives. It has given rise to a version of 'social justice' which is highly capitalistic and market-oriented. 'Equality' means 'equality of opportunity' or 'equal treatment', based upon 'participation' (in waged labour) and 'choice' (in the market); the legitimating principle underpinning this is said to be 'respect for the dignity of the individual'. This version of 'equality' is based upon the 'merit principle', which 'has been a central plank of business and government promotion of age equality'. Age equality is thus good for business. Expanding labour supply, via such 'equality' policies, 'opens up a wide pool of talent from which employers can draw, and yields a diverse workforce with a range of skills and experiences'.[180]

[177] Kirk Mann, *Approaching Retirement. Social Divisions, Welfare and Exclusion* (2001), p. 104.
[178] 'Blunkett Aide in Row Over Race', *Guardian*, 20 Mar. 2004.
[179] Alan Pickering, *Pensions Policy. How Government Can Get Us Saving Again* (2004), p. 1.
[180] Spencer and Fredman, *Age Equality*, pp. 29–36; Fredman and Spencer, *Age as an Equality Issue*, pp. 3, 21, 38–9, 48 (quote).

In this vision of the 'active society' the 'future of old age' would not be a particularly attractive one, and would reflect the widening of social and economic inequality that is taking place in many postindustrial societies. As the recent Hudson Institute Report in the USA warned, twenty-first-century society may consist of 'three worlds': first, a global elite of highly skilled employees commanding 'the highest earnings on the planet', and enjoying 'lifestyles free of material self-denial'; below them, low-skilled workers, subject to the vagaries of the economic cycle; and at the bottom, the permanently idle from the first two worlds.[181] What would emerge from this widening income inequality would be a broadly 'two-tier' retirement experience – the 'two nations' in retirement that Richard Titmuss perceptively warned of nearly half a century ago.[182] For a minority of wealthy retirees, born to the right parents, there would be a long period of education and training (say, up to the age of twenty-five), followed by a thirty-year career in the lucrative, 'core' sector of the labour market; early retirement would occur in one's mid-fifties, bringing a long semi-retirement of perhaps another forty years (part-time working in a 'bridge' job, underpinned by the income from a good final-salary occupational pension, with plenty of time to indulge in leisure pursuits). However, for the majority of poorer retirees – a new 'retirement underclass' – the twenty-first century may offer a short period of full-time education (no further than the age of sixteen), followed by episodic, insecure, low-paid labour market participation (with, accordingly, little opportunity or means to build up funded pension rights) which may last for sixty years – until 'infirmity' retirement occurs, supported only by means-tested social assistance. In essence, this would be a return to the nineteenth-century majority 'retirement experience'.

The most pessimistic interpretation of what is now happening would argue that, in time, older, economically inactive people are going to be forced back into low-paid, casualised jobs by draconian policies, such as the withdrawal of benefit support or the raising of the state pension age. As William Walters points out, the ideal of the 'active society' in many ways represents a reversal of the partial victories gained by working people and their organisations for the right to welfare benefits:

The demand for a right to meaningful work is translated into the obligation to search for, and accept what is often low-paid employment, or participate on public

---

[181] Richard W. Judy and Carol d'Amico, *Workforce 2020: Work and Workers in the 21st Century* (1997), pp. 122–3.

[182] Richard M. Titmuss, 'Pension Systems and Population Change', in Titmuss, *Essays on 'The Welfare State'* (1958), pp. 56–74.

training schemes. These latter obligations are increasingly conditions for the receipt of previously 'social' benefits; workfare is the end point of this logic.[183]

There would be, of course, enormous problems in applying 'workfarist' compulsion to the early retired, some of which can be briefly summarised. First, there is the question of whether suitable jobs exist, or can be created. Unless the 'lump of labour' really is a fallacy, and Britain's labour market is capable of massive expansion, such enforced re-enlistment back into the labour market may only result in a 'substitution effect', whereby subsidised workers displace unsubsidised ones, and nothing is gained. (This is being much discussed with regard to the whole New Deal strategy.) As has been shown, jobless 'fifty-something' men are highly concentrated in de-industrialised regions of Britain, where the problem is one of lack of demand for their labour. Logically, the proper solution is a regional economic policy to re-stimulate that demand; but such demand-side solutions are unlikely to be forthcoming. To be sure, cultural obstacles to the employment of older workers in 'young' jobs are perhaps indicators of widespread ageist attitudes, which could and should be overcome by government re-education policies. A middle-aged, male ex-steelworker based in South Wales may not be hired as a receptionist in a London female beauty parlour because of 'myths and misconceptions' that are irrational and discriminatory in nature; on the other hand, the reasons may have more to do with inappropriate skills, regional mismatches in supply and demand, gendered assumptions and those deeply internalised, 'age-appropriate' expectations that are not really discriminatory. The awkward question is: how far are cultural obstacles responsible for the joblessness that now afflicts nearly one in three men aged 50–64? If they play only a small part, then the current initiatives against age discrimination are not only pointless, they are also dangerously (and perhaps intentionally) misleading. The most damning critique of workfare is that it is merely designed to increase the supply of cheap, exploitable labour competing for a fixed number of jobs, thus driving down wages and displacing less effective workers.

A second difficulty would be the political unsustainability of forcing working-class early retirees back to work, while not applying compulsion to the middle classes on their generous final-salary pension schemes. This would be strongly resisted for its manifest unfairness. There are marked socio-economic differences in life expectancy at the age of 65: citizens in the lower socio-economic groups have a worse chance of living to claim the state pension, and the length of time they spend as pensioners is shorter. Raising

---

[183] Walters, "'Active Society'", p. 226.

the state pension age to, say, 70 would greatly exacerbate these inequalities: for example, nearly one in three men dies before the age of 70 (predominantly in social classes IV and V, and living in those regions where employment prospects for older workers are poorest).[184] An additional problem would be that those aged in their fifties (especially if they have worked all their lives) tend to be viewed as much more 'deserving' by the general public than the younger unemployed, and their unemployment becomes less and less controversial the closer they get to the state pension age.

Third, a central item in a proactive strategy against age discrimination in employment would be individualised performance testing: every year, say, an employee would be given a rigorous, job-related appraisal, and continuation at work would be conditional upon passing it. If 'capacity, not age' really is to be the criterion, capacity will have to be measured at regular intervals. The effect on those employees discarded for being 'unproductive' would be traumatic, causing them to slip down the labour market into permanent economic inactivity, creating even more 'discouraged workers'.

As with so much else, New Labour's policies against age discrimination are riddled with ambiguities. A final thematic paradox is that they illustrate the contradiction between the growth of individual rights, or 'microfreedoms', on the one hand, and the imposition of more work-obligation on the other. Under New Labour, 'self actualisation' has been encouraged by the enhancement of what can be called 'recreational rights', via the liberalisation of soft drugs, pornography, gambling, the alcohol licensing laws and the legal status of same-sex relationships, plus the removal of 'discrimination' in many areas of life. Yet these liberalisations have been accompanied by more coercive, illiberal policies, such as greater state surveillance, rising levels of prison incarceration, restrictions upon asylum seekers, and greater conditionality in welfare receipt. The implication would seem to be that personal freedoms will be enhanced only for those citizens who demonstrate that they are self-supporting through waged labour – and older people must be no exception. When considering the wider rights of older people, therefore, the current age discrimination debate in Britain needs to be examined very critically.

---

[184] 'Increasing Pension Age is "Work Until You Drop"', *Guardian*, 16 June 2004.

Part III

Retirement, health status and work-disability

4   Health status and old age

Introduction

The modern debate on age discrimination has in part been driven by the powerful argument that older people in advanced industrial societies now enjoy better health status than any previous generation. Intuitively, it would seem obvious that this must be so, and there appears to be much supporting evidence. For example, the economic historian Dora Costa, comparing Union Army records from the USA and recent health surveys, concludes that the health of Americans improved 'remarkably' over the course of the twentieth century, owing to the reduction in infectious diseases and occupational hazards, and that functional limitations among older men declined.[1] In both Britain and the USA, death rates have fallen steadily over the past century, and life expectancy at birth has risen dramatically. Most adults can now expect to live healthy, active lives until aged well into their seventies.[2]

'Working capacity' must, therefore, have improved, making it even more morally objectionable than ever to deny older people the right to employment, and a waged income higher than could be produced by any pension scheme. Improvements in survival rates should have increased the heterogeneity in health status that becomes more pronounced with the ageing process. It follows, therefore, that rigorous performance appraisal should be used to grade older workers according to their varying degrees of working capacity, rather than the crude age proxies employed in mandatory retirement policies.

---

[1] Dora L. Costa, 'Understanding the Twentieth-Century Decline in Chronic Conditions Among Older Men', *Demography*, vol. 37, no. 1, Feb. 2000, pp. 53–72; Costa, 'Changing Chronic Disease Rates and Long-Term Declines in Functional Limitation Among Older Men', *Demography*, vol. 39, no. 1, Feb. 2002, pp. 119–37.

[2] For a useful summary re Britain, see Emily Grundy, 'The Health and Health Care of Older Adults in England and Wales, 1841–1994', in John Charlton and Mike Murphy (eds.), *The Health of Adult Britain 1841–1994 Vol. 2* (1997), pp. 183–5.

Adding force to this argument is the changing nature of work. No longer do the majority of the population have to perform physically arduous manual labour in heavy industrial jobs, which in the past resulted in their becoming 'worn out' when aged in their early sixties. New technology and the growth of information-based and service jobs have changed the labour process enormously, making it 'lighter' and less labour-intensive.[3] Each successive cohort of sexagenarians should be healthier than ever, and the jobs open to them should require decreasing amounts of physical effort. It would seem, therefore, that the question of whether older people *could* stay on longer in work must be answered emphatically in the affirmative.

Yet the paradox is that retirement has inexorably spread and retirement ages have fallen steadily over the past 120 years.[4] Why, despite apparent improvements in health status and working capacity, should older people be working less? It is a paradox that has long fascinated social observers: for example, in the 1890s the British poverty investigator Charles Booth was puzzled by the fact that new technology was causing urban industrial workers to become 'worn-out' at progressively earlier ages;[5] again, in 1928 Louis Dublin (President of the American Statistical Association and a statistician at the New York Metropolitan Life Insurance Company) commented that 'there is no logical reason why the increased use of machinery, which requires no severe physical strain to operate, should not lengthen, rather than shorten, the active period of working life'.[6] In 1993 a very similar observation was made by the British Conservative MP David Willetts, who found it 'odd that as life expectations improve and as the physical well being of men in their fifties and sixties gets so much better, they should at the same time be having to give up work earlier'.[7] Another more recent commentator expresses similar puzzlement: 'Given the advances in medical science and improving life expectancy, it is quite extraordinary that there has been such a deterioration in the activity rate for men aged between 50 and 64 over the past twenty years.'[8] Clearly,

---

[3] Martin Neil Bailey, 'Aging and the Ability to Work: Policy Issues and Recent Trends', in Gary Burtless (ed.), *Work, Health and Income Among the Elderly* (1987), pp. 90–2.

[4] John Macnicol, 'Retirement and Health Status: the Paradox', in Helen Bartlett, John Stewart and Jonathan Andrews (eds.), *Historical and Contemporary Perspectives on Health, Illness and Health Care in Britain Since the Seventeenth Century* (1998), pp. 78–87; Henry R. Moody, 'The Contradictions of an Aging Society: From Zero Sum to Productive Society', in Robert Morris and Scott A. Bass (eds.), *Retirement Reconsidered: Economic and Social Roles for Older People* (1988), pp. 16–17.

[5] John Macnicol, *The Politics of Retirement in Britain 1878–1948* (1998), pp. 48–59.

[6] Louis I. Dublin, *Health and Wealth. A Survey of the Economics of World Health* (1928), p. 161.

[7] David Willetts, *The Age of Entitlement* (1993), pp. 31–2.

[8] Sean Rickard, *A Profits Warning. Macroeconomic Costs of Ageism* (n.d. c. 2000), p. 8.

those very technological developments which have made work lighter and less labour-intensive have simultaneously displaced older people from the labour market.

To some, the apparent improvements in health status and working capacity mean that older workers *should* stay on in work past state pension ages, thereby contributing to the general good via economic productivity, increased tax revenues and forgone social security benefits. It is an argument partly rooted in the currently fashionable nostrums of 'work-obligation', 'rights and responsibilities' and the 'active society', which have emerged in all industrialised societies with the growth of hypercasualised, low-paid, insecure jobs and the emphasis on achieving economic growth by maximising labour supply. At a time when public expenditure is under severe pressure, and faced with the costs of maintaining an ageing population after the second decade of the twenty-first century, surely it is right for older citizens to 'earn their keep'? Surely the paradoxical situation of apparently improving working capacity yet declining economic activity will eventually prove both economically unsustainable and morally indefensible – particularly if retirement ages keep falling and longevity continues to improve?

Projections on future health status and working capacity are going to be of enormous importance in determining the cost of health care and social security systems in Western societies.[9] As sickness is gradually postponed to the end of the human lifespan, and as, therefore, medicine increasingly becomes 'geriatric medicine', the health status of old people will become an increasingly accurate proxy for overall population health. The debate on health status and working capacity has also been central to the whole retirement debate. For example, the clinician James Fries's assumption of steadily improving health status in old age led him in 1983 to suggest that there should be no mandatory retirement ages whatsoever.[10] Free market economists in the USA, like Donald Parsons, have also put forward the ingenious argument that, since working capacity has improved, the spread of early retirement must be attributable to the incentive effect of social security (with the implication that social security should be cut back, in order to free up labour supply).[11] In 1983, measures were introduced to raise the pension eligibility age in the USA to 66 by the year 2009, and 67

[9] Kenneth G. Manton, Burton H. Singer and Richard M. Suzman, 'The Scientific and Policy Needs for Improved Health Forecasting Models for Elderly Populations', in Manton, Singer and Suzman (eds.), *Forecasting the Health of Elderly Populations* (1993), p. 3.

[10] James F. Fries, 'The Compression of Morbidity', *Milbank Memorial Fund Quarterly/Health and Society*, vol. 61, no. 3, 1983, p. 415.

[11] Donald O. Parsons, 'The Decline in Male Labor Force Participation', *Journal of Political Economy*, vol. 88, no. 3, June 1980, pp. 119–20.

by 2027; these were also predicated on the assumption that gains in aggregate health status in the older American population had improved working capacity, and that therefore it was not unreasonable to expect older workers to delay retirement in the future.[12]

The purpose of this section is to explore the difficult and paradoxical problem of whether or not health status and working capacity in old age have improved in both Britain and America over the past 100 years. In particular, it examines the interplay between retirement, health status and working capacity, with a view to answering the key question: can arguments derived from medical evidence be used to justify the re-enlistment of older workers into paid employment?

Health status and old age

At every age, health is a function of the interaction of endogenous, intrinsic or genetic factors with exogenous, extrinsic or environmental ones.[13] However, the precise balance between each is the subject of great controversy. Current debates on longevity tend to polarise between demographers and social scientists on the one hand, who argue that about 120 years is the absolute maximum length of the human lifespan, with most deaths in the future being distributed around the age of 85, and molecular biologists on the other, who maintain that, if only cell deterioration could be arrested, the human lifespan could be extended to hundreds of years – perhaps even a thousand.[14] Spectacular breakthroughs in our understanding of the ageing process are promised almost daily. But there are good grounds for caution: it is one thing to extend the life of rats, worms or fruit-flies in laboratory experiments; applying this to the complexity of human societies will be quite another.[15] And there is little point in extending the human lifespan unless 'disability-free life expectancy' or 'active life expectancy' can also be extended.

Even greater controversy occurs over the question of whether health status in old age is improving. The debate over what has happened, and

---

[12] Kenneth G. Manton and Beth J. Soldo, 'Disability and Mortality Among the Oldest Old: Implications for Current and Future Health and Long-Term Care Service Needs', in Richard M. Suzman, David P. Willis and Kenneth G. Manton (eds.), *The Oldest Old* (1992), p. 202. For another general discussion, see James M. Porteba and Lawrence H. Summers, 'Public Policy Implications of Declining Old-Age Mortality', in Burtless, *Work, Health and Income*, pp. 19–58.

[13] Christina R. Victor, *Health and Health Care in Later Life* (1991), p. 3.

[14] Biological theories of ageing are very well discussed in a special edition of *Scientific American*, vol. 11, no. 2, Summer 2000.

[15] Richard A. Miller, 'Extending Life: Scientific Prospects and Political Obstacles', *Milbank Quarterly*, vol. 80, no. 1, 2002, pp. 155–74.

what is going to happen, is exceedingly complex, and will be developed more fully later in this section. Broadly speaking, approaches to the biology of ageing tend to be divided between genetic determinism, nutritional determinism and lifestyle determinism. The first and second rather imply that, where our health status and age of death are concerned, the die is cast from the moment of conception: our health status in old age may be primarily a function of endogenous, unalterable factors such as our DNA, or of the nutrition we received in our mother's womb and of our exposure to infections in the first year of life.[16]

It is the third approach – the so-called 'use-it-or-lose-it' model – which has aroused most interest on the part of social scientists, gerontologists and medical demographers, since it holds that the biological processes of ageing are *not* inevitable, in the sense that they can be significantly delayed or modified. It is a truism in gerontology that the biology of ageing is always mediated through social processes and attitudes. 'Normal' ageing – divorced from its socio-economic context – is very difficult to define.[17] Thus Emily Grundy has observed that 'Many of the health problems of older adults may have more to do with a poor environment and cumulative exposure to various hazards than with the effects of ageing (senescence) alone.'[18] Likewise, the eminent British geriatrician John Grimley Evans argues that the biological processes of ageing have to be distinguished from those external factors that make old people appear 'different': the latter 'are not due to ageing but are frequently mistaken for it'.[19] For those who believe that academic social science should exert a beneficial effect upon social policy, the idea of citizens taking control of their own destiny – with the help of governments – is very appealing. As Maddox, Clark and Steinhauser put it, 'For social scientists, the variables of greatest interest in understanding the dynamics of aging processes and of aging "successfully" are largely structural and external to the individual.'[20] Much the same optimism can be seen in Jacob Siegel's declaration that the present gap between average life expectancy and the maximum observed human lifespan suggests 'that knowledge of the causes, prevention, and treatment of the most chronic diseases is quite limited and that much remains to be

---

[16] D. J. P. Barker, *Mothers, Babies and Health in Later Life* (1994).

[17] V. Korenchevsky, 'The Problem of Ageing. Basic Difficulties of Research', *British Medical Journal*, 8 Jan. 1949, p. 66.

[18] Grundy, 'Health and Health Care', p. 183.

[19] John Grimley Evans, 'Age Discrimination: Implications of the Ageing Process', in Sandra Fredman and Sarah Spencer (eds.), *Age as an Equality Issue* (2003), p. 11.

[20] George L. Maddox, Daniel O. Clark and Karen Steinhauser, 'Dynamics of Functional Impairment in Late Adulthood', *Social Science and Medicine*, vol. 38, no. 7, 1994, p. 925.

done in the way of medical research'.[21] This 'use-it-or-lose-it' position maintains, therefore, that, if only the health status of the general population could be raised to that of the highest socio-economic groups (such as Harvard graduates), through persuasion or policy, disability-free life could be extended into extreme old age, with a consequent lengthening of the working life.

Much evidence has accumulated over recent decades which appears to indicate that many factors associated with the ageing process previously considered intrinsic and thus unchangeable are in fact extrinsic and amenable to external influences.[22] For example, in all industrial societies, blood pressure rises with age such that 'normal' levels are age-adjusted; but in non-industrial societies (such as among nomadic shepherds), or in closed communities largely insulated from the stress of modern urban life (such as monasteries), this is not so.[23] Again, the loss of higher frequencies in hearing in modern societies is more a function of environment than of decrements inevitably brought about by the ageing process.[24] Muscle deterioration can be countered with exercise: there have been many instances of middle-aged and old people taking up physical activity – even marathon running – with beneficial results. Intellectual functioning can be maintained in old age by fresh mental challenges, such as learning a new language or merely continuing old hobbies at a demanding level. Vision loss can be countered by laser treatment or spectacles, the mobility of the physically disabled can be improved by powered wheelchairs, and future developments in bionic technology, transplant surgery and all kinds of 'gerontechnology' may go a long way towards counteracting the physical declines associated with the ageing process.[25] Times of national need (such as the Second World War) have demonstrated that older people can be quickly trained for demanding jobs: they certainly possess the latent cognitive and physical ability.

These and countless other examples suggest that many facets of the ageing process could be arrested by technology, lifestyle changes and

---

[21] Jacob S. Siegel, *A Generation of Change. A Profile of America's Older Population* (1993), pp. 222–3.

[22] J. Grimley Evans, 'Human Ageing and the Differences Between Young and Old', in J. Grimley Evans *et al.*, *Health and Function in the Third Age. Papers Prepared for the Carnegie Inquiry into the Third Age* (1993), p. 7.

[23] Richard G. Wilkinson, *Unhealthy Societies. The Afflictions of Inequality* (1996), pp. 189–90.

[24] Grimley Evans, 'Human Ageing', pp. 7–8.

[25] Jan-Erik Hagberg, 'Old People, New and Old Artefacts – Technology for Later Life', in Britt-Marie Oberg, Anna-Lisa Narvanen, Elisabet Nasman and Erik Olsson (eds.), *Changing Worlds and the Ageing Subject. Dimensions in the Study of Ageing and Later Life* (2004), pp. 161–84.

manipulations of the environment.[26] If medical interventions could significantly delay the onset or mitigate the effects of heart disease, cancers, strokes and respiratory diseases – which currently account for some 70 per cent of deaths in British people aged 65+[27] – then health status in old age would improve markedly. Perhaps more importantly, there would be wider gains: the happiness, self-esteem, social confidence and quality of life of older adults would also improve (themselves factors that make for a psychological predisposition to longevity). As noted in an earlier chapter, historical examples of extreme longevity have often been cited to illustrate what could be achieved in the future. The key question is not so much why these heroic figures survive to an active old age; it is why the vast majority of their contemporaries do not. Montaigne's dictum that 'men do not usually die, they kill themselves' reflects the demographic truism that premature mortality, rather than survival, holds the key to understanding how to extend the human lifespan. The tantalising possibility is that, if only such premature mortality could be prevented, then the achievements of these heroic survivors would become the norm, and extreme longevity would be enjoyed by the large majority of the populations of Western societies.

However, there is an opposing view, which is more complex and less reassuring. The comfortable model of unproblematic success in improving health status may seem intuitively correct, but it is open to considerable debate. Throughout history, discourses on ageing have always been marked by a sharp dualism between notions of 'positive' or 'successful' ageing on the one hand, and metaphors of decay and decrepitude on the other.[28] Several interacting factors have contributed to this more pessimistic view.

First, since the mid nineteenth century there has occurred a long-run 'epidemiological transition', whereby the old quick-killing diseases of the early industrial era (notably epidemics) have been replaced by chronic, degenerative conditions of longer duration. Hence roughly three out of every four deaths in the USA today occur as a result of degenerative diseases, and at advanced ages.[29] These diseases appear to have very

---

[26] Sidney M. Stahl and Jacqueline Rupp Feller, 'Old Equals Sick: an Ontogenetic Fallacy', in Sidney M. Stahl (ed.), *The Legacy of Longevity. Health and Health Care in Later Life* (1990), p. 25.

[27] Victor, *Health*, pp. 47–8.

[28] Mike Featherstone, 'Post-Bodies, Aging and Virtual Reality', in Mike Featherstone and Andrew Wernick (eds.), *Images of Aging: Cultural Representations of Later Life* (1995), p. 227.

[29] S. Jay Olshansky and A. Brian Ault, 'The Fourth Stage of the Epidemiologic Transition: The Age of Delayed Degenerative Diseases', *Milbank Quarterly*, vol. 64, no. 3, 1986, p. 361.

long-term origins – perhaps resulting from early life exposures[30] or genetic factors. Their diagnosis and prognosis is thus extremely problematic. For example, arthritis is the most prevalent condition among American women aged 45+; yet, notes Verbrugge, it 'is actually a term for over 100 specific conditions; the preeminent one is osteoarthritis. Its aetiology, pathogenesis and successful control are still mysteries.'[31]

It has long been known that, as the Roman Celsus put it, 'old age is more exposed to chronic diseases, youth to acute ones'.[32] As early as 400 BC, Hippocrates observed that

old men suffer from difficulty in breathing, catarrh accompanied by coughing, strangury, difficult micturation, pains at the joints, kidney disease, dizziness, apoplexy, cachexia, puritis of the whole body, sleeplessness, watery discharges from the bowels, eyes and nostrils, dullness of sight, cataract, hardness of hearing.[33]

What has changed since the mid nineteenth century has been that increasing numbers of the population have been exposed to these degenerative diseases associated with advanced years. The measurement of aggregate health status at the population level has thus moved from an emphasis upon the relatively simple indicator of mortality to much more complex and flawed morbidity measures;[34] as a result, the psycho-social and environmental influences upon sickness have become ever more important. 'Health' has become an increasingly multi-dimensional and elusive concept and its measurement more difficult.

In the case of old people, several measures of health status can be applied. The most obvious starting-point would be materialist indicators. Heights and weights have been widely used in economic history, and can be very effective in making comparisons across time (for example, in the health of schoolchildren). They may have a part to play in measuring the health status of old people.[35] Birth weights appear to show a close

[30] Kenneth G. Manton, Eric Stallard and Larry Corder, 'Changes in the Age Dependence of Mortality and Disability: Cohort and Other Determinants', *Demography*, vol. 34, no. 1, Feb. 1997, pp. 135–6.

[31] Lois M. Verbrugge, 'Recent, Present and Future Health of American Adults', in L. Breslow, J. E. Fielding and L. B. Lave (eds.), *Annual Review of Public Health*, vol. 10, 1989, pp. 342–3, 354.

[32] Quoted in Trevor H. Howell, *Our Advancing Years* (1953), p. 31.

[33] Quoted in Gerald Bennett and Shah Ebrahim, *The Essentials of Health Care of the Elderly* (1992), p. 59.

[34] Richard G. Brooks, *Health Status Measurement: a Perspective on Change* (1995), p. 17; Michael Bury, *Health and Illness in a Changing Society* (1997), p. 116.

[35] For an application of anthropometric data on heights and weights, see Bernard Harris, 'Growing Taller, Living Longer? Anthropometric History and the Future of Old Age', *Ageing and Society*, vol. 17, pt. 5, Sept. 1997, pp. 491–512.

correlation with subsequent health status and intellectual ability, and may well have a causal effect on very late life.[36]

Second, there are measures of functioning at the everyday level. 'Activities of daily living' (ADLs) relate to activities such as bathing, dressing, toileting, continence and feeding; 'instrumental activities of daily living' (IADLs) relate to activities such as shopping, cooking, housekeeping, laundry, use of transport, managing money, self-dispensation of medication, and the use of the telephone.[37] Many other intricate measures of mobility, frailty, independence and quality of life have been constructed to evaluate the functional impairment of older people in their day-to-day social and domestic environment (such as the Duke University Center Health Profile). One obvious disadvantage of such indicators is that they fail to capture the psycho-social dimensions of health, being relatively immune to background social and economic factors. (Of course, this is also their great advantage.)[38] Another disadvantage is that they tend not to record the degree of difficulty involved in accomplishing the stipulated tasks. Measures of disability can also be combined with mortality rates and life expectancy data to produce a calculation of 'disability-free life expectancy' or 'health expectancy' (the expectation of years of life in various health states).

However, in the final analysis health is a quality of life, as encapsulated in the World Health Organization's famous definition that health is 'a state of complete physical, mental and social wellbeing and not merely the absence of disease and infirmity'.[39] Arguably, therefore, morbidity indicators need to be used. However, these are equally problematic. Over the past 100 years, age-specific mortality declines have been accompanied by increasing health care utilisation rates. Higher public expectations of what constitutes 'good' health and a host of psycho-social factors have meant that self-reported health appears to have worsened since the 1970s, with more recorded disability and long-term sickness, while functional measures such as ADLs and IADLs have shown health to be improving. This does not necessarily invalidate survey-based health measures: as Lois

---

[36] Barker, *Mothers*, ch. 4.

[37] These are well discussed in Brooks, *Health Status*, esp. ch. 2. For an example of their application, see Eileen M. Crimmins and Yasuhiko Saito, 'Getting Better and Getting Worse. Transitions in Functional Status Among Older Americans', *Journal of Aging and Health*, vol. 5, no. 1, Feb. 1993, pp. 3–36.

[38] On the other hand, if ADL/IADL measures rely upon individuals' assessments of their own mobility they may produce results that are contaminated by changing expectations and environmental modifications. See Vicki A. Freedman and Linda G. Martin, 'Understanding Trends in Functional Limitations Among Older Americans', *American Journal of Public Health*, vol. 88, no. 10, 1998, p. 1457.

[39] Quoted in Brooks, *Health Status*, p. 7.

Verbrugge observes, 'People seem to be able to sum up their own health better than health professionals, maybe sensing incipient diseases that have not crossed clinical thresholds, the real severity of diagnosed conditions, and their body's overall physiological reserve.'[40] However, it does mean that the results of self-reported health surveys cannot necessarily be taken at face value.

A second cautionary point is that gains in mortality since the mid nineteenth century have been largely in childhood; adult longevity has increased much less. 'Progress' has thus meant more individuals surviving to adulthood, rather than dramatic extensions of the lifespan. The replacement of epidemics by degenerative diseases has resulted in the survival of more adults with 'health impaired' lives, and this increasing number of 'impaired survivors' may lower aggregate health status.

Third, it cannot be assumed that progress in public health will inevitably continue. Positive developments, such as new pharmaceuticals, non-invasive microsurgery, organ transplants, genetic screening, improved living standards, and so on, may be offset by negative factors, such as environmental pollution, new work-related illnesses (for example, repetitive strain injury), health impairments caused by poor food hygiene, widening income inequality and even new epidemics (of which AIDS and SARS may be only a portent) exacerbated by factors such as increasing transglobal travel and global warming. Twenty-first-century advanced industrial societies appear to be more competitive than any previous society, and there are increasing numbers of citizens who are becoming 'burned-out' as a result: thus an ICM Research survey in Britain in 2002 revealed that an estimated 12,000,000 people – 20 per cent of the population – were on anti-depressants, the number of prescriptions for anti-depressant drugs having doubled between 1991 and 2001.[41] Again, claims to disability benefits in Britain have tripled since the 1970s. Just as the twenty-first-century labour market may become more like its nineteenth-century counterpart (with the growth of poorly paid, casualised jobs), so the new century's 'public health problem' may uncannily mirror that of Victorian times. There may also be health-related 'problems of civilisation', such as the burgeoning concern that sedentary lifestyles in Western societies and consumption of high-fat 'fast-foods' (especially among today's children) are raising levels of

---

[40] Verbrugge, 'Recent, Present and Future', p. 337.

[41] 'Happiness is a Warm Friend', *Observer*, 19 May 2002; Office for National Statistics, *Social Trends No. 33 2003 Edition* (2003), p. 134. This can be attributed to several factors, including the normalisation of pharmaceutical consumption and the marketing techniques of drug companies.

obesity.[42] By the year 2001, 21 per cent of males in England, and 24 per cent of females, were obese and a further 47 per cent of males and 33 per cent of females were 'overweight'.[43] Adult obesity in England has increased by nearly 400 per cent since the early 1980s, and childhood obesity has tripled. This is engendering great concern that conditions such as diabetes, hypertension, heart disease and even cancers may increase in incidence, posing great problems for health care systems in the future: life expectancy at every age may decrease, with the alarming possibility that some children will die before their parents.[44] Furthermore, even if all human beings led completely 'risk-free' lifestyles in environmentally perfect surroundings, there would probably still be considerable variation in health status and age of death, attributable to endogenous factors.

A final factor is that the data on morbidity are contaminated by powerful behavioural, environmental and psycho-social factors. Demand for health care is affected by an enormous number of variables, including the level and availability of health services and diagnostic procedures, the existence of new medical technology, individuals' definitions of their own health status and their thresholds for self-referral, professional thresholds for referral to specialist care, circumstantial factors such as stress, and – most significantly for this study – labour market demand.[45] A final problem is that the distribution of morbidity is patterned according to factors such as gender, race, marital status, locality, age, culture and socio-economic status. These variations render generalisations about the aggregate health status of a population relatively useless. All in all, the difficulties attendant upon measuring health status are so many and varied that one economist has aptly commented that 'true states of health are not directly observable'.[46]

We cannot, therefore, assume that the aggregate health status of older adults in Britain and the USA has necessarily improved. And when we then move to a consideration of working capacity, a further difficulty is encountered. 'Working capacity' can be defined as the juxtaposition of the functional abilities of an individual with the functional requirements of a job. There are thus two elements in the equation, and within these two elements

---

[42] Christine L. Himes, 'Obesity, Disease and Functional Limitation in Later Life', *Demography*, vol. 37, no. 1, Feb. 2000, pp. 73–82.

[43] Office for National Statistics, *Social Trends No. 33*, p. 140.

[44] See, for example: 'The Diabetes Timebomb', *Guardian*, 30 May 2000; 'Children Will Die Before Their Parents', *Guardian*, 27 May 2004.

[45] M. J. Goldacre, 'Disease in the Third Age: a Profile from Routine Statistics', in Grimley Evans *et al.*, *Health and Function*, p. 45.

[46] Gary Burtless, 'Introduction and Summary', in Burtless, *Work, Health, and Income*, p. 6.

are many variables: there will be huge variation in the functional abilities of individuals, depending on genetic inheritance, socio-economic status, lifestyle/environmental factors, and personality; the functional requirements of jobs will also vary enormously, and over time.

Throughout history, individuals' self-assessments of their own working capacity have been profoundly shaped by numerous interacting factors. Prominent among these factors is labour market demand: when jobs are plentiful, more people will define themselves as capable of working; when jobs are scarce, more people define themselves as 'work-disabled'. Ill-health has always been a socially acceptable reason for de facto unemployment. Recorded ill-health and disability are thus partly reflective of external economic factors. In the light of this, confident assertions that health status and working capacity have improved over the last 100 years, such as to justify a longer working lifespan, need to be examined critically. These issues will be explored in the following three chapters.

5   From the late nineteenth century to the 1940s

The quest for longevity

Throughout history, mankind has been fascinated by the possibility of achieving immortality, via the 'quest for longevity' or 'prolongevity'.[1] In medieval times, even the most omnipotent ruler had to face the humiliating prospect of death, along with the lowliest peasant. The possibility of cheating death became a growing obsession in human societies – particularly during the eighteenth-century Enlightenment, with its faith in the perfectibility of mankind.[2] Paradoxically, to achieve near-immortality, and become at one with the angels, has been a recurring goal of post-Enlightenment scientific rationalism. Social history is replete with stories of extreme old age, many of them apocryphal or exaggerated. Figures like Thomas 'Old' Parr, of Shropshire, became legends: his age was claimed to be 152 years and 9 months when he died in London in 1635 (and was examined as a freak of nature by William Harvey). Parr was said to have married for the first time at the age of 80, and again at 132; in the interim, he allegedly performed penance for fathering a child out of wedlock. Disappointingly, it is likely that Parr was in fact three generations of one family.[3] A similar heroic individual was Christian Jacobsen of Denmark, who died in 1772 allegedly aged 145 and claimed to have lived under seven Danish kings.[4] Such mythical centenarians have always had a strong appeal, since they appear to stand as exemplars of what could be achieved in a perfect world.

---

[1] Gerald J. Gruman, *A History of Ideas About the Prolongation of Life: the Evolution of Prolongevity Hypotheses to 1800* (1966).

[2] See, for example, C. W. Hufeland, *The Art of Prolonging Life* (1797).

[3] William J. Thoms, *Human Longevity. Its Facts and Its Fictions* (1873), pp. 85–6, 308–12 (Harvey's autopsy report on Parr); John Burn Bailey, *Modern Methuselahs* (1888), pp. 404–5. Examples of extreme longevity are entertainingly discussed in Robert E. Pieroni, 'Centenarians', in Erdman B. Palmore (ed.), *Handbook on the Aged in the United States* (1984), pp. 3–16.

[4] Louis I. Dublin and Alfred J. Lotka, *Length of Life: a Study of the Life Table* (1936), pp. 3–4.

As several writers have observed,[5] Enlightenment optimism has continued into the twentieth and twenty-first centuries, the aim of much geriatric medicine being to achieve the miraculous slowing-down of the ageing process. As one expert commented, 'For many scientists and medical research workers the problem of ageing is fascinating not only because it affects the well-being of every man and woman, but also, and often chiefly, because it is one of the greatest and most fundamental mysteries and riddles in biology and medicine.'[6] The 'prolongevity project' has thus attracted a vast amount of medical research and public interest. One estimate is that there are now some 300 different biological theories of ageing.[7] Many examples of ageing and longevity are also to be found in fiction, such as Anthony Trollope's *The Fixed Period* (1882) – a classic of dystopian literature – or Aldous Huxley's brilliantly sardonic satire *After Many a Summer* (1939), and as the theme of populist texts, such as Walter B. Pitkin's *Life Begins at Forty* (1932) (which promised to reveal the secret of how to stay 'vital' until extreme old age). Today, researchers continue to examine, in great detail, the variety of endogenous (biological) and exogenous (social) factors that appear to bestow extreme longevity upon the inhabitants of particular geographical locations – the Caucasus in Russia, regions of Southern Ecuador, or the village of Talana in Sardinia. One day, the secrets of longevity may be fully revealed. For the moment, much is promised, but little is actually delivered. The disappointing truth is that, in the past, the social factors that have correlated most closely with extreme longevity have been illiteracy, poor birth recording and a cheerful tendency of local inhabitants to tell researchers exactly what they imagine those researchers want to hear.[8]

The debate on health status and old age from the nineteenth century to the Second World War

It is an oft-repeated truism that the hundred years after the 1880s was accompanied by an increasing 'medicalisation' and 'problematisation' of

[5] Stephen Katz, 'Imagining the Life-Span: from Pre-Modern Miracles to Postmodern Fantasies', in Mike Featherstone and Andrew Wernick (eds.), *Images of Aging: Cultural Representations of Later Life* (1995), p. 65; Stephen Katz, *Disciplining Old Age. The Formation of Gerontological Knowledge* (1996), pp. 39–48. A particularly good account of the early American pioneers of geriatrics is to be found in W. Andrew Achenbaum, *Crossing Frontiers. Gerontology Emerges as a Science* (1995), ch. 1.

[6] V. Korenchevsky, 'The Longest Span of Life Based on the Records of Centenarians in England and Wales', *British Medical Journal*, 5 July 1947, p. 14.

[7] Kathryn Brown, 'How Long Have You Got?', *Scientific American*, vol. 11, no. 2, Summer 2000, p. 11.

[8] For a discussion of the problems of verifying claims to extreme longevity, see Bernard Jeune and James W. Vaupel (eds.), *Validation of Exceptional Longevity* (1999).

old age.[9] In a general sense, this is undeniable. As old age, retirement and state pensions grew in importance as social issues, so was there increasing concern over the particular health problems of older adults. Thus G. M. Humphry (Professor of Surgery at the University of Cambridge) commented in 1885 that 'old age acquires a gradually increasing interest, as advancing civilisation enables a larger number of persons to attain to it, and affords them additional means of enjoying it, and profiting by it'.[10] However, this concern was more finely balanced between the 'care' and 'control' functions of geriatric medicine than many post-Foucaultians allow. Andrew Achenbaum rightly argues that, while a 'medicalisation' process did take place, the early triumvirate of American geriatricians (Elie Metchnikoff, G. Stanley Hall and I. L. Nascher) also had aspirations to raise the status of old people and meet their particular needs: they 'believed that scientific advances in senescence would pave the way for more positive assessments of growing older; they expected science someday to make it possible for people to affix constructive meanings and purposes to late years'.[11]

The slowly growing number of centenarians in late Victorian society held up the tantalising prospect of the democratisation of longevity. Nevertheless, difficult questions remained unanswered. Just what was 'degeneration', and where could it be most easily observed in the body? What was the maximum possible human lifespan, and under what conditions might it be achieved by a large proportion of the population? Which cells degraded quickest? Was cancer related to senility, and thus a symptom of it? Was 'centenarian pathology' merely a case of 'simple and general atrophy', or was it the catastrophic failure of one vital organ?[12] These and other questions were deeply puzzling.[13] Central to the whole debate was the issue of whether old age was normal (involving 'natural decay') or pathological (a collection of mutually reinforcing specific diseases – what today might be termed 'multiple pathology' or 'comorbidity'). If old age was the latter, then the identification and conquest of those diseases would bestow the gift of longevity on mankind – increasing the human lifespan to perhaps 200 years.[14]

---

[9] This is a central theme in Katz, *Disciplining Old Age*.

[10] G. M. Humphry, 'The Annual Oration on Old Age and the Changes Incidental to It', *British Medical Journal*, 9 May 1885, p. 927.

[11] Achenbaum, *Crossing Frontiers*, p. 49.

[12] Sir James Crichton-Browne, 'Old Age', *British Medical Journal*, 3 Oct. 1891, p. 734. Crichton-Browne's (pp. 727–36) article is – for the time – unusually long and interesting.

[13] See, for example, Hastings Gilford, 'The Nature of Old Age and of Cancer', *British Medical Journal*, 27 Dec. 1913, pp. 1617–20.

[14] Bailey, *Modern Methuselahs*, p. 19.

However, the biology of ageing was still a minority medical interest, and geriatric medicine was in its infancy: Ignatz L. Nascher, who is generally credited with inventing the term 'geriatrics',[15] had great difficulty getting his ideas accepted in the world of medicine.[16] The period from the late nineteenth century to the 1940s is somewhat bereft of texts on health status and old age, even if a small number of doctors were intrigued by the question of why human beings reached maturity at a certain age, and then experienced a slow decline. The maximum human lifespan could be five times the period of growth to maturity (i.e. five times twenty-one), or it could conform to the Pythagorean model of four twenty-year parts, or the Shakespearean seven ages.[17] Growth, equilibrium and decline seemed to be the normal three-stage pattern, but there was much disagreement about the timing or inevitability of the last stage. Optimists believed that the progress of medical science would permit larger numbers to survive longer, thereby allowing definite conclusions to be drawn. For example, G. M. Humphry conducted a survey of over 500 people aged 80+ (males and females in equal numbers) and 52 centenarians, to ascertain shared characteristics. His aim was to record the inevitable decline in physical and mental ability that accompanied the ageing process after the body had attained maturity, but also to point to the marked variations in health status in any age-group. He listed the specific manifestations of bodily decrements brought about by the ageing process: a thinning of the skull, a calcification of the cartilages, a hardening of the arteries, a lessening in the power of concentration and 'quickness' in the brain, and so on.[18]

In looking backwards, one must be wary of imposing the condescensions of posterity upon the past. Though medical science was, on the face of it, less 'developed' than it is today, most nineteenth-century commentators were well aware of the methodological difficulties that attended the measurement of health status in old age. Then, as now, many realised that the answer to the problem of how to extend the human lifespan would not be found in the few who survived to extreme old age, but in the many who did not. In a famous passage, the late-nineteenth-century medico-legal expert George M. Beard summed up the problem of assessing the effect of the ageing process on the mental faculties. Examining the few individuals who remained mentally active in advanced years might be

---

[15] I. L. Nascher, *Geriatrics. The Diseases of Old Age and Their Treatment, Including Physiological Old Age, Home and Institutional Care, and Medico-Legal Relations* (1914).
[16] Achenbaum, *Crossing Frontiers*, pp. 46–7.
[17] Bailey, *Modern Methuselahs*, p. 18.
[18] Humphry, 'Annual Oration', pp. 927–31; 'Supplement', *British Medical Journal*, 11 Dec. 1886.

methodologically flawed, argued Beard, since they were not a representative sample. Yet clinical tests were equally fraught with difficulties:

If physiology alone could solve these problems – if it were possible for the microscope to so reveal the complex mechanism of the brain, and if chemistry could so analyse its intricate and manifold constituents as to make it a human possibility to determine, from the brain itself, both the general and special functions of which it is capable, and the modifications which these functions undergo by age, by disease, and external conditions – then, by a sufficient number of post-mortem examinations, these hard questions could be scientifically answered.[19]

However, it was not possible to obtain evidence from such post-mortems. Instead, medicine had to rely upon observations of older people in their social settings – and this meant that such observations were a comment on the exogenous or environmental factors, rather than the endogenous ones attributable to old age per se.

From the mid nineteenth century, advice on how to achieve longevity proliferated. Much of it was, at best, straightforward common sense, and, at worst, a set of banal homilies relating to temperance, mental alertness and physical activity.[20] Such advice was termed 'gerocomy' by one commentator, who attempted to identify the specific pathologies of old age as 'diseases of sedentary and advanced life'.[21] Others produced a plethora of suggestions. Chronic bronchitis in elderly patients should involve keeping the toxicity of the blood as low as possible, assisting healthy respiration by surrounding the patient with pure air, maintaining a sparse diet and vigorous circulation, and encouraging breathing exercises.[22] Arnold Lorand's 'twelve commandments for old age' consisted of open air and sunshine, good diet, a daily bath, a daily bowel movement, cotton underwear, early bedtime and morning rising, sleeping in a darkened and quiet room, one day's rest a week, not worrying, getting married, moderation in alcohol, tobacco, tea and coffee, and avoidance of overheated places.[23] Since many of the ailments of old age were caused by over-feeding, food should be reduced 'as maturity glides into senility', according to Dr George Keyworth. Like other commentators, Keyworth cited specific

[19] George M. Beard, *Legal Responsibility in Old Age, Based on Researches into the Relation of Age to Work* (1874), p. 4, reprinted in Gerald J. Gruman, *The 'Fixed Period' Controversy. Prelude to Ageism* (1979).

[20] Thomas Bailey, *Records of Longevity: with an Introductory Discourse on Vital Statistics* (1857), p. 6.

[21] J. Milner Fothergill, *The Diseases of Sedentary and Advanced Life: a Work for Medical and Lay Readers* (1885), pp. 133–295.

[22] Harry Campbell, 'The Treatment of Chronic Bronchitis in the Elderly and Aged', *British Medical Journal*, 12 Oct. 1901, pp. 1063–4.

[23] Arnold Lorand, *Old Age Deferred: the Causes of Old Age and its Postponement by Hygienic and Therapeutic Measures* (1910), pp. 457–8.

(and possibly unrepresentative) examples of those who had attained extreme old age by watching their diet, and offered mundane advice (exercise, bowel movement, moderate wine-drinking).[24] Interestingly, many late-nineteenth-century texts recommended a small food intake – something that is now being systematically researched as 'calorie restriction'.

Much of the prevailing advice was slightly patronising in tone, portraying old age (following Shakespeare) as a kind of second infancy. Aldred Scott Warthin's recommendation – tinged with a rural romanticism – was that

Creative mechanical work of some kind offers one of the best outlets to the old man's restlessness; and of all the occupations that may offer, that of gardening, of growing and planting and tending growing things, is the very best form of exercise and avocation adapted to the needs of the aged individual. There is also a very definite psychologic relationship shown in this return of the old man to the soil.[25]

Such sentiments expressed the truism that doctors should not allow older people to vegetate in an indolent or bed-ridden state, and should try and encourage them to find 'light employment' that would keep them physically active and mentally alert, thus investing their lives with meaning and self-worth.[26] Sir Humphrey Rolleston's 1922 text on *Medical Aspects of Old Age* – unusual for the time, in that it dealt with the biology of ageing – surveyed the state of knowledge on longevity and recommended the maintenance of an active mind and body, rather than abrupt retirement.[27]

Extreme longevity caused great puzzlement to late-nineteenth-century commentators. Some very old people were to be found in the most insanitary conditions (which had killed off many of their contemporaries in childhood and youth), and some paragons of rectitude died young.[28] The mix of endogenous and exogenous factors was perplexing. 'Nothing can be more capricious than longevity', observed John Burn Bailey, who could find no evidence that it was inherited: in that respect, it was as unpredictable as genius status. Longevity could be experienced by both

the voluptuary and the ascetic; the son of affluence and the child of poverty; the man whose existence is regulated by rule, and he whose habits defy all method; the

---

[24] George Hawson Keyworth, 'Notes on Disease in Advanced Life', *British Medical Journal*, 31 Jan. 1903, pp. 240–1.

[25] Aldred Scott Warthin, *Old Age, the Major Involution: the Physiology and Pathology of the Aging Process* (1929), p. 181.

[26] F. Martin Lipscomb, *Diseases of Old Age* (1932), pp. 456–7. See also Alfred Worcester, *The Care of the Aged, the Dying and the Dead* (1935).

[27] Sir Humphrey Rolleston, *Medical Aspects of Old Age* (1922; 1932 edn), pp. 56, 58.

[28] Keyworth, 'Notes'.

man of the world and the recluse; the daring adventurer and he who clings to the safety of home; the married man burdened with a large family, and the bachelor free as air.[29]

G. M. Humphry argued that there was a large genetic component in longevity, but environmental factors were also present – 'freedom from exposure to the various casualties, indiscretions, and other causes of disease to which illness and early death are so much due'.[30] Likewise, the *British Medical Journal* commented that senility of cells was 'not the penalty of advanced life only, but frequently ensues upon a combination of faults of heredity and errors in living'.[31] G. Stanley Hall's famous text, *Senescence: the Last Half of Life* (1922) – a notable early example of advice on 'positive ageing' – also suggested that heredity was the principal factor in longevity, but warned that obeisance to this view might weaken the confidence of doctors that they could prolong the lifespan; social and psychological factors were also important, including encouraging the over-seventies to feel that they had a useful role still to play.[32] Likewise, Lawrence Frank argued that ageing consisted of both involuntary processes internal to the body – the inevitable modification of cells, tissues and fluids – and also external factors such as toxins, traumas and nutritional inadequacies.[33]

Death in extreme old age could be attributed to general decay – a concept not unlike the modern idea of 'natural death'[34] – but premature mortality (say, before the eighth decade) was a puzzle, since it appeared to involve the catastrophic failure of only one vital organ, with the others still healthy and carrying what today would be termed substantial 'organ reserve'. This, again, echoes modern theories: as a leading demographer of today has observed, 'The human organism is a complex multicomponent system, each having its own ageing rate. The death of the individual organism therefore will be determined by the fastest aging rate of the individual components.'[35] Longevity might, therefore, depend upon a 'balance' of the internal organs, with all functioning well simultaneously: hence 'each organ must be sound in itself, and its strength must have a due

---

[29] Bailey, *Modern Methuselahs*, p. 3.   [30] Humphry, 'Annual Oration', p. 928.
[31] 'Disease in Old Age', *British Medical Journal*, 31 Jan. 1903, p. 270.
[32] G. Stanley Hall, *Senescence: the Last Half of Life* (1922), pp. 244, 246–7.
[33] Lawrence K. Frank, 'Foreword', in E. V. Cowdry (ed.), *Problems of Ageing: Biological and Medical Aspects* (1939), p. xiii. Cowdry's text is a comprehensive study of old age by various American medical authorities.
[34] James F. Fries, 'Aging, Natural Death and the Compression of Morbidity', *New England Journal of Medicine*, vol. 303, no. 3, 17 July 1980, pp. 130–5. Rolleston (*Medical Aspects*, p. 7) considered natural death in humans very rare.
[35] Kenneth G. Manton, 'Changing Concepts of Morbidity and Mortality in the Elderly Population', *Milbank Memorial Fund Quarterly/Health and Society*, vol. 60, no. 2, 1982, p. 223.

relation to the strength of the other organs'.[36] The organism of some vertebrates was able to resist the ravages of time much longer than mankind could under the social conditions of the 1900s, and extreme old age in humans could involve physical decay yet mental alertness, or vice versa.[37] As Hastings Gilford put it:

A man of 70 may die of senile decay, and yet many of his organs may to the naked eye, and even to the microscope, be as sound and as free from evidence of degeneration as the normal organs of youth. Indeed, it is conceivable that the senescence which is responsible for his death may be confined to one organ or even to part of one organ.[38]

The challenge for medical science would be to ensure that all the organs within the body achieved the lifespan of the longest-lived organs. Quite why some outlived others was a puzzle. For example, the normal lifespan of the human eye exceeded that of the body as a whole, even if the eye's vision efficiency declined.[39] Slow impairments afflicted all human beings as they aged (such as the loss of hearing of the upper frequencies).[40]

The epidemiological transition

From the late nineteenth century onwards, there was a growing realisation that increased longevity might not bring improved health. As Humphry put it, 'decay and disease are, by civilisation, substituted for quick and early death'.[41] In 1891, Sir James Crichton-Browne noted with concern that falls in mortality since 1859 had chiefly been among the younger age-groups; among those aged 45+ the decline was insignificant, and mortality rates for those aged 65–75 had actually increased. While death rates for some diseases (notably epidemics) had fallen, those for cancers and diseases of the heart, nervous system and kidneys had risen. He favoured an environmental explanation. These degenerative diseases were traceable 'to wear and tear, to the stress and strain of modern life'. The 'high pressure of civilisation' was causing men and women to 'grow old before their time'. Death rates for those aged 65+ were higher in urban than in rural areas, apparently demonstrating that modern competitive society was inimical to longevity. (This gloomy prognostication probably reflected contemporary concerns over urban degeneration.) Because women did not live as competitive lives as

---

[36] Humphry, 'Annual Oration', p. 928.
[37] Elie Metchnikoff, *The Prolongation of Life: Optimistic Studies* (1907), p. 14.
[38] Gilford, 'The Nature', p. 1617.
[39] Jonas S. Friedenwald, 'The Eye', in Cowdry, *Problems*, p. 521.
[40] Stacy R. Guild, 'The Ear', in Cowdry, *Problems*, p. 532.
[41] Humphry, 'Annual Oration', p. 928.

did men, argued Crichton-Browne, they had a longer life expectancy. Interestingly, he was convinced that both men and women were incurring degenerations associated with old age at progressively younger ages – spectacles were being used earlier in life, teeth were being lost sooner, 'senile insanity' was increasing in incidence, as were other physiological ailments.[42] Unscientific though much of this was (being based upon anecdotal evidence), it was interesting for its pessimistic tone, reflecting the unease that was creeping into medical and scientific literature in both Britain and the USA. One American who wrote prolifically and authoritatively on the changing epidemiological pattern was Dr Louis I. Dublin. Dublin observed with concern that those diseases which predominated in old age – cancer, nephritis and heart disease – had not been brought under control: for Americans aged 45+, mortality from heart disease was increasing.[43]

It followed, therefore, that the biology of ageing in an individual was profoundly affected by that individual's position in society and the socio-economic context in which they lived – including their conditions of work. What is intriguing about the late-nineteenth- and early-twentieth-century debate on the biology of ageing is how the construction of the problem in medical terms often related – implicitly or explicitly – to the physical requirements of industrial jobs as the labour process changed. Thus Malford Thewlis argued that if old men were given a little work to do to keep them active (for example, as a nightwatchman, janitor or gardener), with some remuneration and plenty of encouragement, the ageing process could be delayed.[44] As a book reviewer in the *British Medical Journal* put it in 1942, 'Economic and social insecurity play a large part in hastening mental deterioration in older persons. We are apt to draw the unwarranted conclusion that many of their mental and emotional characteristics are biologically inevitable when they really result from external social conditions.' The physician should therefore not only treat organic disease but also direct attention towards 'maintaining his patient as a useful member of society. This will lead him beyond the strict domain of medicine.'[45] As early as 1939, the philosopher John Dewey was suggesting exactly what some recent commentators[46] – sadly unaware of gerontology's history – have

---

[42] Crichton-Browne, 'Old Age', pp. 728–30.
[43] Louis I. Dublin, *Health and Wealth. A Survey of the Economics of World Health* (1928), pp. 138–9; Louis I. Dublin and Alfred J. Lotka, 'The History of Longevity in the United States', *Human Biology*, vol. 6, no. 1, Feb. 1934, p. 65.
[44] Malford W. Thewlis, *Geriatrics: a Treatise on Senile Conditions, Diseases of Advanced Life, and Care of the Aged* (1919), pp. 53, 55.
[45] 'Care of Ageing Tissues', *British Medical Journal*, 2 May 1942, p. 554.
[46] For example, Bryan S. Turner, 'Aging and Identity: Some Reflections on the Somatization of the Self', in Featherstone and Wernick, *Images*, p. 246.

urged: that there was a need to determine exactly how biological processes interacted with economic, political and cultural ones, especially now that new industrial conditions were placing a decreasing emphasis upon experience and judgement.[47] The problem was that researchers could not control for changing industrial conditions; in addition, the discipline of 'industrial gerontology' (as it came to be known) was still in its infancy. Productivity declines with age could be inferred from comparing the output of older workers with that of younger ones, but ultimately productivity at any age depended more on the efficiency of production methods (including the use of new technology) in any particular industry, and many other variables, than on an individual's working capacity. As later researchers into age discrimination were to find, 'proof' was difficult to obtain, especially in an atmosphere of workplace insecurity in the high-unemployment 1930s. Two American researchers commented: 'Decade to decade measurement of achievement in adulthood has not been reported in any systematic or large scale way in industry or business. Men are naturally hesitant about subjecting themselves to tests that may show occupational or skill decrement with age and so perhaps threaten their economic security.'[48] An intriguingly similar viewpoint was put to the 1893–5 Royal Commission on the Aged Poor (chaired by Lord Aberdare) in Britain by James David Grout, a 'wire-worker', in his oral evidence. When asked if he had come across instances where older workmen had been 'squeezed out' of employment on account of their age, Grout replied, 'That is an awkward question to answer, because you would have to get it admitted that the man was excluded from his trade because of old age, and so far as I can hear no one would admit that it was actually in consequence of old age.'[49]

The debate on the 'worn-out' older worker

Late-nineteenth- and early-twentieth-century labour markets tended to be structured around hierarchies of not just skill, gender and sector, but also age. As manual workers grew older, they often had to adjust to diminishing physical strength and working capacity by moving to progressively lighter jobs. The pre-Fordist response by small employers was to keep such workers on for as long as possible, if they had served the firm for many years. Workers who did not enjoy such stability of employment had to

---

[47] John Dewey, 'Introduction', in Cowdry, *Problems*, pp. xxiii–xxvi.
[48] Walter C. Miles and Catharine C. Miles, 'Principal Mental Changes With Normal Aging', in Edward J. Stieglitz (ed.), *Geriatric Medicine: Diagnosis and Management of Disease in the Aging and in the Aged* (1941), p. 114.
[49] *Royal Commission on the Aged Poor*, 1895, C-7684-II, Vol. III, *Minutes of Evidence*, p. 742.

achieve this for themselves, by moving from job to job. Lady (Gertrude) Bell's classic study *At the Works* (1907) described this age-based de-skilling process:

> The man who has had a strenuous and important post, requiring the utmost vigilant thought, is obliged, perforce, to accept some inferior job, that of a labourer, perhaps, at much less wages, and he is bound to be less competent at it than a labourer who is younger ... It is, no doubt, always a bitterness to a man to have to content himself with a lighter, less well-paid, and less responsible job than the one he occupied when he was hale and vigorous.

It also discussed the extent to which younger relatives had to look after the aged who had become industrially obsolescent.[50] Likewise, Louis Dublin commented in 1913 that 'Many who become incapacitated for continued work at the dusty trades often enter other and lighter work, dropping thus in the scale of economic efficiency and later succumb to other conditions of middle life.'[51]

However, in the late nineteenth and early twentieth centuries British and American industries began to undergo profound structural changes, and technological innovations began to displace older workers in greater numbers. This process was exacerbated by more scientific management regimes, with a greater emphasis on individual productivity. Retirement around the age of 65 became an accepted method of dispensing with the services of workers who were increasingly judged industrially obsolete in a more competitive economic environment.[52]

By the end of the nineteenth century, the plight of the older deindustrialised male worker was beginning to attract increasing attention. Why was it that older men appeared to be 'worn out' at earlier ages, when all the accepted social indicators (falling mortality, rising real wages, improvements in diet and sanitation, and so on) indicated that they should be getting healthier? The most common explanation was that the 'pace' and competitiveness of modern life, both in society at large and in industrial working practices, had increased in intensity. As Louis Dublin observed, 'The unceasing whirl of high-speed machinery, the persistent noises of the shop and the necessary nervous accommodation to the rapid movements of the machines result, after long periods of time, in distinct psychoses.'[53] Some even argued that this was having a biological impact: for example, in 1903 the *British Medical Journal* commented that 'The increasing wear and

---

[50] Lady (Gertrude) Bell, *At the Works* (1907), pp. 108–9 and ch. V.
[51] Louis I. Dublin, *Possibilities of Reducing Mortality at the Higher Age-Groups* (1913), p. 1269.
[52] John Macnicol, *The Politics of Retirement in Britain 1878–1948* (1998), ch. 2.
[53] Dublin, *Possibilities*, p. 1268.

tear of life, due to the feverish activity of the day, cannot fail to shorten the existence of the average adult by using up too rapidly the cell-reproductive possibilities with which his organism was originally endowed.'[54]

The most interesting forum for discussion of this problem in Britain was the oral evidence given to the 1893–5 Aberdare Commission. Witness after witness testified that, although living standards generally were rising, the 'pace' of industry was speeding up: older workers were being 'left behind' and appeared to be becoming 'worn out' at an earlier age; the answer was a state system of old age pensions. The poverty researcher Charles Booth argued that life ran 'more intensely' now than in the past 'and the old tend to be thrown out'; 'new men, young men' were now needed 'to take hold of the new machines or new methods employed. The community gains by this, but the old suffer.' A man of 60 or 65 might 'not be a worse man at that age than his father was', but he had to do more 'in order to keep pace with the way the work is done now'.[55] H. Allan (a carpenter from Birmingham) testified that, in urban areas like Birmingham, a man aged 55 'is looked upon as almost played out, and the competition of younger men is so great that he has very little chance if he gets out of employment at that period of life of ever getting on again at his own trade'.[56] Another witness from Birmingham (Alfred Jephcott, an engineer) declared that, if a man had grey hairs on his head, it was increasingly difficult for him to obtain a job.[57] Numerous witnesses were convinced that new production methods had improved productivity but had also made work more stressful, to the disadvantage of older workers.

To what extent did diminishing employment opportunities affect the self-defined health status of older men in Britain at this time, causing more of them to judge themselves to be 'work-disabled'? In examining this question – which could be a major historical project in its own right – one is, of course, hampered by the lack of reliable records of sickness. The British National Health Insurance scheme commenced in 1913, and initially covered only about 14,000,000 men and women wage-earners. As a former Chief Medical Officer, Sir George Newman, commented in 1939, 'It is strange but true that previous to the introduction of the insurance system we had no direct means in England of knowing the incidence of sickness, apart from three particular bodies of data: those obtained by the notification of certain infectious diseases, the school medical service, and the examination of recruits in the Army and Navy.'[58]

---

[54] 'Disease in Old Age', p. 269.   [55] *Royal Commission on the Aged Poor*, pp. 579–80.
[56] Ibid., p. 880.   [57] Ibid., p. 797.
[58] Sir George Newman, *The Building of a Nation's Health* (1939), p. 408.

Even more problematic is the lack of sickness records for older people. The National Health Insurance scheme initially covered workers up to the age of 70. After 1928, however, eligibility ceased at age 65. One of the few sources available in Britain is friendly society sickness benefit claims. A celebrated, if flawed, survey by Alfred Watson (a consultant actuary to the Manchester Unity of Oddfellows – one of Britain's largest friendly societies – and later Government Actuary)[59] demonstrated that sickness benefit claims had risen between 1846–8 and 1893–7 for members of all ages, but particularly among those aged 65+.[60] While some of this could be explained by the unfolding of the epidemiological transition, and the replacement of quick-killing epidemics by chronic degenerative diseases of later life, it is likely that older men who were becoming displaced from the workforce through diminishing labour market demand were rationalising their joblessness by ill-health – very similar to what has happened in Britain and the USA in recent years.[61] For example, a letter to the *Oddfellows Magazine* in 1895 from a 'Grand Master' of an Oddfellows Society branch warned that many friendly society lodges were now paying sickness benefits to their aged members 'who have not been labouring under any specific illness, but have on account of their age simply been rendered incapable of following their ordinary employment'.[62]

Unfortunately, systematic investigation into the 'worn-out' older worker was uncommon. In the 'Industry Series' of his classic poverty survey, *Life and Labour of the People in London*, Charles Booth researched the age profiles of different occupations in late-Victorian London. Booth was intrigued by the varying rates at which workers 'aged' (in relation to the demands of their jobs), but his conclusions, while interesting, were rather general.[63] One of the few examples of systematic research was the article by Sir James Crichton-Browne in the *British Medical Journal* for 1891. As indicated above, Crichton-Browne was convinced that the stresses of modern life generally were lowering the health status of those increasing numbers who survived to old age. He recorded the output of factory operatives, and noted how it varied with age. A turner of buttons reached maximum productivity at the age of 30, making 6,240 vest buttons in one day. After that age, 'strive as he may', the operative could not increase his productivity, which began to diminish at the age of 45. Crichton-Browne blamed 'the minute division of labour in factories and

[59] John Macnicol, 'Alfred William Watson (1870–1936)', *New Dictionary of National Biography* (2004).
[60] Alfred W. Watson, *An Account of an Investigation of the Sickness and Mortality Experience of the I.O.O.F. Manchester Unity During the Five Years 1893–1897* (1903).
[61] Macnicol, *Politics of Retirement*, pp. 125–31.
[62] A. W. Page, letter in *Oddfellows Magazine*, vol. xxvi, no. 243, Mar. 1895, p. 82.
[63] Macnicol, *Politics of Retirement*, pp. 48–59.

workshops these days': the highly specialised tasks necessitated by the new factory discipline imposed an excessive strain on a few parts of the body, wearing them out prematurely – in effect, what would now be termed repetitive strain injury: 'In primitive employments such as agriculture and navigation, all the muscles of the body are brought into play from time to time in ever varying combinations, but in the industries which modern civilisation has created, small groups of muscles have to repeat their actions with distressing and monotonous iteration.' He cited the instance of a penknife maker in Sheffield, who had to deliver 28,000 accurate strokes of a hammer each day, with consequent degeneration of those particular muscles.[64] If premature mortality was caused by the failure of one organ, the new Fordist industrial conditions were inimical to longevity since the work involved was tending to apply excessive wear and tear to one small part of the body. Death rates in old age were higher in urban areas 'in which high pressure existence prevails', compared with rural areas 'in which life is still comparatively tranquil'.[65]

By the 1930s, declines in cognitive and physical ability with age were being more scientifically measured in both Britain and the USA. For example, an extended study was conducted at the Psychology Department of Stanford University, in California, with a grant from the Carnegie Corporation of New York. The results pointed to measurable declines, but also considerable heterogeneity of ability within any given age-group. If measured intelligence increased with chronological age through childhood and youth, by how much did it decline with ageing in adulthood?[66] Speed of reaction decreased with age, the average 70-year-old being between one-quarter and one-third slower than the adult mean. However, Walter Miles, the chief researcher in the Stanford project, found that the range of individual differences in capacity and achievement at any given age was greater than the average year-by-year decrements: one-quarter to one-third of old people were just as capable as the average adult, and thus individualised testing for ability, rather than chronological age, should be used as a measure.[67] A further difficulty was that the inevitable ability declines associated with ageing could be counterbalanced by other positive factors: for example, losses in measured intelligence were to an extent offset by the development of experience and critical judgement.[68] Much depended upon the social context: one researcher argued

[64] Crichton-Browne, 'Old Age', p. 732.   [65] Ibid., p. 729.

[66] Catharine Cox Miles and Walter R. Miles, 'The Correlation of Intelligence Scores and Chronological Age From Early to Late Maturity', *American Journal of Psychology*, vol. 44, no. 1, Jan. 1932, pp. 76–8.

[67] W. R. Miles, 'Correlation of Reaction and Co-ordination Speed with Age in Adults', *American Journal of Psychology*, vol. 43, no. 3, July 1931, pp. 389–90.

[68] Walter R. Miles, 'Psychological Aspects of Ageing', in Cowdry, *Problems*, pp. 568–70.

that 'the *ability* to learn depreciates very slowly indeed if the *will* to learn is retained', and bemoaned the fact that, in the USA, adult education was 'in a deplorable state'.[69]

The problems of older workers in inter-war Britain

The 1920s and 1930s were the great decades of the social survey in Britain.[70] Against a backdrop of mass unemployment, the economic circumstances of low-income working-class families were scrutinised in enormous detail. However, the focus in much of this research was on family poverty where the male breadwinner was unemployed; an important subsidiary interest was the health and nutrition of children. Poverty and ill-health in old age received little attention, the assumption being that state old age pensions were an adequate protection against poverty; pensioners were considered to be marginal to the labour market.[71] Again, as Charles Webster has pointed out, much inter-war social legislation benefited groups other than the old.[72]

The problem of male unemployment at younger ages was so overwhelming in the inter-war years that work-disability in old age tended to be overlooked. By the 1930s there was, however, a growing discussion of the more specific problem of the 'worn-out' older worker, especially in the high-unemployment depressed areas where global economic forces had resulted in large-scale closure of industries. In such areas were concentrated the traditional staple industries that had been the leading sectors of Britain's industrial revolution – coal mining, iron and steel production, shipbuilding, heavy manufacturing. They also had the highest proportions of older workers (apart from agriculture). These industries responded to the world-wide recession by reducing workforces, lowering production costs and increasing output through the introduction of new, labour-saving technology.[73] Older workers were displaced from these industries, forming a concentration of long-term unemployed in the depressed areas.

In the 1930s, some 'expert' opinion took the view that older workers represented the core of the overall manpower problem in the depressed areas. They were said to be so health-impaired and unproductive that they

---

[69] Edward J. Stieglitz, 'Orientation', in Stieglitz, *Geriatric Medicine*, p. 26.

[70] The debate on retirement in the USA in the inter-war years and after is dealt with in a later chapter.

[71] Macnicol, *Politics of Retirement*, ch. 12.

[72] Charles Webster, 'The Elderly and the Early National Health Service', in Margaret Pelling and Richard M. Smith (eds.), *Life, Death and the Elderly* (1991), pp. 165–6.

[73] *Report of the Commissioner for the Special Areas in England and Wales for the Year Ended 30th September 1938*, Cmd. 5896, pp. 25–7.

would be better pensioned off, and the two most notable proposals for generous retirement pension schemes – those by the trades unionist Ernest Bevin and by the independent research body Political and Economic Planning – had the explicit aim of streamlining British industry by encouraging older workers to retire so that their jobs could be taken by the young unemployed.[74] By the late 1930s, 'worn-out' older workers were being seen in some quarters as hindering the recovery of the British economy. As the research organisation Political and Economic Planning put it, 'It is not often recognised how closely the problem of the depressed area is bound up with the problem of the elderly worker. In a sense, wherever the elderly worker exists there is an actual or potential distressed area, due to his greater exposure and reduced resistance to economic blizzards.'[75]

Unemployment in Britain slowly fell from its peak of just under 3,000,000 in 1933, but rose slightly in 1938–9. By the end of the 1930s, therefore, there were growing concerns about the long-term unemployed in general, and older workers in particular: men aged 45+ were a rising proportion of the total unemployed and might, it was feared, find it difficult to re-enter industrial life once prosperity returned. Then, as now, older men had only slightly higher unemployment rates than younger men; but once unemployed, they took much longer to find new employment. Hence only 8.5 per cent of applicants to the Unemployment Assistance Board aged 16–24, and 15.8 per cent of those aged 25–34, had been unemployed for three years or more in 1937, compared with 34.1 per cent of those aged 55–64. But of these older men, the proportions unemployed for three years or more in the old staple industries were much higher: 68.7 per cent in engineering, 68.3 per cent in mining and 61.1 per cent in shipbuilding.[76] The Unemployment Assistance Board's 1938 Annual Report somewhat controversially viewed unemployed men aged 45+ as increasingly difficult to re-absorb back into industrial employment, given that long-term unemployment was having a deleterious effect on their health and morale. (Men aged 45+ formed nearly half of the Board's male applicants.)[77] In the high-unemployment Special Areas in 1936–7, unemployment fell fastest among men aged 18–34, and slowest

---

[74] Ernest Bevin, *My Plan for 2,000,000 Workless* (1933); Political and Economic Planning, *The Exit from Industry* (1935).

[75] Political and Economic Planning, *The Exit*, p. 5.

[76] *Report of the Unemployment Assistance Board for the Year Ended 31st December 1937*, Cmd. 5752, pp. 71–4.

[77] *Report of the Unemployment Assistance Board for the Year Ended 31st December 1938*, Cmd. 6021, pp. 2–3, 30, 59, 63. For a criticism of this view that men were 'old' at 45, see Joan S. Clarke, *The Assistance Board* (1941), p. 3.

among men aged 55+. Such older men, it was feared, might become
chronic 'discouraged workers', with obsolescent skills, sub-standard
health and low motivation. When industries in the depressed areas began
to expand again, they would only take on younger men.[78] The 'most
serious problem' in these depressed areas was said to be 'the older man
who is never likely again to obtain employment in the ordinary way',[79] and
there were demands in Parliament for an official enquiry into the labour
market problems of older men.[80]

However, within a very short time the situation was reversed. During the
Second World War, the voracious demands of a wartime economy resulted
in unemployment falling to insignificant levels. Many older people were
re-enlisted back into the labour market, often performing important wartime work.[81] In the absence of a 1941 census, the extent of wartime working
by men and women over pensionable age can only be inferred. The evidence
from returned National Insurance cards (and therefore confined to insur-
able employment) shows a rise from 322,000 to 622,000 (or nearly 100 per
cent) in the number of men aged 65+ in employment between 1939 and
1945.[82] The 1947 Nuffield Survey found that its sample of 455 firms had
experienced a 313 per cent increase in male employees aged 65+ between
1939 and 1945, though this result was probably exaggerated.[83] A more
cautious contemporary estimate was that 1,478,000 men aged 60+ were in
all forms of employment in England and Wales in mid-1945, compared with
1,282,000 in 1931.[84] Unfortunately, a comparison of 1945 with 1931 was of
limited value, since the 1930s recession and economic restructuring
undoubtedly led to a faster rate of labour market exit by older workers:
had 1939 been taken as a baseline, the wartime increase in older men's
employment would have been dramatically revealed.

It was clear, therefore, that, when given the opportunity, older workers
proved themselves fit and healthy enough to perform quite physically

---

[78] *Report of the Commissioner for the Special Areas in England and Wales for the Year Ended
30th September 1937*, Cmd. 5595, pp. 25, 89–93. A whole section of this report was devoted
to 'The Problem of the Older Man'.

[79] G. Gillen (Commissioner for the Special Areas) to Lord Rushcliffe (Unemployment
Assistance Board), 24 May 1937, PRO AST 7/317.

[80] For example, J. J. Tinker in *H of C Deb.*, 5s, vol. 345, 3 April 1938, col. 2444.

[81] For brief examples of this work, see Nuffield Foundation, *Old People. Report of a Survey
Committee on the Problems of Ageing and the Care of Old People Under the Chairmanship of
B. Seebohm Rowntree* (1947), ch. 6. The wartime work by older people remains tantalis-
ingly unresearched.

[82] Macnicol, *Politics of Retirement*, pp. 23–4.

[83] Nuffield Foundation, *Old People*, p. 152.

[84] Geoffrey Thomas, *The Employment of Older Persons* (UK Social Survey Report, 1947),
tables 2 and 3. Because of overall population growth, this was in fact a decline in economic
activity rates from 63 per cent to 53 per cent.

rigorous jobs: 'many persons who in former times would have retired are still capable of productive labour', concluded the 1947 Nuffield Survey.[85] In this upbeat atmosphere, the 1942 Beveridge Report argued quite the contrary to what many had argued a decade earlier: Beveridge's notional justification for proposing a retirement condition for receipt of the new, universal state pension was that this would encourage older workers to stay on in work as long as possible, thus benefiting the economy, the social security budget, and themselves (although there are strong grounds for arguing that Beveridge had other motives as well).[86] The empirical justification for this proposed new retirement condition was Beveridge's examination of the records of the Amalgamated Engineering Union and the Friendly Society of Iron Founders – from which he deduced that, since the late nineteenth century, the age of voluntary superannuation had risen slightly, by between one and four years (followed by an increasing period of retirement, which placed a growing strain on their superannuation funds). Beveridge disagreed strongly with what he called 'the popular impression that the growing pace of industry is rendering people unfit earlier and earlier in life',[87] and argued that there was 'no statistical evidence that industrial development is making it harder for people to continue at work later in life than it used to be'.[88] Working capacity must have improved, and thus it was not unreasonable to expect older workers to delay retirement. It was an optimistic view of the labour market, and for much of the 1950s it seemed justified.

---

[85] Nuffield Foundation, *Old People*, p. 93.
[86] Macnicol, *Politics of Retirement*, pp. 357–68.
[87] Beveridge memorandum, 'Pensions Finance', 16 July 1942, Beveridge Papers VIII 33.
[88] *Social Insurance and Allied Services*, Cmd. 6404, 1942, p. 99.

Introduction

The twenty years after the end of the Second World War witnessed in both Britain and America a lively and detailed debate on old age.[1] In Britain, the first modern social surveys explicitly on old age were published;[2] geriatric medicine took off with the establishment of the National Health Service; state pensions continued to be a major fiscal and political issue; there were serious concerns over retirement, population ageing and future 'dependency ratios'; and in a way that was uncannily similar to the 1990s, British governments made concerted attempts – ultimately unsuccessful – to persuade older workers to remain longer in work. As two contemporaries observed, the problems of old age were suddenly discovered in the 1940s and 1950s, after a period of relative neglect.[3] In some ways, this concern was odd, given that the 1950s were years of relative full employment and economic growth. However, we should be wary of the benefits of hindsight: Britain had only recently emerged from all the disruptions and privations of the Second World War, preceded by two decades of major recession, and in the late 1940s it was a society struggling to adjust to peacetime economic conditions.

The British economy of the 1950s was one in which manual working-class jobs were steadily declining and new, service-based jobs were expanding. Many of these service-based sectors were experiencing labour shortages: as is well known, the National Health Service and London Transport had to recruit workers from New Commonwealth countries to fill vacant jobs. The minimum school leaving age had been raised from 14 to 15 in 1947, and National Service removed from the labour market a large number of young men of prime working age.

---

[1] The debate in the USA in this period is dealt with in a later chapter.
[2] John Macnicol and Andrew Blaikie, 'The Politics of Retirement, 1908–48', in Margot Jefferys (ed.), *Growing Old in the Twentieth Century* (1989), pp. 21–2.
[3] Peter Townsend and Dorothy Wedderburn, *The Aged in the Welfare State* (1965), p. 10.

The maximisation of labour supply was thus central to postwar economic policy, and was a driving force behind the debate on retirement, health status and working capacity. Could older workers be persuaded to stay on in employment slightly longer, and thus ease the perceived labour shortages? 'Workers are wanted almost everywhere and this demand seems certain to increase', warned the Ministry of Labour booklet, *Employment of Older Men and Women* (1952), adding, somewhat apocalyptically, that 'the encouragement of the employment of the elderly is a pressing necessity; we cannot afford that the willing and able worker should stand idle'. In a foreword, the Minister of Labour, Walter Monckton, stressed that the need to extend the working life was of paramount importance because of the ageing of the population and the prevailing labour shortages.[4]

Concerns over an ageing population

In the 1930s, concerns over Britain's ageing population had risen to a crescendo, profoundly affecting discussions of old age and pensions. The tendency in such discussions was to view the retired as a passive 'burden' of 'consumers' who contributed little or nothing to the economy, in contrast to the 'producers' of working age.[5] Key social policy documents in wartime – notably, the 1942 Beveridge Report – had also been strongly affected. In response, a Royal Commission on Population was established in 1944, and reported in 1949. However, the British birth rate rose from 1942 onwards, heralding the beginning of the 'baby boom', and much of the concern over falling fertility had disappeared by the time the Royal Commission's report was published. Hence, despite its excellent analysis of population trends, the report failed to merit even a Parliamentary debate.

Nevertheless, concern over an ageing population permeated much expert thinking on retirement, health status and working capacity in the 1950s. It fuelled the whole retirement debate – particularly the crucial question of whether more workers could be persuaded to remain longer in work, thus diminishing the overall pensions bill, raising income tax revenue and increasing labour supply. Male expectation of life at age 65 had only risen by about one year since 1838–54,[6] but the combination of past high birth rates and improved survival had increased the number of men aged 65+ and women aged 60+ from 2,750,000 in 1911 to 6,620,000 in

---

[4] Ministry of Labour and National Service, *Employment of Older Men and Women* (1952), pp. 2, 4.

[5] John Macnicol, *The Politics of Retirement in Britain 1878–1948* (1998), pp. 259–64.

[6] Richard M. Titmuss, 'Pension Systems and Population Change', in Titmuss, *Essays on 'The Welfare State'* (1958), p. 58.

1951.[7] One official report warned that, in 1911, one in fifteen of the population were men aged 65+ and women aged 60+; by 1951, this had become two in fifteen, and by 1977 it was expected to be three in fifteen.[8] (Such alarmism was misleading and at times opportunistic: for example, the diminished proportion of children in the population over the same period had of course improved the combined neontic and gerontic dependency ratios.) As a result, there were concerted – but ultimately futile – attempts by government agencies to persuade employers to retain older workers, and a considerable volume of research was conducted into retirement, health status and working capacity. A central question addressed by this research was how much latent working capacity there existed among healthy, work-fit men who had taken retirement (some being forced to retire). Just how large was the 'reserve of labour' (as three researchers put it)[9] beyond retirement age, and should social policy be redesigned so that this reserve could be utilised?

The Royal Commission on Population's report reinforced the image of a 'burden' of increasingly dependent retirees: the extent to which they consumed more than they produced made retirees 'a factor in reducing the average standard of living of the community'. It therefore suggested that

the old should, if possible, do more than hitherto to maintain themselves, or rather, contribute more by their exertions to the general economic effort of the community. Indeed, further improvement in the national standard of living may depend increasingly on how far this object can be attained. There can be no doubt that many men are fully capable of discharging the duties of ordinary paid employment for several years after what is becoming the normal retiring age of 65. Many more would be capable of part-time work in some capacity.

Since standards of health and fitness in old age would improve in the future, 'a prolongation of the period of capacity for work is a natural counterpart of a prolongation of the period of life', and the average level of fitness currently associated with the age of 65 would characterise the age of 68, or 70; but such extension of the working life was envisaged as following 'naturally on the basis of individual choice'.[10] The demographic concerns expressed by the Royal Commission were reflected in many discussions of ageing in the 1940s and 1950s, although, given the background of steady economic growth, the pessimism that had characterised the debate in the

---

[7] V. George, *Social Security: Beveridge and After* (1968), p. 148.
[8] *National Advisory Committee on the Employment of Older Men and Women. First Report,* Cmd. 8963, 1953, p. 9.
[9] R. G. Brown, Thomas McKeown and A. G. W. Whitfield, 'Observations on the Medical Condition of Men in the Seventh Decade', *British Medical Journal,* 8 Mar. 1958, p. 561.
[10] *Report of the Royal Commission on Population,* Cmd. 7695, 1949, pp. 113–14.

1930s became decreasingly evident. For example, J. H. Sheldon, a leading authority on health problems in old age, warned in 1950 that 'from the domestic point of view the community is already bearing about as big a burden of old age as it can manage'. Sheldon pointed to the gap between the 'official' (i.e., age-65) and the 'natural' onset of old age (the age 'at which the physical independence of adult life becomes so compromised that there is a definite limitation of activity'), and suggested that working for as long as possible was important both for society and for the health and happiness of the individual.[11] Many other commentators in the 1950s criticised a fixed retirement age, and suggested that flexible retirement would be both more humane and economically desirable.[12] The prevailing medical orthodoxy was, not surprisingly, that old people should keep as active and fit as possible.[13] However, if old age was 'a quality of mind and body whose time of onset varies from individual to individual rather than a mere quantity expressed by a term of duration applicable to all',[14] it would be very difficult to design a retirement policy that was flexible enough to take account of these individual variations.

The most notable official response to the concerns over an ageing population was the appointment in July 1953 of a committee on the 'Economic and Financial Problems of the Provision for Old Age', under the chairmanship of Sir Thomas Phillips (a retired civil servant, who had been Permanent Secretary at the Ministry of Labour and then the Ministry of National Insurance). The Phillips Committee's 1954 report ranged over a number of areas – future population projections and dependency ratios, the funding of state pensions, retirement trends – and it repeatedly portrayed pensioners as a passive 'burden' on the rest of society.[15] A crucial question considered by it was whether future improvements in health status among the old would enable the postponement of retirement, and how much labour supply would thereby be created. It pointed to the 'regrettable lack of precise evidence' as to the physical capacity of men and women to continue at their normal trade during the first five years of

[11] J. H. Sheldon, 'The Role of the Aged in Modern Society', *British Medical Journal*, 11 Feb. 1950, pp. 319–21. For demographic concerns, see also: Trevor H. Howell, 'Social Medicine in Old Age', *British Medical Journal*, 16 Mar. 1946, p. 399; J. H. Sheldon, *The Social Medicine of Old Age. Report of an Inquiry in Wolverhampton* (1948), p. 1; W. P. D. Logan, 'Work and Age: Statistical Considerations', *British Medical Journal*, 28 Nov. 1953, pp. 1190–1.

[12] See, for example, Logan, 'Work and Age', p. 1193.

[13] Marjory Warren, 'Activity in Advancing Years', *British Medical Journal*, 21 Oct. 1950, pp. 921–4.

[14] Sheldon, *Social Medicine*, p. 1.

[15] *Report of the Committee on the Economic and Financial Problems of the Provision for Old Age*, Cmd. 9333, 1954, p. 27.

pensionable age. Eventually, it recommended 'some increase' in minimum state pension ages: after a transition period, these should be 68 (men) and 63 (women).[16] (Oddly, it did not recommend restoring 65 as the women's pensionable age, although this had been set at 60 only fourteen years earlier.) But the report recognised that savings in pension costs would be offset by higher expenditure on unemployment and sickness benefits, and by a reduction in contribution income that would be actuarially justified by a shortened pensionable period. It also concluded that post-ponement of retirement would add relatively little to total labour supply: a 'major change' in retirement habits would be needed to add a mere 1 per cent (or 240,000 in number) to the total workforce.[17] Not mentioned in the report – but picked up by critics of it – was the political difficulty of proposing a rise in working-class retirement ages, while for middle-class retirees on occupational pensions the trend was in the opposite direction. As Richard Titmuss pointed out, taxpayers were having to finance generous pension schemes for public sector employees, which allowed them to retire at 60. For example, civil servants (like Sir Thomas Phillips) were able to retire at the age of 60, despite the fact that, since this age was established (in 1859), average expectation of life at 60 had increased to seventeen years for men and twenty for women.[18] Raising the retirement ages remained a political non-starter in the 1950s, as did most of the Phillips recommendations.[19] Thus the Conservative Party's 1955 general election manifesto reassured voters that there would be no change in the minimum retirement age.[20]

The development of geriatric medicine

Had geriatric medicine been better developed in Britain at this time, it might have been the arena in which research on the interface between the biology of ageing and working capacity was conducted. But it was not. Before the National Health Service, the status of geriatric medicine was extremely low. Long-stay, chronically ill older patients with few financial resources – in other words, the majority – were placed in local authority

---

[16] Ibid., pp. 49, 50–1.

[17] Ibid., and p. 24. The report wrongly predicted little change over the coming twenty-five years in the economic activity rates of women aged 15–44.

[18] Richard M. Titmuss, 'Social Administration in a Changing Society', in Titmuss, *Essays*, pp. 25–6. For a critique of the Phillips Committee's report, see: Titmuss, 'Pension Systems', pp. 56–74; Brian Abel-Smith and Peter Townsend, *New Pensions for the Old* (1955).

[19] Leslie Hannah, *Inventing Retirement: the Development of Occupational Pensions in Britain* (1986), pp. 54–5.

[20] George, *Social Security*, p. 151.

hospitals (which before 1929 had been run by the Poor Law, and bore all the marks of less eligibility). A late-1940s description of one ex-Poor Law hospital (the Western Road Infirmary in Birmingham) is chilling: aged patients sat around listlessly in 'an atmosphere of profound apathy'; over half of them were bedfast; many of them seemed to be suffering from pathological conditions which were degenerative or genetic in origin, and about which nothing was done.[21] Looking back at this pre-NHS era, two recent commentators give a graphic description:

Many of the hospitals of the time were old workhouses from the Poor Law period and before admission patients had to be declared destitute by a Poor Law Relieving Officer. The long term wards were the dumping ground for alcoholics, psychiatric patients, the chronically sick, children, the elderly and the destitute. The elderly residential patients waited to die in the most uncivilised conditions – nights spent in cramped dormitories of 20–30 beds and days spent sitting on benches looking at their feet. Men and women, husbands and wives, were segregated. The ammoniacal smell of urine, stale tobacco, unwashed clothes and bodies hung heavy in the air. Hopelessness pervaded everywhere.[22]

By contrast, there were relatively few geriatric patients in voluntary hospitals, where medical students were taught and the most prestigious consultants worked. The result was that little research was undertaken into the medical needs of older patients, and many doctors went through their training receiving little instruction in geriatric medicine. Yet older patients were 'a rich mine of clinical material for teaching and investigation', as one doctor put it, adding that the exclusion of geriatric patients from the wards of teaching hospitals was responsible for 'serious defects in the training of medical students'.[23] In the 1920s and 1930s, pioneers in geriatric medicine – including Marjory Warren in Britain, and Ignatz Nascher and Malford Thewlis in the USA – had been conspicuous by their rarity.[24]

In the 1950s, the National Health Service benefited greatly from advances in pharmaceutical developments (for example, penicillin and streptomycin) which reduced the burden on the Service of long-stay infectious patients. Given the high cost of hospital treatment, the effect of these pharmaceutical advances on the funding of the NHS was marked, enabling

---

[21] A. P. Thomson, 'Problems of Ageing and Chronic Sickness', *British Medical Journal*, 30 July 1949, pp. 244, 246.

[22] U. K. Ghosh and K. Ghosh, 'The History of Geriatric Medicine in Scotland', *Scottish Medical Journal*, vol. 42, no. 5, Oct. 1997, p. 158.

[23] A. P. Thomson, 'Problems of Ageing and Chronic Sickness', *British Medical Journal*, 6 Aug. 1949, pp. 301, 304.

[24] Trevor H. Howell, *Our Advancing Years* (1953), pp. 132–6, 149; Stephen Katz, *Disciplining Old Age. The Formation of Gerontological Knowledge* (1996), pp. 83–8; Pat Thane, *Old Age in English History. Past Experiences, Present Issues* (2000), pp. 436–8.

it to devote more resources to new areas of medical intervention that improved mobility and quality of life, especially in middle-aged and older adults. Medicine all over the industrialised world began to turn its attention to new developments, such as hip replacements, kidney dialysis and organ transplants. In addition, new medical technology was continuing to reduce both infant mortality and maternal mortality rates. The prospect of nearly all babies surviving birth and infancy, then to experience a largely disability-free adulthood, became more and more enticing. The unfolding of the epidemiological transition was vividly illustrated by the fact that hospital wards and personnel formerly devoted to tuberculosis patients could now be allocated to geriatric care.[25]

There is no doubt, therefore, that the foundation of the NHS greatly benefited old people (as also it benefited working-class women and children), opening up new developments in geriatric medicine. They were a generation who had suffered all the cumulative privations of a deficient health care system before 1948 – bad teeth, uncorrected eyesight, untreated disabilities, poor hospital provision, and so on.[26] Thus a pioneering researcher into the health problems of older people could attest in 1954 that the provision of spectacles under the NHS had been by far the most beneficial aid to the activity of old people.[27] However, there were some who viewed the progressive developments with caution, noting that they might only lead to a postponement of the onset of disease, and that the NHS might find itself concentrating more and more on the health problems of the very old (the treatment of which might turn out to be very expensive) as the epidemiological transition unfolded. For example, Derek Walker-Smith (Minister of Health) warned in 1958 that 'If one is less likely to die of diphtheria as a child, or from pneumonia as an adult, one has a greater chance of succumbing later to coronary disease or cancer ... By increasing the expectation of life, we put greater emphasis on the malignant and degenerative diseases which are characteristic of the later years.'[28] As a result of these morbidity changes and a steadily ageing population, the proportion of total NHS expenditure devoted to those aged 65+ rose from 20 per cent in 1951–2 to nearly 50 per cent in 1988.[29]

---

[25] Ghosh and Ghosh, 'History', p. 159.

[26] Charles Webster, 'The Elderly and the Early National Health Service', in Margaret Pelling and Richard M. Smith (eds.), *Life, Death and the Elderly* (1991), pp. 167–8.

[27] J. H. Sheldon, 'The Social Philosophy of Old Age', in *Old Age in the Modern World. Report of the Third Congress of the International Association of Gerontology, London 1954* (1955), p. 18.

[28] Quoted in Rudolf Klein, *The New Politics of the National Health Service* (1995 edn), p. 28. For a similar warning in the USA, see Nathan W. Shock, *Trends in Gerontology* (1951), pp. 11–12.

[29] John Appleby, *Financing Health Care in the 1990s* (1992), p. 64.

However, geriatric medicine was to remain something of a 'cinderella service' within the NHS. It had less prestige than other specialisms, attracting one of the lowest proportions of merit awards and holding out few prospects for private medicine (other than private nursing homes).[30] It was often seen as a refuge for doctors who had 'failed' in other branches of medicine.[31] 'How will you feel about giving up medicine?' was allegedly the question asked at interview of the successful applicant for a consultant geriatrician's post in the mid-1950s.[32] One anonymous authority commented in retrospect that 'Geriatric medicine came into the world because of the hardness of men's hearts ... the British medical establishment of the 1950s saw the speciality as no more than a device for coping with the old workhouse hospitals and their unfortunate residents'.[33] From its very beginnings, there has always been controversy over whether geriatric medicine should exist as a separate specialism (thus perhaps marginalising old age), or whether it should be part of mainstream medical practice.[34]

Geriatric medicine thus established itself slowly in Britain. In 1947, fourteen consultants founded the Medical Society for the Care of the Elderly (later the British Geriatrics Society); yet only in 1965 was the first clinical chair of geriatric medicine established.[35] In *The Social Medicine of Old Age* (1948) – a ground-breaking survey of the medical conditions of a sample of old people – J. H. Sheldon complained that so little was known about 'normal' ageing, in contrast to the specialism of paediatrics.[36] A. N. Exton-Smith's *Medical Problems of Old Age*, published as late as 1955, claimed to be the first British textbook on diseases of the old. In the USA, geriatric medicine appears to have been more advanced: for example, when Malford Thewlis's *Geriatrics: a Treatise on Senile Conditions, Diseases of Advanced Life, and Care of the Aged* was published in 1919, there was already a New York Geriatrics Society.

A number of surveys were carried out in Britain in the 1940s and 1950s into the health status of old people. The hope was that clinical

---

[30] See, for example, *Report of the Royal Commission on the National Health Service*, Cmnd. 7615, 1979, pp. 236, 430.

[31] John Grimley Evans, 'Geriatric Medicine: a Brief History', *British Medical Journal*, vol. 315, 25 Oct. 1997, p. 1076.

[32] Ghosh and Ghosh, 'History', p. 159.

[33] Quoted in Emily Grundy, 'The Health and Health Care of Older Adults in England and Wales, 1841–1994', in John Charlton and Mike Murphy (eds.), *The Health of Adult Britain 1841–1994 Vol. 2* (1997), p. 195.

[34] B. E. Shenfield, *Social Policies for Old Age. A Review of Social Provision for Old Age in Great Britain* (1957), p. 180.

[35] Webster, 'The Elderly', p. 170. This was at Glasgow University, and was held by Fergus Anderson.

[36] Sheldon, *Social Medicine*, p. 187.

examinations of older workers could inform retirement policy (which, it was felt, had hitherto been handicapped by the lack of such knowledge), by ascertaining how many of them were still 'work fit' when aged in their sixties.[37] However, many such studies ended up as a mere cataloguing of health defects, their authors finding it impossible to disentangle all the variables that might influence health status. Hence J. H. Sheldon's famous survey was mainly a record of morbidity prevalence.[38] Likewise, Pemberton and Smith tried to ascertain the extent to which male patients aged 50–64 in one teaching hospital were subsequently able to return to work; but their study said little about the labour market context.[39] Most of these surveys came to obvious conclusions: the principal diseases of old age were those affecting the heart and arteries, strokes, bronchitis, arthritis, prostate and bladder problems, and so on.[40] Similarly, Brown, McKeown and Whitfield's study of 1,062 men aged 60–9 in Birmingham discovered that the most common causes of disability were bronchitis (often related to a history of cigarette smoking), defective hearing and hypertension. However, it was difficult to move beyond such simple observations without closely scrutinising an individual's performance at work.[41] A general review by le Gros Clark of published research into health status, morbidity and disability concluded that about four out of five men aged in their late sixties were 'thoroughly mobile and alert in mind', but warned that all of these surveys had used different methodologies, which limited their comparative value.[42]

Research into working capacity

During the late 1940s and 1950s, considerable research was conducted into older workers (overwhelmingly male), notably at the universities of London, Liverpool, Bristol and Cambridge.[43] The most famous venue was the Nuffield Research Unit into the Problems of Ageing, established in 1946 at the Psychological Laboratory, Cambridge University. Though the Unit encountered some initial teething problems, by the early 1950s it

---

[37] Brown, McKeown and Whitfield, 'Observations', p. 555.
[38] Sheldon, *Social Medicine*.
[39] John Pemberton and Joan C. Smith, 'The Return to Work of Elderly Male Hospital In-Patients', *British Medical Journal*, 6 Aug. 1949, pp. 306–8.
[40] I. M. Richardson, *Age and Need. A Study of Older People in North-East Scotland* (1964), p. 13.
[41] Brown, McKeown and Whitfield, 'Observations', pp. 556–8.
[42] F. le Gros Clark, *Work, Age and Leisure. Causes and Consequences of the Shortened Working Life* (1966), ch. 9 and p. 116.
[43] Shirley Dex and Chris Phillipson, 'Social Policy and the Older Worker', in Chris Phillipson and Alan Walker (eds.), *Ageing and Social Policy: a Critical Assessment* (1986), p. 46.

was conducting a number of research projects into the changes in working capacity that accompanied old age. Much of this research was rather ponderous and not particularly illuminating. Laboratory experiments were undertaken to measure the average decline in functional ability with age, particularly with regard to speed, complexity and physical demands,[44] but applying the results to the 'real world' of the workplace was fraught with methodological difficulties, for several reasons.

First, there was an enormous range of variables at both the individual and the environmental level. The human organism, as 'a piece of anatomical and physical machinery', did experience slow physical decline after about the age of 30,[45] but, as always, averages concealed the considerable heterogeneity in health status and functional ability between individuals, caused by factors such as social class, gender, age, personality, genetic inheritance and lifestyle/risk factors (particularly, for that generation, cigarette smoking). Environmental factors included the stress and 'pace' of the job, its remuneration and status, the number of previous job changes, an individual's educational level, the employer's retirement policy, job opportunities and sectoral labour market demand in the region, and prevailing cultural expectations. Even within these, there were subvariables, making for 'a continuous chain of interactions between organism and environment'. For example, different age-groups had different educational backgrounds and even childhood experiences (the 'cohort effect'), which might determine skill levels: this made comparison highly problematic.[46] Much depended upon the particular requirements of a specific job. A further complication was that older workers internalised prevailing attitudes and expected themselves to decline in ability; they might even do this unconsciously, and therefore deny it in a research interview.[47]

Second, measuring health status and working capacity by clinical examinations or laboratory experiments was one thing; transferring this to the 'real world' situation of employment was quite another. The latter was methodologically (and perhaps ethically) very difficult. Most studies thus confined themselves to surrogate tests, and were flawed as a result. 'Fitness for employment' was a concept that needed to encapsulate not only physical fitness per se, but also the worker's attitude towards the job and, crucially, the functional requirements of the job itself. Hence what le Gros Clark called 'industrial senescence' could only be defined as the

[44] A. T. Welford, 'Extending the Employment of Older People', *British Medical Journal*, 28 Nov. 1953, pp. 1195–6.

[45] A. T. Welford, *Skill and Age. An Experimental Approach* (1951), p. 5.   [46] Ibid., p. 8.

[47] Welford, 'Extending', pp. 1193–7; Welford, *Skill and Age*, p. 7.

inability of a man to 'maintain either the pace or the standard of work commonly demanded in his accustomed job'.[48] The working environment was therefore all-important to study; but its ever-changing nature (for example, with the continuous introduction of new technology) made such a study highly problematic.

Third, because the decision to continue working or to retire was so influenced by physical fitness, it was extremely difficult to assess the precise effect of retirement upon health status. 'The literature is overwhelming in its indications that retirement is detrimental to the health of older persons', declared Anderson and Cowan confidently.[49] This reflected the prevailing view in the 1950s and 1960s that retirement hastened premature mortality, since death rates in the year following retirement were high.[50] However, this was in fact caused by social selection: those who retired earliest tended to have the lowest health status before retirement, and thus shorter life expectancy after it; conversely, those who continued working past age 65 were probably (but not necessarily)[51] fitter, and this would have been so whether or not they continued working.[52] Research results that showed little loss of productivity with age could be artefactual, since those workers still employed at later ages would tend to be the most 'work-fit'.[53] Thus the prevailing argument that retirement worsened health status could neither be proved nor disproved. A further problem was the one inherent in all self-definitions of health status: interviewees tended to rate their health in relation to what they expected as the norm for their age and, since disability rises with age, 'good health' for those aged in their seventies was a lower objective standard than for those ten years younger.[54]

These methodological constraints greatly limited the usefulness of research into working capacity. If applied to one relatively stable trade, research could offer some answers. For example, among building workers, the attrition in working capacity with age was obvious: 100 per cent were

---

[48] F. le Gros Clark, *Ageing Men in the Labour Force. The Problems of Organising Older Workers in the Building Industry* (1955), p. 1.

[49] W. Ferguson Anderson and Nairn R. Cowan, 'Work and Retirement. Influences on the Health of Older Men', *The Lancet*, vol. CCLXXI, 29 Dec. 1956, p. 1346.

[50] Shenfield, *Social Policies*, p. 83.

[51] Some who were in poor health continued working for as long as possible for financial reasons. Anderson and Cowan, 'Work and Retirement', p. 1345.

[52] Richardson, *Age and Need*, p. 117.

[53] R. M. Belbin, 'Difficulties of Older People in Industry', *Occupational Psychology*, vol. 27, no. 4, Oct. 1953, p. 178.

[54] Richardson, *Age and Need*, p. 11. For a recent discussion of this problem, see Office for National Statistics. Social Survey Division, *Living in Britain. Results from the 1998 General Household Survey* (2000), p. 85.

'still effective' at age 60, 83 per cent at 65, and 32 per cent at 70.[55] However, many workers moved from job to job, and past experiences could have a major effect on both laboratory tests of working capacity and workplace experiments.[56] In addition, experience increasingly compensated for declining skill and strength with age – but at different rates for different individuals.[57] In certain trades, an apparent decline in manual dexterity might be more due to increasing difficulty in perceiving situations and making appropriate decisions, or even to a decline in motivation.[58]

The retirement debate in the 1950s

In 1946 a retirement condition for receipt of the state pension was introduced. This applied only for the first five years of retirement, in the case of both men and women, and its effect on the rate at which retirement spread thereafter seems to have been minimal. In 1921, the economic activity rate of men aged 65+ had been 58.8 per cent; by 1951, this had fallen to 31.1 per cent, and by 1961 it was 24.4 per cent. In the following decade, the fall was only slight, reaching 23.5 per cent in 1971. Male retirement ages were inexorably lowering: thus between 1921 and 1961 the economic activity rate of men aged 70+ fell from 41.2 per cent to 14.9 per cent – a faster rate than for men aged 65–9 (from 79.8 per cent to 39.0 per cent). By contrast, the economic activity rates of men aged 55–9 and 60–4 rose slightly in the 1950s, and then declined somewhat in the 1960s. Significantly, women aged 55–9 and 60–4 virtually doubled their economic activity rates between 1951 and 1971, consequent upon the growth of feminised jobs. As in other times, older workers experienced slightly higher unemployment rates than did younger; but, once unemployed, they were out of work for much longer.[59]

Patterns of retirement in the 1950s were complex. The age of 60 (women) and 65 (men) did not mark an abrupt transition: instead, there was a considerable age-spread. Ages of retirement have always been widely distributed, and over the past 120 years this distribution has moved

[55] F. le Gros Clark, *The Later Working Life in the Building Industry. A Study of 320 Ageing Maintenance Workers* (1954), pp. 5, 9. See also F. le Gros Clark, *Bus Workers in Their Later Lives* (1957).

[56] J. Szafran and A. T. Welford, 'On the Problem of Generalised Occupational Transfer Effects in Relation to Studies of Ageing', *Quarterly Journal of Experimental Psychology*, vol. 1, pt. 4, Oct. 1949, pp. 160–6.

[57] Welford, *Skill and Age*, pp. 8–9.

[58] G. C. de la Mare and R. D. Shepherd, 'Ageing: Changes in Speed and Quality of Work Among Leather Cutters', *Occupational Psychology*, vol. 32, no. 3, July 1958, pp. 204–9.

[59] See, for example, 'Age-analysis of Employed Persons', *Ministry of Labour Gazette*, vol. LIX, no. 6, June 1951, pp. 224–6.

down the age range. Analysis of a 1 per cent sample of the 1951 census showed that, of men aged 60–4, 87 per cent were still working full-time, and 10 per cent retired (with 3 per cent working part-time); of men aged 65–9, the split was more or less even, with 48 per cent working full-time, and 47 per cent retired; of men aged 70 +, 20 per cent were working full-time and 70 per cent were retired.[60] Ages of retirement also varied regionally, and by occupation. In 1951, retirement occurred earliest among men in hard, manual occupations. (The exception was agriculture, which still had jobs that the old could perform.) Thus among men aged 70 +, the proportions retired were 96 per cent in rail transport, 94 per cent in fishing and 92 per cent in mining and quarrying; by contrast, in agriculture it was 59 per cent, among directors and managers it was 63 per cent and among commercial travellers it was 72 per cent.[61] Within working-class occupations, what le Gros Clark and Dunne termed 'survival rates' (i.e. working to one's late sixties) varied according to the stress of the work: for example, watchmakers, precious metals workers and makers of musical instruments had much better survival rates than did coal-face workers, signalmen and construction engineers. The authors observed that 'the capacity of men to continue beyond their mid sixties depends mainly ... upon the actual jobs they have to do'.[62]

From the late 1940s, there were concerted governmental attempts, spearheaded by the Ministry of Labour, to persuade older workers to stay on in work and employers to retain them for as long as possible. This policy had the support of the British Employers' Confederation and the Trades Union Congress. The TUC had long argued that available jobs should be redistributed to younger workers,[63] but opposed compulsory retirement: 'capacity, not age' should be the criterion, and those 'practices or traditions' which placed age barriers in the way of older people obtaining work should be removed.[64] Several official reports on retirement were published – notably a thorough, if rather unsubtle, analysis by the Ministry of Pensions and National Insurance (MPNI), based upon a sample size of 28,952;[65] two reports by a National Advisory Committee

[60] Logan, 'Work and Age', p. 1192. See also Ministry of Pensions and National Insurance, *National Insurance Retirement Pensions. Reasons Given for Retiring or Continuing at Work* (1954), p. 6.

[61] Logan, 'Work and Age', p. 1192.

[62] F. le Gros Clark and Agnes C. Dunne, *Ageing in Industry* (1955), pp. 140–1.

[63] Sarah Harper and Pat Thane, 'The Consolidation of "Old Age" as a Phase of Life, 1945–1965', in Jefferys, *Growing Old*, pp. 48–9.

[64] A. Roberts, 'British Trade Union Attitudes to the Employment of Older Men and Women', in *Old Age in the Modern World*, pp. 320–5. Roberts was a member of the TUC General Council.

[65] *Reasons Given for Retiring or Continuing at Work*.

of experts chaired by Harold Watkinson (Parliamentary Secretary to the Ministry of Labour);[66] and regular publications by the Ministry of Labour.

Governmental reasoning in the 1950s was uncannily similar to what it is today: older people were healthier and fitter than ever before, at higher ages; it was 'certain' that a considerable proportion of those over minimum retirement age wished to continue working; remunerative activity in old age was good for people's self-esteem and psychological well-being; demographic, labour-supply and other macro-economic considerations necessitated as much postponement of retirement as possible. Remedial action seemed tantalisingly easy: more flexible retirement ages; the removal of compulsory, fixed-age retirement; alteration of occupational pension regulations; more enlightened personnel policies; and so on.[67] As in today's debate, the 'irrationality' model of age discrimination dominated: many 'unjustifiable' age barriers to employment existed, and the extent to which one particular industry employed older workers was said to be explicable by personnel policies, rather than the nature of the work. Some of these age barriers were formal (for example, specific age limits, which were much more common in white collar than in manual occupations), but most were informal. Employers were thus urged to drop such 'irrational' and economically dysfunctional practices.[68] The 'long-standing prejudices' of employers and others were to be dispelled by a campaign to achieve 'a better understanding of the issues'. To this end, the Ministry of Labour and other government departments attempted to enlighten employers: for example, in an episode exactly mirroring the 1990s, 165,000 copies of the Ministry of Labour booklet, *Age and Employment*, were distributed to employers; the positive qualities of older workers – accuracy, attention to detail, experience and judgement, better time-keeping – were highlighted; and publicity was given to the small number of 'success stories' where employers had deliberately retained older workers.[69]

Most of the 1950s research focused on male workers in the first five years of retirement who still had the ability to work. There was much debate over the size of the 'reserve of labour' in this age-group. The official view (which, as we shall see, was to be contested by independent researchers) was optimistic – no doubt influenced by the wartime re-enlistment of older workers. In 1951, the number of men aged 65–9 still in work (*c.* 400,000)

[66] *National Advisory Committee. First Report; National Advisory Committee on the Employment of Older Men and Women. Second Report,* Cmd. 9628, 1955.
[67] Ministry of Labour and National Service, *Employment of Older Men and Women,* esp. pp. 3–5.
[68] *National Advisory Committee. First Report,* p. 20.
[69] Ibid., p. 13; *National Advisory Committee. Second Report,* pp. 6–7.

almost balanced the number who were jobless (*c*. 450,000); of the latter, the number said to be incapable of work through ill-health was only 100,000.[70] The crucial question, therefore, was whether the remaining *c*. 350,000 men who were 'work-fit' could be persuaded to delay retirement, either by staying on longer in their existing jobs, or by moving to alternative, 'lighter' jobs consistent with their diminishing physical abilities. There was some movement to lighter work after the age of 60, especially if the normal lifetime job was set at the 'pace' of young workers (for example, assembly line work):[71] le Gros Clark estimated that, by their mid-sixties, roughly 20 per cent of manual workers had made the transition to lighter work.[72] This process, which has been termed 'life cycle deskilling',[73] had been a feature of earlier labour markets, especially in the nineteenth century, and was the norm in the rural economy. Changing one's job was a way of accommodating to the gradual decline in physical capacity. By the 1950s, this was becoming less and less possible; as will be shown, many researchers noted that such light, alternative jobs were disappearing. Nevertheless, the hope was that employers might set aside alternative jobs as a specially protected labour market niche for older employees. Interestingly, this was something Beveridge had suggested as far back as 1909.[74]

However, the problem became more difficult when the reasons for retirement were examined. A full historical analysis of retirement in the 1950s would need to scrutinise, in great detail, industry-by-industry changes in age structure, and has yet to be undertaken. Different firms had different retirement policies, depending on the nature of their economic activity, and within occupational groupings there were variations in the way in which individuals experienced the diminution of working capacity that resulted in industrial senescence.[75] For the moment, it is useful to consider (albeit rather generally) the factors that might plausibly have played a part.

First, there is the possible effect of the National Insurance retirement pension. This can be discounted. The inducement effect of the state retirement pension was conspicuous by its absence in the MPNI survey's

---

[70] *National Advisory Committee. First Report*, pp. 11–12.
[71] Ruth A. Brown, 'Age and "Paced" Work', *Occupational Psychology*, vol. 31, no. 1, Jan. 1957, p. 11.
[72] F. le Gros Clark, *Age and the Working Lives of Men* (1959), pp. 36–7.
[73] Roger L. Ransome and Richard Sutch, 'The Impact of Aging on the Employment of Men in American Working-Class Communities at the End of the Nineteenth Century', in David Kertzer and Peter Laslett (eds.), *Aging in the Past: Demography, Society, and Old Age* (1995), pp. 303–27.
[74] W. H. Beveridge, *Unemployment, a Problem of Industry* (1912 edn), p. 211.
[75] Acton Society Trust, *Retirement. A Study of Current Attitudes and Practices* (1960), p. 2.

listing of reasons for retirement, and the Watkinson Committee's first report was dismissive of it[76] – hardly surprising, given its low relative value: it remained, for a single person, at roughly 18 per cent of average male manual earnings throughout the 1950s.[77] Throughout the postwar period, surveys consistently showed that some 60 per cent of pensioner households had incomes at or only just above the national assistance/supplementary benefit/income support level. Cole and Utting's survey, conducted in the late 1950s, found that nearly 60 per cent of income units in their sample of retirees received £5 or less per week, whereas only 19 per cent of income units in the UK population as a whole had incomes this low.[78] Peter Townsend illustrated the effect of moving from waged income to pension income in his survey of old people in Bethnal Green: the average income of those who continued working full-time was £7.16s per week, but those who were retired averaged only £2.10s per week.[79] Nor is it plausible to argue, as some have,[80] that increased wealth-holding by older people encouraged retirement: Cole and Utting found that just under a third of pensioner income units in their sample had no assets, and half had less than £100.[81]

The wide distribution of retirement ages after the age of 60 meant that the pensionable age of 65 did not mark a sudden change for the majority of men. The MPNI survey found that, out of 12,009 people in its total sample who reached minimum pensionable age at the time of the survey, only 4,834 claimed the retirement pension, and 7,175 continued working.[82] Independent research confirmed that roughly half of men aged 65–9 remained at work.[83] The study by le Gros Clark of a sample of 315 men aged 60+ in the building industry contained 97 men aged 64 and 65; of these, only six appeared to be contemplating retirement, indicating that building workers did not appear to be taking the state pension age very seriously.[84] Overwhelmingly, research in the 1940s and 1950s indicated that most older workers (particularly manual working-class ones) were

---

[76] *National Advisory Committee. First Report*, pp. 32–5.
[77] For the slight variations in annual relative values, see table in Ruth Lister, *Social Security: the Case for Reform* (1975), p. 34.
[78] See, for example, Dorothy Cole, with John Utting, *The Economic Circumstances of Old People* (1962), p. 47, for the late 1950s. For the late 1990s, see Philip Agulnik, 'Pension Reform in the UK: Evaluating Retirement Income Policy' (University of London (LSE) Ph.D. thesis, 2001), pp. 61–2.
[79] Peter Townsend, *The Family Life of Old People. An Inquiry in East London* (1963 edn), p. 176.
[80] Hannah, *Inventing*, p. 125.   [81] Cole and Utting, *Economic Circumstances*, p. 67.
[82] *Reasons Given for Retiring or Continuing at Work*, p. 6.
[83] For example, Logan, 'Work and Age', p. 1192.
[84] F. le Gros Clark, *The Working Fitness of Older Men. A Study of Men Over Sixty in the Building Industry* (n.d., c. 1955), p. 27.

very reluctant to retire.[85] Peter Townsend's verdict that retirement was 'a tragic event for many men' which, as it approached, was viewed with 'uneasiness and ill-concealed fear' was based upon the fact that his area of research, Bethnal Green, was overwhelmingly working-class.[86]

Most workers who continued working past pensionable age did so for reasons of financial need: in the MPNI enquiry, it was the most important reason (44.7 per cent) for men staying on in work, and, of those who were retired compulsorily by their employer between ages 65 and 69, nine out of ten expressed a desire to continue working.[87] The 'general impression' obtained by the Watkinson Committee was that 'the great majority prefer to stay at work as long as they have the health and opportunity to do so'.[88] Thus the state pension tended to be absolved from blame. By contrast, private pensions were criticised, especially for their lack of flexibility and transferability, and their apparent encouragement of earlier retirement:[89] for example, the Acton Society Trust found that working-class occupations with company pension schemes tended to have more compulsory retirement.[90] The irrelevance of the retirement condition's actuarial incentive was demonstrated by the fact that only 0.7 per cent of men stayed on in work after age 65 in order to enhance the value of their state pension.[91]

This evidence of a reluctance to retire and a fear of financial hardship also casts doubt upon a second possible factor: that a 'retirement tradition' or an 'expectation of retirement' took hold of popular consciousness in the 1950s, became internalised, and thus acted as a powerful causal agent,[92] or that twentieth-century retirement was 'invented' by collective consumer choice, involving a voluntary 'reduced dependence of the old on income from employment'.[93] While such social expectations did matter, and no doubt played some part in accelerating existing trends, they were not of prime causal importance. They were more a rationalisation of the inevitable.

[85] See, for example, Geoffrey Thomas and Barbara Osborne, *Older People and Their Employment* (1951), p. v.
[86] Townsend, *Family Life*, pp. 157–8.
[87] MPNI, *Reasons Given for Retiring or Continuing at Work*, pp. 9, 10.
[88] *National Advisory Committee. Second Report*, p. 10.
[89] *National Advisory Committee. First Report*, pp. 32–5.
[90] Acton Society Trust, *Retirement*, p. 22.
[91] MPNI, *Reasons Given for Retiring or Continuing at Work*, p. 9. The size of the enhancement in the value of the pension resulting from postponed retirement had never been actuarially fair, but it is unlikely that this was a reason.
[92] Sarah Harper, 'The Emergence and Consolidation of the Retirement Tradition in Post-War Britain', in Michael Bury and John Macnicol (eds.), *Aspects of Ageing. Essays on Social Policy and Old Age* (1990), pp. 12–29; Harper and Thane, 'Consolidation', pp. 43–61; Thane, *Old Age*, pp. 404–6.
[93] Hannah, *Inventing*, p. 124.

A third possible factor is the existence of compulsory, fixed-age retirement policies on the part of employers. These played some part, but the evidence revealed that they applied only in a minority of cases. The MPNI survey found that only 28.4 per cent of men in its sample who retired at the minimum pensionable age, and 23.5 per cent of those retiring at ages 65–9, were retired or discharged by an employer.[94] Formal age limits on job vacancies were uncommon in manual jobs, although where they existed they made age-65 retirement more likely. Age limits and compulsory retirement policies were more prevalent in white-collar and clerical jobs.[95] It is clear, therefore, that governmental efforts to persuade employers to drop formal age limits and be more 'flexible' would have made relatively little difference, even if employers had paid any attention.

Of course, much of the contemporary research into the extent of compulsory retirement was of limited value, since it failed to probe deeply enough into the complexity of human motivation and the rapidly changing economic context. For example, a perennial difficulty in analysing retirement is that the distinction between 'involuntary' and 'voluntary' retirement is always problematic. Simple opinion surveys, like the official enquiries of the 1950s, rarely uncover the full complexity of employee–employer relationships that constitute a 'decision to retire'. As the Watkinson Committee's second report commented, 'A man may not always know the real reason for his retirement or discharge, for his employer may prefer to attribute it to an age limit rather than to hurt his feelings by telling him it is due to inefficiency or decline in capacity.'[96] Likewise, Peter Townsend attested that it was 'extremely difficult' to ascertain the exact causes of retirement: 'the reasons for leaving work were sometimes found to be other than those first stated'.[97]

Great problems were encountered in determining how many compulsorily retired men were actually discharged because of ill-health, and vice versa.[98] An illustration of this interpretative difficulty was Anderson and Cowan's study of a sample of 323 men who had reached the age of 65, and had attended the Rutherglen Consultative Health Centre for Older People in Scotland.[99] Of these, 243 (75 per cent) had retired. Among the retirees,

[94] *Reasons Given for Retiring or Continuing at Work*, pp. 6, 9.
[95] *National Advisory Committee. First Report*, p. 18, and *National Advisory Committee. Second Report*, p. 12; 'Age of Compulsory Retirement from Work', *Ministry of Labour Gazette*, vol. LVII, no. 4, April 1949, pp. 121–2.
[96] *National Advisory Committee. Second Report*, p. 12.   [97] Townsend, *Family Life*, p. 163.
[98] Le Gros Clark, *Age and the Working Lives*, pp. 39–40.
[99] For the work of the Centre, see W. Ferguson Anderson and Nairn R. Cowan, 'A Consultative Health Centre for Older People. The Rutherglen Experiment', *The Lancet*, vol. CCLXIX, 30 July 1955, pp. 239–40.

83 had been compulsorily retired, 89 had retired voluntarily and 71 had retired through ill-health. Of the 89 voluntary retirees, 30 had done so because the work was 'heavy and beyond the physical capacity of the individual', and 3 because the mental strain of the work was intolerable and alternative suitable employment was not available. In other words, 33 of the 89 notionally voluntary retirees had retired because the work was beyond their physical or mental powers. Thus, out of the total of 243 retirees in the sample, 187 (or nearly three-quarters) had retirement forced upon them for one reason or another. As the authors perceptively noted, 'voluntary retirement may be in the nature of compulsion, owing not to the employer but to the character of the work'.[100] It is thus likely that compulsory, fixed-age retirement was more common in the 1950s than the official surveys revealed.

Fourthly, ill-health might have been a reason. It was certainly accorded much prominence in the 1950s surveys. The MPNI survey found that, of men in its sample retiring at the age of 65, 25.2 per cent gave 'chronic illness' as a reason, a further 24.8 per cent gave 'ill-health', and 3.6 per cent gave 'strain of work'. These causes also accounted for over half of retirements between ages 65 and 70.[101] Cole and Utting likewise found ill-health cited as the most common cause (38.8 per cent) of men aged 65+ stopping full-time work.[102] Logan concluded that 'one of the most important factors to be taken into consideration in determining whether an elderly man is still employable is the amount of time he is liable to lose from work on account of sickness'. The monthly Survey of Sickness conducted in England and Wales between 1944 and 1951 showed that the incidence of sickness was *not* significantly higher in the 65+ age-group, compared with the 16–64 age-group. However, it was of longer duration, and thus probably more work-disabling (particularly from an employer's point of view).[103]

In the 1950s, as before and since, ill-health was often used as a face-saving and socially acceptable rationalisation of increasing work-disability and under-performance, a general feeling of being 'worn-out', or the disappearance of a job. In Pearson's study, the majority of men in the sample who said that they wished to retire at age 65 gave infirmity or ill-health as the reason, but the impression gained was 'that many such men were suffering from general malaise and strain rather than specific disabilities'.[104] Contemporary researchers thus treated reported infirmity

---

[100] Anderson and Cowan, 'Work and Retirement', p. 1344.
[101] *Reasons Given for Retiring or Continuing at Work*, pp. 6, 9.
[102] Cole and Utting, *Economic Circumstances*, pp. 44–5.
[103] Logan, 'Work and Age', pp. 1192–3.
[104] Margaret Pearson, 'The Transition from Work to Retirement (2)', *Occupational Psychology*, vol. 31, no. 3, July 1957, p. 147.

retirement with some caution. In the MPNI survey, those citing chronic illness or ill-health as a reason for retiring at the minimum pension age could be divided into, first, those with recent records of long-term sickness, and, second, those giving ill-health as a very general 'catch-all' reason, which 'obviously covered conditions ranging from a general sense of growing old or not feeling fit to very serious illness'. Yet six out of ten such men had not had more than twelve days of recorded incapacity for work during the eight months prior to the survey.[105] Either such men struggled on to retirement, stoically putting up with health defects, or, more likely, they rationalised enforced retirement by self-defined ill-health. The official surveys failed to settle this question – if, indeed, it could have been settled with existing methodology.

Ill-health as a cause of work-disability retirement cannot be examined in isolation; it must be considered in the context of the demands of the job and the expectations of the employer. The decision by an employer to retire an employee was taken within a particular economic and social context. As has been shown, in the 1950s the 'pace' and 'strain' of the job tended to determine the time of retirement, with heavy manual occupations instigating earliest labour market withdrawal.[106] The interaction between perceived ill-health and labour market demand is shown by the fact that, in regions where there were the highest proportions of men staying on in work after age 65, there was also the lowest proportion of men suffering from chronic illness, and vice versa.[107]

Complexity of motive: 'adjusting to the inevitable'

It is clear, therefore, that there was considerable complexity of motive among retirees and employers, and the extent to which individuals possessed some control over their retirement remains uncertain. The reasons for retirement were complex, overlapping and opaque. Then, as now, the results of surveys could not necessarily be taken at face value, given that human beings have an unerring tendency to impose retrospective justification on events, and make the best of the inevitable; their memory of past events may also be unreliable. Most contemporary researchers fully understood this.[108] Hence Margaret Pearson found a majority of her sample of men supported their firm's fixed-age retirement policy, yet, paradoxically, a majority also expressed a desire to continue working (mainly for reasons of financial hardship). However, once they had

---

[105] *National Advisory Committee. Second Report*, p. 11.   [106] Ibid., p. 12.
[107] MPNI, *Reasons Given for Retiring or Continuing at Work*, p. 46.
[108] See, for example, Cole and Utting, *Economic Circumstances*, p. 44.

retired, they displayed a 'rather passive acceptance of their new way of life'.[109] Likewise, I. M. Richardson's survey in the North-East of Scotland discovered multiple layers of meaning and motive. One man interviewed 'said he retired because his job was a strain, but later in the interview he maintained that the real reason was the need of his crippled wife for his services at home'. Non-work factors such as family responsibilities played a part, but were difficult to ascertain. The majority in the sample were satisfied with their retirement, but this was class-differentiated and also varied according to the length of retirement, 'indicating, as one would expect, that men "learn to like retirement"'. Richardson perceptively concluded that 'Since experience after an event may modify memory of the event itself, too much should not be made of these retrospective reasons for retiring.'[110]

These pieces of contemporary evidence do not support the suggestion that the continued fall in the economic activity rates of men aged 65+ in the full-employment 1950s demonstrates that retirement since the Second World War has been largely caused by 'supply-side' factors, and in particular the desire of British citizens to cease working: Pat Thane, for example, confidently asserts that declining labour market demand can be 'ruled out' as a factor in the postwar spread of retirement.[111]

It is certainly true that, in the 1950s, retirement spread in spite of a tight overall labour market and the sustained governmental efforts to persuade older workers to stay on longer in work. However, analysis of the labour market at the aggregate level is misleading. One must take account of the sectoral, regional and gendered shifts in labour market demand in this period. Certain sectors of the economy – notably service jobs, attracting young workers and women – were expanding rapidly, with a growing demand for labour, while others were contracting or were stable. Older workers in the 1950s, like older workers before and since, were concentrated in Britain's traditional manufacturing industries which were experiencing considerable technological change. They therefore continued to be displaced, or not replaced once they retired. Regional differences in labour market demand were examined in the MPNI survey, and it was found – not surprisingly – that prosperous areas like Inner London and the Midlands had the highest proportions of men remaining in work after age 65. (These were the regions with the lowest unemployment in 1951.)[112] The variation

---

[109] Margaret Pearson, 'The Transition from Work to Retirement (1)', *Occupational Psychology*, vol. 31, no. 2, April 1957, pp. 85–6; Pearson, 'The Transition (2)', p. 148.
[110] Richardson, *Age and Need*, pp. 74–5, 77.   [111] Thane, *Old Age*, p. 387.
[112] Roger Middleton, *The British Economy Since 1945. Engaging with the Debate* (2000), p. 54.

between regions was not great,[113] but this may have been because the defined regions were very large. Smaller-scale local labour market variations appeared to observers to exert a strong influence on retirement rates. Thus in Birmingham in the early 1950s, nearly two-thirds of men aged 65–9 were in work (as compared with the 1951 national average of 48 per cent) because of that city's greater job opportunities.[114] Conversely, on Merseyside, with relatively high unemployment, it was very difficult for older jobless men to find alternative employment.[115] The same was true for Glasgow.[116]

A logical conclusion to draw is that the postwar economic boom was less reflected in the economic activity rates of men aged 65+ than in those of men and women aged 55–9 and 60–4, which (as has been noted) were increasing, owing to buoyant labour market demand and the expansion of feminised jobs.[117] Those who researched the question of whether older men could delay retirement repeatedly stressed that this could only happen if alternative, lighter jobs existed – but they did not.[118] Such jobs were scarce, uneconomic, part-time, or were taken by younger workers with disabilities.[119] In addition, they hardly made a major contribution to the British economy. Indeed, all employed men aged 65–9 were only 2.7 per cent of the male labour force.[120] Essentially, the labour market niche formerly occupied by workers aged 65+ was diminishing in size – a process that had been gradually taking place since the late nineteenth century. 'Light' jobs that had formerly been a refuge for industrially 'worn-out' older workers – jobs like night watchman, messenger or storeman – were disappearing in the face of automation.[121] As one observer accurately commented, suggestions that new jobs could be created for the old were 'disarmingly simple, but they do not really face the situation'.[122] Clark and Dunne concluded, on the basis of their research sample, taken from 32 occupations, that a minimum of 20 per cent of men aged 55–64 would have to be found alternative, lighter jobs if they were to continue working beyond their mid-sixties: this would mean that a national total of 400,000 such jobs would have to be created – which was a practical

[113] It ranged from 67.8 per cent staying on in Inner London to 55.2 per cent in the South-West. MPNI, *Reasons Given for Retiring or Continuing at Work*, p. 46.
[114] Brown, McKeown and Whitfield, 'Observations', p. 558.
[115] Pearson, 'The Transition (2)', p. 140.
[116] Cole and Utting, *Economic Circumstances*, p. 44.
[117] Interestingly, Shenfield was sceptical that this employment boom would be sustained. Shenfield, *Social Policies*, pp. 8–9.
[118] For example, Anderson and Cowan, 'Work and Retirement', p. 1345.
[119] Sheldon, 'The Role of the Aged', p. 322; Pearson, 'The Transition (2)', pp. 140–1.
[120] Shenfield, *Social Policies*, p. 25.   [121] Thane, *Old Age*, p. 391.
[122] J. M. Mackintosh, 'New Jobs for Old', *The Lancet*, vol. CCLXI, 1 Dec. 1951, p. 1033.

impossibility.[123] As already noted, the Phillips Committee had also been pessimistic about the practicality of recreating such 'lost' jobs. Le Gros Clark concluded that, since mechanised industries were technically and organisationally unable to employ their older workers, proposals to raise retirement ages were pointless.[124] No matter how large the theoretical 'reserve of labour' was, ultimately the determining factor was the lack of suitable jobs. When all was said and done, the retirement debate in the 1950s, complex though it was, was shaped by prevailing labour market trends.

Conclusion

The twenty years after the Second World War constitute a curious episode in the history of retirement in Britain. A buoyant economy temporarily reversed the slow trend to male early retirement that had commenced in the 1880s, but economic growth was most pronounced in those new developing sectors that employed younger people and women. Hence the labour market niche occupied by men aged 65+ continued to contract, though this process temporarily slowed in the 1960s. Contemporary surveys were methodologically limited, but they did reveal – as would be expected – that, within the over-arching context of declining labour market demand, retirement had a differential impact according to a myriad of factors, such as class, gender, occupation, health status, genetic or lifestyle influences, region, skill, work stress, employers' personnel policies, and so on.

The period witnessed a lively debate on retirement, health status and working capacity. Intuitively, it was believed that health status and working capacity had improved, but this was impossible to demonstrate independently of the economic and labour market context – so much so that judgements about the health status of older workers were ultimately judgements about the availability of suitable jobs. Hence suggestions for raising retirement ages were futile, and politically non-viable. There was some discussion of age discrimination, but it had little effect. Employers were much more likely to be influenced by economic factors than by government propaganda. A vivid illustration of this was Belbin's finding that older workers in his research sample who were rejected for re-training were not rejected for reasons of age discrimination, but because of 'a policy originating and being operated at a local level and based on the results of

---

[123] Le Gros Clark and Dunne, *Ageing*, p. 145.
[124] Le Gros Clark, *Age and the Working Lives*, p. 66. For an excellent sceptical discussion, see Shenfield, *Social Policies*, pp. 81–4.

experience in the allocation of labour between various operations'.[125] In other words, employers were behaving rationally, and the 'irrationality' model of age discrimination – upon which the government's strategy was based – was irrelevant.

Two further factors prevented the re-enlistment of older workers back into work. First, the retired are always 'last in the queue' in the reserve army of labour[126] (being employed in industrial sectors that are in steady decline), and thus the long-run trend to jobless retirement has only been temporarily reversed in very exceptional times, such as the two World Wars. Second, for the majority of older workers – predominantly working-class – the financial impossibility of living solely on a state retirement pension meant that they postponed retirement for as long as possible. Ill-health (either 'genuine', or masking joblessness) and loss of working capacity were the most common reasons for retirement between the ages of 60 and 69. Independent research seemed to show that the retired population in this age-group contained only a small number who considered themselves 'work-fit'; hence the 'reserve of labour' appeared to be much smaller than the government claimed. For example, Brown, McKeown and Whitfield calculated that, of their sample of men aged 65–9 in Birmingham, 86.0 per cent were judged by doctors to be fit for some employment – and 64.8 per cent were actually employed.[127] The 'reserve of labour' was largest in skilled and sedentary, white-collar occupations, where retirees were most likely to have been encouraged into permanent retirement by relatively generous occupational pension schemes.

By the late 1950s, it was believed that the inexorable progress of automation was destroying many labour-intensive jobs; hence the need to retain older workers diminished considerably, and much of the research into working capacity was wound up.[128] Indeed, the idea of a 'leisured society' began to feature in public debates. For example, in his famous 'white heat of technology' speech at the 1963 Labour Party Annual Conference, Harold Wilson warned that automation was proceeding at such a pace that some 10,000,000 new jobs would have to be created by the mid-1970s just in order to compensate. However, if properly controlled, automation could bring great benefits: the choice was between 'the blind imposition of technological advance, with all that means in terms of

---

[125] Belbin, 'Difficulties', p. 179.
[126] John Macnicol, 'Old Age and Structured Dependency', in Bury and Macnicol, *Aspects*, pp. 35–6.
[127] Brown, McKeown and Whitfield, 'Observations', p. 561.
[128] Dex and Phillipson, 'Social Policy', pp. 47–8.

unemployment, and the conscious, planned, purposive use of scientific progress to provide undreamed-of living standards and the possibility of leisure, ultimately on an unbelievable scale'.[129] Within a few years, however, the British economy was beginning to experience the prelude to that second industrial revolution that was to hit it ten years later. As one commentator aptly put it, the late 1960s and early 1970s 'marked the reversal of the postwar long wave of economic expansion in Britain, and the onset of accelerating negative de-industrialisation'.[130] Unemployment began to rise from 1966, with regional unemployment 'black spots' emerging.[131] The pace of technological change in British industry accelerated, with the aim – as in the 1930s – of reducing labour costs and shrinking workforces; in the process, older workers began to be shed, and (as has already been noted in a previous chapter) the 1965 Redundancy Payments Act was designed to facilitate this. Thus from the early 1970s the economic activity rates of men aged 55–64 began to fall precipitously.

This economic transformation was occurring across the advanced industrial world, though with differences in timing. As early as 1962 the Organisation for Economic Co-operation and Development held a Technical International Seminar on 'Age and Employment' at Stockholm, which discussed, among other things, the recent 'acceleration in technological change' in industrial production, which was a 'new and growing problem' affecting men in the second half of their working lives, i.e. aged 40–55.[132] By the late 1950s and 1960s, contemporary observers were warning of what might lie ahead. As early as 1951, Richard Titmuss pointed out that, for civil servants and other government employees who retired at 60, the state had 'accepted the responsibility of making generous provision for a period of years amounting to nearly half the working life of these professional, technical and administrative workers'. And, perhaps anticipating that early retirement might spread down the occupational structure, he warned of an impending social problem: 'For millions of people an extra span of life has come into being with its own economic and social needs. Provision for this span now comes into conflict with the needs of other age spans.'[133] 'For more and more people', observed Titmuss,

[129] Harold Wilson, *Purpose in Politics* (1964), pp. 17–18.
[130] Ron Martin, 'Industrial Restructuring, Labour Shake-out and the Geography of Recession', in Mike Danson (ed.), *Redundancy and Recession. Restructuring the Regions?* (1986), p. 3.
[131] Registered unemployment in the UK was 291,674 in 1966, and 539,149 in 1967. By the mid-1970s, it was around 800,000.
[132] Organisation for Economic Co-operation and Development, *Age and Employment* (1962), pp. 44, 46–7.
[133] Titmuss, 'Social Administration', pp. 26, 29.

'work and death are becoming increasingly separated by a functionless interregnum'.[134] Likewise, in the 1960s Frederick le Gros Clark – who, as has been shown, was a leading authority in the postwar debate on retirement, health status and working capacity – drew attention to emerging labour market trends. Interestingly, he believed that the increase in women's employment was one of the 'social revolutions of our time', which would have momentous consequences in the future.[135] He also warned of 'the technological revolution we are just entering' in industrial production methods – a revolution that would surely displace more older workers – and he presciently observed that, in the future 'we shall soon find it necessary to treat retirement (at all events in its early stages) as a comprehensive way of life with its own unique code of social rights. For it will often represent a long period of time and will embrace a large section of the population.'[136] Subsequent decades were to prove that these warnings had been correct.

---

[134] Quoted in Pearson, 'The Transition (2)', p. 149.
[135] F. le Gros Clark, *Woman, Work and Age* (1962), p. 13.
[136] Le Gros Clark, *Work, Age and Leisure*, p. 22.

7   The recent debate

Introduction

The profound economic changes that have re-shaped Western economies since the 1970s have generated renewed interest in the debate on health status and old age. For a variety of reasons outlined in earlier chapters – the spread of male 'early' retirement, the rise in disability benefit claims, concern over health, social security and pension costs, alarmism over an ageing population in the future, the transition to new labour markets – the question of whether older workers 'could' or 'should' stay on longer in work has become central to public debate. If older workers are healthier than ever before, so it is argued, it is not unreasonable to expect them to stay in work a little longer.[1] Retirement ages should thus be raised, and policies to persuade older workers to remain longer in the labour market should be introduced – including policies to combat age discrimination in the workplace. In addition, the ascendancy of 'supply-side' free market economics since the 1980s has meant that the alleged behavioural effects of welfare benefits have been put under scrutiny. The implication is that early retirement schemes have become too attractive an incentive, and should be cut back. Since working capacity has improved, it is argued, this should cause little hardship: older workers should be capable of supporting themselves through waged labour.

Accordingly, there has emerged since the 1980s a wide-ranging debate over the projected future health status of older people in advanced industrial societies. Until the 1960s, mortality gains in the USA had been slow. Official projections in the 1970s thus consistently underestimated the future size of the older population.[2] However, mortality rates fell much more rapidly from the 1960s: for example, in the USA between 1950 and

[1] 'Health Transitions and the Compression of Morbidity', in Dorothy M. Gilford (ed.), *The Aging Population in the Twenty-First Century. Statistics for Health Policy* (1988), p. 94.
[2] Kenneth G. Manton, 'The Dynamics of Population Aging: Demography and Policy Analysis', *Milbank Quarterly*, vol. 69, no. 2, 1991, p. 311.

1992 age-standardised death rates from heart disease declined by 53.0 per cent, stroke mortality by 70.4 per cent and clinically diagnosed hypertension prevalence in older people was also reduced.[3] By the early 1980s it was apparent in both Britain and the USA that life expectancy in old age *was* improving – albeit slowly – while morbidity rates for middle-aged and older adults appeared to be worsening,[4] levels of disability (self-reported, or benefit-supported) appeared to be rising,[5] and health care utilisation rates were increasing, raising the gloomy possibility of rapidly rising medical and institutional costs. Again, evidence seemed to suggest that poor health was the most frequently cited, and growing, reason for the spread of early retirement: for example, the longitudinal National Health Interview Survey in the USA found that the proportion of men aged 45–64 who reported that they were 'unable to perform their major activity' (i.e. working) had risen from 4.4 per cent in 1960–1 to 10.8 per cent in 1980.[6] Examining the group aged 50–69 in the USA, Jacob Feldman discovered that the proportion of men reporting themselves as unable to work through illness increased between 1970 and 1980. Sub-dividing into age-groups, among those aged 50–4, it had risen from 5.3 per cent to 7.7 per cent; aged 55–9, from 8.4 per cent to 12.7 per cent; aged 60–4, from 15.0 per cent to 18.9 per cent; and aged 65–9, from 21.9 per cent to 25.2 per cent.[7] Was population health status actually worsening? Was the apparent increase in work-disability caused by declining health status per se, or was it driven by background social and economic factors?[8] And if increasing numbers of older men were defining themselves as 'work-disabled', how viable were proposals to raise pension-eligibility ages?

Essentially, the debate has centred on two questions: By how much is life expectancy in old age increasing? And by how much is the period of disability-free, active life extending? It is therefore mostly concerned with

[3] Kenneth G. Manton, Eric Stallard and Larry Corder, 'Changes in the Age Dependence of Mortality and Disability: Cohort and Other Determinants', *Demography*, vol. 34, no. 1, Feb. 1997, p. 136.

[4] Lois M. Verbrugge, 'Longer Life But Worsening Health? Trends in Health and Mortality of Middle-aged and Older Persons', *Milbank Memorial Fund Quarterly/Health and Society*, vol. 62, no. 3, 1984, p. 491.

[5] Barbara L. Wolfe and Robert Haveman, 'Trends in the Prevalence of Work Disability from 1962 to 1984, and Their Correlates', *Milbank Quarterly*, vol. 68, no. 1, 1990, p. 53; Edward H. Yelin and Patricia P. Katz, 'Making Work More Central to Work Disability Policy', *Milbank Quarterly*, vol. 72, no. 4, 1994, pp. 598–9.

[6] Martin Neil Baily, 'Aging and the Ability to Work: Policy Issues and Recent Trends', in Gary Burtless (ed.), *Work, Health, and Income Among the Elderly* (1987), p. 75.

[7] Jacob J. Feldman, 'Work Ability of the Aged Under Conditions of Improving Mortality', *Milbank Memorial Fund Quarterly/Health and Society*, vol. 61, no. 3, 1983, p. 432.

[8] For a general discussion, see Thomas N. Chirikos, 'Accounting for the Historical Rise in Work-disability Prevalence', *Milbank Quarterly*, vol. 64, no. 2, 1986, pp. 271–301.

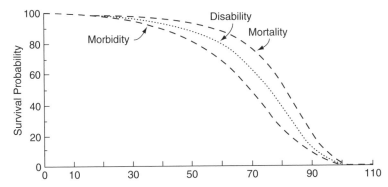

Figure 7.1. The mortality (observed), morbidity (hypothetical) and
disability (hypothetical) survival curves for US females in 1980.
Source: WHO, *The uses of epidemiology in the study of the elderly.* Report
of the WHO Scientific Group on the Epidemiology of Aging, Technical
Report Series, 706. Geneva: WHO, 1984, p. 29.

the 'oldest old' (those aged 75+) who experience the highest rates of morbidity and disability. However, this has an important policy implication, in
that if the health of the 'oldest old' were to improve, those aged in their fifties
and sixties would presumably also experience an improvement and would
thus be more able to stay on at work past 'normal', age-65 retirement.

The debate is highly complex, and only its main outlines can be delineated
here. Essentially, it hinges upon the inter-relationship between the three
parallel curves of morbidity, disability and mortality (relating prevalence to
age). If the first two curves can be moved 'to the right' (or up the age range),
and the survival curve remains static (or moves less rapidly), disability-free life
expectancy will increase. However, if the survival curve moves rightwards,
and the others do not (or they move more slowly), the prevalence of chronic
illness will increase.[9] The nature and timing of the inter-relationship between
these curves is crucial. As three authorities have put it, 'If mortality declines
because health problems are prevented or because their onset is delayed,
population health will improve with the decline in mortality. If the treatment
of existing diseases merely prevents their progression or eliminates death
at a later stage, some deterioration in population health is expected.'[10]

[9] Jean-Marie Robine, Colin Mathers and Nicholas Brouard, 'Trends and Differentials in
Disability-Free Life Expectancy', in Graziella Caselli and Alan D. Lopez (eds.), *Health and
Mortality Among Elderly Populations* (1996), p. 187; 'Health Transitions', pp. 99–100.

[10] Eileen M. Crimmins, Mark D. Hayward and Yasuhiko Saito, 'Changing Mortality and
Morbidity Rates and the Health Status and Life Expectancy of the Older Population',
Demography, vol. 31, no. 1, Feb. 1994, p. 160.

Hence increasing availability of kidney dialysis machines would lead to extensions of life of sub-optimal quality.[11] Another example is offered by Jacob Feldman. Before the use of insulin in the management of diabetes, few diabetic patients lived more than three or four years after diagnosis. With better management regimes, however, 'The greatly improved survival of diabetic patients has resulted in an extremely large increase in the prevalence of the condition and such disabling complications as vision loss and cardio-vascular problems.'[12]

All projections of future health status are thus highly problematic. The whole topic is a methodological minefield, the empirical evidence is patchy and there is 'a lack of consensus on definitions of health, morbidity and disability, and on the standardisation of calculation procedures'.[13] Given that ageing is a long *process*, and that health problems in old age may originate very early in life, detailed longitudinal studies are needed; these are still comparatively rare. Existing surveys, conducted over time, have often used differently-worded questions, making temporal comparisons well-nigh impossible. For example, the National Health Interview Survey (NHIS) in the USA – surveying *c.* 100,000 persons, and commencing in 1957 – changed the design of its questions in 1982. In addition, there are innumerable psycho-social factors which contaminate the data. Thus an apparent rise in reported morbidity could be attributable to several causes: a real increase in the incidence of chronic diseases; earlier diagnosis; earlier accommodations of those diseases (for example, more willingness to claim disability benefits); improved survival, resulting in more years of impaired health; less institutionalisation; changes in research questionnaires; higher expectations on the part of the public; and greater willingness to play the 'sick role'.[14]

Interpreting past data is hard enough; even greater problems arise in attempting to predict the precise future balance of positive and negative factors. As noted in chapter 4, improvements in health status caused by therapeutic interventions and better lifestyles may be negated by the rise of new conditions. Modern work-related diseases (such as repetitive strain injury) may 'wear out' workers as quickly as those of nineteenth-century

---

[11] James M. Porteba and Lawrence H. Summers, 'Public Policy Implications of Declining Old-Age Mortality', in Burtless, *Work, Health, and Income*, p. 27.

[12] Feldman, 'Work Ability', p. 442.

[13] Jean-Marie Robine and Karen Ritchie, 'Healthy Life Expectancy: Evaluation of a New Global Indicator for Change in Population Health', *British Medical Journal*, vol. 302, 23 Feb. 1991, p. 460.

[14] Verbrugge, 'Longer Life', pp. 507–8; Monroe Berkowitz, 'Functioning Ability and Job Performance as Workers Age', in Michael E. Borus, Herbert S. Parnes, Steven H. Sandell and Bert Seidman (eds.), *The Older Worker* (1988), p. 102.

industrial life. Levels of stress (brought about by factors such as an increasingly insecure labour market, urban living, or a competitive market economy) may increase, resulting in more conditions with psycho-social origins. New epidemics may prove relatively uncontrollable, and may increase mortality rates in certain population sub-groups. Illnesses among the middle-aged and young-old may be conquered, with the result that high levels of morbidity may be concentrated in the 'oldest old'. Thus Olshansky and Carnes warn:

> As diseases and disorders of older ages are successfully postponed, it is predicted that new or infrequently observed diseases and disorders that may be more difficult to conquer will be revealed. Although modifying risk factors may produce further reductions in death rates from fatal diseases (as has been observed in low mortality countries), the health benefits should be neither synergistic nor additive. Instead, gains in life expectancy should follow a biologically based law of diminishing returns.[15]

Future 'progress' may therefore involve only brief extensions of the human lifespan, terminated by 'substitute morbidity and mortality': we will live just a little longer, and then die of something else. For example, cardio-vascular diseases may be replaced by more cancers. As John McCallum has warned, these immediate-future trends have no historical precedents, and will pose a major challenge to policy-makers.[16] We may indeed be entering a 'fourth stage' of the epidemiological transition – one that we do not fully understand.[17] Finally, much of this epidemiological modelling is based upon whole population data, thus ignoring the substantial inequal-ities of class, race, gender and region in morbidity and mortality. For example, there are important gender differences in morbidity, disability and mortality (women have higher levels of reported sickness during their lifetimes, yet live longer than men) and in the prevalence of particular conditions (women are more likely than men to report conditions of disability, such as osteoporosis and arthritis, whereas men are more likely to report potentially fatal conditions, such as heart disease; women also spend a larger proportion of their lives in a physically disabled state).[18]

---

[15] S. Jay Olshansky and Bruce Carnes, 'Prospect for Extended Survival: a Critical Review of the Biological Evidence', in Caselli and Lopez, *Health and Mortality*, p. 55.

[16] John McCallum, 'Health and Ageing: the Last Phase of the Epidemiological Transition', in Allan Borowski, Sol Encel and Elizabeth Ozanne (eds.), *Ageing and Social Policy in Australia* (1997), pp. 59, 67, 72.

[17] S. Jay Olshansky and A. Brian Ault, 'The Fourth Stage of the Epidemiologic Transition: The Age of Delayed Degenerative Diseases', *Milbank Quarterly*, vol. 64, no. 3, 1986, pp. 355–91.

[18] Eileen M. Crimmins, Mark D. Hayward and Yasuhiko Saito, 'Differentials in Active Life Expectancy in the Older Population of the United States', *Journal of Gerontology: Social Sciences*, vol. 51B, no. 3, 1996, p. S119.

The three models

Bearing all these problems in mind, three broad models of ageing and health have been posited. These are often presented as separate and opposed, but to an extent they overlap and each may be 'correct' in different temporal contexts. First, there is the optimistic 'compression of morbidity' model, in which increasing proportions of the populations of Western societies will enjoy disability-free lives to their eighth decade and will then experience 'natural death' around the age of 85. Reductions in 'health-risk' behaviours and improvements in medical technology will increasingly postpone chronic illness to the period just before death. Morbidity will thus become 'compressed' at the end of the lifecourse. Presumably, mortality will also become compressed with variability in ages of death being inexorably reduced. Like the celebrated 'one-hoss shay', our bodies will suddenly fall apart, having functioned perfectly up to that point.

This thesis was most famously suggested by the clinician James F. Fries in 1980[19] – although it has a long history[20] – and developed subsequently by him, initiating a lively (and often bitter) controversy in medical circles. Fries's ideas were derived in part from the demographic truism that gains in life expectancy at birth over the past 100 years have been attributable to falling infant and childhood mortality; the further one moves up the age ranges, the less dramatic have been the improvements.[21] Projecting into the future, Fries argued that the 'survival curve' will therefore become 'rectangularised', and sickness will increasingly become concentrated in the last few years of extreme old age. Genetic heterogeneity will mean that there will still be a distribution on either side of this average experience,[22] but the growth of self-help health regimes (such as more nutritious eating and more aerobic exercise) and the reduction in risk factors (such as cigarette smoking and animal fat consumption), plus increasingly effective medical technology, will remove many of the harmful exogenous factors inimical to longevity.[23] Given that death is inevitable, this scenario can be judged both realistic and optimistic – the best we could hope for. Fries argued that it would result in a reduced period of infirmity and an improved quality of life in old age, plus lowered health care expenditure, while not significantly affecting

---

[19] James F. Fries, 'Aging, Natural Death and the Compression of Morbidity', *New England Journal of Medicine*, vol. 303, no. 3, 17 July 1980, pp. 130–5.

[20] It is traceable at least back to the biologist Raymond Pearl's published ideas in 1923.

[21] James F. Fries, 'The Compression of Morbidity', *Milbank Memorial Fund Quarterly/ Health and Society*, vol. 61, no. 3, 1983, pp. 400–1.

[22] Ibid., p. 404.

[23] James F. Fries, 'The Compression of Morbidity: Near or Far?', *Milbank Quarterly*, vol. 67, no. 2, 1989, p. 211.

mortality. He suggested 'that the number of very old persons will not increase, that the average period of diminished physical vigour will decrease, that chronic disease will occupy a smaller proportion of the typical life span, and that the need for medical care in later life will decrease'.[24]

Fries was not wholly optimistic. New existential challenges would have to be faced, such as the fact that disease and death, occurring later in life, would become increasingly unavoidable, and medical intervention in the patient without organ reserve would be recognised as futile.[25] Again, Fries acknowledged that future patterns of morbidity could be complex and uncertain: new epidemics might appear, and widening inequality might worsen the health status of the lowest socio-economic groups.[26] However, his influential thesis emphasised the enormous potential power that human beings in advanced industrial societies may possess to counter the seemingly inevitable decrements associated with ageing, and thus it appeared to substantiate the 'use-it-or-lose-it' recipes of 'positive' ageing.[27]

A second, contrasting model is the 'failure of success' model, which argues that increasing life expectancy at birth has resulted in more survivors with health-impaired lives ('marginal survivors'), carrying a burden of accumulated 'health insults'. Ernest Gruenberg suggested in 1977 that life-saving technology and bio-medical research had outstripped health-preserving technology, and the result had been a steady worsening of health status in Western populations. Future reductions in mortality would thus be accompanied by a rise in the incidence of disability and chronic illness. Although often labelled the 'pessimistic' view, Gruenberg's interestingly discursive article ended with a plea for more research into the preventible causes of chronic illness in old age.[28] Another broadly pessimistic contribution came from Morton Kramer, who warned that the prevalence of chronic illnesses and mental disorders was rising 'at an alarming rate'. Whereas a pandemic of communicable diseases rose to a peak and then declined, this new one showed no signs of tailing off: it was a product both of technological advances in medicine which had saved the lives of those at risk from these conditions, and of the increasing duration

[24] Fries, 'Aging, Natural Death', p. 130.
[25] Ibid., p. 133. John R. Wilmoth and Shiro Horiuchi, 'Rectangularisation Revisited: Variability of Age at Death Within Human Populations', *Demography*, vol. 36, no. 4, Nov. 1999, pp. 482, 490.
[26] Fries, 'The Compression of Morbidity: Near or Far?', p. 225.
[27] George L. Maddox, Daniel O. Clark and Karen Steinhauser, 'Dynamics of Functional Impairment in Late Adulthood', *Social Science and Medicine*, vol. 38, no. 7, 1994, p. 925. For a useful summary of the debate, taking a broadly 'optimistic' view of changes in health status between 1961 and 1981, see Erdman B. Palmore, 'Trends in the Health of the Aged', *The Gerontologist*, vol. 26, no. 3, June 1986, pp. 298–302.
[28] Ernest M. Gruenberg, 'The Failures of Success', *Milbank Memorial Fund Quarterly/Health and Society*, vol. 55, no. 1, 1977, pp. 3–24.

of such conditions consequent upon improving longevity.[29] Much in the same vein, Schneider and Brody argued that mortality rates of the US population aged 85+ were falling faster than those of any ten-year age-group between ages 55 and 85, while morbidity in the upper age ranges appeared to be increasing,[30] and Colvez and Blanchet concluded that the level of 'activity limitation' in the US population had increased, with a continuous rise in the demand for health care.[31] Likewise, Bebbington, using General Household Survey (GHS) responses in Britain, found an increase in self-reported disability between 1985 and 1988.[32]

A third model is something of a middle way – the 'dynamic equilibrium' model, most notably argued by Kenneth Manton. In this, the gains in longevity will indeed be accompanied by the survival of more people with 'impaired lives' – in other words, the 'epidemiological transition' will continue – but improving disease management regimes and reductions in 'health-risk' behaviours will result in gradual improvements in aggregate health status. Following the dictum that it is never too late in life to improve one's health status, awareness of the importance of regular exercise, good diet, stress avoidance and other elements of a healthy lifestyle are spreading throughout populations of Western societies, and should have an inexorable 'cohort effect', raising the health status of successive generations.[33] Manton (whose position has become noticeably more 'optimistic' in the past decade) has thus declared that 'Reclassification of processes from endogenous to exogenous is occurring with increasing frequency owing to rapid increases in scientific knowledge.'[34]

Manton has argued that much of the debilitation and morbidity experienced at advanced ages is the result of health-related behaviours and risk-factor exposures occurring earlier in life – 'the result of a lifelong accumulation of exogenous insults to the physiology of the individual'.

[29] M. Kramer, 'The Rising Pandemic of Mental Disorders and Associated Chronic Diseases and Disabilities', *Acta Psychiatrica Scandinavica*, 62, 1980 (Suppl. 283), pp. 382–97.

[30] Edward L. Schneider and Jacob A. Brody, 'Aging, Natural Death and the Compression of Morbidity: Another View', *New England Journal of Medicine*, vol. 309, no. 14, 6 Oct. 1983, pp. 854–5.

[31] Alain Colvez and Madeleine Blanchet, 'Disability Trends in the United States Population 1966–76: Analysis of Reported Causes', *American Journal of Public Health*, vol. 71, no. 5, May 1981, pp. 464–71.

[32] A. C. Bebbington, 'The Expectation of Life Without Disability in England and Wales', *Population Trends*, no. 66, Winter 1991, pp. 26–9.

[33] Kenneth G. Manton, 'Changing Concepts of Morbidity and Mortality in the Elderly Population', *Milbank Memorial Fund Quarterly/Health and Society*, vol. 60, no. 2, 1982, pp. 183–244.

[34] Kenneth G. Manton, Eric Stallard and H. Dennis Tolley, 'Limits to Human Life Expectancy: Evidence, Prospects, and Implications', *Population and Development Review*, vol. 17, no. 4, December 1991, p. 622.

The risk factors at younger ages are well known – high blood pressure, obesity, drinking alcohol to excess, cigarette smoking, lack of exercise, high blood sugar levels – and if the incidence of these could be reduced through health education campaigns producing more responsible behaviours, chronic illness in later life would also be reduced.[35]

There is evidence that this is happening in Western societies, giving grounds for a guarded optimism that the increased survival of relatively unhealthy sections of the US and UK populations has been offset by a general lowering of mortality, consequent upon reductions in 'health-risk' behaviours, permitting more health-robust people to survive.[36] Lung cancer deaths among older adults are decreasing in those countries (such as the UK) which launched anti-smoking campaigns some years ago.[37] Hence death rates from cancer among men in England and Wales have fallen from 2,700 per million population in the late 1960s to 1,900 per million in 2001.[38] Many examples of the apparent success of preventive measures have been documented. Early-life physical activity lowers the risk of stroke. Blood pressure can also be reduced by dietary changes and the relatively benign pharmaceuticals that are available today: for example, it has been estimated that a 5 mmHg reduction in mean population diastolic blood pressure, attainable by reducing the mean daily salt intake in the population by 50 mmol/l, might cut the incidence and mortality from strokes by 20 per cent, and halve the number of patients requiring pharmacological treatment of hypertension.[39] There is some evidence that the more the years of education, the lower the risk of developing Alzheimer's disease at late ages (though the precise causal mechanisms are unclear).[40] Bone density, determined by both nutrition and the level of weight-bearing physical activity up to menopause, appears to be related to the risk of fractures in old age.[41] Breast cancer is influenced by age of first pregnancy. Cigarette smoking greatly increases the risk of lung cancer. Many other examples exist.[42]

---

[35] Kenneth G. Manton, 'Life-Style Risk Factors', *Annals of the American Academy of Political and Social Science*, vol. 503, May 1989, pp. 72–88.

[36] Porteba and Summers, 'Public Policy Implications', pp. 44–9.

[37] Graziella Caselli and Alan D. Lopez, 'Health and Mortality Among the Elderly: Issues for Assessment', in Caselli and Lopez, *Health and Mortality*, p. 12.

[38] Office for National Statistics, *Social Trends No. 33 2003 Edition* (2003), p. 135.

[39] N. U. Weir and M. S. Dennis, 'Meeting the Challenge of Stroke', *Scottish Medical Journal*, vol. 42, no. 5, Oct. 1997, p. 145. (This edition of the journal is devoted to health care in old age.)

[40] For example, it is possible that a more highly educated old person performs better on the mental tests for Alzheimer's, and thus disguises the severity of their condition.

[41] M. E. T. McMurdo, 'Physical Activity and Health in Old Age', *Scottish Medical Journal*, vol. 42, no. 5, Oct. 1997, pp. 154–5.

[42] Manton, Stallard and Corder, 'Changes', p. 135.

Methodological and interpretative problems

Most participants in the 'compression of morbidity' debate have been interested in the interpretative problems, which focus upon two questions: whether the idea of 'natural death' and a fixed human lifespan is correct; and whether chronic illness is increasingly being postponed to later life, with 'disability-free life expectancy' therefore lengthening. There is little doubt that, in Western societies, more individuals are surviving to very extreme old age. However, it is the quality of life in those final years that is crucial. How can that quality of life be measured? What methodological problems arise from the process of measurement? Five particularly relevant points will be considered here: together, they suggest that one should be cautious about pronouncing a simple, over-optimistic verdict on future trends.

The first is whether health care costs will fall in the future, as the compression of morbidity brings about a reduced period of chronic illness at the end of the average lifespan. This is often averred.[43] However, the problem is that there are a number of factors which will probably continue to push up health care costs in the future, the most important of which is the tendency of successive cohorts to have higher expectations of their health care systems – a product of secondary factors such as rising living standards, the availability and quality of health services, the invention of new medical technologies and the role of the medical profession.[44] For example, one complication in measuring trends in the health status of older Americans is that the debate took off at a time when their access to health care markedly improved, following the introduction of Medicare in 1965: improving access naturally led to increasing usage. The interaction between behavioural/lifestyle changes, changes in the demand for health care and the resultant levels of public expenditure is by no means simple. For example, a significant reduction in cigarette smoking would ensure that more citizens survive to old age, thus increasing health and social security expenditure at higher ages[45] – contrary to what Fries predicted.

---

[43] See, for example, John Grimley Evans, 'Age Discrimination: Implications of the Ageing Process', in Sandra Fredman and Sarah Spencer (eds.), *Age as an Equality Issue* (2003), p. 18.

[44] Malcolm Hodkinson, 'Active Life Expectancy and Disability', in J. Grimley Evans *et al.*, *Health and Function in the Third Age. Papers Prepared for the Carnegie Inquiry into the Third Age* (1993), pp. 52–3.

[45] Thus a 2001 report for the Czech government by the tobacco company Philip Morris suggested that premature mortality through smoking-related deaths saved it £100,000,000 per annum in health care and pension costs.

A second problem is the question of whether medical intervention is the prime determinant of mortality reductions. As a clinician, Fries assumed that a combination of improving medical technology and lifestyle alterations holds the key to longevity. However, a substantial body of evidence, following the pioneering work of Thomas McKeown,[46] has cast doubt on the historical role of medical intervention in reducing mortality.

Third, there is convincing evidence that socio-economic status and educational levels are much more significant predictors of impairment in later life, rather than chronological age per se,[47] and these variables further complicate the analysis.[48] Nearly all advanced industrial societies are experiencing widening economic inequality, and this is impacting adversely on their most deprived sub-groups. For example, working-class African-American males in the northern US urban ghettos are suffering rising mortality rates, falling life expectancy and worsening absolute health status: thus in the 1980s black men in Harlem had a worse chance of survival beyond the age of 40 than males in Bangladesh.[49] Again, in Britain male life expectancy at birth in 1997–8 ranged from 78.5 years for professionals to 71.1 years for unskilled manual workers.[50] It is likely that, in the future, this patterned distribution will become more complex, rendering generalisation less and less meaningful. Aggregate health status could worsen because of a decline in the health status of an increasingly impoverished sub-group suffering severe economic deprivation. Future projections will thus have to take account of complex variables such as income, wealth, pension support, employment status, migration and even emotional well-being: for example, the bereavement of a co-resident partner can result in the loss of health-promotion assistance and support. These variables will increase heterogeneity in health status, and therefore in ages of death.

The fourth critical point is perhaps the most devastating. If genetic or early-life nutritional factors, rather than lifestyle ones, are crucial, then the survival curve will not become rectangularised: inherent biological influences will mean that people will continue to die at very different ages. As has been shown, Fries anticipated that there would be a distribution on either side of the survival curve; but if this distribution is very wide, it will

---

[46] Thomas McKeown, *The Modern Rise of Population* (1976).

[47] Maddox, Clark and Steinhauser, 'Dynamics', pp. 932–3; Richard Wilkinson, *Unhealthy Societies: the Afflictions of Inequality* (1996).

[48] George L. Maddox and Daniel O. Clark, 'Trajectories of Functional Impairment in Later Life', *Journal of Health and Social Behavior*, vol. 33, June 1992, p. 115.

[49] Colin McCord and Harold P. Freeman, 'Excess Mortality in Harlem', *New England Journal of Medicine*, vol. 322, no. 3, 18 Jan. 1990, pp. 173–7.

[50] Office for National Statistics, *Social Trends No. 33*, p. 130.

invalidate the idea of 'natural death'. Only if an entire population adopted an 'ideal type' lifestyle, in accordance with the 'risk-factor model', and there were no genetic heterogeneity, would the survival curve become perfectly rectangularised. (Even then, it would be absurd to envisage all human beings dying at exactly the same age.) This scenario has been criticised on several grounds. First, there is the impracticality of persuading an entire population to live lives of complete moral rectitude, eschewing all 'risk-factor' behaviours. Risk is relative, not absolute. In practice, most individuals live lifestyles with varying degrees of health-risk behaviour (for example, swimming every day, yet also smoking cigarettes), and this creates enormous problems of research methodology: just how are these variations to be classified? Second, the available medical evidence is not comforting: research into population sub-groups leading 'ideal type' healthy lives (such as Mormon high priests, Seventh Day Adventists, or inmates of religious orders) shows that substantial variation in ages of death occurs, implying that genetic or early-life factors are important.[51] (One methodological difficulty is that even inhabitants of such closed communities may have led very diverse lifestyles, with varying degrees of health-risk behaviours, before they joined the community.) Third, mortality rates at younger ages are now so low in most advanced industrial societies that the demographic effects of further reductions would be negligible.[52] Thus even if the US population lived the kind of ideal lifestyle prescribed by the 'risk-factor' model, resulting in the complete elimination of all deaths below the age of 50 (only 12.4 per cent of all deaths), life expectancy at birth would rise by a mere 3.5 years. A survival curve based on life expectancy at birth of 85 years could be achieved only if mortality rates declined by 65 per cent for the population aged 50+ − a theoretical possibility, but not a practical one: 'major breakthroughs' would have to occur in the treatment of fatal degenerative diseases in the population aged 50+. A life expectancy at birth of 100 years could only be achieved if death rates at all ages declined by a massive 85 per cent.[53] This is frankly utopian.

A final interpretative complication is that medical intervention and general environmental factors can have varying impacts on different population cohorts. Thus Manton, Stallard and Corder point out that initially the use of diuretics to control hypertension had adverse side-effects

[51] Manton, Stallard and Tolley, 'Limits', pp. 612–13.
[52] Emily Grundy, 'The Health and Health Care of Older Adults in England and Wales, 1841–1994', in John Charlton and Mike Murphy (eds.), *The Health of Adult Britain 1841–1994 Vol. 2* (1997), p. 184.
[53] S. Jay Olshansky, Bruce A. Carnes and Christine Cassel, 'In Search of Methuselah: Estimating the Upper Limits to Human Longevity', *Science*, vol. 250, pt. 2, 1990, pp. 634–40; Olshansky and Carnes, 'Prospect for Extended Survival', pp. 44, 51–2, 54.

(aggravating cardiac arrhythmias and diabetes) and failed to reduce total mortality: since then, anti-hypertension drugs have improved vastly. Different cohorts will also have different lifetime exposures to infections and other risk factors, and will experience differences in the quality of health care, food availability, real wages, housing, and so on. Manton, Stallard and Corder thus found 'significant differences' in the mortality and disability experiences of three elderly cohorts that they examined, using data from the 1980s.[54] Summing up this interpretative problem, Crimmins, Hayward and Saito conclude:

> When medical science and technology first address a chronic disease, the initial effect probably is felt on the death rates of fairly sick people. As progress is made against chronic diseases, either fatal or nonfatal, the progression of these diseases may be arrested at earlier stages. Eventually the understanding of the disease process may advance to the point where the age of onset of problems is increased and people are restored to better health. Such a situation would lead to a decline in the proportion of the population dependent.[55]

It is likely, therefore, that each of the three broad models outlined above may be 'correct' or 'incorrect' at different points in history.

Much hinges on the potential 'modifiability' of the ageing process (or 'plasticity of ageing'). There is an enormous debate about the salience of lifestyle/risk-factor influences, vis-à-vis genetic or other endogenous factors. For example, although physical exercise appears to have some beneficial effect on mortality (particularly on coronary heart disease),[56] the effect may not be great: Paffenbarger et al., in an article strongly supportive of the importance of physical exercise, examined a sample of Harvard graduates aged 45 to 84, and found that, between 1977 and 1985, those who took up moderately vigorous physical activity and ceased smoking gained only 2.49 additional years of life;[57] likewise, Barker has argued that recent trials of the effects of lifestyle interventions – including exercise, weight loss, smoking cessation and dietary changes – reduce the incidence of coronary heart disease by less than 8 per cent.[58] Increasing knowledge of the precise balance between endogenous and exogenous

---

[54] Manton, Stallard and Corder, 'Changes', pp. 135–57.

[55] Crimmins, Hayward and Saito, 'Changing Mortality', p. 173.

[56] Ralph S. Paffenbarger, Robert T. Hyde, Alvin L. Wing and Chung-Cheng Hsieh, 'Physical Activity, All-Cause Mortality and Longevity of College Alumni', *New England Journal of Medicine*, vol. 314, no. 10, 6 Mar. 1986, pp. 605–13.

[57] Ralph S. Paffenbarger, Robert T. Hyde, Alvin L. Wing, I-Min Lee, Dexter L. Jung and James B. Kampert, 'The Association of Changes in Physical-Activity Level and Other Lifestyle Characteristics with Mortality Among Men', *New England Journal of Medicine*, vol. 328, no. 8, 25 Feb. 1993, p. 543.

[58] D. J. P. Barker, *Mothers, Babies and Health in Later Life* (1994), p. 2.

factors may in the future help resolve what Maddox has called 'the Cartesian dualism of person and environment'[59] (something which, as was shown earlier, intrigued commentators a century ago). For now, however, there is still much uncertainty. To take but one example: recently, two entirely different explanations have been posited for women's greater longevity. One is biological: that women possess stronger immune systems (with higher levels of T-cells) than do men. The other is social: that men lead more stressful, competitive lifestyles that are inimical to longevity, and that as more women enter the labour market in the future, suffering equivalent levels of stress, their relative longevity will be shortened.

The 'Fries/anti-Fries' debate has ranged deep and wide in the last twenty years, reflecting both the problematic nature of the empirical evidence and the perennial difficulties of interpreting that evidence. However, a summary of the positive and negative evidence can be made, covering both old people and the all-age population. Essentially, the paradox is that objective indicators demonstrate that population health appears to be improving, whereas measures based upon self-reporting show it to be worsening.

The empirical evidence: Britain

In Britain, death rates at older ages have been falling in recent years. For men aged 55, there was no improvement until after 1951, but for women of that age the improvement began twenty years earlier.[60] Life expectancy at birth has, of course, risen greatly. Thus in Britain in 1901, it stood at roughly 45 years (male) and 49 years (female); by 2001 these expectations had risen to 75.7 years (male) and 80.4 years (female). However, given that increasing life expectancy at birth is largely a function of decreasing infant and childhood mortality, life expectancy at age 65 has only increased by some 6 years for men since 1901 (to nearly 16 additional years in 2001), and by just over seven years for women (to 19 additional years).[61] These rises have been most rapid in recent decades. Thus in contrast to Fries's contention (above) that 'the number of very old persons will not increase', the number of centenarians in Britain increased from 300 to 4,400 between 1951 and 1991 (a rate of about 7 per cent per annum), and is projected to rise to a massive 45,000 in 2031 (80 per cent of whom will be women).[62]

---

[59] George Maddox, 'Aging Differently', *The Gerontologist*, vol. 27, no. 5, 1987, p. 559.
[60] Grundy, 'Health and Health Care', p. 192.
[61] Office for National Statistics, *Social Trends No. 33*, p. 130.
[62] Roger Thatcher, 'Trends and Prospects at Very High Ages', in Charlton and Murphy, *Health of Adult Britain*, pp. 205–10.

This is partly because of improved survival, but mainly because of the larger cohorts moving into extreme old age.

As measured by 'activities of daily living', disability-free life expectancy at higher ages also rose between 1980 and 1994 – for example, from 11.6 years to 13.5 years for men aged 65–9, and from 14.4 years to 15.6 years for women aged 65–9.[63] By this measure, healthy life expectancy as a proportion of total life expectancy at age 65–9 rose for both males and females between 1976 and 1991.[64] Another piece of evidence on the positive side is that fully 60 per cent of men aged 65–79 in private households in England rated their health as 'good' or 'very good' in 2000.[65] Finally, improving health status might be reflected in the fact that the average height of the British population is increasing: British men aged 20–5 are an average of 7 cm taller than men aged 70–5.[66]

However, contradictory and slightly pessimistic results have been obtained from surveys of self-reported health status. The *Health and Lifestyle Survey*, first conducted in 1984–5,[67] found that 78 per cent of males and 75 per cent of females aged 65+ thought that people were healthier than in their parents' time.[68] When conducted again in 1991–2, there was found to be an improvement in self-reported health status, although there was also an increased prevalence of certain conditions between the two surveys (asthma, diabetes among men, migraine among women, coronary problems in later age). However, the problems inherent in self-reported measures of health were highlighted by the warning: 'Whether these self-reported prevalences represent true rises (as in some cases they are thought to be) or whether they are diagnostic and identification changes, can be ascertained only where there is other evidence within the Survey.'[69]

National surveys of sickness and health care usage were undertaken after the Second World War,[70] but the most reliable since the 1970s has been the GHS. (Even then, it is less than perfect because it omits those old people in institutions, whose health will tend to be poorer.) This has shown

---

[63] Office for National Statistics, *Social Focus on Older People* (1999), p. 64.

[64] Margaret Bone, Andrew C. Bebbington, Carol Jagger, Kevin Morgan and Gerry Nicolas, *Health Expectancy and Its Uses* (1995), p. 20.

[65] National Centre for Social Research, *Health Survey for England 2000. The Health of Older People. Summary of Key Findings* (2002), p. 7.

[66] Office for National Statistics, *Social Focus on Older People*, p. 69. To an extent, of course, height falls with the ageing process.

[67] B. D. Cox et al., *The Health and Lifestyle Survey* (1987).

[68] Christina R. Victor, *Health and Health Care in Later Life* (1991), p. 95.

[69] Brian D. Cox, Felicia A. Huppert and Margaret J. Whichelow (eds.), *The Health and Lifestyle Survey: Seven Years On* (1993), esp. pp. 49, 51, 54, 61, 328 (quote).

[70] For a useful summary, see Grundy, 'Health and Health Care', pp. 193–8.

a slow rise in self-reported long-standing illness for all ages between 1972 and 2000, from 21 per cent of all respondents to 32 per cent. (These responses of course vary by socio-economic status, with lower social classes reporting poorer health.) The rise could in part be explained by increasing levels of economic inactivity: 46 per cent of men and 37 per cent of women who were economically inactive reported a limiting illness in 2000, compared with 10 per cent of working men and 11 per cent of working women. However, above state pension ages there has also been no apparent improvement: 48 per cent of individuals aged 65–74 reported a long-standing illness in 1972, and 59 per cent in 1998.[71] Likewise, the Health Survey for England shows a slight deterioration in self-reported health and an increase in reported acute sickness between 1995 and 1998.[72] However, the GHS definition of 'limited long-standing illness' includes relatively minor conditions. This has led Bone *et al.* to conclude that 'there has been a relentless increase in the expectation of unhealthy life', supporting the pessimistic view that there will be a growing demand for health and social services as the population ages in the future.[73]

It should not surprise one, therefore, that health care utilisation rates have risen in Britain. The GHS shows that the proportion of adults and children who had seen a General Practitioner in the 14 days prior to interview rose from 12 per cent in 1971 to a peak of 17 per cent in 1993, and then fell slightly to 14 per cent in 2000.[74] This must derive from rising public expectations of what constitutes 'good health', exacerbated by the fact that the number of general practitioners in Britain has increased by one-third over that period.[75] Likewise, 'finished consultant episodes' in National Health Service hospitals have risen from 5,693,000 in 1981 to 8,204,000 in 2001–2 (for acute conditions):[76] this rise reflects productivity improvements, consequent upon new medical technologies, rather than a worsening of health status.[77]

[71] Office for National Statistics. Social Survey Division, *Living in Britain. Results from the 2000 General Household Survey* (2001), pp. 75–7; Office for National Statistics. Social Survey Division, *Living in Britain. Results from the 1998 General Household Survey* (2000), pp. 19, 86–7, 91. See also *Independent Inquiry into Inequalities in Health. Report* (Chairman: Sir Donald Acheson) (1998), pp. 10, 13.

[72] Department of Health, *Health and Personal Social Services Statistics. England. As at 1st June 2002* (2002), table A5.

[73] Bone *et al.*, *Health Expectancy*, p. 24.

[74] Office for National Statistics. Social Survey Division, *Living in Britain. Results from the 2000 General Household Survey*, pp. 7, 79.

[75] Office for National Statistics, *Social Trends No. 28 1998 Edition* (1998), p. 143.

[76] Office for National Statistics, *Social Trends No. 34 2004 Edition* (2004), p. 122.

[77] For example, between 1981 and 2001–2, the mean duration of bed stay in National Health Service hospitals fell from 8.4 days to 4.9.

The difference between ADL- or IADL-measured health status and self-reported health status in Britain may be explained by a number of factors: rising public expectations, improved diagnostic techniques and earlier diagnosis, an increase in the supply of medical personnel, the fact that the NHS focuses more on serious conditions (which ADLs measure) rather than minor ones (which constitute 'limited long-standing illness'), and so on. At any rate, the divergent results make it very difficult to pronounce a clear verdict on health trends.

The empirical evidence: the USA

'Overall, most signs point toward worsening health', wrote Lois Verbrugge in 1989,[78] reflecting the pessimistic view that emerged in the USA in the 1980s. As already noted, life expectancy at age 65 hardly improved in the USA until the 1960s. However, mortality declines in the 1970s and 1980s appeared to be accompanied by an increase in disability prevalence rates (except among those aged 75+),[79] and in health care utilisation rates. In 1983, only three years after Fries's original article, Robert Butler argued that there was no evidence to substantiate his claims regarding future mortality, morbidity and the need for health care: contrary to Fries, the number of very old persons was in fact increasing, morbidity rates in the older population were not improving, the proportion of the average life-span spent in chronic illness was increasing and the need for health care in later life was not diminishing.[80] Certainly, the number of centenarians in the USA has continued to increase, contrary to Fries's projections, and variability in ages of death is still pronounced (although, of course, historically it has been reduced).[81]

However, Verbrugge and others fully recognised that the appearance of deteriorating health could well be artefactual. In an interesting article, Waidmann, Bound and Schoenbaum questioned the appearance of worsening health in the 1970s followed by improving health in the 1980s, arguing that significant background factors were at work in the former

[78] Lois M. Verbrugge, 'Recent, Present and Future Health of American Adults', in L. Breslow, J. E. Fielding and L. B. Lave (eds.), *Annual Review of Public Health*, vol. 10, 1989, p. 338.

[79] Eileen M. Crimmins, Yasuhiko Saito and Sandra Reynolds, 'Further Evidence on Recent Trends in the Prevalence and Incidence of Disability Among Older Americans from Two Sources: the LSOA and the NHIS', *Journal of Gerontology: Social Sciences*, vol. 52B, no. 2, 1997, p. S59.

[80] Robert N. Butler, 'The Relation of Extended Life to Extended Employment since the Passage of Social Security in 1935', *Milbank Memorial Fund Quarterly*, vol. 61, no. 3, 1983, pp. 420–9.

[81] Wilmoth and Horiuchi, 'Rectangularisation Revisited', pp. 475–95.

decade, such as improvements in prevention and early detection, expansion of disability income maintenance programmes (which encouraged more marginal workers with pre-existing health impairments to define themselves as 'work-disabled' and leave the labour force) and a decrease in institutionalisation rates. For example, prevalence levels of self-reported hypertension rose between 1971 and 1986, caused by better and earlier clinical diagnosis. In general, the magnitude of change in health status in the 1970s was greater than could plausibly be explained by mortality declines. Waidmann, Bound and Schoenbaum argued that it was highly unlikely that mortality declines throughout the 1970s and 1980s could have produced seemingly opposed results: if the 'failure of success' scenario were correct, self-reported health would have continued to worsen.[82]

Empirical analysis supporting a more 'optimistic' position has been forthcoming recently, such as Freedman and Martin's verdict that there had been declines in functional limitations among older Americans between the mid-1980s and the mid-1990s (the smallest gains being for those aged 50–64, the largest for those aged 80+);[83] some reported disabling conditions increased in prevalence, but had become less debilitating over time.[84] In an important article published in 1997, Crimmins, Saito and Ingegneri surveyed the disabled population, using NHIS data (adjusted to take account of the changes in questionnaire wording from 1981), and found a small, but significant, increase in the level of disability in the non-institutional population between 1970 and 1980. However, between 1980 and 1990 there was little change in disability levels in most age-groups, and an actual decrease in those aged 60–9. The authors therefore found an improvement in disability-free life expectancy between 1980 and 1990. Men aged 65 could expect a further 13.0 years of life in 1970, of which 6.6 years would be disability-free; by 1990, this had risen to 15.1 years, of which 7.4 years would be disability-free.[85]

---

[82] Timothy Waidmann, John Bound and Michael Schoenbaum, 'The Illusion of Failure: Trends in the Self-Reported Health of the US Elderly', *Milbank Quarterly*, vol. 73, no. 2, 1995, pp. 253–87.

[83] Vicki A. Freedman and Linda G. Martin, 'Understanding Trends in Functional Limitations Among Older Americans', *American Journal of Public Health*, vol. 88, no. 10, 1998, pp. 1457–62.

[84] Vicki A. Freedman and Linda G. Martin, 'Contribution of Chronic Conditions to Aggregate Changes in Old-Age Functioning', *American Journal of Public Health*, vol. 90, no. 11, 2000, pp. 1755–60.

[85] Eileen M. Crimmins, Yasuhiko Saito and Dominique Ingegneri, 'Trends in Disability-Free Life Expectancy in the United States, 1970–90', *Population and Development Review*, vol. 23, no. 3, September 1997, pp. 555–72.

Conclusion: health trends in Britain and the USA

By the end of the 1990s, many commentators in Britain and the USA were observing some improvement in health status among older people – or were recognising that 'health' was such a complex, multi-dimensional concept, and its measurement riddled with methodological difficulties, that outright pessimism was not justified. Crimmins, for example, highlighted the 'mixed trends' in evidence, and argued that worsening health should not necessarily be seen as a lack of progress, but as 'an expected epidemiological stage' that might be followed by a period of health gains; indeed, there might be improvement in some health indicators, but deterioration in others.[86] Likewise, Karen Dunnell, in her brief but effective summary of UK trends in health, responded to the question 'are we healthier?' with the following succinct statement:

At a simple level, the answer could be that almost universal improvements in mortality rates and increasing life expectancy suggest that we are indeed healthier. However, surveys of reported and measured health status suggest that there is no comparable general improvement in health. In addition, several behaviours related to poor health show little signs of change. The answer to the question can only be that some things are better, some worse and some have stayed the same.[87]

If a clear verdict on health status per se is, therefore, difficult to pronounce with confidence, one needs to turn to the more specific area of disability and work-disability.

Disability and work-disability

In all advanced industrial societies, work-disability has once again become the subject of public debate: the period since the early 1970s has witnessed a rise in disability benefit claims among the working-aged – but at significantly different rates of increase – and these rises have engendered much public discussion.[88]

In Britain, economic support for disabled people is provided via a confusing mixture of benefits: some, such as incapacity benefit (before 1995, called invalidity benefit, or IVB), are contributory, National

---

[86] Eileen M. Crimmins, 'Mixed Trends in Population Health Among Older Adults', *Journal of Gerontology: Social Sciences*, vol. 51B, no. 5, 1996, S223–5.

[87] Karen Dunnell, 'Are We Healthier?', in Charlton and Murphy, *Health of Adult Britain*, p. 180.

[88] For a useful table, illustrating these rises, see Richard V. Burkhauser, Andrew J. Glenn and David C. Wittenburg, 'The Disabled Worker Tax Credit', in Virginia P. Reno, Jerry L. Mashaw and Bill Gradison (eds.), *Disability: Challenges for Social Insurance, Health Care Financing, and Labor Market Policy* (1997), p. 48.

Insurance-based, and are thus self-funding to an extent; others are contingent (such as the disability living allowance), or are means-tested (such as income support). At 1996–7 prices, expenditure on the total range of disability benefits in Britain rose from £5.4bn in 1979–80 to £22.4bn in 1997 (of which incapacity benefit made up about one-third), and the numbers claiming invalidity/incapacity benefits tripled in the twenty years to 1998.[89] By May 2002, a total of 2,365,000 people were claiming incapacity benefit.[90] In the five years to spring 1997, the number of people in Britain who wanted a job but were not seeking one because of long-term sickness or disability more than doubled, from 304,000 to 685,000.[91] In the USA, the number of people receiving disability benefits of all kinds increased from 3,652,000 in 1974 to 7,254,000 in 1994.[92] Cross-national variations in claim levels, and their rate of increase, tend to reflect variations in national labour markets, differing levels in benefits and conditions for their receipt, and background cultural factors (such as how each society wishes its disabled people to be treated). Clearly, the Netherlands has experienced a spectacular increase (despite some attempts to rein it back). By 1994, one in ten Dutch citizens of working age was in receipt of disability benefits, and the 'Dutch disease', as it has been rather contemptuously termed,[93] was arousing alarm in some quarters.

The increase in disability benefit claims has thus occurred for complex and inter-related reasons – and not simply because of a relaxation in eligibility conditions, as is often supposed. To be sure, in some countries (for example, the Netherlands), eligibility conditions have been slightly eased since the 1970s. However, this cannot be a major causal factor since claims have also risen in countries where eligibility conditions have been tightened. There is probably now a greater willingness to self-define minor conditions as 'disability', resulting from higher health expectations and a more competitive labour market. For example, sub-optimal mental health could be disguised in the predominantly blue-collar, industrial labour market of the 1950s in a variety of undemanding jobs (such as factory storekeeper); but such a condition will have a more work-disabling effect in a predominantly service-based post-industrial economy where

---

[89] Richard Berthoud, *Disability Benefits. A Review of the Issues and Options for Reform* (1998), pp. 10–11; *New Ambitions for Our Country: a New Contract for Welfare*, Cm. 3805 (1998), p. 14.

[90] Department for Work and Pensions, *Work and Pensions Statistics 2002* (2002), p. 125.

[91] Office for National Statistics, *Social Focus on the Unemployed* (1998), p. 10.

[92] Edward D. Berkowitz and Richard V. Burkhauser, 'A United States Perspective on Disability Programmes', in Leo J. M. Aarts, Richard V. Burkhauser and Philip R. de Jong, *Curing the Dutch Disease. An International Perspective on Disability Policy Reform* (1996), p. 75.

[93] Aarts *et al.*, *Curing*.

inter-personal 'soft skills' are important. Undoubtedly, greater levels of mental and physical stress are being experienced by the whole of society: Tania Burchardt argues that this could explain the fact that the prevalence of disability in Britain has risen among both those in work and those not in work, in different age-groups and across the range of impairment severity.[94]

However, a major causal factor has undoubtedly been economic restructuring and consequent shifts in sectoral labour market demand. This has led to a shake-out of labour from long-established, declining industries (notably, manufacturing, mining and construction), in which were concentrated workers who were older and less 'work-fit'; economic growth has been in the service and financial sectors, with younger and more feminised workforces.[95] These displaced workers tended to be doubly disadvantaged by physical or mental impairments and by limited skills or educational levels[96] – those whom a leading US researcher has termed a 'contingent labor force'.[97] Since the 1970s, the number of jobseekers in the UK and US economies has increased, consequent upon the 'baby boom' generation reaching working age, the growth of part-time jobs, the increased number of married women working, and changes in family structure.[98] Employers in the 1980s and 1990s were thus able to be more choosy in their selection of employees, and those with physical or mental disabilities increasingly found themselves marginalised.[99] Older male workers have not been the only ones affected: young, unskilled men (particularly those from ethnic minorities) have also found greater difficulty gaining jobs. Hence between 1977 and 1997 in Britain the economic inactivity rates of men aged 16–19 remained the same, at just over 35 per cent, despite improving economic conditions.[100] Indeed, between 1984 and 1996 the gap between disabled and non-disabled employment rates in Britain grew faster for the 25–49 age-group than for the 50+ age-group.[101] All in all, the transition to a post-industrial economy has created a sharper polarisation between labour market 'winners' and 'losers'.

[94] Tania Burchardt, *Enduring Economic Exclusion. Disabled People, Income and Work* (2000), pp. 35, 41.
[95] Edward H. Yelin, 'The Recent History and Immediate Future of Employment Among Persons with Disabilities', *Milbank Quarterly*, vol. 69, supplements 1/2, 1991, pp. 135–7.
[96] Jerry L. Mashaw, 'Findings of the Disability Policy Panel', in Reno, Mashaw and Gradison, *Disability*, p. 26.
[97] Yelin, 'Recent History', pp. 135–6.
[98] Leo J. M. Aarts, Richard V. Burkhauser and Philip R. de Jong, 'Introduction and Overview', in Aarts *et al.*, *Curing*, p. 2.
[99] Berthoud, *Disability Benefits*, pp. 32–3.
[100] Christina Beatty and Stephen Fothergill, *The Detached Male Workforce* (1999), p. 6.
[101] Burchardt, *Enduring Economic Exclusion*, p. 17.

Downward pressure on social security expenditure has led to a growing apprehension over the rise in disability benefit claims since the 1970s, and demands that more 'work-obligation' should be attached to receipt of such benefits via 'welfare to work' provisions. In one sense, this continues the tradition of assisting the registered disabled back to work that, in Britain, began with the 1944 Disabled Persons (Employment) Act and followed with the introduction of the Disability Working Allowance in 1992 and the 1995 Disability Discrimination Act (although these measures are much criticised for their ineffectiveness). However, it also reflects the growth of workfarism. A stricter medical test was introduced in 1995, when incapacity benefit replaced invalidity benefit. The 1997 Labour government adopted a more proactive approach, consisting of both 'carrots' and 'sticks'. The rights of disabled people were strengthened via initiatives such as the Disability Rights Task Force and Disability Rights Commission, and anti-discrimination legislation in Britain is now being made more effective; but this was balanced by the New Deal for Disabled People and other policies to encourage working by disabled people.[102] Under New Labour, disabled people must attend an interview with a 'personal adviser', but are not yet obliged to take a suggested job if they do not wish to. It remains to be seen whether more compulsion will be introduced in the future. In the USA, the 1990 Americans with Disabilities Act requires employers to make reasonable accommodations for workers with handicaps,[103] and there has been some development of in-work benefits. Particular concern has been expressed over the fact that the pathway into disability benefit tends to be, for older men, a 'one-way street': recipients are likely to remain claiming such benefits until they become eligible for retirement pensions, becoming the hard core of the 'discouraged workers'. Hence in Britain, disabled people of working age are about four times as likely to be economically inactive as those without a disability.[104] What is often forgotten is that they experience substantial labour market disadvantages in an increasingly competitive economy.[105]

However, this is much more than a fiscal concern. As indicated in previous chapters, the last ten years have seen Western governments espouse economic policies that are designed to maximise labour supply and enhance human capital. An important reason for concern over the so-called 'disability explosion' has therefore been that disability benefits

[102] *New Ambitions*, ch. 6.
[103] Richard V. Burkhauser, 'US Policy Toward Workers With Handicaps', in Olivia S. Mitchell (ed.), *As the Workforce Ages. Costs, Benefits and Policy Challenges* (1993), p. 214.
[104] Office for National Statistics, *Social Focus on the Unemployed*, p. 18.
[105] Burchardt, *Enduring Economic Exclusion*, p. 61.

have removed marginal workers who could form a supply of cheap labour for the new, hypercasualised and peripheral jobs that are developing alongside the high-tech, high-skilled 'core' jobs.

These concerns – and particularly the labour-supply ones – led to a growing critique from free-market economists in the 1980s over the alleged 'work disincentive' effects of 'over-generous' disability benefits. As one American commentator put it, 'The disability insurance program offers sizeable incentives for workers with limited disabilities to report more severe ones ... poor health provides a socially acceptable explanation for failure to work full time'.[106]

In small part, this critique was correct: over at least the past 100 years, older workers forced into early retirement have tended to use ill-health to mask joblessness. Being made redundant, or just having to survive in an increasingly competitive labour market, will tend to encourage a more critical assessment of one's own health and working capacity. To this, the existence of disability benefits may add a small incentive effect: for example, the high level of disability benefit claims in the Netherlands has been partly a product of that country's higher benefit:wages replacement rate (compared, say, to Britain);[107] again, the fact that incapacity benefit in Britain is not means-tested appears to act as a slight incentive to claim it rather than income support. However, such an excessively 'rational choice', behavioural analysis rests upon the unrealistic assumption that older workers possess the power to 'choose' their precise moment of early retirement, and it ignores the economic and labour market context. There is abundant historical evidence (notably, the example of the Second World War) showing that a tight labour market and a re-stimulation of the old heavy industries would draw back into employment many of those currently considered 'unemployable' through ill-health, disability and deficient skills; and today, among all the economically inactive in Britain, disabled people are more likely than non-disabled people to want a job.[108] Indeed, the Blair government has used this very argument to justify its more proactive workfarist policies, claiming that up to 1,000,000 disabled people would like to return to work if they were given the right assistance.[109]

[106] Gary Burtless, 'Introduction and Summary', in Burtless, *Work, Health, and Income*, p. 8. See also Martin Feldstein, 'The Social Security Explosion', *The Public Interest*, no. 81, Fall 1985, pp. 94–106; Donald O. Parsons, 'The Decline in Male Labor Force Participation', *Journal of Political Economy*, vol. 88, no. 3, June 1980, p. 123.

[107] Susan Lonsdale and Mansel Aylward, 'A United Kingdom Perspective on Disability Policy', in Aarts *et al.*, *Curing*, p. 112.

[108] 'Disabled People and the Labour Market', *Labour Market Trends*, vol. 109, no. 12, Dec. 2001, p. 542.

[109] *New Ambitions*, p. 52.

The increase in disability benefit claims since the 1970s in all advanced industrial societies has also been in part the result of governmental willingness to use disability benefits to conceal the real level of unemployment, against a background of massive economic restructuring and workforce downsizing. For example, in Britain, the policy of the Conservative governments in the 1980s was to encourage such older, displaced workers to claim disability benefits, in order to massage the unemployment figures (which had become politically embarrassing). Trades unions supported this policy, since it redistributed available jobs to younger workers; employers found it an easy and cheap way of dispensing with unproductive or redundant workers. As Mark Priestley reminds us, categories like 'disability' and 'retirement' have historically been used to control labour supply.[110] Thus in Britain in 1998, 7 per cent of the working-age population were claiming benefits on grounds of incapacity, and 5 per cent as unemployed; some argued that the true level of unemployment was therefore 12 per cent.[111] Again, although disability benefit claims are more common in the upper age ranges, this concentration has not increased, despite the falling economic activity rates of older men: men aged 55–64 accounted for 60 per cent of earnings-replacement benefit recipients in 1978–9, and 56 per cent in 1992–3.[112] Thus unemployment at all ages has been a causal factor. Finally, the 'welfare as incentive' model glosses over the fact that disabled people on benefits suffer a low standard of living;[113] if there is an apparent preference for non-working, it is only because available jobs are unattractive, low-paid or hard to find in particular localities.

Several points must be borne in mind when considering the complex and symbiotic relationship between self-defined health status and labour market demand. First, a distinction must be made between work-disability and disability per se. All disability is the gap between personal capability and the requirements of particular tasks: the World Health Organization's International Classification thus defined disability as 'any restriction or lack ... of ability to perform an activity in the manner or within the range considered normal for a human being'.[114]

---

[110] Mark Priestley, 'Adults Only: Disability, Social Policy and the Life Course', *Journal of Social Policy*, vol. 29, pt. 3, July 2000, pp. 426–7.

[111] 'Analysis: Disability', *Guardian*, 24 Nov. 1998.

[112] Berthoud, *Disability Benefits*, p. 30.

[113] Jean Martin and Amanda White, *The Financial Circumstances of Disabled Adults Living in Private Households* (1988).

[114] Quoted in Lois M. Verbrugge, 'The Iceberg of Disability', in Sidney M. Stahl (ed.), *The Legacy of Longevity. Health and Health Care in Later Life* (1990), p. 56.

Disability is thus a continuum, from very severe conditions to very slight ones: definitions involve setting a threshold, and relating functional ability to the practical requirements of an individual's 'normal' environment.[115] On the other hand, work-disability is more specific, being the inability to perform particular job-related tasks. There are two very obvious elements in the equation – the health of the individual, and the demands of the job. As a leading analyst of the problem summarises it: 'Work disability exists only when an impairment, in conjunction with the person's other abilities, the demands of work, and the broader environment, make her or him unable to perform the tasks of work. Consequently, changes in the broader environment affect the prevalence of work disability and the demands placed on disability benefit programs.'[116]

An individual's self-defined health status thus interacts with the work environment in a highly complex way. Measuring either in isolation is difficult enough; measuring the interaction between the two may be well-nigh impossible. Labour market demand is constantly changing, in that there is always change in both the specific requirements of a job (for example, through the introduction of new technology) and the economic background (which can be affected by global economic forces over which the individual has no control). As Martin Neil Baily succinctly puts it, 'The ability of the population to perform a given job interacts with the demands of the jobs that the economy provides. Exogenous changes in technology can bring about shifts in job requirements, and endogenous responses by employers to the capabilities of the work force can do the same.'[117]

The most controversial variable that may influence self-defined work-disability is, of course, the inducement effect of an early exit incentive or a disability benefit scheme, but their interaction with other factors will be complex, so that 'identical health impairments will produce different retirement decisions depending upon financial resources, and ... identical financial resources will produce different decisions depending on health conditions'.[118]

Labour market conditions may also exert not an overt but a subtle 'background effect', which will influence judgements by professional gate-keepers (notably, doctors) regarding the degree of work-disability. Thus Lonsdale and Aylward correctly observe that 'a labour market consideration may not necessarily have to be explicitly articulated to have an

[115] Jean Martin, Howard Meltzer and David Eliot, *The Prevalence of Disability Among Adults* (1988), pp. xi, 6.
[116] Mashaw, 'Findings of the Disability Policy Panel', p. 26.
[117] Baily, 'Aging and the Ability', p. 90.
[118] Herbert S. Parnes, 'The Retirement Decision', in Borus *et al.*, *Older Worker*, p. 136.

effect'.[119] Finally, temporal comparisons are fraught with difficulties: experiments may be conducted by different methodologies, new technology alters the labour process, there may be increasing heterogeneity in functional ability among the subjects (making averages misleading), and so on.[120]

Second, recorded disability in general is highly age-specific. In Britain in the late 1960s, it was found that there were just over 3,000,000 people aged 16+ in private households in Britain who suffered some degree of physical, mental or sensory impairment; of these, 1,750,000 were aged 65+, and fewer than 100,000 were aged under 30.[121] The Office of Population Censuses and Surveys study of 1984 – using a definition with a fairly low threshold – found that, of the 6,000,000 persons in Britain with at least one form of disability, 69 per cent were aged 60+ and only 31 per cent were aged 16–59.[122] A more recent survey, published in 1998, estimated the total number of disabled adults in private households in Britain as c. 8,600,000, of which c. 4,830,000 – or 56 per cent – were aged 60+.[123] Perhaps as many as one in five of the working-age population in private households was disabled in mid-2000.[124] This apparent rise in numbers cannot necessarily be taken as real: it of course reflects changing definitions. However, the concentration among older adults is consistent across all studies. Only a minority of disabled people are of conventional working age: in Britain, the majority are over retirement age, and live on retirement pensions (perhaps supplemented by the attendance allowance).[125] Contrary to the popular image of a disabled person as wheelchair-bound and young, disability is much more a condition of old age. The form taken by this kind of disability is thus the chronic illness associated with the gradual 'wearing out' of the body. (The connection between morbidity, disability and mortality is demonstrated by the fact that, in extreme old age, disability rates fall, since by then mortality has winnowed out those with the most health-impaired lives.)[126] The breakdown of medical conditions by age reflects this. In the USA, the majority of disability benefit recipients are aged 50–64, with circulatory disorders, musculoskeletal diseases, mental disorders and neoplasms accounting for some 70 per cent of all

[119] Lonsdale and Aylward, 'United Kingdom Perspective', p. 111.
[120] Harold Sheppard, 'Work and Retirement', in Robert H. Binstock and Ethel Shanas (eds.), *Handbook of Aging and the Social Sciences* (1976), p. 294.
[121] Amelia I. Harris, *Handicapped and Impaired in Great Britain, Pt. I* (1970), p. 59.
[122] Martin, Meltzer and Eliot, *Prevalence*, p. 27.
[123] Cited in Berthoud, *Disability Benefits*, p. 5.
[124] Breda Twomey, 'Disability and the Labour Market: Results from the Summer 2000 LFS', *Labour Market Trends*, vol. 109, no. 5, May 2001, p. 241.
[125] Berthoud, *Disability Benefits*, p. 7.   [126] Hodkinson, 'Active Life Expectancy', p. 49.

conditions; in younger recipients, mental disorders predominate.[127] Disability at younger ages is more commonly the result of accident (often a road accident), injury (for example, a sports injury) or congenital birth defect. Interestingly, disability rights activists, positing the 'social model' of disability which locates the problem of disability in the negative attitudes of the non-disabled, are likely to be this latter group.[128] Hence, disability rights activists tend to reject the medical sociologists' view that disability is a form of illness.[129]

A third point to note is that the attempts hitherto made to define and classify disability have been only partially successful. As has been shown, social security-based definitions are strongly affected by eligibility criteria and labour market conditions; and they underestimate the prevalence of disability in women.[130] Mobility and frailty indicators are subject to differences in classification country-by-country and over time. In the 1970s, the World Health Organization (WHO) tried to impose some definitional uniformity on this complex, multi-faceted problem: it came up with a threefold classification into 'impairment' (parts or systems of the body which do not function properly, such as hearing or sight), 'disability' (restrictions or lack of ability to undertake activities considered normal – including work) and 'handicap' (the disadvantage experienced by an individual as a result of the impairment or disability).[131] However, these notionally accurate categories have been criticised for overlapping greatly.[132] And the disability rights lobby, which grew in organisational strength in the 1980s and 1990s, has argued that the WHO categories are political constructs, fashioned by 'expert', medicalised definitions in a 'normal' society where disability is labelled and stigmatised.[133]

The prevalence of disability per se in a population is therefore likely to be the result of a number of factors: its demographic structure, particularly its average age; its educational, race, marital and socio-economic status; economic conditions; the availability and value of disability benefits; expectations of 'good health'; and so on.[134] Hence the ageing of a population will by itself increase disability prevalence rates,[135] and improved rates

[127] Berkowitz and Burkhauser, 'A United States Perspective', p. 82. For similar UK statistics, see Department for Work and Pensions, *Work and Pensions Statistics 2002*, p. 127.

[128] For example, Mike Oliver, *The Politics of Disablement* (1990).

[129] Michael Oliver, *Understanding Disability. From Theory to Practice* (1996), pp. 33–4.

[130] Susan Reisine and Judith Fifield, 'Expanding the Definition of Disability: Implications for Planning, Policy and Research', *Milbank Quarterly*, vol. 70, no. 3, 1992, p. 505.

[131] Victor, *Health*, pp. 60–1.   [132] McCallum, 'Health and Ageing', pp. 60–1.

[133] David Field, 'Chronic Illness and Physical Disability', in Steve Taylor and David Field (eds.), *Sociology of Health and Health Care* (1997 edn), pp. 128–30.

[134] Wolfe and Haveman, 'Trends', pp. 53–61.

[135] Burchardt, *Enduring Economic Exclusion*, p. 34.

of survival into later adulthood will also increase the proportion of 'health-impaired' older workers.[136] There are also many different types of disability: individuals' own personal circumstances are complex,[137] meaning that help with labour market re-entry must be precisely tailor-made, and there are considerable flows in and out of 'the disabled state': only a small proportion of working-age people who experience disability are long-term disabled (though they make up a high proportion of all disabled at any one time), but a large proportion of people experience a spell of disability at some point in their working lives.[138]

As indicated above, work-disability is also complex in its causes, but labour market effects are very strong. Hence Yelin and Katz argue that work-disability needs to be explained by the nature of work itself: the individual work histories of disabled people, shifts in the overall (and sectoral) demand for labour, changes in the nature of work, and so on.[139] More recently, studies have demonstrated that the growth of disability benefit claims in Britain may be, as Berthoud argues, 'part of a much wider and systematic shift in employment patterns, rather than a characteristic of the particular benefit under consideration'.[140] Thus Holmes, Lynch and Molho found receipt of invalidity benefit closely associated, in men, with: being older; having a history of claims for sickness benefit; living in areas of poor housing, unfavourable employment structures, and high unemployment (notably Wales); having been registered as unemployed; having been on low pay in the last job; and so forth. Likewise, married women were significantly more likely to come onto invalidity benefit if they lived in areas of high female unemployment and poor job opportunities.[141] An additional factor is increasing programme duration. This alone will increase numbers since the 'outflows' from disability benefit reliance and into employment tend to be blocked (especially in areas of poor job prospects).[142] However, it may prove to be the case, as Beatty and Fothergill suggest, that in the future the numbers of

---

[136] Feldman, 'Work Ability', p. 434; Wolfe and Haveman, 'Trends', p. 53.

[137] Sue Yeandle, *Personal Histories: the Context for Joblessness, Disability and Retirement* (1999), p. 17.

[138] Tania Burchardt, 'The Dynamics of Being Disabled', *Journal of Social Policy*, vol. 29, pt. 4, Oct. 2000, pp. 645–68.

[139] Yelin and Katz, 'Making Work More Central', pp. 615–16. For the UK, see David Piachaud, 'Disability, Retirement and Unemployment of Older Men', *Journal of Social Policy*, vol. 15, pt. 2, April 1986, pp. 145–62.

[140] Berthoud, *Disability Benefits*, p. 32.

[141] Phil Holmes, Mauricea Lynch and Ian Molho, 'An Econometric Analysis of the Growth in the Numbers Claiming Invalidity Benefit: An Overview', *Journal of Social Policy*, vol. 20, no. 1, Jan. 1991, pp. 87–105.

[142] Lonsdale and Aylward, 'United Kingdom Perspective', p. 102.

work-disabled may diminish as the last generation of de-industrialised blue-collar manual workers moves into retirement age.[143]

The geographical distribution of working-age disability in Britain reflects economic conditions, with the highest levels being found in the North-East of England and Wales (where there was a concentration of heavy industries such as coal mining and heavy manufacturing), and the lowest in the South-East.[144] A map of disability in Britain thus fits exactly with one of unemployment and economic inactivity: Beatty and Fothergill point out that there is 'an uncanny resemblance between the geography of sickness-related claimants and the geography of unemployment-related claimants'.[145] While these traditional blue-collar industries may have 'worn out' workers relatively rapidly, thus giving rise to more health problems,[146] the fact that the highest levels of work-disability occur in areas which had been dependent upon old, manufacturing industries now in recession indicates that such benefits are being used by de-industrialised, unemployed men who observe their local labour market offerings and conclude – correctly – that there is little realistic chance of their ever working again. For example, Beatty and Fothergill found that, in Barnsley, 40 per cent of long-term incapacity benefit claimants had worked in the coal mining industry. Again, in 2002 the proportions of men aged 50–64 who were jobless and claiming sickness-related benefits was 36 per cent in Manchester, 38 per cent in Liverpool, 44 per cent in Glasgow and 51 per cent in Merthyr Tydfil.[147] Sickness and disability are now the most likely reasons for male (particularly older male) economic inactivity in Britain. It is clear, therefore, that the apparent increase in work-disability in Britain and the USA is the product of several inter-related factors, one of the most important of which is the massive economic restructuring that has occurred since the 1970s, removing heavy industrial jobs and effectively de-skilling many older men.

Conclusion

This four-chapter section has addressed the difficult question: if older workers are healthier than ever, 'could' or 'should' they remain in work

---

[143] Christina Beatty and Stephen Fothergill, *Incapacity Benefit and Unemployment* (1999), p. 45.

[144] 'Disabled People and the Labour Market', p. 541.

[145] Beatty and Fothergill, *Incapacity Benefit*, p. 15.

[146] 'Disabled People and the Labour Market', p. 541.

[147] Christina Beatty and Stephen Fothergill, 'Moving People Into Jobs. Jobcentre Plus, New Deal and the Job Shortfall for the Over 50s' (unpublished paper, Centre for Regional Economic and Social Research, Sheffield Hallam University, 2004), p. 12.

longer? Over at least the past 100 years, there has been a lively debate on this very question, with many attempts to explore the complex interaction between self-defined health status and labour market demand. Much research was conducted in the 1950s in both Britain and America (considered in the next chapter) over the question of how the working life could be extended (given that health status and working capacity seemed to have improved), and how the barriers to the employment of older people (including the alleged age discriminatory practices of employers) could be removed.

However, with the slow unfolding of the epidemiological transition, 'health' has become an increasingly multi-dimensional, elusive concept, affected by many variables external to the individual. The 'compression of morbidity' debate shows that answering even the simple question 'are we healthier than in the past?' is extremely difficult. The measurement of working capacity is even more problematic. As has been argued earlier, working capacity consists of two elements: the functional ability of an individual, and the functional requirements of a job. There is a complex set of variables on each side, and a symbiotic relationship between each set of variables. On the one hand, individuals' self-definitions of health are influenced by factors such as prevailing health expectations, medical technology, diagnostic techniques, the availability of health care, thresholds for self-referral to a doctor, doctors' thresholds for referral to specialist care, and so on. On the other hand, an individual's working environment will be affected by factors such as market demand for the product (local, national and global), new technology, workforce rationalisation and downsizing, the performance of rival firms, and, crucially, the existence of a job.

In answering the question '*could* older workers stay on in work?' one thus becomes trapped within a philosophical conundrum analogous to Hobbes's 'state of nature' or Rawls's 'original position': if we cannot judge health status and work-disability independent of labour market demand, we cannot decide whether or not 'working capacity' has improved sufficiently to justify the re-enlistment of older males into the workforce. The question '*should* older workers stay on in work?' is, on the other hand, a political and moral question relating to distributive justice. We must bear in mind that the question is increasingly being asked at a time when new post-industrial labour markets are demanding an expansion of labour supply. The answer to it depends upon how willing a society is to support its unwaged, dependent populations.

Part IV

America's Age Discrimination in Employment Act

Introduction

In 1967, America passed its historic Age Discrimination in Employment Act (the ADEA). With subsequent amendments, this Act has outlawed age discrimination in employment (with some exceptions) and has abolished mandatory retirement for all but a few stipulated occupations. It stands as the most comprehensive legislative action against age discrimination, and is often referred to in the British debate. This two-chapter section will trace the long-term origins of the Act (going back to the 1920s), including the lively debate on age discrimination and the problems of older workers that took place in the 1950s and 1960s. It will then consider the reasons behind the 1967 Act – itself something of an aberration in a country with far less employment protection than Britain. The operation of the Act from 1967 to the present will then be examined, and its 'success' in relation to its notional aims will be evaluated. An examination of the ADEA tells us much about the dilemmas and difficulties of action against age discrimination.

The spread of retirement in the USA

In common with all advanced industrial societies, the United States of America experienced a steady fall in the labour force participation rates[1] of men aged 65+ from the late nineteenth century to the 1990s. Basically, retirement has slowly spread down the age structure. Bearing in mind all the caveats about using census data as an indicator of actual labour force participation,[2] we can see a steady downward trajectory in the labour force participation rates of men aged 65+ between 1890 and 1970 (Table 8.1).

---

[1] In the USA the term 'labor force participation rate' is used where 'economic activity rate' is used in the UK.

[2] In the UK, census data both over- and under-recorded the actual labour force participation of older men. See John Macnicol, *The Politics of Retirement in Britain 1878–1948* (1998), pp. 24–5. Some scholars have suggested that US census data under-estimated the extent of

Table 8.1. *The labour force participation of men aged 65+ in the USA, numbers and rates, 1890–1970.*

Year	Number	Rate (per cent)
1890	846,000	68.3
1900	987,000	63.1
1920	1,383,000	55.6
1930	1,795,000	54.0
1940	1,838,000	41.8
1950	2,373,000	41.4
1960	2,231,000	30.5
1970	2,092,000	24.8

Source: US Department of Commerce and US Bureau of the Census, *Historical Statistics of the United States. Colonial Times to 1970, Part 1* (1975), pp. 131–2. The year 1910 does not appear on the original of this table.

The labour force participation rates of men aged 45–64 dropped only slightly in this period, from 92.0 per cent in 1890 to 87.2 per cent in 1970, though their numbers increased from 3,937,000 to 17,434,000 as a consequence of the expansion of the total US workforce. By contrast, women aged 65+ increased their low labour force participation rates only very slightly, from 7.6 per cent in 1890 to 10.0 per cent in 1970.

Like their colleagues in other societies, American social historians have debated the reasons for the spread of modern 'jobless' retirement. It is beyond the scope of this study to explore this debate in depth. As noted in a previous chapter, some favour explanations that place more emphasis on declining labour market demand[3] – implying that, initially, retirement was caused by structural economic and labour force changes – while others stress supply-side factors that made the 'retirement decision' one of individual choice, such as the federal pension system established by the 1935 Social Security Act,[4] rising levels of personal wealth,[5] a desire for leisure at

true retirement before 1930, and that therefore the labour force participation rates of older US men remained relatively unchanged between 1870 and 1930. For a discussion, see: Roger L. Ransome and Richard Sutch, 'The Labor of Older Americans: Retirement of Men On and Off the Job, 1870–1937', *Journal of Economic History*, vol. 46, no. 1, Mar. 1986, pp. 1–30; Carole Haber and Brian Gratton, *Old Age and the Search for Security. An American Social History* (1994), p. 13; Dora L. Costa, *The Evolution of Retirement. An American Economic History, 1880–1990* (1998), pp. 7–9.

[3] See, for example: William Graebner, *A History of Retirement. The Meaning and Function of an American Institution, 1885–1978* (1980); Judith C. Hushbeck, *Old and Obsolete. Age Discrimination and the American Worker, 1860–1920* (1989).

[4] Haber and Gratton, *Old Age*.

[5] Costa, *Evolution*.

the end of the working life, or the early retirement inducements introduced by employers since the 1970s.

Old age as a social problem

American historians of old age are thus in considerable dispute over the exact causes and timing of the spread of modern mass retirement. There has also been a minor debate over the veracity of contemporary accounts of the economic plight of America's aged. Some revisionist historians have argued that social reformers of the 1920s and 1930s exaggerated the impoverishment of older people, either because they were genuinely mistaken or for political reasons.[6] There is even the suggestion that 'European ideas' were imported into the USA by such reformers, and threatened the 'traditional American values' of 'thrift, self-reliance and the market system'.[7]

However, social observers in the first half of the twentieth century were in little doubt that the economic circumstances of older people were worsening relative to the rest of society, and it was from this that interest in age discrimination grew. As far back as the late nineteenth century, it began to be noticed that significant new developments were rendering the older worker industrially obsolete, surplus to requirements and 'worn out' at an earlier age: population was migrating to urban areas from rural communities (where workers had been able to move to lighter, less demanding occupations as they aged – particularly if they owned the land upon which they worked); industry was becoming more concentrated in larger units of production, with impersonal, hierarchically structured and bureaucratically run workforces; artisans and craftsmen found themselves de-skilled by new mass-production methods, and were being forced to join the ranks of waged labourers in factories; the labour process became more specialised and intensive; technological innovation was leading to a 'speeding up' of production methods; and older workers were suffering labour force displacement in increasing numbers, often by enforced retirement not of their choice.[8]

These growing numbers of 'worn-out' older workers had come to the notice of social reformers. In a study published in 1912, Lee Welling

---

[6] See, for example, Haber and Gratton, *Old Age*, pp. 133–4. Such assertions rest upon the bold claim that the retrospective analysis of economic evidence can disprove the verdicts of contemporaries. They also cannot explain the appearance of senior citizen movements in the 1930s, notably the Townsend Movement.

[7] Carolyn L. Weaver, *The Crisis in Social Security. Economic and Political Origins* (1982), pp. 35–6.

[8] For an excellent summary, see Hushbeck, *Old and Obsolete*.

Squirer estimated that some 1,250,000 of the 4,000,000 US citizens aged 65+ were dependent upon public and private charity: they were the 'worn-out, indigent veterans of the industrial army of the United States'.[9] In *Misery and its Causes* (1909), Edward T. Devine observed that employers were allowed to 'scrap' their older workers much in the same way that they 'scrapped' outmoded machinery. Devine concluded: 'It has been in this respect a callous age, that it has not recognised that such rapid wearing out of human lives as does take place should be a burden upon the industry in which it occurs rather than upon charity or upon wives and children.'[10] Many of this generation of social reformers were advocates of social insurance on the European model. Hence Isaac Rubinow discussed 'the old man's problem in modern industry', arguing that 'economic old age' now arrived much earlier than 'physiologic old age', and that federal social insurance via old age pensions would help relieve the growing problem of old age dependency.[11] Rubinow campaigned actively for a federal social security system, as did Abraham Epstein, author of a remarkably thorough survey of the conditions of older people, *Facing Old Age* (1922).[12] (Epstein was instrumental in founding the American Association for Social Security in 1927.) Other commentators noted that even middle-aged men were becoming 'old before their time', and that their employment position was increasingly precarious:[13] for example, a Pennsylvania Commission on Old Age Pensions of 1918–19 specifically investigated the apparent decline in working capacity of workers aged 40+.[14] It seemed paradoxical that new labour-saving machinery, which should have lengthened the working life, was in fact shortening it, so that the industrial worker was 'old and worn-out' at an age when the farmer was still productive: there also seemed to be 'a very widespread and intense prejudice against the employment of older workers'.[15]

Despite these concerns, very little was done for America's aged population until the late 1930s.[16] Most had to suffer their poverty in stoical silence, relying as best they could on families, neighbours, charities and

---

[9] Lee Welling Squirer, *Old Age Dependency in the United States: a Complete Survey of the Pension Movement* (1912), pp. 3–4.

[10] Edward T. Devine, *Misery and its Causes* (1909), p. 130.

[11] I. M. Rubinow, *Social Insurance* (1913), ch. 20.

[12] Abraham Epstein, *Facing Old Age: A Study of Old Age Dependency in the United States and Old Age Pensions* (1922).

[13] Hushbeck, *Old and Obsolete*, p. 122.   [14] Epstein, *Facing Old Age*, p. 16.

[15] Louis I. Dublin, *Health and Wealth. A Survey of the Economics of World Health* (1928), pp. 159–61.

[16] The exception was the federal pension system for military veterans, which by the 1920s was costing $260,000,000. Weaver, *Crisis*, p. 31.

almshouses.[17] Research studies on the older worker were remarkably few in number.[18] However, one estimate was that, in the late 1920s, 30 per cent of those aged 65+ were dependent upon others for support (mainly their own relatives and children).[19] (This problem appears to have aroused considerable concern in the early 1930s.)[20] Yet these families could ill afford such support: the Brookings Institution calculated that three-fifths of US families in 1929 earned less than $2,000 per annum.[21] By 1929, old age pensions were paid by a mere eleven states; only 1,000 recipients shared a total of $222,000.[22] These schemes tended to be administered with brutally strict eligibility criteria: for example, a household means test usually operated, and a pension would not be paid if there were any surviving children who were judged capable of rendering support.[23] By 1932, seventeen states had old age pension laws: yet about 73 per cent of state pensioners (receiving 87 per cent of total pension expenditure) were to be found in only three relatively wealthy states – California, Massachusetts and New York.[24] The economic recession of the 1930s placed an even greater strain upon such familial and charitable support. A survey by the Social Security Board in 1937 put the level of reliance on others as even higher, using a broader definition of 'dependency' to include the newly-introduced federal old age assistance: nearly 65 per cent of the 7,816,000 people in the US aged 65+ were judged to be 'dependent' upon public assistance, federal assistance, private charity, almshouses and – principally – friends or relatives.[25] By the 1930s, the pattern of the twentieth century had become established: older workers suffered only slightly higher rates of unemployment than their younger counterparts; but once unemployed,

[17] W. Andrew Achenbaum, *Social Security: Visions and Revisions* (1986), pp. 14–15.

[18] An exception was Solomon Barkin, *The Older Worker in Industry: a Study of New York State Manufacturing Industries* (1933).

[19] Estimate by Abraham Epstein, cited in Abraham Holtzman, 'Analysis of Old Age Politics in the United States', *Journal of Gerontology*, vol. 9, no. 1, Jan. 1954, p. 59.

[20] 'Extent, Distribution and Causes of Old-Age Dependency', *Monthly Labor Review*, vol. 30, no. 4, April 1930, pp. 9–23; Mary Conyngton, 'Extent and Distribution of Old-Age Dependency in the United States', *Monthly Labor Review*, vol. 38, no. 1, Jan. 1934, pp. 1–10.

[21] Holtzman, 'Analysis', p. 58.

[22] James T. Patterson, *America's Struggle Against Poverty 1900–1994* (1994), p. 29.

[23] See, for example: Alton A. Linford, *Old Age Assistance in Massachusetts* (1949), ch. 3; Jackson K. Putnam, *Old-Age Politics in California. From Richardson to Reagan* (1970), pp. 9–10.

[24] Jill Quadagno, *The Transformation of Old Age Security. Class and Politics in the American Welfare State* (1988), p. 72; Florence E. Parker, 'Experience Under State Old-Age Pension Acts in 1933', *Monthly Labor Review*, vol. 39, no. 2, August 1934, pp. 255–72; Weaver, *Crisis*, pp. 60–1.

[25] 'Economic Status of the Aged', *Monthly Labor Review*, vol. 46, no. 6, June 1938, pp. 1348–9.

they found it increasingly difficult to gain re-employment and were likely to become 'discouraged workers'. In April 1940, for example, 14 per cent of workers aged 45–64 were unemployed, compared with 12 per cent of those aged 25–44; but 54 per cent of the older group had been unemployed for six months or longer, more than three times the proportion of the younger group.[26]

The social and economic problems of older workers received little attention from governments. For much of the first half of the twentieth century, American capitalism flourished in an almost totally unregulated labour market. The victories won by labour unions tended to be at local or firm level, with the federal government reluctant to become involved. As Paul Burstein has perceptively observed, American culture contains an unresolved conflict between egalitarian ideals and the reality of substantial discrimination[27] – what Gunnar Myrdal, in the context of race, called the 'American dilemma'. Discriminations based upon race, gender and age were little addressed.

The main developments at federal level took place in the mid-1930s, with the launching of President Franklin D. Roosevelt's New Deal. As is well known, the Wall Street crash of 1929 and subsequent recession in the 1930s were traumatic for American confidence, appearing to call into question the whole basis of free-market capitalism. The official unemployment figure was 12,800,000 in 1933, equivalent to 25 per cent of the labour force; the true figure was probably nearer 15,000,000. Even in 1939, some 9,700,000 Americans were recorded as unemployed. In response to this economic crisis, Roosevelt's New Deal combined reflationary, job-creation measures with new social insurance schemes. Included in the 1935 Social Security Act was old age insurance and old age assistance: after a brief qualifying period, the first federally supervised social insurance pensions were paid out in 1940. Even then, only 20 per cent of America's population aged 65+ were initially covered. (Old age assistance was payable from 1936 and was the major source of support for the retired until the increase in social security benefits and coverage that took place in 1950; but old age assistance levels varied greatly from state to state.) This provision of 'old age security' was in part an attempt to remove older workers from industry and re-distribute their jobs to the young unemployed.[28] Interestingly, a mandatory retirement condition had been

---

[26] Ewan Clague, 'Labor Force Trends in the United States', *Journal of Gerontology*, vol. 7, no. 1, Jan. 1952, p. 95.

[27] Paul Burstein, *Discrimination, Jobs and Politics. The Struggle for Equal Opportunity in the United States Since the New Deal* (1985), pp. 1–2.

[28] Graebner, *History of Retirement*, pp. 184–90.

considered for receipt of old age insurance; it was abandoned, but amendments in 1939 set an earnings limit (thereafter termed the 'retirement test'), which amounted to the same thing.[29]

In the area of employment protection, some minimal advances were made via the 1926 Railway Labor Act, the 1935 National Labor Relations Act (which prohibited discrimination against members of labour unions) and the 1938 Fair Labor Standards Act.[30] In 1941, one of the most important figures in African-American politics, A. Philip Randolph (President of the Brotherhood of Sleeping Car Porters), pressurised President Roosevelt into issuing Executive Order 8802, which outlawed racial discrimination in the defence industry. Though of limited effectiveness, this law was a precedent.[31]

Growth of interest in age discrimination

If one cares to look hard enough, one can discover a fine thread of concern over age discrimination in employment running back to the early 1900s, despite the federal government's lack of interest. A law against age discrimination in employment was passed in the state of Colorado as early as 1903, and other states slowly followed suit. Sometimes, there would be limited, and ineffective, legislation, such as the State of New Jersey's 1930 law covering those aged 40+ applying for employment in state, county or municipal services (with some exceptions).[32] There was also considerable discussion of the problem. For example, in 1938 the New York State Legislature produced a *Preliminary Report on Age Discrimination in Employment of the Middle Aged*, after several months of committee hearings involving employers, labour unions, veterans' organisations, and so on. Twenty-one possible sources of discrimination were investigated, including the displacement of workers by modern machinery, the higher cost of employing older men, physical decline, the 'speed-up' in industry, lack of relevant education and skills, and the absence of industrial re-training programmes. The report commented, regarding older workers, that 'It is common knowledge ... that for the past 20 years, except during the World War, a large number of employable men and women without work have been constantly in quest of jobs which did not exist.'[33]

[29] Achenbaum, *Social Security*, pp. 24, 32, 107.
[30] Mack A. Player, *Federal Law of Employment Discrimination in a Nutshell* (1981), p. 8.
[31] Burstein, *Discrimination*, p. 8.
[32] 'Age Discrimination Barred in Public Employment in New Jersey', *Monthly Labor Review*, vol. 30, no. 6, June 1930, p. 106.
[33] 'Causes of Discrimination Against Older Workers', *Monthly Labor Review*, vol. 46, no. 5, May 1938, pp. 1138–43.

However, bills introducing measures to combat age discrimination in employment failed to pass the New York State Assembly and Senate, despite continuing interest in the problems of older workers: for example, in the early 1950s the New York State Joint Legislative Committee on Problems of the Aging published two lengthy volumes, full of upbeat articles and photographs chronicling old age 'success stories'.[34] The state of Massachusetts did pass an age discrimination in employment law in 1937, but it was largely inoperable since proven discrimination carried no penalty provisions: by 1950, only two cases had been considered under it.[35] Other states that passed laws (of varying effectiveness) were: New York in 1958; Connecticut and Wisconsin in 1959; California, Ohio and Washington in 1961; New Jersey in 1962; Michigan and Indiana in 1965.[36]

The Second World War

During the Second World War, there was a massive re-enlistment of older men into the civilian labour force, owing to the stimulation to labour market demand occasioned by a wartime economy, and to military call-up.[37] Between 1940 and 1945, military enlistment resulted in jobs being vacated and filled by marginal workers.[38] As a result, there was considerable postponement of retirement, a return of old age insurance beneficiaries to employment and a diminution of old age assistance rolls.[39] Total recorded unemployment in the USA fell from 8,000,000 in 1940 to less than 1,000,000 in 1944, and the total labour force (civilian and military) expanded from 56,100,000 in 1940 to 66,210,000 in 1945. Whereas in 1940, 1,838,000 men aged 65+ had been in the labour force, by 1942 this figure had risen to 2,190,000, and by 1945 it was 2,460,000. Women aged 65+ increased their labour force participation at an even higher rate, from

---

[34] New York State Joint Legislative Committee on Problems of the Aging, *No Time to Grow Old* (1951) and *Age Is No Barrier* (1952).

[35] Joseph T. Drake, *The Aged in American Society* (1958), p. 117; Kenneth J. Kelley, 'Massachusetts Law Against Age Discrimination in Employment', in New York State Joint Legislative Committee, *No Time to Grow Old*, pp. 173–5.

[36] Raymond F. Gregory, *Age Discrimination in the American Workplace: Old at a Young Age* (2001), p. 16.

[37] Mary T. Waggaman, 'Improved Employment Situation of Older Workers', *Monthly Labor Review*, vol. 54, no. 1, Jan. 1942, pp. 59–69; Jacob Perlman and Howard I. Kumin, 'Employment and Earnings Under Old-Age and Survivors Insurance During the First Year of the War', *Social Security Bulletin*, vol. 8, no. 3, Mar. 1945, p. 10.

[38] Philip M. Hauser, 'Changes in the Labor-Force Participation of the Older Worker', *American Journal of Sociology*, vol. LIX, no. 4, Jan. 1954, p. 316.

[39] Mary T. Waggaman, 'Older Workers in Wartime', *Monthly Labor Review*, vol. 59, no. 1, July 1944, pp. 24–38.

279,000 in 1940 to 490,000 in 1945.[40] All older workers saw their employment prospects improve: by 1944, some 6,700,000 men and women aged 55–64, and 2,900,000 aged 65+ were in the labour force – nearly 2,000,000 more than in 1940.[41] Other groups previously on the periphery of the labour force – youths, disabled people, the least skilled ethnic minorities – also found jobs during the War.[42] 'In the tight wartime labour market, this "marginal" group has become a genuine asset', was one apposite comment.[43] Not surprisingly, work-disability prevalence decreased: between 1940 and 1950 the proportion of males of all ages recorded as 'unable to work' fell from 5.8 per cent to 4.4 per cent, and for men aged 65+ from 39.9 per cent to 29.1 per cent. The stimulus of a wartime economy had subtly changed the definition of 'employability'.[44]

These developments temporarily ended discussion of age discrimination. During the War employers greatly relaxed their normal hiring criteria, dropped upper age limits to employment and introduced individualised testing for job competence in the case of older workers – exactly what old age pressure groups were to suggest many years later.[45] Even the maximum age limits for civil service examinations were relaxed. One famous example was the programme run by the Harvard University Graduate School of Business Administration, which successfully re-trained middle-aged men for more responsible positions in industry; it was discovered that these men were quick to learn new skills and were able to offer new ideas using the wisdom born of experience.[46] The lesson to be drawn, noted Ross McFarland, was that 'the value of each worker will vary with his physiological age or fitness rather than his chronological age ... The older worker should be made to feel that he is needed and wanted, by correcting some of the fictions that form the basis of

[40] US Department of Commerce and US Bureau of the Census, *Historical Statistics of the United States. Colonial Times to 1970, Part 1* (1975), p. 131.

[41] Gertrude Bancroft, 'Older Persons in the Labor Force', *Annals of the American Academy of Political and Social Science*, vol. 279, Jan. 1952, p. 56.

[42] 'Social Security in Review', *Social Security Bulletin*, vol. 8, no. 2, Feb. 1945, p. 1. A full breakdown of these new workers by age and gender is given in 'Characteristics of Extra Workers in the Labor Force, April 1944', *Monthly Labor Review*, vol. 59, no. 2, Aug. 1944, pp. 270–8.

[43] Michael T. Wermel and Selma Gelbaum, 'Work and Retirement in Old Age', *American Journal of Sociology*, vol. LI, no. 1, July 1945, p. 20.

[44] Hauser, 'Changes', p. 314.

[45] Nathan W. Shock, 'Older People and Their Potentialities for Gainful Employment', *Journal of Gerontology*, vol. 2, no. 2, April 1947, p. 97; Evan K. Rowe and Thomas H. Paine, 'Pension Plans Under Collective Bargaining, Part II', *Monthly Labor Review*, vol. 76, no. 5, May 1953, pp. 488–9.

[46] Harold Sheppard, 'Work and Retirement', in Robert H. Binstock and Ethel Shanas (eds.), *Handbook of Aging and the Social Sciences* (1976), p. 296.

discrimination against him.'[47] There were hopes that the wartime experience might encourage employers to drop the pre-war 'prejudices' that had been based upon erroneous notions of older workers.[48] Significantly, though, older workers were still 'last in the queue' in the reserve army of labour: the rate at which they were absorbed into the wartime economy was slower than for younger workers and women.[49]

The 1940s and 1950s

By the 1940s and 1950s, it had become clear that retirement was a con-sequence of long-run declining labour market demand (institutionalised by mandatory retirement) or ill-health (often concealing joblessness), with the Second World War being only a brief interlude. The employment problems of older men could no longer be seen, as they had in the 1930s, as the product of a specific recession. One knowledgeable authority commented: 'as obvious as Cyrano's nose, the main barrier to the employment of older workers is simply the lack of available jobs'.[50] A survey of 2,380 male old age benefit recipients conducted in 1941–2 by the Bureau of Old-Age and Survivors Insurance found that more than half had been laid off by their employers, while another one-third had retired through ill-health; only some 5 per cent had retired voluntarily.[51] In 1949 Ewan Clague noted that 'the trend towards earlier withdrawal from the labor force has been pri-marily a result of economic compulsion rather than individual choice',[52] and in an important 1952 article on labour force trends he warned that older workers' economic activity rates were declining while the period they spent in retirement was lengthening. Clague observed that

If this lengthening of the retirement period resulted from a real preference for leisure in old age instead of continued gainful activity and from an increasing financial ability to retire, we could count this as a very salutary development. However, the information available to us on this subject points to the opposite conclusion. It appears that earlier retirement has been forced upon older workers as a result of a lack of suitable employment opportunity. Our experience during

---

[47] Ross A. McFarland, 'The Older Worker in Industry', *Harvard Business Review*, vol. XXI, no. 4, Summer 1943, pp. 512–13, 519.

[48] Wermel and Gelbaum, 'Work and Retirement', p. 20.

[49] Clague, 'Labor Force Trends', p. 96.

[50] Albert J. Abrams, 'Barriers to the Employment of Older Workers', *Annals of the American Academy of Political and Social Science*, vol. 279, Jan. 1952, p. 65.

[51] Edna C. Wentworth, 'Why Beneficiaries Retire', *Social Security Bulletin*, vol. 8, no. 1, Jan. 1945, p. 16; W. H. Stead, 'Trends of Employment in Relation to the Problem of Aging', *Journal of Gerontology*, vol. 4, no. 4, Oct. 1949, p. 295.

[52] Ewan Clague, 'The Working Life Span of American Workers', *Journal of Gerontology*, vol. 4, no. 4, Oct. 1949, p. 286.

World War II, for example, provides ample evidence that many older persons flock back into the labor market when their services are in demand.[53]

Clague and others dismissed the possibility that old age insurance benefits induced older workers to retire.[54] All the available evidence pointed to the fact that 'Most old people work as long as they can and retire only because they are forced to do so ... without earnings they do not have resources enough to live at the level to which they are accustomed, or even to meet the cost of their basic needs'.[55] In 1952, the average federal old age and survivors insurance pension level was $502 per annum for a single retired worker, and $816 per annum for a retired worker and wife; by contrast, official Social Security Administration estimates for a 'modest but adequate' minimum income for a retired couple ranged from $1,620 to $1,908 per annum, depending upon state[56] – and this was after the 1950 increases, which raised benefit levels by 77 per cent. Of the 4,100,000 households in the US with incomes under $1,000 per annum in 1950, 32 per cent were headed by a person aged 65+.[57] It was therefore highly implausible that the federal social security pension induced workers to retire.[58] As one historian rightly remarks, until the 1960s, social security 'was still basically a poverty programme'.[59]

By the 1950s, therefore, most commentators considered it unlikely that the long-run trend in declining labour market demand would be reversed.[60] For example, Wilbur Cohen[61] saw no evidence that employment opportunities would improve, such as to offset future rising pension

---

[53] Clague, 'Labor Force Trends', p. 94. See also Ewan Clague, 'Do American Workers Save for Retirement?', in George B. Hurff (ed.), *Economic Problems of Retirement: a Report on the Fourth Annual Southern Conference on Gerontology held at the University of Florida, 27–28 January 1954* (1954), pp. 10–13.

[54] Clague, 'Labor Force Trends'; Bancroft, 'Older Persons', p. 52. See also Drake, *The Aged*, p. 71.

[55] Margaret L. Stecker, 'Beneficiaries Prefer to Work', *Social Security Bulletin*, vol. 14, no. 1, Jan. 1951, pp. 15, 17. One of the few studies of the 1950s to argue that retirement was largely voluntary was Peter O. Steiner and Robert Dorfman, *The Economic Status of the Aged* (1957), esp. pp. 49–50.

[56] Wilbur J. Cohen, 'Income Maintenance for the Aged', *Annals of the American Academy of Political and Social Science*, vol. 279, Jan. 1952, p. 159.

[57] Robert M. Ball, 'Old Age Retirement: Social and Economic Implications', *Social Security Bulletin*, vol. 13, no. 9, Sept. 1950, p. 4.

[58] Solomon Barkin, 'Should There Be a Fixed Retirement Age? Organised Labor Says No', *Annals of the American Academy of Political and Social Science*, vol. 279, Jan. 1952, p. 78.

[59] Quadagno, *Transformation*, p. 153.

[60] One notable exception was Peter F. Drucker, 'Population Trends and Management Policy', *Harvard Business Review*, vol. XXIX, no. 3, May 1951, pp. 73–8.

[61] Wilbur Cohen (1913–87) was a social welfare expert who served as Director of the Social Security Administration's research bureau; between 1961 and 1969 he was Assistant Secretary of the Department of Health and Welfare.

costs.[62] The stimulation to the US economy occasioned by the Korean War improved the employment situation of older male workers: in 1950, some 535,000 more men aged 65+ were in employment compared with 1940, and their labour force participation rate was almost the same – 41.4 per cent (1950), as against 41.8 per cent (1940). However, this was only temporary. Thereafter, low unemployment and a tight labour market failed to arrest the continuing downward fall in their labour force participation rates.

Because of this, greater attention was paid to those factors over which policy might have some control: mandatory retirement and age discriminatory employment practices came under increasing criticism as being both socially unjust and economically dysfunctional, in the minority of cases where workers retained high industrial value after 'normal' retirement age. There began to be increasing calls for individualised testing for job competence,[63] 'objective criteria' for hiring and retirement, a shorter working week, more part-time jobs, schemes to allow the tapering-off of work in middle age, more 'counselling, rehabilitation and training' for older workers, the abandonment of employers' 'prejudices', more research into the employment problems of older workers, and so on.[64] A perennial suggestion was that a sheltered labour market niche might be reserved for older workers, much as the Dodge Division of the Chrysler Corporation had an 'old man's department' where very senior employees could work at their own pace.[65] The wide-ranging discussion of all these issues in America at this time is evident in the burgeoning literature: for example, Nathan Shock's *A Classified Bibliography of Gerontology and Geriatrics* (1951) listed over 3,000 references on the economic, psychological and social aspects of ageing.[66]

In 1950, a National Conference on Aging was convened by Oscar Ewing, Head of the Federal Security Agency. The Conference examined, among other things, the problems of older workers, and concluded that 'while numerous surveys report that employers concede that older workers are more reliable, absent less often, have fewer accidents, and even produce as much as younger workers, discriminatory age barriers

---

[62] Wilbur J. Cohen, 'Government Policy Concerning Private and Public Retirement Plans', in Hurff, *Economic Problems*, pp. 56–7.

[63] For example, Drucker, 'Population Trends', p. 76.

[64] Clark Tibbitts, 'Retirement Problems in American Society', *American Journal of Sociology*, vol. LIX, no. 4, Jan. 1954, p. 303.

[65] Wermel and Gelbaum, 'Work and Retirement', p. 21.

[66] Nathan W. Shock, *A Classified Bibliography of Gerontology and Geriatrics* (1951). This extraordinary work contains a total of 18,036 publications (though there is some double-counting) on every aspect of gerontology and geriatrics.

persist'.[67] The *Journal of Gerontology* – perhaps the best indicator of trends in research – regularly contained articles on the problems of older workers, anticipating almost uncannily the issues that were to be discussed several decades later, as did the *American Journal of Sociology* (including an interesting special edition specifically on old age in January 1954). On a popular level, too, there was expressed concern. For example, the 19 October 1953 edition of *Time* magazine ran a story on the problems of older workers (including the hope that many corporations were reviewing 'prejudices' against older workers and policies on mandatory retirement), and the December 1946 edition of *Fortune* considered the question of an ageing population and whether 'the long life can be made the good life'.[68] In 1949 Ewan Clague warned that, if working life continued to shorten while chronological life lengthened, social security pensions would have to be raised in value; Clague discussed the desirability of phased retirement, via 'flexible' employment policies geared to the specific needs of individual workers.[69]

Another two authors considered the possibility of flexible retirement ages, to overcome the problem of workers 'ageing' at different rates; interestingly, they warned that individualised testing could allow employers to practise favouritism or negative discrimination.[70] The January 1952 edition of the *Annals of the American Academy of Political and Social Science* was devoted to old age, and contained articles on the social and psychological needs of 'the aging', barriers to the employment of older workers, the pros and cons of mandatory retirement and flexible retirement, housing, continuing education, family life, and so on.[71] One particularly interesting text was Joseph Drake's *The Aged in American Society* (1958), which contained quite a detailed discussion of employment issues and explored the ambiguities of age discrimination with remarkable acuity. Like most of his contemporaries, Drake was slightly puzzled why, with a buoyant economy and virtual full employment, retirement continued to spread. His conclusion was that labour market withdrawal was forced upon individuals by employers' mandatory retirement policies or by

---

[67] Quoted in Sara E. Rix, 'Public Policy and the Older Worker: Fifty Years of More or Less Benign Neglect' (paper to the 48th Annual Scientific Meeting of the Gerontological Society of America, Los Angeles, November 1995), p. 4.

[68] 'The Older American Worker. The US Must Make Better Use of Him', *Time*, 19 Oct. 1953, p. 100; 'The Aging Population', *Fortune*, vol. XXXIV, no. 6, Dec. 1946, pp. 250–4.

[69] Clague, 'Working Life Span', pp. 285–9.

[70] Evan K. Rowe and Thomas H. Paine, 'Pension Plans Under Collective Bargaining, Part I', *Monthly Labor Review*, vol. 76, no. 3, Mar. 1953, p. 246.

[71] *Annals*. The rather quaint title of the edition was the 'Social Contribution of the Aging' – a reflection of the desire of the editor, Clark Tibbitts, to present a message of 'positive' ageing.

ill-health. There appeared to be four principal obstacles to the employment of older males: cultural or social factors (including irrational stereotypes of incompetence); personal deficiencies (such as ill-health); barriers erected by labour unions, who wished jobs to go to their younger members; and personnel policies in industry (notably mandatory retirement). Age discrimination, where it existed, was not confined to formal employment regulations, but was also (probably in a more virulent form) 'in the personal attitudes and prejudices of the hiring agent or the personnel manager'. It was, he admitted, very difficult to ascertain whether employers' views of older workers were based on false stereotypes or on broad generalisations which had an approximate accuracy.[72] Another interesting discussion was Albert Abrams's analysis of direct and indirect discrimination against older workers. With regard to the latter, he cited research into 'help wanted' advertisements: for example, an analysis of 3,474 male job advertisements in the New York Times revealed that 38.2 per cent included age limits.[73] (Abrams conducted quite thorough research into age discrimination in the 1950s.)[74] Involuntary retirement was thus the most common form of retirement; this was often rationalised by individuals as ill-health or failing working capacity, though it might originate in the discontinuation of a job.[75] By the late 1950s, therefore, most informed commentators realised that the spread of retirement since the late nineteenth century had occurred for a complex mix of reasons – the most important being declining labour market demand – and that its effect on individuals, in terms of their psychological well-being, varied greatly.[76] However, legislative action against age discrimination in employment might have some beneficial effect at the margins.

By the early 1960s, the impact of enforced retirement and inadequate social security was arousing comment. Although the War on Poverty of that decade was primarily concerned with poverty and economic marginalisation among younger adults, old age poverty was projected into national debates. For example, in his famous The Other America (1962), Michael Harrington devoted a whole chapter to the topic, and cited Bureau of the Census statistics showing that, in 1958, 60 per cent of Americans aged 65+ had incomes of less than $1,000 per annum, where

---

[72] Drake, The Aged, pp. 71–2, 83–99.   [73] Abrams, 'Barriers', p. 63.
[74] See, for example, A. J. Abrams, 'Discrimination Against Older Workers in Various Countries', in Old Age in the Modern World. Report of the Third Congress of the International Association of Gerontology, London 1954 (1955), pp. 291–5.
[75] Margaret S. Gordon, 'Changing Patterns of Retirement', Journal of Gerontology, vol. 15, no. 3, July 1960, p. 301.
[76] Wayne E. Thompson, Gordon F. Streib and John Kosa, 'The Effect of Retirement on Personal Adjustment', Journal of Gerontology, vol. 15, no. 2, April 1960, pp. 165–9.

the federal standard of adequacy for a retired couple in an urban area in 1959 ranged from \$2,681 to \$3,304 per annum.[77] (One-sixth of older Americans were recorded as having no income at all.)[78] A Department of Health, Education and Welfare survey in 1963 showed the median income of non-married persons aged 65+ to be only \$1,130 per annum, and that of married couples \$2,875.[79] Old age poverty was, of course, sharply differentiated by race and gender. Retrospective analysis shows that, in 1959, the poverty rates for Americans aged 65+ were: white men, 27.8 per cent; non-white men, 62.9 per cent; white women, 48.4 per cent; non-white women, 73.4 per cent.[80]

A vital ingredient: the growth of old age pressure groups

Old age pressure groups of the 'representational' variety (that is, mass movements) face certain intrinsic problems: their members tend to have low incomes, and thus cannot afford to fund expensive campaigns; their ability to exert industrial muscle (via strikes) is limited; membership turn-over is considerable, owing to illness and mortality; infirmity among members can limit their ability to demonstrate;[81] and in the politics of welfare distribution, the old tend to be accorded low status because of their diminished human capital and labour market value. Old age pressure groups also face a difficult dilemma: by campaigning for special treatment and extra resources, they may thereby 'ghettoise' and 'problematise' old age.[82] To add to these inherent difficulties, the economic prosperity of the 1950s, the existence of social security (albeit offering very low pensions) and the general atmosphere of political quiescence in that decade served to dampen down political activism.

There had been some 'grey activism' before the 1950s. The most famous example was the Townsend Movement, started in Long Beach, California, by Francis Townsend, a retired doctor. Then, as now, California had acted as an economic magnet. In the 1920s, many older people had moved

[77] Michael Harrington, *The Other America* (1962), p. 104 and ch. 6.
[78] Margaret S. Gordon, 'The Income Status of Older Persons', in William Haber and Wilbur J. Cohen (eds.), *Social Security. Programs, Problems, and Policies* (1960), p. 109.
[79] Leonore A. Epstein and Janet H. Murray, *The Aged Population of the United States. The 1963 Social Security Survey of the Aged* (1967), p. 39.
[80] Elizabeth Evanson, 'Social and Economic Change Since the Great Depression: Studies of Census Data, 1940–1980', *Focus* (University of Wisconsin-Madison Institute for Research on Poverty), vol. 11, no. 3, Fall 1988, p. 3.
[81] Henry J. Pratt, *The Gray Lobby* (1976), pp. 40–1; Andrew Blaikie, 'The Emerging Political Power of the Elderly in Britain 1908–1948', *Ageing and Society*, vol. 10, pt. 1, Mar. 1990, p. 20.
[82] Carroll L. Estes, *The Aging Enterprise* (1979), p. 17.

there – only to find that the subsequent depression left them in dire poverty. By 1940, some 69 per cent of aged persons in California were unemployed, and there was considerable job insecurity among the 45–64 age-group.[83] Long Beach contained many retirees living on fixed incomes (from investments, savings and so on), and these incomes had become seriously eroded by the stock market crash of 1929. These retirees were also relatively well educated and vociferous.[84] Townsend's idea was to build a mass movement based upon the central demand of a $200 per month pension for all aged 60+, financed by a 2 per cent tax on all business transactions: the pension was to be spent within a fixed brief period, in order to stimulate demand. One of the Townsend Movement's immediate attractions was that it promised several things – a reflation of economic activity, a dispersal of purchasing power, an alleviation of old age poverty, and job redistribution to the young unemployed. Though its influence on the passage of the 1935 Social Security Act has been exaggerated, the Townsend Movement grew rapidly and for a time showed the potential power of a future grey lobby.[85] As noted in a previous chapter, it aroused some concern in certain quarters, appearing to symbolise a new kind of single-issue politics that might change the landscape of American democracy.

However, the seeds of a large-scale grey lobby were planted in 1947, when the National Retired Teachers' Association (NRTA) was founded by Ethel Percy Andrus. Ethel Andrus had retired in 1944, aged fifty-nine, as Principal of the Abraham Lincoln High School in East Los Angeles – a multi-ethnic, inner-city school which she transformed by personal dynamism and energy. These were qualities which she was to bring to pressure group politics. Andrus's retirement had not been voluntary: she left early to care for a sick mother, and, because of this, only received a pension of $60 per month (though she also enjoyed some family money). A major problem faced by retirees in the 1940s and 1950s was that of obtaining health insurance to cover the risks of illness, disability or accidents in old age: no insurance company would accept them. In 1955 Ethel Andrus met an insurance salesman, Leonard Davis, who was willing to broker such policies. In 1958, Andrus and Davis founded the American Association of Retired Persons (AARP) as an insurance-selling partner to the NRTA,

[83] Putnam, *Old-Age Politics*, p. 7.
[84] Henry J. Pratt, *Gray Agendas: Interest Groups and Public Pensions in Canada, Britain and the United States* (1993), p. 61.
[85] Robert H. Binstock, 'The Politics of Aging Interest Groups', in Robert B. Hudson (ed.), *The Aging in Politics. Process and Policy* (1981), p. 53; Quadagno, *Transformation*, p. 108; Putnam, *Old-Age Politics*, pp. 49–71.

and for non-teacher retirees. The AARP's method of funding itself was peculiarly American. The two sides of this organisation worked together, expanding the insurance business, setting up pharmaceutical, travel and educational facilities, giving advice on financial, medical and other matters to members, and putting pressure on governments. By the time of Andrus's death in 1967, she had become a national figure, and the NRTA/AARP membership continued to grow.[86] By 1973, there were over 6,000,000 members; now the figure is closer to 35,000,000 (membership being open to those aged 50+).[87] The AARP has become the second largest organisation in the USA after the Catholic Church, with an annual budget in 1993–4 of $470,000,000. This success did bring its critics, who objected to the emphasis on for-profit insurance selling, its excessive political power and its apparently munificent wealth.[88]

Today the AARP campaigns actively for America's seniors, pursuing a wide variety of aims. It staunchly defends federal social security, and argues against the view that a fiscal crisis is approaching; it supports improvements in health and social care provision; interestingly, it conveys a message of 'positive ageing', emphasising that older Americans should do all they can to reap the rewards of the 'longevity bonus'; and it campaigns against all remaining mandatory retirement provisions, arguing for their replacement by individualised testing in occupations such as airline pilots.[89] It has been joined by other pressure groups, such as the Alliance for Retired Americans, the Older Women's League and the National Council on the Aged.

The 1950s and early 1960s: a summing-up

It can be seen, therefore, that the 1940s and 1950s were decades in which American gerontologists analysed the problems of older workers with remarkable incisiveness: the bibliography in Joseph Drake's seminal study is eloquent testimony to this.[90] By the mid-1960s, pressure for effective federal action had built up strongly, and it is worth pausing to consider the reasons behind this, which were complex and often contradictory.

---

[86] 'The Story of AARP', *Modern Maturity*, Aug.–Sep. 1974, pp. 55–62; 'Memorial Edition', *Modern Maturity*, Jan. 1968.
[87] AARP, *Annual Report 1999* (1999).
[88] Dale Van Atta, *Trust Betrayed: Inside the AARP* (1998).
[89] AARP, *The Public Policy Agenda 1999* (1999); AARP, *Annual Report 1998* (1998) and *Annual Report 1999* (1999).
[90] Drake, *The Aged*.

First was the contention that age was one of several disadvantages experienced in the labour market and in wider social attitudes.[91] Thus the official report that preceded the unsuccessful 1962 Equal Employment Opportunity Bill argued that fully 50 per cent of US citizens in search of jobs suffered some kind of employment discrimination because of race, religion, skin colour, national origin, ancestry or age.[92] By the early 1960s, many advocates of the cause of older people sought the abolition of mandatory retirement,[93] citing the accumulating evidence that, although working capacity probably did decline slowly with age, heterogeneity increased – making for wider ability differentials: job competence should therefore be measured by individualised testing. Presenting age as one of several structured inequalities was to give the ADEA the moral under-pinning necessary to win public acceptance in America's highly competi-tive, individualistic society, and it enabled campaigners to present their case in terms of social justice.

A second argument was that, although unemployment rates were higher among young than among middle-aged men, the latter's experi-ence of joblessness was qualitatively worse.[94] Youth unemployment was a growing problem in the 1950s and early 1960s (particularly among African Americans), and was one reason for the War on Poverty's measures to re-socialise the jobless back into the labour market via community action programmes. (In 1961, unemployment reached its highest level since the Second World War.) Thus in 1964 the unemploy-ment rate for males aged 14–19 was just under 15 per cent, whereas for men aged 45–54 it was only slightly over 3 per cent (with, of course, substantial black:white differentials). However, the average older worker, once unemployed, experienced a longer period of joblessness: in 1964, only 15.2 per cent of male workers aged 14–24 had been unem-ployed for 27 weeks or more, whereas the proportion for males aged 45–64 was 28.0 per cent. The older worker's unemployment, especially if commencing past the age of 55, was likely to become permanent, carrying with it greater psychological shocks and feelings of uselessness – the

[91] W. Andrew Achenbaum, 'Putting ADEA Into Historical Context', *Research on Aging*, vol. 13, no. 4, Dec. 1991, pp. 465–6.

[92] House Report No. 1370, 87th Cong. 2nd Sess., 1962, in US Equal Employment Opportunity Commission, *Legislative History of the Age Discrimination in Employment Act* (1981), p. 1.

[93] For example, statement by Louis Kaplan, President of the Gerontological Society of America, in *The Aged and the Aging in the United States. Hearings Before the Subcommittee on Problems of the Aged and Aging of the Committee on Labor and Public Welfare, United States Senate, June 16, 17 and 18 1959* (1959), p. 100.

[94] James P. Northrup, *Old Age, Handicapped, and Vietnam-era Antidiscrimination Legislation* (1980), p. 7.

classic 'discouraged worker' syndrome.[95] Once in such a state, problems tended to 'cluster' and become mutually reinforcing as 'age plus something else'.[96] In particular, health could deteriorate; or poor health could be used as 'an acceptable pride-saving excuse' for early retirement.[97] The recorded lower rates of unemployment among older workers also reflected the fact that many of them had ceased to look for work. It was increasingly seen as imperative to remove as many as possible of the barriers to the re-employment of older unemployed men: one such barrier was the existence of formal age limits in job advertisements. Surveys in the late 1950s and early 1960s showed that anywhere between 25 per cent and 40 per cent of these 'help wanted' advertisements stipulated upper age limits.[98] The ADEA thus sought to address the particular problems that long-term joblessness inflicted on older workers and on the economy in general. Curiously, it was *not* a response to falling labour force participation rates among middle-aged men, since these had remained more or less stable since the Second World War. In 1947, 95.5 per cent of men aged 45–54, and 89.6 per cent aged 55–64, were in the labour force; by 1964, these rates had hardly changed, at 95.7 per cent and 85.6 per cent respectively. As in all industrial societies, middle-aged American women had increased their labour force participation rates over the same period: for those aged 45–54, from 32.7 per cent to 51.4 per cent; and for those aged 55–64, from 24.3 per cent to 40.2 per cent.[99] It was only from the 1970s that the labour force participation rates of older men began to fall.

A third important impulse – giving an enormous boost to the 'social justice' case – was that the whole civil rights movement was beginning to take off in the late 1950s. As will be shown later in this chapter, age discrimination was seen as complementary to race and sex discrimination. By the early 1960s the civil rights movement had grown to such proportions

---

[95] US Department of Labor, *The Older American Worker. Age Discrimination in Employment. Report of the Secretary of Labor to the Congress Under Section 715 of the Civil Rights Act of 1964* (1965), pp. 97–102.

[96] State of California, Department of Employment and Citizens' Advisory Committee on Aging, *A Survey of the Employment of Older Workers – 1964. A Report to the California Legislature, 1965 Session* (1965), p. 70.

[97] Statement by Michael Batten, Director of Consultant Services in Industrial Gerontology at Kirschner Associates, in *Age and Sex Discrimination in Employment and Review of Federal Response to Employment Needs of the Elderly. Hearing Before the Subcommittee on Retirement Income and Employment of the Select Committee on Aging, House of Representatives, Dec. 10 1975* (1976), p. 26.

[98] National Council of Senior Citizens, *The Nation's Stake in the Employment of Middle-Aged and Older Persons* (1971), p. 10; US Department of Labor, *The Older American Worker*, pp. 7–10.

[99] US Department of Labor, *The Older American Worker*, p. 145.

as to change political behaviour in Washington. The reasons why the ruling Democratic Party took up the cause of civil rights are complex, and can only be summarised here: the strong public support for legislation; the economic modernisation of the South, which was sweeping away the cobwebs of quasi-feudal social relations and slowly fashioning a 'freer' society; the need for the Democratic Party to woo the northern African-American voter; the damage to the United States's reputation by televised pictures of police brutality against civil rights demonstrators flashed round the world; Lyndon Johnson's desire, in the aftermath of the Kennedy assassination, to be seen as a reforming President; and so on. These and other reasons can be debated endlessly: the point is that age discrimination legislation succeeded because it was attached to the coat-tails of civil rights. The civil rights movement was the great engine that drove the whole package of rights-based federal measures in the 1960s and 1970s, ostensibly designed to improve the lot of various disadvantaged groups in American society.

A fourth, and more important, factor was that the American economy was undergoing a period of modernisation, in common with other indus-trialised societies. (Arguably, the civil rights movement was itself a product of this modernisation process.) Service and white-collar occupations were expanding, and blue-collar industrial jobs were beginning to go into rela-tive decline; continued migration of African Americans from the Southern farm economy was putting pressure on unskilled jobs in the Northern cities, worsening unemployment and social problems in the inner-city ghettos; 'pockets of poverty' were developing; technological innovation (then called 'automation') was being introduced at a significantly faster rate in key industries, and was beginning to displace from the labour force both young, unskilled, ethnically disadvantaged workers and older, experi-enced ones.[100] The launching of the Russian Sputnik on 4 October 1957 caused a ripple of alarm in the USA: many believed that Russia was ahead in scientific and aerospace research. However mistaken this view, it did intensify the debate on how to maximise the educational and skills levels of American workers. (Total federal, state and local education spending doubled between 1957 and 1964.)[101] The thrust of economic policy in the 1960s was to direct and assist this process of economic modernisation, while social policy innovations were designed to maintain conditions of social stability and, via community action, re-socialise back into economic usefulness those who were becoming marginalised. Maximising productivity

---

[100] Barbara L. Bessey and Srijati M. Ananda, 'Age Discrimination in Employment. An Interdisciplinary Review of the ADEA', *Research on Aging*, vol. 13, no. 4, Dec. 1991, pp. 413–14.
[101] J. Ronald Oakley, *God's Country: America in the Fifties* (1990), p. 352.

and efficiency in the US workforce was a key theme in economic debates of the 1960s. Improving the technological proficiency and per capita productivity of the US workforce meant not only raising educational and skill levels, but also modernising personnel policies so that productive workers, regardless of their age, were retained. Increasingly, the use of crude age proxies – seemingly based upon irrational, 'false stereotypes' of older workers' industrial obsolescence – and the imposition of mandatory retirement at age 65 were seen as economically dysfunctional, leading to a loss of valuable workers and diminishing the productive power of the economy, as well as forcing growing numbers of people to live in poverty on a low pension.[102] Even though the fall in labour force participation rates of older male workers would be difficult to reverse, some of the obstacles to their employment could be removed by policies to counter age discrimination. These labour supply arguments indicate that the age discrimination debate was being driven by profound economic forces. They were also, of course, explicitly articulated by campaigners for tactical reasons, in order to enlist the backing of employers and economic conservatives and thereby build a broader base of support. At the same time, ageism in social relations appeared to be intensifying with the emergence of a new youth culture: this tendency needed to be countered by a re-education of public opinion. Two experimental psychologists who investigated the 'misconceptions and stereotypes' held by young people about the old concluded that 'old people are living in a social climate which is not conducive to feelings of adequacy, usefulness, and security and to good adjustment in their later years'.[103] Another later commentator declared, 'we have permitted our entire society to become so youth-oriented that those over 45, without jobs, have been swept away in a backwash'.[104]

A final ingredient in the 1950s was the growth of a 'grey lobby' – discussed earlier in this chapter – which in future decades was to exert enormous pressure on politicians in Washington. Indeed, so powerful has this influence been that many politicians regard social security as the untouchable 'third rail' in US politics. The power and influence of old age pressure groups in the US is unique among industrialised nations.

---

[102] See, for example: Bancroft, 'Older Persons', p. 61; G. Hamilton Crook and Martin Heinstein, *The Older Worker in Industry. A Study of the Attitudes of Industrial Workers Toward Aging and Retirement* (1958), p. 4.

[103] Jacob Tuckman and Irving Lorge, 'Attitudes Toward Old People', *Journal of Social Psychology*, vol. 37, May 1953, p. 260.

[104] Statement by William R. Hutton, Executive Director, National Council of Senior Citizens, in *Age Discrimination in Employment. Hearings Before the General Subcommittee on Labor of the Committee on Education and Labor. House of Representatives, August 1, 2, 3, 15, 16 and 17 1967* (1967), p. 91.

A solution in search of a problem? Paradoxical arguments

The arguments for federal legislation were thus powerful, and an examination of the early 1960s debates convincingly refutes the charges made by conservatives in the 1980s (discussed in the following chapter) that the ADEA was a piece of misguided legislation, foisted upon the American public by a small, strident and self-seeking 'grey lobby'. However, these arguments did contain some paradoxes symptomatic of the difficulties inherent in age discrimination, and they are worth exploring briefly. Peter Schuck's somewhat disenchanted verdict that the ADEA was 'a solution in search of a problem'[105] derives from these paradoxes: there was indeed some uncertainty over precisely what problems the Act was attempting to solve.

First, 'social justice' and 'labour supply' arguments were inextricably mixed together. For example, in 1959 Senator Pat McNamara, supporting more measures to help meet older people's housing, income and other needs, placed the problem of age discrimination firmly, if rather hyperbolically, in the context of the economic cold war:

We are living in a time of such international tension that the fate of the free world rests in great measure on the productive capacity of our country. It would seem essential to our survival that we make full use of the assets and contributions of all our citizens to meet the needs of our times.

Yet there is a vast waste of wisdom, experience, and human resources in the compulsory retirement of our older citizens.[106]

It is significant that, when the Secretary of Labor, Willard Wirtz, was instructed on 20 November 1963 to draw up his famous report on *The Older American Worker*, the remit charged him with measuring the consequences of age discrimination on both individuals affected and the economy in general.[107] As Representative John H. Dent put it, in the 1967 Congressional Hearings, the Act's aim was 'to uphold the dignity of the older worker and to require the fullest possible utilisation of our manpower resources ... Age discrimination is not only unnecessary and unjustified, it is injurious both to the nation's economy and to the potential contributions of the persons to whom it is directed.'[108] This duality of motive was also evident in President Lyndon Johnson's 'Older Americans

---

[105] Peter H. Schuck, 'Age Discrimination Revisited', *Chicago-Kent Law Review*, vol. 57, no. 4, 1981, p. 1043.

[106] *The Aged and the Aging*, p. 1.

[107] House Report No. 914, 88th Cong. 1st Sess. (1963) on the Civil Rights Act 1964, in US Equal Employment Opportunity Commission, *Legislative History*, p. 4.

[108] *Age Discrimination in Employment. Hearings, 1967*, p. 6.

Message' of 23 January 1967, in which he outlined the case for legislation. Johnson said:

Hundreds of thousands not yet old, not yet voluntarily retired, find themselves jobless because of arbitrary age discrimination. Despite our present low rate of unemployment, there has been a persistent average of 850,000 people age 45 and over who are unemployed . . .

In economic terms, this is a serious – and senseless – loss to a nation on the move. But the greater loss is the cruel sacrifice in happiness and well-being which jobless-ness imposes on these citizens and their families.[109]

In short, the 1967 Act was seen as striking a careful balance between enhancing the employment rights of older workers and maximising the supply of skilled labour.

A second – and related – feature of the 1967 Act was its reflection of the prevailing optimism that 'arbitrary' or 'irrational' age discrimination was essentially the result of employers' misconceptions about the health and working capacity of older workers. Although (as argued earlier in this book) this has always been a rather simplistic view of employer motiv-ation, it appears to have prevailed within Congress.[110] As Achenbaum puts it, employers in the 1960s were seen to be suffering from 'structural lag': their attitudes lagged behind the actual improvements in older people's health status that had occurred since the Second World War.[111] Hence Willard Wirtz argued that age discrimination in employment was the result of a failure on the part of employers to realise 'how technology and the life sciences have combined to increase the value of older people's work' and to adjust pension planning and seniority provisions in collective bargaining agreements to 'the facts of life and the increasing mobility of labor'.[112] He could find no significant evidence of the kind of personal animus or intolerance that occurred in the case of race, colour, religion or national origin, and which was based on considerations entirely unrelated to a person's ability to perform a job.[113] Therefore, only age discrimination in the workplace was to be tackled. Reflecting the 'labour supply' con-siderations, Wirtz repeatedly emphasised that the Act would not protect those workers between the ages of 40 and 65 who were incompetent: the underlying aim was that such workers would be weeded out by

---

[109] Contained in US Equal Employment Opportunity Commission, *Legislative History*, pp. 60–1.
[110] Cathy Ventrell-Monsees, 'How Useful Are Legislative Remedies: America's Experience with the ADEA', *Aging International*, vol. XX, no. 3, Sept. 1993, p. 42.
[111] Achenbaum, 'Putting ADEA', p. 465. The term 'structural lag' originated with Matilda White Riley.
[112] *Age Discrimination in Employment. Hearings, 1967*, p. 7.
[113] US Department of Labor, *The Older American Worker*, p. 5.

individualised testing. 'Putting it more simply, if a person can't "cut it", that person will have to live with the consequences', he warned.[114] And looking back in 1986, the Chair of the Senate Committee on Aging (Senator John Heinz) pointed out that the Act 'does not require employers to keep unfit or unproductive employees. All that the ADEA requires is that the employer make individualised assessments where it is possible and practical to do so.'[115] In other words, the ADEA only outlawed 'unjustified' or 'arbitrary' age discrimination; age discrimination that was economically justified was quite permissible.

The 'irrationality' model prevailed, therefore: in time, it was hoped, the Act would dispel the myths and misconceptions held by employers. Yet there were many observers who realised that the actions of employers could not be explained away quite so simplistically. In some circumstances, older workers might be preferred over younger ones – for example, in specialised retail outlets, where their 'knowledge, confidence, dependability, maturity and general handling of customers' was better.[116] Willard Wirtz himself acknowledged that, while his survey of 540 firms revealed that one in four operated clear upper age limits in hiring, the two most common reasons for this were 'physical requirements' (34.2 per cent of cases) and 'job requirements' (25.1 per cent). Three out of five firms made exceptions to their upper age limits, if labour supply considerations justified it. The majority of firms which operated no age restrictions in fact hired relatively few older workers. Employers tended to shy away from individualised testing for eminently rational reasons (expense and inconvenience), although there could be an 'irrationality' element in their tendency to make snap judgements about an older worker's physical abilities.[117] In short, the patterned distribution of jobs by age could well have a rational basis.

Finally, no-one seems to have tackled the difficult issue of whether, or how far, the Act would actually improve the job prospects of older workers. Wirtz himself admitted that male early retirement was primarily affected by overall levels of unemployment, by technological innovation and by the general state of the economy. There was no clear evidence that the employment situation of older workers was better in those US states with age discrimination legislation.[118] As noted in chapter 1, mandatory

---

[114] *Age Discrimination in Employment. Hearings, 1967*, p. 10.
[115] Quoted in Daniel P. O'Meara, *Protecting the Growing Number of Older Workers: the Age Discrimination in Employment Act* (1989), p. 345.
[116] State of California, *A Survey*, p. 49.
[117] US Department of Labor, *The Older American Worker*, pp. 7–15.
[118] Statement by Peter J. Pestillo, US Chamber of Commerce, in *Age Discrimination in Employment. Hearings, 1967*, p. 61.

retirement actually affected only a very small proportion of American workers in the 1960s. A major factor was, of course, the long-run decline in labour demand in traditional blue-collar industries like coal mining, railroads and agriculture, which were contracting; newer expanding industries, such as electronics, aerospace and atomic energy, tended to have 'youthful' age profiles and absorbed the increasing supply of labour as the 'baby boom' generation reached working age.[119] Several witnesses at the 1967 Congressional Hearings emphasised that many complex factors were involved – for example, the state of the economy, the possible higher cost of employing older workers, the expense of job re-training, pension scheme rules, mandatory retirement, seniority systems – and that the Act could never be an instant panacea: Wirtz's laconic warning was that 'any exuberant certainty on this score would be an attempt at deception', and a representative of the US labour movement emphasised that the Act 'would only mark a beginning in dealing with the problems of older workers'.[120] Some witnesses suggested a federal job-creation scheme for older unemployed workers,[121] or tax credits for employers who employed older workers,[122] but such suggestions were deemed too radical. Nevertheless, the vast majority of witnesses at the August 1967 Hearings were strongly supportive of legislation. Sailing through largely untroubled waters, therefore, the Act passed into law quite easily.

---

[119] US Department of Labor, *The Older American Worker*, pp. 35, 67.

[120] *Age Discrimination in Employment. Hearings, 1967*, pp. 8 (Wirtz), 417 (written evidence by Kenneth Meiklejohn, Legislative Representative, AFL-CIO).

[121] As suggested by Claude Pepper (ibid., p. 423). This would have provided part-time paid jobs in community service programmes for workers aged 60+ who were unable to secure full-time employment, or for those needing to supplement an inadequate retirement income.

[122] Statement by Representative Roman Pucinski, ibid., p. 408.

9   From 1967 to the present

The 1967 Age Discrimination in Employment Act and after

The sequence of events leading up to the 1967 Age Discrimination in Employment Act can now be described briefly. The growing interest in the employment problems of older workers was reflected in the world of politics by several failed attempts to introduce age discrimination legislation at federal level, to supplement the state laws. As early as 1951, Senator Jacob Javits submitted an Age Discrimination in Employment Bill in the House of Representatives, of which he was then a member. On becoming a Senator in 1957, Javits tried again in the Senate; and he was to do so regularly thereafter.[1] An attempt to prohibit age discrimination in employment was made via the 1962 Equal Employment Opportunity Bill, but this was blocked by the House Rules Committee.[2] Likewise, attempts by Javits and other Senators in the early 1960s to amend the 1938 Fair Labor Standards Act failed, though in 1964 age discrimination in employment was made illegal where work was being carried out under federal contracts.[3] As is well known, the solid phalanx of Republicans and conservative Southern Democrats in both Houses made legislative innovation in the Eisenhower and Kennedy years difficult, if not impossible.

Originally, age discrimination was to have been included in the 1964 Civil Rights Bill: conservative Southern senators, both Republican and Democrat, tried to make the Bill unworkable by overloading it with additional provisions. By this tactic, sex discrimination was added, but survived intact. Age discrimination did not survive, the proposal to add the word 'age' being outvoted in the Senate with twenty-eight votes in favour

---

[1] Statement by Javits in 1967, in US Equal Employment Opportunity Commission, *Legislative History of the Age Discrimination in Employment Act* (1981), p. 117.

[2] US Equal Employment Opportunity Commission, *Legislative History*, p. 1; Daniel P. O'Meara, *Protecting the Growing Number of Older Workers: the Age Discrimination in Employment Act* (1989), p. 11.

[3] US Equal Employment Opportunity Commission, *Legislative History*, pp. 46–7.

and sixty-three against.[4] (It was decided that age could not be included under Title VII of the Civil Rights Bill since all workers would eventually fall within the protected group, age being a 'relative characteristic', unlike the 'immutable characteristics' of sex and race.)[5] However, this opposition by liberals was tactical, for the 1964 Civil Rights Act also contained a provision instructing the Secretary of Labor, Willard Wirtz, to conduct a study of age discrimination in employment.[6] This Wirtz duly did, and his report on *The Older American Worker* was published in June 1965.[7]

The Age Discrimination in Employment Act which passed into law on 15 December 1967 (becoming effective on 12 June 1968) had three explicit aims, as outlined in Section 2(b): (1) to promote the employment of older persons based on their ability rather than age, partly through re-educating employers; (2) to prohibit 'arbitrary' age discrimination in employment; (3) to help employers and workers find ways of solving problems arising from the impact of age on employment. The Secretary of Labor was authorised to initiate a re-education programme, and by this and other means to expand employment opportunities. These re-education and employment promotion measures were said to be 'vital to the overall effectiveness of the bill'.[8] However, they were never properly implemented. As noted, the focus was overwhelmingly on job protection rather than countering ageism in social relations. However, supporters of the ADEA have always argued that changing public attitudes and dispelling ageism in employment practices could only ever be a long, slow process. Thus Schuster, Kaspin and Miller point out that the ADEA 'acquired the role of educator ... value changes evolve more quickly when present values become costly to maintain'.[9]

Another important point to note is that initially the ADEA was *not* about old age. Reflecting the underlying labour-supply motives, it was a job-protection measure for middle-aged workers. The protected group was initially set at ages 45–65, but the Senate agreed to a House change

---

[4] Lawrence M. Friedman, *Your Time Will Come: the Law of Age Discrimination and Mandatory Retirement* (1984), p. 14.

[5] O'Meara, *Protecting*, pp. 1–2; US Equal Employment Opportunity Commission, *Legislative History*, pp. 6–8.

[6] US Equal Employment Opportunity Commission, *Legislative History*, p. 6.

[7] US Department of Labor, *The Older American Worker. Age Discrimination in Employment. Report of the Secretary of Labor to the Congress Under Section 715 of the Civil Rights Act of 1964* (1965).

[8] House Report No. 805, 90th Cong. 1st Sess., 23 Oct. 1967: *Age Discrimination in Employment Act of 1967. Report from the Committee on Education and Labor*, in US Equal Employment Opportunity Commission, *Legislative History*, pp. 74–6.

[9] Michael Schuster, Joan A. Kaspin and Christopher S. Miller, *The Age Discrimination in Employment Act: an Evaluation of Federal and State Enforcement, Legal Processes and Employer Compliance. A Final Report to the AARP Andrus Foundation* (1989), p. 13.

lowering the qualifying age to 40, since this was when most expert witnesses considered age discrimination in employment became evident. (The upper age limit was, however, subject to review by the Secretary of Labor; it was thus always 'on the agenda'.) Initially, therefore, the ADEA was not concerned with mandatory retirement, since the 'normal' retirement age of 65 was the upper age limit for protection. This age limit was raised to 70 in 1978.[10] Only in 1986 – nearly twenty years later – was mandatory retirement abolished for all but a few occupations, and by then this provision was largely irrelevant, given the small proportion of citizens who were still economically active when aged in their late sixties and seventies. (In 1990, only 16.3 per cent of men and 8.6 per cent of women aged 65+ were still in the labour force.) As will be shown later in this chapter, by the late 1980s employers were using other methods to get rid of their unwanted older employees and restructure their workforces – notably, by offering attractive early retirement incentives, which purported to be 'voluntary'.[11]

Initially, the ADEA only covered private employers – federal, state and local governments were excluded – with more than twenty-five employees. Employment agencies and labour unions were also covered. Most focus in the Act was on the prohibitory clauses. It was unlawful for an employer 'to fail or refuse to hire or to discharge any individual or otherwise discriminate against any individual with respect to his compensation, terms, conditions or privileges of employment, because of such individual's age'.[12] Advertisements containing age specifications were unlawful if they could be shown to discourage the employment of older workers (unless, of course, they fixed a *minimum* age limit which was under 40).[13] Employers were prohibited from retaliating against an employee who had complained of discrimination or who had brought an age discrimination law suit. Even age-based workplace harassment was outlawed.[14] For discrimination to occur, there need not be a clear-cut case of an older employee being replaced by a younger one. Non-promotion, firing, non-hiring, exclusion from a re-training programme, and so on, could all be enough to establish a prima facie case. An interesting point is that the ADEA allowed age-based targeting in the allocation of social security benefits by age, whereas Title VII did not allow it regarding gender and race.

---

[10] L. M. Friedman, *Your Time*, pp. 82–3. For the background arguments, see *Mandatory Retirement: the Social and Human Costs of Enforced Idleness. Report by the Select Committee on Aging. Ninety-Fifth Congress, August 1977* (1977).

[11] Jill S. Quadagno and Melissa Hardy, 'Regulating Retirement Through the Age Discrimination in Employment Act', *Research on Aging*, vol. 13, no. 4, Dec. 1991, pp. 470–1.

[12] *The Age Discrimination in Employment Act of 1967*, Section 4 (a).

[13] Terms such as 'young', 'college student' or 'girl' would thus be suspect.

[14] Sally Dunaway, 'Thirty Years Later: the ADEA, an Essential Shield for the Older Worker' (unpublished AARP paper, April 1998), p. 5.

Remedies for violations of the ADEA included injunctive relief (a court order prohibiting further discrimination), reinstatement, back pay with interest, front pay, attorney's fees, compensatory damages and punitive damages.

The enlargement of the ADEA's coverage was quite gradual. In 1974, Congress extended its protection to employees of federal, state and local governments, and firms employing over twenty employees were henceforth included: this meant that the Act's coverage of workers aged 40–65 rose from just under half in 1974 to nearly 70 per cent in 1976. In 1978, the upper age limit was raised, and trial by jury was introduced (generally benefiting plaintiffs);[15] in 1984 US citizens working for American corporations overseas were covered; and in 1986 the upper age limit was removed (with some exceptions). Mandatory retirement was thus abolished for all but a small number of occupations where public safety was the issue – basically, airline pilots, firefighters and law enforcement officers – and for tenured faculty at universities.[16] (This exemption ran until 31 December 1993, and was then reviewed: in 1996 Congress passed the Age Discrimination in Employment Amendments, confirming the right of state and local governments to set mandatory retirement ages for public safety employees.) There was also exemption for high-level executives who had held such a position for more than two years, and whose pension and benefits amounted to at least $44,000 per annum. The 1990 Older Workers Benefit Protection Act restored and clarified the ADEA's protection of employee benefits. Some other exemptions have always existed: the ADEA does not protect elected officials or their personal staff, appointees on a policy-making level, and those appointees' immediate legal advisors. As O'Meara drily comments, Congress 'has thereby afforded itself the unmitigated right to discriminate on the basis of age'.[17] Needless to say, the ADEA has also done nothing to affect minimum age stipulations for activities like voting, alcohol consumption, sexual intercourse, and so on, as well as age-related matters such as the school curriculum. There are also statutory minimum ages for such offices as President (35), Congressman (25) and Senator (30), as well as minimum and maximum ages for jury service.

Enforcing the ADEA

Enforcement of the ADEA was initially performed by the Wage and Hour Division of the Department of Labor. The original intention had been to

---

[15] O'Meara, *Protecting*, p. 33. Henceforth, the selection of sympathetic jurors became a legal tactic. It is possible that jurors are more sympathetic to plaintiffs since they themselves may well have had experience of age discrimination at work. The right to trial by jury arose from *Lorillard* v. *Pons* (1978).

[16] Joseph E. Kalet, *Age Discrimination in Employment Law* (1990), p. 5.

[17] O'Meara, *Protecting*, p. 341.

establish a special agency similar to the Equal Employment Opportunity Commission (EEOC) – the body responsible for enforcement of the 1964 Civil Rights Act – but an amendment by Senator Javits placed the task with the Department of Labor, partly reflecting Javits's view that the ADEA was essentially an employment protection measure and partly because the EEOC was experiencing a backlog of Title VII cases. Enforcement was transferred to the EEOC in 1978. At this time, the EEOC, chaired by Eleanor Holmes Norton, was said to be processing complaints quickly and efficiently. However, under the chairmanship of Clarence Thomas in the 1980s there were increasing complaints by groups such as the AARP and the Older Women's League that enforcement was slow and ineffective. On several occasions, the AARP provided statistical evidence of the increasing tardiness with which ADEA complaints were being processed. Official Hearings were held to consider the charges that the ADEA was not being properly enforced.[18] In part, this critical onslaught reflected dislike of Thomas's conservative views (he was a Reagan appointment). Thomas's defence was that staff cuts meant that the EEOC was having to process more complaints with fewer personnel;[19] this was a point made repeatedly by other EEOC representatives. The steady growth in complaints has undoubtedly been a perennial problem for the EEOC. For example, by 1991, the EEOC was operating with 400 fewer staff than in 1980, yet had 75 per cent more charges to process.[20] Thus by the mid-1990s a backlog of some 120,000 pending charges had built up.[21]

The processes for dealing with an age discrimination complaint involve negotiating a set of 'procedural wrinkles'[22] which reflect the Act's attempt to build in a measure of 'conciliation, conference and persuasion' between the parties involved. For an individual to bring a private action under the ADEA, a 'charge' (in writing) must first be filed with the EEOC within 180 days of the alleged act of unlawful discrimination or, in a case where an alleged discriminatory action occurs in a state which has its own age discrimination law and authority administering the law, within 300 days. This basically continues the system that operated when the Department of

---

[18] *Twenty Years of the Age Discrimination in Employment Act: Success or Failure? Hearings Before the Special Committee on Aging, United States Senate, September 10 1987* (1988), esp. pp. 61–72.

[19] Ibid., pp. 81–4.

[20] Statement by James H. Troy (EEOC), in *Age Discrimination in the Workplace: a Continuing Problem for Older Workers. Hearing Before the Select Committee on Aging. House of Representatives, September 24 1991* (1992), p. 89.

[21] US Equal Employment Opportunity Commission, *Annual Report 1995* (1995), p. 20.

[22] L. M. Friedman, *Your Time*, p. 20. For a full account of procedures, see: O'Meara, *Protecting*, ch. IV; US Equal Employment Opportunity Commission. Technical Assistance Program, *Age Discrimination* (1995), Section B.

Labor had responsibility. The EEOC then has 60 days to investigate the charge and eliminate any illegal practices by informal methods, conciliation, etc. No civil action can be commenced by an individual until this 60-day period has elapsed. After this, an individual can bring a private action in the federal court. The EEOC itself files law suits in remarkably few ADEA cases: for example, in the fiscal year 1996, these amounted to less than 1 per cent of the 15,665 ADEA charges received.[23] The EEOC also investigates wider instances of age discrimination in employment, and issues interpretative guidelines and regulations for employers and employees.[24] Mainly in order to discourage an employer from impeding the investigation, conciliation and enforcement process, liquidated damages against a defendant are doubled where there is a 'wilful' violation (that is, where the employer has shown 'knowledge or reckless disregard' of the fact that the ADEA has been contravened). Class actions are possible, but more difficult than in Title VII cases. (Class actions most often take place where there are large-scale layoffs.)[25]

Complaints received by the Secretary of Labor steadily rose, from 1,031 in 1969 to 5,121 in 1976. In his very useful summary of the first ten years of the Act's working, Marc Rosenblum suggested three main reasons for this increase: growing awareness on the part of workers (particularly after several big age discrimination court cases were reported in the press); extensions of the Act's coverage; and recessions and downsizings, which began to affect the American economy from the mid-1970s.[26] Increasing awareness is indicated by the difference in results between two surveys carried out by the Department of Labor: the first, in 1981, found 30 per cent of all employees aware of the ADEA; the second, in 1985, found 50 per cent aware.[27]

The principal defences

One verdict on the ADEA can be pronounced with total confidence: it has produced a spate of litigation, in which complex legal arguments have

[23] *Developments in Aging: 1996. Volume 1. Report of the Special Committee on Aging. United States Senate* (1997), p. 79.

[24] Mack A. Player, *Federal Law of Employment Discrimination in a Nutshell* (1981), p. 111.

[25] For example, in 1998 the pharmaceutical company Hoffman-La Roche had to pay $13,650,000 to settle the claims of 476 employees laid off in 1985 because of company downsizing. Bureau of National Affairs, *Employment Discrimination Report*, vol. 10, no. 3, 21 Jan. 1998, p. 75.

[26] Marc Rosenblum, *The Next Steps in Combating Age Discrimination in Employment: With Special Reference to Mandatory Retirement Policy. A Working Paper Prepared for Use by the Special Committee on Aging, United States Senate* (August 1977), p. 7.

[27] Cathy Ventrell-Monsees, 'How Useful Are Legislative Remedies: America's Experience with the ADEA', *Aging International*, vol. XX, no. 3, Sept. 1993, p. 43.

become intertwined with the latest (and ever-changing) medical evidence on health status and working capacity. Anti-discrimination legislation in the USA has historically been drafted in fairly general language (in contrast, say, to health and safety regulation), and thus has had to be clarified by litigation in the courts.[28] Consequently, much of the legal controversy in the early years of the ADEA was over procedural issues; then it moved to 'age-substantive' issues – the fundamental and very difficult questions of what constitutes proof in cases of age discrimination, and how the main defences defined in the Act are to be interpreted. The hybrid nature of the Act creates problems: for example, whereas a Title VII plaintiff must show that his or her replacement was outside the protected group, in ADEA cases the replacement can be within the protected group: a woman cannot file a sex discrimination case if she is replaced by another woman, but this does not necessarily apply where a sixty-year-old is replaced by a forty-year-old.

There were three important exceptions to the ADEA's coverage, all of which were to be the subject of great legal dispute in the three decades after 1967. These were borrowed from Title VII, and permitted age discrimination: (1) Where age is a bona fide occupational qualification (BFOQ) reasonably necessary to the normal operation of the particular business, or where the differentiation is based on reasonable factors other than age (RFOA); (2) To observe the terms of a bona fide seniority system or any bona fide employee benefit plan such as a retirement, pension, or insurance plan, which is not a subterfuge to evade the purpose of the Act, except that no such employee benefit plan can excuse the failure to hire any individual; (3) To discharge or otherwise discipline an individual for good cause.

As in all anti-discrimination legislation, proof of intent and motive is always problematic in ADEA cases, given that evidence tends to be circumstantial. Clear empirical evidence of age discrimination is often difficult to obtain. If a defendant articulates a reasonable, non-discriminatory justification for his or her actions, the presumption of discrimination dissolves, and the burden of proof falls on the plaintiff. Statistical evidence can be important – for example, where the average ages of those dismissed are clearly higher than those retained by a firm. (Certain analytical techniques, such as non-parametric tests, can be used to decide whether the age pattern of terminated employees justifies a charge of discrimination.)[29] In a recent case brought against several Hollywood studios by twenty-eight

---

[28] James P. Northrup, *Old Age, Handicapped, and Vietnam-era Antidiscrimination Legislation* (1980), p. 51.

[29] For an interesting elaboration, see Barbara L. Bessey and Srijati M. Ananda, 'Age Discrimination in Employment. An Interdisciplinary Review of the ADEA', *Research on Aging*, vol. 13, no. 4, Dec. 1991, pp. 437–44.

television writers aged 40+, the average age of the writing staff on night-time television series was compared unfavourably with the average age of the Writers' Guild of America membership.[30] However, 'statistical discrimination' is generally hard to prove since there is a natural tendency in all firms for senior employees to be replaced by junior ones: this is inherent in the very process of ageing, since age is a 'continuous variable'. Between-group differences in earnings or employment may be the result of discrimination; but they may also reflect differentials in education, skills, productivity and so on.[31] Employees who under-perform and fail to secure promotion will languish at the same level in a firm for several years and will therefore tend to be older than others who have been more recently promoted to that level: they may feel resentment, but discrimination will not be the cause.[32] Again, it has long been the case that the average age of a workforce primarily reflects the type of business engaged in by the firm: new industries have younger age profiles than old ones.

In the legal debates, the relativities of age have been judged qualitatively different from the immutabilities of race and gender:[33] unlike the latter, all will become members of the protected group eventually (unless they die prematurely), and therefore drawing the boundaries round the protected group is difficult. If a 55-year-old is unfairly replaced by a 25-year-old, the evidence of age discrimination may be clear-cut; if, however, a 55-year-old is replaced by a 45-year-old (and both thereby fall within the protected group), the decision may still be age discriminatory, but winning an ADEA case could be difficult. In such cases, the requirement is that there must be sufficient 'daylight' between the two ages, and the courts have paid close attention to this.[34] For example, in a 1998 case in Colorado, a 2 years and 9 months age difference between a discharged employee and his replacement was insufficient to establish a prima facie case.[35] A further problem is that there may be 'mixed motive' cases (discrimination may be one of several reasons for a personnel decision) or 'multiple discrimination' (or 'compounded discrimination') cases,[36] involving members of minority

[30] Bureau of National Affairs, *Employment Discrimination Report*, vol. 15, no. 18, 8 Nov. 2000, p. 633.
[31] Report of the Secretary of Labor, *Labor Market Problems of Older Workers* (1989), p. 55.
[32] Bessey and Ananda, 'Age Discrimination', pp. 422–3.
[33] O'Meara, *Protecting*, pp. 93–4.   [34] Kalet, *Age Discrimination*, p. 24.
[35] Bureau of National Affairs, *Employment Discrimination Report*, vol. 10, no. 6, 11 Feb. 1998, p. 187.
[36] US Equal Employment Opportunity Commission. Technical Assistance Program, *Theories of Discrimination. Intentional and Unintentional Employment Discrimination* (1995), p. A-6. For an analysis of age and sex discrimination cases, see American Association of Retired Persons, *Employment Discrimination Against Midlife and Older Women. Volume II: An Analysis of Discrimination Charges Filed With the EEOC* (1997).

groups, women and handicapped individuals.[37] An older ethnic minority woman may bear a double, or triple, burden of age, sex and race discrimination, both overt and subtle.[38] Finally, some plaintiffs may use the ADEA opportunistically. Isolated cases may more reflect individual grudges – on the part of either the employer or the employee – than the patterned behaviour in a firm that the ADEA is attempting to alter. Lawrence Friedman cites one such case: a 51-year-old administrator of a nursing home was fired and replaced by a 34-year-old; the real motive was probably because the administrator had been the son-in-law of the nursing home's owners, and then got divorced.[39]

Some forms of proof are more straightforward, such as remarks uttered at the workplace: if older employees are referred to as 'old codgers', 'past their best', 'worn-out geriatrics', 'old ladies with balls',[40] and so on, and then are dismissed, a prima facie case can be established. Three examples will suffice. In April 1998 the Massachusetts Appeals Court upheld a $624,504 judgement on behalf of a 60-year-old employee who was told by his company's president, 'You've been doing a good job, but I want a younger man.' Another case concerned a 61-year-old grandmother who was rejected for a part-time sales job with a children's clothing retail chain, having been called for interview on the basis of her (age-unspecified) job application; when the store manager saw how old she was, he conducted only a cursory interview with her while sitting on a park bench. The humiliating circumstances of the interview were enough. Again, a pharmaceutical company vice-president's remark that 'we need to get rid of the old guys' permitted an ADEA case to be brought by a salesman who was demoted and replaced by two younger men.[41]

Not surprisingly, the ADEA has given rise to a plethora of legal cases where the 'smoking gun' of proof has been the subject of bitter wrangles. This was to an extent anticipated, especially by the Act's few critics: for example, Senator Peter Domenick warned in 1967 that the federal government was opening up a 'can of legal worms'.[42] Interpretation by the courts has been crucial: the ADEA created 'doors' which could be prised open by the courts via key decisions. The most important of these became

---

[37] US Commission on Civil Rights, *The Age Discrimination Study* (1977), p. 13.

[38] Statement by Joan Kurianski (Executive Director, Older Women's League), in *Age Discrimination in the Workplace*, p. 108.

[39] Case of *Simmons* v. *McGuffey* (1980), cited in L. M. Friedman, *Your Time*, p. 47.

[40] This particular gem is quoted in Bessey and Ananda, 'Age Discrimination', p. 429.

[41] Bureau of National Affairs, *Employment Discrimination Report*, vol. 10, no. 14, 8 April 1998, p. 449; ibid., vol. 10, no. 1, 7 Jan. 1998, pp. 22–3; ibid., vol. 15, no. 11, 20 Sept. 2000, p. 383.

[42] Quoted in W. Andrew Achenbaum, 'Putting ADEA Into Historical Context', *Research on Aging*, vol. 13, no. 4, Dec. 1991, p. 466.

'landmark' rulings by the US Supreme Court (which, incidentally, has always displayed a slight hostility to the ADEA). To an extent, such rulings always reflect the prevailing political culture at any one time, since Supreme Court judges do not exist in a social vacuum, and are political appointees; thus the interpretation of the ADEA has subtly changed over time. These legal interpretations render analysis of the ADEA difficult: one is forced to trawl through a list of complex litigation issues best understood by highly experienced lawyers.[43] In this chapter, space does not permit a detailed exploration of all the legal nuances; only the general principles will be outlined.

ADEA defences have been affected by the wider discussion in Title VII litigation over disparate treatment and adverse impact.[44] The former refers to situations where there is intentionally less favourable treatment because of an individual protected characteristic, such as age: most ADEA cases have fallen under this heading. Adverse impact refers to cases where there is no intent to discriminate, yet a facially neutral policy has an adverse impact on the protected group and that policy cannot be justified by 'business necessity'. Proof of a discriminatory motive is not required in such cases.[45] For example, a rigorous test of physical strength may eliminate most women from the position of firefighter, but would be justified by business necessity. Again, a policy of not allowing employees to have beards might have an adverse impact on an ethnic minority group, but would be permissible if it pertained to work-relevant factors, such as safety or hygiene. However, it can in practice prove very difficult to determine when the adverse impact becomes legally significant.

In the wider civil rights debate, the key legal case defining adverse impact was *Griggs* v. *Duke Power Company* (1971). Here, a company with a long history of not employing African Americans was subject to a complaint under Title VII for requiring job applicants to possess a high school diploma and a pass score in two professionally recognised tests that were, in effect, intelligence tests. Data presented at the trial demonstrated that these neutral employment requirements had a substantially greater impact on blacks than on whites. Since blacks were less likely than whites to possess such an educational qualification – because of poorer educational facilities and the strong correlation between parental income and a child's educational attainment – this qualification was

---

[43] For example, see L. Steven Platt and Cathy Ventrell-Monsees, *Age Discrimination Litigation* (2000), which is a detailed guide for plaintiffs.

[44] Sometimes called 'disparate impact'. For an elaboration, see Albert G. Mosley and Nicholas Capaldi, *Affirmative Action. Social Justice or Unfair Preference?* (1996), pp. 6–7.

[45] Kalet, *Age Discrimination*, p. 67; Bessey and Ananda, 'Age Discrimination', pp. 424–36.

eventually held by the Supreme Court, in a unanimous ruling, to be discriminatory, despite the company's protestations that there was no intent to discriminate. A pre-employment test that was not job-related was discriminatory. Policies that were facially neutral or 'fair in form but discriminatory in operation' were contrary to Title VII.[46] In other words, outcome mattered more than intent. The legal touchstone, again, was business necessity. Interpretations of the ADEA have followed similar reasoning, even though it has been argued that, since age is a relative characteristic, older people have not experienced a long-term history of discrimination such as can be used to justify the adverse impact principle in racial discrimination cases.

Of the three principal ADEA defences, most discussion has centred on BFOQ and RFOA, with the 'employee benefit plan' defence experiencing some legal clarification. (The 'good cause' defence is the least problematic, since it is subject to the same kind of proof that would operate in any unfair dismissal case – for example, persistent lateness, unprofessional conduct, abuse towards a colleague, and so on.) In BFOQ, an employer admits age discrimination, but offers an explanation that the courts will find acceptable – what is known as an 'affirmative defence'. On the other hand, in RFOA cases the employer denies that age played a part, and contends that job performance or some other non-age-related factor was used.[47] The defendant's prima facie case is acknowledged.

In BFOQ cases, an employer must: (1) Demonstrate that the job requirements allegedly being fulfilled less and less effectively because of advancing age are necessary to the essential operation of the business; (2) Establish that substantially all persons over the determined age would be unable to undertake safely or efficiently the duties of the job in question, or that it would be impractical or impossible to deal with older employees on an individual basis. Thus if an employer conducts proper, well-designed performance evaluations clearly related to the requirements of the job, there is no violation of the ADEA; by contrast so-called 'pen and paper' tests that do not have direct relevance are discriminatory. Here we see the intention of the Act to outlaw only 'unreasonable' or 'arbitrary' discrimination: federal courts have tended to take the view that age discrimination in employment is justified if there is any rational basis for it.[48]

---

[46] Ray Marshall, Charles B. Knapp, Malcolm H. Liggett and Robert W. Glover, *Employment Discrimination: the Impact of Legal and Administrative Remedies* (1978), p. 5; O'Meara, *Protecting*, pp. 132–3.

[47] O'Meara, *Protecting*, p. 147.

[48] Rosenblum, *The Next Steps*, p. 8; *Mandatory Retirement: the Social and Human Costs*, p. 16.

The public safety defences

The instances in which BFOQ applies have been steadily narrowed down since 1967 to occupations where public safety is at risk (notably, airline pilots, helicopter pilots, uniformed police officers, bus drivers, firefighters and prison guards), or where age is necessary for authenticity (for example, actors and actresses, or persons promoting products to a particular age-group). A series of important cases hinging upon medical evidence and performance testing helped clarify the scope of permissible BFOQ categories, as did the virtual elimination of mandatory retirement in 1986. (Firefighters, police officers and prison guards were granted special exemptions, which ran until 31 December 1993.) For example, two notable cases – *Hodgson* v. *Greyhound Lines, Ltd* (1974), and *Usery* v. *Tamiami Trail Tours, Inc.* (1975) – established that bus companies could keep upper age limits for applicants as bus drivers, on the public safety justification. However, the most interesting BFOQ cases were those relating to airline pilots, police officers and firefighters.

These debates began relatively innocuously in the mid-1960s, over the question of whether youth was a bona fide occupational qualification for airline stewardesses. At that time, many airlines stipulated a maximum age (often 30 or 32) for their (female) stewardesses, attaching numerous conditions regarding appearance, grooming, length of hair, lipstick and even dental bridges. These were enforced by rigorous physical examinations. The justification was that weary middle-aged businessmen (the most lucrative of airlines' customers) wanted to be served in-flight refreshment by pretty young women; yet in reality stewardesses were there 'to perform significant actions with respect to emergency situations, and ill or deranged passengers'.[49] By the end of the 1960s, age barriers for airline stewardesses had been removed. However, weight and height remained bona fide occupational qualifications.

The case of airline pilots was much more complex. In the 1950s, air travel became considerably faster with the spread of jet planes. It was considered vital that pilots' health and reaction times be monitored regularly, given the catastrophic consequences of pilot error, illness or death in flight. Thus in 1959 the Federal Aviation Administration fixed the mandatory retirement age at 60 for commercial airline pilots.[50] A long period of debate has followed, with several important court cases confirming the 1959 decision. Most attention has been focused on the possibility of a heart attack, and the reliability of medical testing that claims to predict this.

---

[49] Statement by Herbert Levy, Attorney for the Air Line Pilots Association, in *Age Discrimination in Employment. Hearings, 1967*, p. 104.
[50] William E. Thoms and Frank J. Dooley, *Airline Labor Law: The Railway Labor Act and Aviation After Deregulation* (1990), p. 137.

The debate over airline pilots can be summarised quickly. One school of thought contends that medical testing is now so good that, with regular and intensive examination, the likelihood of a heart attack in men aged in their forties and fifties can be predicted with sufficient accuracy. Thus one expert witness claimed in 1991 that the 'revolution' that has taken place in the understanding of the biology of ageing means that individualised testing can now be so accurate as to render mandatory retirement medically and scientifically unjustified 'in any profession or job', including that of airline pilot.[51] It is therefore discriminatory to maintain the mandatory retirement age at 60 for those who wish to continue working and are in good health. While few argue that it should be abolished completely, the suggestion is that the mandatory retirement age for airline pilots could be raised by a few years with no threat to passenger safety.

Another school of thought contends that medical testing is too flawed for public safety to be put at risk, and that there have been enough instances of pilots passing their medicals only to have a heart attack shortly after. However, the arguments are not all about health. A further complication is the existence of complex structures of seniority. On large airlines, the older pilots are allocated the long-haul, prestige routes. The younger pilots work their way up to these as they age, and look forward to them. All pilots thus have a vested interest in preserving a retirement age of 60. It is the classic argument for mandatory retirement – that it frees up paths to promotion, seniority and status.

The right of commercial airlines not to hire older pilots has been upheld by the courts. For example, in *Murnane* v. *American Airlines* (1981) the court upheld the airline's policy of not hiring flight officers over the age of 40, on the justification that, since it was company policy to move a flight officer to a captain's position only after sixteen years of service, flight officers could not be appointed above the age of 40.[52] As already noted, Federal Aviation Administration regulations stipulate that civil aviation pilots must retire at age 60. However, this does not apply to flight engineers, one of whom is normally present in the cockpit, alongside the captain (pilot) and first officer (co-pilot). In 1978, following the raising of the ADEA's upper age limit to 70, Trans World Airlines (TWA) proposed a scheme whereby pilots reaching the age of 60 would be able to 'bid' for flight engineer positions instead of retiring outright. (The retirement age of a TWA flight engineer was set at 70.) The success of these bids was determined by seniority, with unsuccessful bidders being forced to retire. By contrast,

[51] Statement by Professor T. Franklin Williams, in *Age Discrimination in the Workplace*, pp. 39–45.
[52] Thoms and Dooley, *Airline Labor Law*, p. 138.

pilots below the age of 60 could transfer to flight engineer status with no such restrictions. Three TWA pilots were forced – for different reasons – to retire through being unsuccessful bidders. Interestingly, the Air Line Pilots Association (ALPA) opposed this proposed new arrangement, insisting that both pilots and flight engineers should be retired at age 60. The three plaintiffs thus filed an action against both TWA and the ALPA, their own trade union. The court's eventual decision was that denying freedom of transfer to pilots above the age of 60 violated the ADEA. The case of *Western Airlines* v. *Criswell* (1985) established that Western's policy of fixing an upper age limit of 60 for flight engineers also violated the ADEA. In coming to this decision (which was viewed as a significant narrowing of the BFOQ defences), the court emphasised the increasing heterogeneity in health status, cognitive ability and working capacity that accompanies the ageing process, and ruled that employers should accordingly make every reasonable effort to conduct individualised testing. Western Airlines' case was, of course, greatly weakened by the fact that other airlines permitted flight engineers to work past the age of 60.[53]

In the case of police officers, the legal decisions have largely supported mandatory retirement. A landmark case was *Massachusetts Board of Retirement* v. *Murgia* in 1976. As a Massachusetts state policeman, Robert Murgia was required to take vigorous physical examinations, made stricter after the fortieth birthday. Having passed these, he was obliged to retire at 50, in accordance with the Massachusetts State Police Department's mandatory retirement rule for uniformed police. Since the ADEA did not at that time cover public employees, Murgia rested his case on the Fourteenth Amendment (which guarantees 'equal protection' for all US citizens). Eventually, Murgia lost. The court decided that physical ability *does* decline with age, and that, in the case of uniformed police officers, a certain level of physical ability was a bona fide occupational qualification. The protection of the public was the key issue. Once again, a test that was job-related was a rational basis for mandatory retirement, confirming the ADEA's aim of allowing 'justified' age discrimination.[54] The lesson was that if an employer conducts proper job-related performance tests, a charge of discrimination is unlikely to succeed.[55]

The public safety exemption established under the 1986 Act expired on 31 December 1993, and then came under review, via bills permitting state and local police and fire departments to return to the practice of

---

[53] Joel W. Friedman and George M. Strickler, *Cases and Materials on the Law of Employment Discrimination* (1987), pp. 611–21; O'Meara, *Protecting*, pp. 147–55.

[54] Player, *Federal Law*, p. 75.

[55] Schuster, Kaspin and Miller, *Age Discrimination in Employment Act*, p. v.

mandatory retirement. Opinion was even more polarised than ever: for example, the point was made that police needed to be fitter and mentally more alert in the 1990s than in the past, given that offenders tended to be younger and more violent. (In the ADEA, 'law enforcement officer' basically means a policeman who apprehends and detains criminals, rather than one in a desk job.) In the Senate's Committee on Labor and Human Resources proceedings of 8 March 1996 there occurred a debate which encapsulated the difficulties involved in the whole public safety issue.

Expert witnesses were in sharp disagreement. Captain Thomas Miller, a firefighter with twenty-eight years of experience, spoke on behalf of the International Association of Firefighters and supported a maximum age limit. Even the best fitness regimen, he argued, could not prevent the deterioration of ability that occurs with age. Standard fitness tests (such as climbing three flights of stairs carrying a hose) could never replicate the 'real world experiences' of a firefighter, involving 'extreme temperature fluctuations, smoke, stress, fatigue, and the speed at which a person must go from a sedentary state to a state of full exertion'.

However, an opposing point of view came from Frank J. Landy, a Professor of Psychology, on behalf of the American Psychological Association. Landy had directed a study (mandated by Congress) into the feasibility of substituting tests for crude age proxies. His study examined over 5,000 research results, and found that, overall, age was a poor predictor of physical and mental ability: some 30-year-olds could not climb flights of stairs pulling a charged fire hose, while some 60-year-olds could. Furthermore, argued Landy, experience was an important contributor to effective work performance, especially in dangerous firefighting situations. Individualised testing should thus be the determinant of retirement decisions.

These opposing statements were followed by a debate of sharp disagreement. Loren Myhre, a research psychologist who had studied over 1,000 firefighters in a twenty-year period, argued that most tests for firefighters were deficient and that, where public safety was concerned, mandatory retirement was essential since, in the aggregate, cardio-vascular fitness did decline markedly with age. In reply, Landy pointed out that, in 1994, only thirteen out of the 265,000 paid firefighters in the USA had had heart attacks while on the job. Of these, only two were aged over 55; eight had a prior history of heart disease, and should not have been on duty – regardless of their age.[56] The arguments were unresolved and, in the final analysis, public safety considerations meant that age remained a BFOQ.

---

[56] *Age Discrimination in Employment Amendments of 1995: Hearing of the Committee on Labor and Human Resources. United States Senate, March 8 1996* (1996), pp. 1–72.

The RFOA defence is more common, and has been applied to a wider variety of cases. Employers may use a factor such as poor work performance (for example, inability to reach certain sales targets). EEOC regulations do not offer much guidance on how such defences might be interpreted; instead, the EEOC tends to proceed more on a case-by-case basis. Recently, there has been concern that the RFOA defence is being steadily widened. For example, in *Hazen Paper Co.* v. *Biggins* (1993), the Supreme Court upheld the right of an employer to dismiss a 62-year-old man just weeks before his pension would have vested; it ruled that no disparate treatment existed, since the employer's decision was based upon a factor other than the employee's age.[57] The higher cost of employing someone was not originally intended to be an RFOA defence, but has crept in – most notably, in the 1997 case of *Michael J. Marks* v. *Loral Corp. et al.*, in California, where high salary costs were allowed: a California appellate court ruled that older, highly paid employees could be replaced by younger, lesser-paid ones, and this was confirmed by the Court of Appeal. Supporters of the ADEA were concerned that henceforth plaintiffs would have to demonstrate that an employer's defence of economic considerations was a pretext for age discrimination.

The 1980s: downsizing and recession

The ADEA came up against the greatest challenge to its stated intentions during the 1980s, when the American economy experienced massive re-structuring, involving widespread downsizing of firms, corporate mergers, redundancies and recession. Increasing global economic competition necessitated reductions in the unit costs of labour, often achieved by technological innovations in production methods that displaced marginal workers. As in other advanced industrial economies, the impact upon older workers was disproportionate since they tended to be concentrated in those sectors (notably manufacturing) that suffered the greatest contraction, or had higher salary costs. The 'great American jobs machine' was still producing replacement jobs at an impressive rate – the civilian workforce increased from 110,204,000 in 1982 to 131,056,000 in 1994 – but these new jobs tended to be more insecure, lower-paid, service industry-based, and filled by young workers (often women).[58] The jobs that were

---

[57] Howard C. Eglit, 'The Age Discrimination in Employment Act at Thirty: Where It's Been, Where It is Today, Where It's Going', *University of Richmond Law Review*, vol. 31, 1997, pp. 693–4.
[58] See, for example, Report of the Secretary of Labor, *Labor Market Problems*.

lost – a total of 43,000,000 between 1976 and 1993, according to one source[59] – were not only industrial, but also white-collar corporate jobs which disappeared as a consequence of the outsourcing of production to overseas locations where labour was cheaper. The effect on those middle-class, middle-aged American men who were made redundant was often traumatic, involving an abrupt shock to their psychological well-being.[60] A study by James Medoff, a Harvard economist, found that workers aged 35–54 were 45 per cent more likely during the 1980s to suffer permanent job loss than their equivalents in the 1970s.[61] Again, a Bureau of Labor Statistics study of displaced workers between 1979 and 1984 showed that, of 5,100,000 who were made redundant, only 41 per cent of those aged 55–64 were re-employed, as opposed to 70 per cent of those aged 20–4.[62]

In their restructuring programmes of the 1980s, employers had to show that the employees who left either were terminated on the basis of their relative contributions to the business, or went voluntarily (via early exit incentives), or were in a job that was eliminated. These 'reduction in force' (RIF) cases had to be handled very carefully by employers. Any hint that downsized older workers were being replaced by younger ones would lead to expensive age discrimination claims. (Such a fate befell the Rank Xerox Corporation.)[63] The 'bona fide employee benefit plan' defence in the ADEA could not be used to instigate 'involuntary retirement', and thus it was carefully circumvented. Large firms came up with extensive early retirement programmes, and relied on the simple, cheap and convenient criterion of age in allocating redundancies – often with attractive early retirement schemes. These would be on offer to employees only for a short period,[64] and had to be constructed very carefully: for example, any threat of dismissal against those employees refusing to go 'voluntarily' would be taken by the courts to be 'constructive discharge'.[65] However, it was possible for an employee voluntarily to sign away his or her rights to appeal to the EEOC (providing this was 'knowing and voluntary'), in return for a greatly enhanced early retirement pension, and this was the

---

[59] Louis Uchitelle and N. R. Kleinfield, 'The Price of Jobs Lost', in The New York Times, *The Downsizing of America* (1996), pp. 4, 18.

[60] For a recent exploration of this human problem, see Richard Sennett, *The Corrosion of Character: The Personal Consequences of Work in the New Capitalism* (1998).

[61] Cited in Eglit, 'Age Discrimination in Employment Act', p. 604.

[62] Statement by Rep. Marilyn Lloyd, in *Displaced Older Workers. Hearing Before the Select Committee on Aging. House of Representatives, July 24 1985* (1985), p. 8.

[63] Statement by Jules Lusardi, former Rank Xerox employee, in *Twenty Years*, p. 14.

[64] O'Meara, *Protecting*, p. 185.

[65] Schuster, Kaspin and Miller, *Age Discrimination in Employment Act*, p. 8.

strategy used by some large corporations.[66] In response, there was introduced the 1990 Older Workers Benefit Protection Act, which added new
requirements to be met if an employee agreed to waive his or her ADEA
rights.[67]

Thus in 1986 the Exxon Corporation (the US's largest oil company)
offered immediate retirement to employees aged 50+ with more than
fifteen years of service, on enhanced terms. The offer was available during
a brief 'window', from 22 April to 30 May.[68] The downsizings of the 1980s
raised again the question of whether employers really were basing their
personnel decisions upon irrational 'myths and misconceptions', or
whether they were just relying on the cheapest and quickest method of
deciding where the axe of redundancy should fall. At a time when labour
costs had to be cut, employers were behaving rationally by laying off older
workers who were more expensive to employ (particularly with regard to
health insurance costs). Essentially, employers were using crude age
proxies much as they had done in the 1950s. Thus from the 1980s, many
early retirements that appeared to be voluntary (and were cited to justify
supply-side explanations of 'retirement behaviour') were in fact caused by
economic restructuring and thus more 'involuntary'. Public opinion surveys in the 1980s that found the 'retirement decision' to be largely voluntary, and induced by early exit incentives, should thus be treated with some
scepticism. Compared with the underlying economic causes, the effect of
such incentives was only secondary, and after the event.

The increasingly obvious plight of the displaced older worker in the
1980s and 1990s once again aroused concerns about the loss to the US
economy of valuable skilled personnel,[69] and led to calls from interest
groups for more federal protection for older workers (via new re-training
programmes). The EEOC was flooded with ADEA complaints from regions
where traditional manufacturing industries had been concentrated (such as
Pittsburgh, home of the steel industry),[70] and age discrimination cases rose
from just over one-tenth of all charges filed with the EEOC in 1980 to a
quarter in 1991.[71] As Martin A. Corry (AARP) argued in 1991, age

---

[66] For a discussion of reductions in force, early retirement incentives, waivers of claims
against the ADEA and the vexed question of what constitutes 'voluntary' redundancy,
see Raymond F. Gregory, *Age Discrimination in the American Workplace: Old at a Young
Age* (2001), chs. 3, 4 and 5.
[67] Eglit, 'Age Discrimination in Employment Act', p. 698.
[68] Quadagno and Hardy, 'Regulating Retirement', pp. 471–2.
[69] See, for example, American Bar Association. The Commission on Legal Problems of the
Elderly, *Downsizing in an Aging Work Force* (1992), p. 11.
[70] Letter from Eugene V. Nelson, Area Director of the Pittsburgh Area Office of the EEOC,
in *Twenty Years*, p. 36.
[71] Evan J. Kemp, Chair of EEOC, in *Age Discrimination in the Workplace*, p. 83.

discrimination issues were more important than ever, because of 'a contracting economy and mergers and acquisitions that prompt reductions in
labor costs'.[72] At the same time, however, there was a sense of powerlessness
in the face of global economic forces and the transformation of the US
economy from a predominantly manufacturing base to new service industries (in which older workers were less likely to be employed). Representative
Olympia J. Snowe thus pointed out that the declines in the labour force
participation rates of older men were 'likely not voluntary, but rather a
result of the economy and of patterns in the labor force which militate
against the employment of older persons'.[73] As the economist Stephen
Sandell perceptively observed, the events of the 1980s demonstrated that
age discrimination was only one of many problems faced by older workers.[74]
Most of the contributors to a volume edited by Sandell, *The Problem Isn't
Age* (1987), agreed.[75] Remedial action by further anti-discriminatory legislation could therefore only have a limited effect.

Attacks by conservatives in the 1980s

A sea-change in political ideology swept through American public life with
the accession of Ronald Reagan to the Presidency in 1980. Neo-classical
economics rapidly became the new orthodoxy, and was adopted with
almost religious fervour by its adherents.[76] Many notionally independent
think-tanks swung round to a broadly 'supply-side' position in their
analysis of social problems and policy solutions. Social benefits were
increasingly said to have a corrosive effect on human behaviour – allegedly
offering 'perverse incentives' that rewarded idleness instead of work – and
on labour supply, at a time when the new emergent capitalism required
more low-paid, 'flexible' workers. Hence Martin Feldstein argued:

Now there is widespread agreement that the conditions of unemployment, retirement, a low level of accumulated assets, and high medical bills are in part the result
of rational choices by the individuals affected. It is recognised that the social
insurance programmes themselves distort incentives and thereby contribute to
the very problems that they are intended to solve.[77]

---

[72] Statement by the AARP, ibid., p. 97. See also, Dunaway, *Thirty Years Later*, pp. 13–15.
[73] *Displaced Older Workers*, p. 16.
[74] Ibid., pp. 42–4. For useful discussion, see American Bar Association, *Downsizing*.
[75] Stephen H. Sandell (ed.), *The Problem Isn't Age. Work and Older Americans* (1987).
[76] A good example of this zealotry is David A. Stockman, *The Triumph of Politics* (1986).
[77] Martin Feldstein, 'The Social Security Explosion', *The Public Interest*, no. 81, Fall 1985,
p. 95. The most celebrated attack was Charles Murray, *Losing Ground: American Social
Policy, 1950–1980* (1984).

Moreover, conservative critics tended to blame the 1960s for all of America's prevailing social ills, and looked back – nostalgically, romantically and misguidedly – at the 1950s as a free-market nirvana.

Not surprisingly, the ADEA did not escape unscathed in this massive and concerted attack upon all federal social policies. The theoretical underpinning of this attack was Edward Lazear's celebrated analysis of mandatory retirement, which argued that it was a business necessity: mandatory retirement enabled firms to dispense with the services of older employers who, because of their age and seniority, were paid more than their marginal value and productivity.[78] At a time when the US economy was experiencing massive re-structuring and workforce reductions, with downward pressure on wages, the encouragement of labour mobility and wage elasticity was seen by neo-classical economists as vitally important. The ADEA was said to restrict both, and accordingly it came under attack from employers and free-market economists.

Conservatives in the 1980s began to articulate several powerful criticisms: that the 1967 Act had been an ill thought-out, knee-jerk reaction to the broader pressure from the civil rights movement; that the perceived problem of 'age discrimination' which caused such debate among liberals in the 1960s was in fact a simplistic rationalisation of complex shifts in labour market demand, or of technological changes that displaced older workers; that age discrimination was in practice very difficult to prove, being associated with reasonable and publicly acceptable personnel decisions relating to seniority systems, promotion and age stratifications in a firm; that the arguments of advocates often confused rationality and irrationality on the part of employers; that the federal government had cleverly abrogated responsibility by ensuring that its role was merely supervisory (for example, compensation was paid by employers, rather than the federal government); that it was too easy for politicians such as Claude Pepper to court popularity by continually extending the Act's coverage; and that the ADEA had made employers reluctant to hire older workers.

Thus in 1982 the conservative *Fortune* magazine attacked the ADEA as 'one of the weirder products of the Great Society mind-set', arguing that 'all personnel decisions are probabilistic'. Employers, it was said, were acting reasonably when they hired a 30-year-old in preference to a 60-year-old, since the former had more potential for growth.[79] Richard Epstein's critique was in line with the growing attack by conservatives on all federal affirmative action and anti-discrimination measures: in a perfect free market,

---

[78] Edward P. Lazear, 'Why Is There Mandatory Retirement?', *Journal of Political Economy*, vol. 87, no. 6, Dec. 1979, pp. 1261–84.
[79] Daniel Seligman, 'The Case for Ageism', *Fortune*, 20 Sept. 1982, p. 47.

argued Epstein, 'irrational' or 'arbitrary' discrimination could never occur, since it would be contrary to the economic interests of employers. (Underpinning this argument was the assumption that employers always behave rationally.) Congress had never attempted to understand the logical business reasons for personnel decisions that appeared superficially to be discriminatory, argued Epstein: often, 'discrimination' was in reality 'a rational response to the frictions that necessarily arise out of long-term employment contracts'.[80] In similar vein, Peter Schuck maintained that employers acted quite reasonably in using age proxies in personnel decisions, since in the aggregate working ability *does* decline with age: age proxies were cheaper and more convenient than a complex programme of individualised testing.[81] Similar objections came from leading industrialists in the 1980s: David Braithwaite (Director of Corporate Employment, the US Steel Corporation) and Robert Thomson (Chairman of the Labor Relations Committee of the US Chamber of Commerce) argued that mandatory retirement was an integral part of human resource and personnel decisions in large firms. By attempting to combine employment protection with Title VII, the ADEA had presented employers with 'the worst of both worlds', argued Thomson. The ADEA was sometimes used as 'a device to shake down innocent employers' by incompetent middle managers aged in their fifties. Many employers had to buy their way out of problems, said Thomson, 'no matter how meritless the charge'.[82] These and other criticisms from conservatives as much reflected the changed political climate of the 1980s as they did the deficiencies of the ADEA. A certain re-writing of history occurred generally in that decade on the part of those who sought to justify welfare cut-backs by presenting the Great Society programme as a naively well-intentioned but ultimately disastrous experiment in social engineering, foisted upon an unsuspecting public by a 'liberal elite'. Given that Louis Harris Associates polls in 1974 and 1981 both found that eight out of ten Americans believed that most employers discriminated against older people, and nine out of ten considered enforced retirement to be unjustified, it was unconvincing to argue that the ADEA had no populist roots.[83] However, the tenets of classical economics appeared to be verified by the

---

[80] Richard A. Epstein, *Forbidden Grounds: the Case Against Employment Discrimination Laws* (1992), pp. 59, 444.

[81] Peter H. Schuck, 'The Greying of Civil Rights Law', *The Public Interest*, no. 60, Summer 1980, pp. 69–93.

[82] *Hearing Before the Subcommittee on Employment Opportunities of the Committee on Education and Labor, House of Representatives, To Amend the Age Discrimination in Employment Act of 1967, 9 September 1982* (1982), pp. 25–39.

[83] Stephen R. McConnell, 'Age Discrimination in Employment', in Herbert S. Parnes (ed.), *Policy Issues in Work and Retirement* (1983), p. 160.

evidence that increasing numbers of employers in the 1980s achieved staff downsizing by the use of early exit incentives, in order to circumvent the ADEA – thereby making the 'retirement decision' appear to be the result of free, unconstrained choice. Thus by the end of the 1980s it had become the new orthodoxy that retirement was largely voluntary and caused by supply-side factors such as early retirement schemes, rather than by declining labour market demand.[84] Certainly, there was an element of truth in the conservatives' charge that the analytical underpinnings of the 1967 Act had been a little confused.

Paradoxically, it was during a conservative administration that the ADEA was extended (in 1986) such that mandatory retirement was virtually abolished. However, the 1980s also witnessed the emergence of more conservative arguments for action to protect older workers – notably, that older workers who remained in employment would contribute to social security, that income from work was better than an inadequate pension, and that technological innovations should make the labour process less physically demanding.[85] Older workers were increasingly being seen as a source of labour in the new post-industrial economy. For example, in the 1991 Congressional Hearings, it was argued that older workers were 'extremely good investments for business', since they were more reliable, absent less often, and showed a willingness to learn.[86] By the 1990s and the turn of the new century, informed commentators in America were articulating concerns identical to those in Britain – that overall labour supply needed to be increased (particularly with regard to highly skilled workers), that more older workers were needed, and that the ageing of the population would cause problems.[87]

Conclusion

A clear verdict on the 'success' or 'failure' of the ADEA is very difficult to pronounce. Such evaluations always depend upon the perceived aim of the policy, and, as has been shown, the ADEA had several discrete aims: to protect the employment rights of older workers (including their right not to suffer harassment in the workplace); to re-educate public opinion – especially employer opinion – away from the use of 'false stereotypes'

---

[84] See, for example, Report of the Secretary of Labor, *Labor Market Problems*, pp. 1–2.
[85] Statement by Malcolm H. Lovell (Under Secretary of Labor, Department of Labor), in *Hearing, 9 September 1982*, pp. 2–3.
[86] Statement by Rep. William J. Hughes, in *Age Discrimination in the Workplace*, p. 11.
[87] Richard W. Judy and Carol D'Amico, *Workforce 2020: Work and Workers in the 21st Century* (1997), pp. 7–8; Robert S. Menchin, *New Work Opportunities for Older Americans* (1993), p. xiii.

regarding older workers' functional abilities (possibly also, in the process, countering wider ageist attitudes); and to improve labour supply, maximise available labour power and thus boost the American economy. Success in relation to some of these aims is unprovable: for example, we cannot construct an historical counterfactual to show how the American economy would have developed without an ADEA. As has been argued earlier, the recessions, downsizings and economic re-structurings that have taken place in the American economy since the late 1970s have affected the job prospects of older Americans far more than the protection offered by the ADEA: its original aim of expanding job opportunities for older workers was always unrealistic – perhaps no more than a political 'sweetener' – and by the 1980s was foundering on the rocks of the post-industrial labour market. Given that retirement has been a long-run trend, caused mainly by structural economic factors, the effect of the ADEA could only ever be limited.

The primacy of economic and demographic factors over legislative ones can be demonstrated by two examples. First, the median age of the US workforce has changed in a U-curve over the last forty years: it was 40.6 years in 1962, 34.6 years in 1980; and is projected to return to 40.6 years in the year 2005.[88] This has nothing to do with the ADEA. It derives from the larger sizes of birth cohorts passing through the workforce and the expansion of feminised jobs, balanced by decreasing labour force participation rates of older males. Second, as shown in Table 9.1, the ADEA has not been able to influence the trend to male 'early' retirement, the fall in the average age of male retirement, the increasing labour force participation of middle-aged women, the replacement of full-time by part-time jobs and the general redistribution of employment, which the US economy shares with other industrialised nations. For example, between 1960 and 1995, the average age of older workers' transition into economic inactivity fell from 66.5 years to 63.6 years for American men, and from 65.1 years to 61.6 years for American women. These rates of decline were very similar to those for Britain over the same period.[89] Once again, we cannot know how things would have been without the ADEA. Criticisms of the ADEA to the effect that it has failed to protect the jobs of older, 'fifty-something' men are, on the face of it, justified;[90] conversely, the ADEA cannot take credit for the recent small rise in the employment rates of older American men.

[88] O'Meara, *Protecting*, p. 21; Eglit, 'Age Discrimination in Employment Act', pp. 666–7.

[89] OECD data, cited in Kirk Mann, *Approaching Retirement. Social Divisions, Welfare and Exclusion* (2001), p. 182.

[90] See, for example, David Willetts, *The Age of Entitlement* (1993), p. 33.

Table 9.1. *US labour force participation rates by age: percentages and numbers (millions).*

	1970	1980	1990	2000	2008**
Men					
Aged 65+	26.8%	19.0%	16.3%	17.5%	17.8%
	2.2m	1.9m	2.0m	2.4m	2.8m
Aged 55–64	83.0%	72.1%	67.8%	67.3%	69.4%
	7.1m	7.2m	6.6m	7.6m	10.8m
Aged 45–54	94.3%	91.2%	90.7%	88.6%	88.8%
	10.4m	9.9m	11.1m	16.0m	19.0m
Women					
Aged 65+	9.7%	8.1%	8.6%	9.4%	9.1%
	1.1m	1.2m	1.5m	1.8m	1.9m
Aged 55–64	43.0%	41.3%	45.2%	51.8%	57.7%
	4.2m	4.7m	4.9m	6.4m	9.8m
Aged 45–54	54.4%	59.9%	71.2%	76.8%	80.0%
	6.5m	7.0m	9.1m	14.5m	17.8m

** = projections
NB. The figures for 1970 differ slightly from those cited at the beginning of the previous chapter, taken from a different source.
Source: US Census Bureau, *Statistical Abstract of the United States: 1999* (1999), p. 411, and *Statistical Abstract of the United States: 2001* (2001), p. 367.

The ability of anti-discrimination legislation to counter profound and long-run economic trends can only ever be limited.

Analysis of legal cases tells us something, but is equally fraught with difficulties. As Howard Eglit observes, in his comprehensive study, 'there is little reason to believe that reported cases are an accurate reflection of the actual incidence of age discrimination in the workplace'.[91] Legal cases are probably only the 'tip of the iceberg', and it is likely that much age discrimination (especially at the hiring stage) occurs without the victim being aware of it. Evidence shows that very few ADEA cases survive preliminary challenges by defendants; and thereafter plaintiffs face several obstacles in their pursuit of a claim, such as personal stress, publicity, potential findings of liability and the defendant settling out of court. For example, in 1999 only 5.3 per cent of ADEA charges were settled in favour of the plaintiff; in 59.4 per cent, 'no reasonable cause' was found, and a further 23.3 per cent were closed administratively.[92] 'The result', notes Eglit,

---

[91] Eglit, 'Age Discrimination in Employment Act', p. 591.
[92] David Neumark, 'Age Discrimination Legislation in the US: Assessment of the Evidence', in Zmira Hornstein (ed.), *Outlawing Age Discrimination. Foreign Lessons, UK Choices* (2001), p. 48.

'is that the most unequivocal instances of discrimination disappear before they ever become subject to public attention, let alone formal recordation in reported judicial opinions'.[93] The steady rise in cases certainly cannot be taken as evidence that age discrimination in employment is increasing.

Nevertheless, analyses of ADEA charges do provide some interesting clues. Initially, the legal actions tended to centre on administrative and procedural issues (with some important principles of defence being established). By the 1980s, the socio-economic profile of plaintiffs was causing comment and leading to some criticism that the ADEA was chiefly benefiting those who would not normally be thought of as victims of discrimination. An individual believing that he or she has been discriminated against can file a complaint with the EEOC on several grounds: race, sex, age, equal pay, religion, national origin and employer retaliation.[94] In the work of the EEOC, age discrimination cases always figure less prominently than those associated with race and gender. For example, in the fiscal year 1995, of all new charges dealt with by the EEOC, 30,047 related to race, 26,214 to sex, 19,811 to disability, and 17,430 to age.[95] Strikingly, age discrimination cases have been dominated by white, male professionals contesting the termination of their employment. The principal reason for this is that age is an accelerator of sex, race and class discrimination: a black woman will find it easier to obtain recourse under Title VII of the 1964 Civil Rights Act.[96]

Hence Lawrence Friedman examined 153 age discrimination cases brought by private plaintiffs which reached the federal circuit courts as of 11 February 1982. Of these, only 16 were brought by women. A mere 10 per cent were brought by blue-collar workers. On the whole, defendants did slightly better than plaintiffs (but this could have reflected the fact that employers will only defend cases they think they can win).[97] Likewise, Daniel O'Meara's survey of cases between 1978 and 1983 revealed 79 per cent of ADEA plaintiffs to be white-collar employees, 14 per cent blue-collar and only 7 per cent clerical.[98] The survey by Schuster, Kaspin and Miller in the late 1980s examined 487 federal cases filed under the ADEA, using content analysis, and found that 82.4 per cent were brought by men and 64.0 per cent by managerial and professional employees, with 55.2 per cent of plaintiffs aged 50–9.[99] Other surveys have confirmed this

[93] Eglit, 'Age Discrimination in Employment Act', p. 595.
[94] Schuster, Kaspin and Miller, *Age Discrimination in Employment Act*, p. 81.
[95] US Equal Employment Opportunity Commission, *Annual Report 1995*, p. 28.
[96] Plaintiffs can, of course, file a 'concurrent' charge, which combines two or more alleged violations of equal employment opportunity statutes.
[97] L. M. Friedman, *Your Time*, pp. 45–7.   [98] O'Meara, *Protecting*, pp. 25–7.
[99] Schuster, Kaspin and Miller, *Age Discrimination in Employment Act*, pp. 31–3.

broad profile of complainants, and have found that most cases involve firing or non-promotion.[100] For example, O'Meara found that 75.9 per cent of cases were over termination of employment, with only 9.4 per cent over refusal to hire, 6.6 per cent over failure to promote and 6.3 per cent over demotion.[101] Slightly contrasting results were forthcoming from a detailed survey of ADEA decisions published in 1996, undertaken by the experienced legal academic Howard Eglit. This seemed to indicate that by the 1990s the socio-economic profile of ADEA litigants was changing, in response to changing workplace demographics. They were younger (probably reflecting the growth of early retirement) and more likely to be women (though men still predominated). A striking feature was that plaintiffs who went to court tended to fare worse than did defendants; but discharge was still the most common cause of dispute, and management or white-collar occupations predominated.[102]

The ADEA has thus been least effective where perhaps it is most needed – at the hiring stage. This is ironic, since age restrictions in job advertisements were most often cited prior to 1967 as evidence of the need for legislation. The reasons are not hard to fathom. Discrimination in hiring is the most difficult to prove, since job applicants possess relatively little evidence of how and why decisions were made (for example, they will be given a censored version of why they were not hired). New applicants do not usually develop the bitterness that terminated employees often do. Finally, damage awards are generally lower in 'refusal to hire' cases, making them less profitable for a private counsel to accept.[103] To some critical observers, the ADEA allows too many job-incompetent male executives aged in their fifties to vent their disgruntlement by bringing an ADEA suit for termination or non-promotion.[104] In this respect, the ADEA has perhaps not been a sensitive enough instrument to tackle the particular problems of women. One reason for women being a small minority of ADEA plaintiffs is that they are least likely to bring a charge relating to termination: they are most likely to encounter discrimination in hiring, promotion, remuneration and fringe benefits.[105]

Thus O'Meara's excellent study, while very sympathetic to the ADEA, offers a somewhat guarded verdict: arguing that it really has done nothing for the long-term unemployed, 'discouraged worker' and may possibly

---

[100] Bessey and Ananda, 'Age Discrimination', p. 422.   [101] O'Meara, *Protecting*, pp. 25–7.
[102] Eglit, 'Age Discrimination in Employment Act', pp. 596–630, 662–3.
[103] O'Meara, *Protecting*, pp. 267–8.
[104] Statement by David Braithwaite, in *Hearing, 9 September 1982*, p. 41.
[105] Lois B. Shaw, 'Special Problems of Older Women Workers', in Michael E. Borus, Herbert S. Parnes, Steven H. Sandell and Bert Seidman (eds.), *The Older Worker* (1988), pp. 55–70.

have made employers less willing to hire older workers, he comments that 'The ADEA, in many respects, is a piece of well-intentioned legislation of the 1960s that has ultimately failed in its primary purpose, the reduction in long-term unemployment among older workers ... the primary impact of the ADEA has been as a wrongful discharge statute for white male professionals and managers'.[106] It is therefore possible to argue that, by protecting white, male, middle-class professionals, the ADEA has worsened the job prospects of women and minorities at the younger end of the labour market: it may unintentionally be at odds with Title VII of the 1964 Civil Rights Act.[107] Again, it is clear that employers have learned how to avoid charges:[108] a disturbing possibility is that the ADEA may merely have driven age discrimination deeper – into the whispered conversations and shared assumptions of personnel managers and corporate executives. From a viewpoint of considerable sympathy towards the problems of older workers, Quadagno and Hardy suggest that, by placing tight constraints on employers, the ADEA may have reduced the flexibility of early retirement programmes and made them less efficient in selecting which workers ought to retire and which be retained.[109] As has been shown, the downsizings of the 1980s were conducted much as they would have been in the 1950s. Acknowledging that 'there is a fairly large hole in our knowledge of age discrimination legislation', especially in comparison with the research conducted on race and gender discrimination, David Neumark has recently argued – on the basis of a state-by-state comparison – that age discrimination laws have improved the employment of protected workers aged under 60 by less than one percentage point, and those aged 60+ by six percentage points; this is hardly a spectacular success, and other studies examined by Neumark reveal similar ambiguous results.[110] However, no confident conclusions pro or con can be drawn from Neumark's analysis, meticulous though it is, because of the enormous methodological difficulties of separating out the effects of the ADEA from other economic and social factors.

Those who work on behalf of age discrimination victims are convinced that the ADEA has brought enormous benefits to older workers in the

---

[106] O'Meara, *Protecting*, p. 48. For a similar critique, see Samuel Issacharoff and Erica Worth Harris, 'Is Age Discrimination Really Age Discrimination?': The ADEA's Unnatural Solution', *New York University Law Review*, vol. 72, no. 4, Oct. 1997, pp. 786–7.

[107] Schuster, Kaspin and Miller, *Age Discrimination in Employment Act*, p. 45.

[108] See, for example, Richard I. Lehr, David J. Middlebrooks and David J. Rutledge (eds.), *How to Avoid Charges of Age Discrimination in the Workplace* (1989); Stephen S. Rappoport, *Age Discrimination: a Legal and Practical Guide for Employers* (1989).

[109] Quadagno and Hardy, 'Regulating Retirement', p. 470.

[110] Neumark, 'Age Discrimination Legislation', pp. 56–9.

USA, and that the ensuing litigation represents but a small proportion of the real problem. Supporters of the ADEA argue that, more than thirty years after its enactment, most blatant age discrimination has disappeared. Whereas in the 1950s employers could freely specify upper age limits, impose mandatory retirement, bar older workers from re-training programmes, summarily dismiss them and indulge in ageist harassment in the workplace, now things are very different.[111] Another interesting defence of the ADEA is offered by Neumark and Stock, in reply to Lazear's critique. They argue that, by obviously protecting the older worker, the ADEA strengthens the bond between worker and firm, to the ultimate benefit of everyone.[112] ADEA supporters maintain that the increase in charges reflects a commendable growth in public awareness of age discrimination, but that much more work still needs to be done: a lawyer experienced in such matters has recently declared that age discrimination in employment 'remains a national disgrace'.[113] Thus a 1997 report from the Senate's Special Committee on Aging argued that older workers still faced too many 'negative stereotypes about aging and productivity', which needed to be combated.[114] The AARP has likewise expressed concern over continuing age discrimination in employment and the increasing use by employers of early exit incentives targeted at older workers; it points out that, of 1 million workers aged 55+ who were displaced from the labour force in 1995–7, only 56 per cent were re-employed by February 1998.[115] As more 'baby boomers' encounter employment problems later in life, and as a larger proportion of the US population becomes covered by the ADEA, so may there be an increasing resort to litigation.

As in all social policy, therefore, a 'verdict' on the ADEA depends very much on what one assumes its original intentions were in the very different world of 1967. Verdicts can also change in response to external circumstances. Thus most British governmental publications in the 1990s – both Conservative and Labour – tended to be unenthusiastic about the ADEA as a model for Britain.[116] Since the year 2000, however, it has become increasingly clear that Britain will have to introduce legislation against age discrimination in employment. Accordingly, the ADEA has been experiencing something of a rehabilitation. Thus *Winning the Generation Game* acknowledges that it has failed to arrest the trend to early retirement in the

[111] See, for example, Ventrell-Monsees, 'How Useful', pp. 42–3.
[112] David Neumark and Wendy A. Stock, *Age Discrimination Laws and Labor Market Efficiency* (National Bureau of Economic Research Working Paper No. 6088, July 1997).
[113] Gregory, *Age Discrimination*, p. 7.   [114] *Developments in Aging: 1996*, p. 77.
[115] AARP, *The Public Policy Agenda 1999* (1999), pp. 4–1, 4–9.
[116] See, for example, Department for Education and Employment, *Action on Age: Report of the Consultation on Age Discrimination in Employment* (1998), para 2.31.

USA, but claims that there is some recent 'positive evidence', in the form of rising employment rates.[117] Likewise, the tendency has been to interpret the essentially ambiguous results contained in Zmira Hornstein's edited survey[118] in an over-favourable light, and a recent British study judges that the ADEA has provided 'the most promising evidence' of the beneficial effect of legislation.[119] There is a slight feeling of clutching at straws here: an economic downturn could worsen the job prospects of older Americans, and pull the rug from under such statements.

As in Britain, there have been many suggestions for how to encourage older Americans to stay on longer in work, and some policies have been forthcoming. Thus, on the one hand, a higher pension-eligibility age is to be phased in and the delayed retirement credit for those working and not claiming a social security pension is being gradually increased. There are many on the political right who would like social security to be radically cut back, or privatised, and for older Americans to retire only when they are financially able to do so. Yet, on the other hand, America's social provision for older people has been relatively successful. Improvements in the social security pension scheme have steadily reduced the poverty rate of Americans aged 65+, from 35.2 per cent in 1959 to 15.7 per cent in 1980 and 9.7 per cent in 1999;[120] mandatory retirement has been abolished in all but a very few occupations; the earnings disregard for pensioners has been raised. Nearly forty years after the ADEA's passage, age discrimination in employment is proving as difficult as ever to identify and eradicate, but possibly the American public has become more aware of how the indignities of age affect older people in the labour market. Frustratingly, the ADEA's greatest likely success – that of educator of public opinion – is also the most difficult to demonstrate. All in all, it is the improved social security income that has transformed the status of older Americans, rather than the ADEA. There may be a lesson here for Britain.

---

[117] Cabinet Office. Performance and Innovation Unit, *Winning the Generation Game: Improving Opportunities for People Aged 50–65 in Work and Community Activity* (2000), pp. 57–8.

[118] Hornstein, *Outlawing*.

[119] Sarah Spencer and Sandra Fredman, *Age Equality Comes of Age. Delivering Change for Older People* (2003), p. 17.

[120] US Bureau of the Census, *Statistical Abstract of the United States: 1976* (1976), p. 420; US Census Bureau, *Statistical Abstract of the United States: 2001* (2001), p. 443.

10 Conclusion

This book has tried to confront the difficulties and ambiguities inherent in ageism and age discrimination, and to analyse critically the current British debate in its comparative and long-term historical context. From this perspective, it can be seen that ageism in social relations and attitudes is a relatively recent concept, emerging with a more 'rights-based' social and political culture in Western societies. As such, the modern ageism debate can be viewed as a belated and welcome recognition of the indignities suffered by many people merely on account of their age. There is substantial anecdotal evidence that ageism is widespread; although hearsay and experiential, this evidence is so powerful that it cannot be ignored. However, ageism is so closely bound up with strongly internalised and widely accepted notions of 'age-appropriate' behaviours and 'stages' in the lifecourse that establishing exactly at what point these notions become 'discriminatory' is difficult. For example, ageism is not as obvious as racism or sexism. Nevertheless, much still needs to be done to re-educate public opinion to respect the rights of older people. Certainly, if we do not combat ageism we are waging war on our future selves.

However, this more 'rights-based' culture has also been associated with the emergence since the 1970s of a new kind of capitalism, and the attendant heightening of competitive individualism. When applied to welfare states, it argues that citizens have an 'obligation' to support themselves by waged labour and welfare purchased through the private market. It is against this background that there has taken place the recent British debate on age discrimination in employment, which is a much more problematic concept. Since the 1930s, there has been a vigorous debate over how far the labour market problems of older workers are the result of 'discrimination' in the accepted sense of the word – the 'unequal treatment of equals', based upon irrational prejudices, myths and misconceptions, false stereotypes or deep-seated fears of the ageing self – and how far they are caused by structural factors endemic to modern labour markets (economic restructuring; mismatches of skill, gender, age and region; lower educational levels; and so on). Although older workers may indeed experience 'discrimination' in certain circumstances, these latter factors are much more important: for example, mandatory retirement and the long-run spread of joblessness among older men are not very convincing examples of age discrimination. The current British debate over older workers is in part a revival of interest: there was a better-informed and more edifying debate in the 1950s, against a background of concerns that working lives needed to be lengthened. But in part it also arises from the macro-economic strategy – hegemonic in Western societies since the 1970s – of expanding labour supply (in both a quantitative and, interestingly, a qualitative sense), particularly in low-waged, 'flexible' employment (for which older workers are seen as particularly suitable).

The difficulties inherent in age discrimination as a concept can be seen in the generational equity and health care rationing debates. Simplistic and politically motivated it may have been, but the generational equity debate of the 1980s and 1990s has yielded some nuggets of conceptual gold. These have served to remind us that there is a complex balance of both positive and negative discriminations in the allocation of public resources and social policies across the lifecourse. These lifecourse divisions are intersected by those of class, gender, ethnicity, region, cohort experience and so on – making it well-nigh impossible to compare completed lives and therefore decide what a 'just' allocation of resources by age should be. Health care rationing illustrates this well. There is powerful anecdotal evidence that ageism has been widespread in the British National Health Service. At the practical level, efforts are belatedly being made to eliminate the more egregious forms of age-based rationing, and to ensure that older people are not excluded from what should be the good clinical practice of treating all citizens as individuals. However, at the philosophical level, deciding what would be a 'just' allocation of health care resources by age is extremely difficult.

Since 1997, the New Labour government has picked up the initiatives on age discrimination in employment begun by its Conservative predecessor, and placed them firmly in its overall macro-economic strategy of raising employment levels, expanding labour supply and applying workfare to those marginal to the labour market. New Labour's rhetoric is often studiously vague, and therefore challenging to analyse. However, where age discrimination is concerned, this overall economic strategy seems to be more important than the 'social justice' case articulated by old age pressure groups: the latter forms little more than a liberal patina on New Labour pronouncements. Viewed in the long term, we are currently (as in the 1950s) in an era in which re-enlisting older people into the labour force and extending the working life is considered essential (for demographic and fiscal reasons). Yet there have been other times (the 1930s, and the

1970s and 1980s) when the opposite strategy has dominated, and 'obligation' has meant older workers withdrawing from paid employment.

The forthcoming British legislation against age discrimination in
employment is, in principle, to be welcomed. Hopefully, it will in time
give new employment protection to workers above the age of 65 and effect
some change in personnel practices, making them less ageist. There are,
however, some key areas where it will have less effect. The 'cultural shift'
that is hoped for rests upon the dubious assumption that many employers
have been behaving irrationally, and that they can be disabused of these
'prejudices'. This is misleadingly simplistic. The abolition of mandatory
retirement is by itself likely to have few tangible outcomes, since it now
affects only a small number of workers. Future employment levels among
older people remain conjectural, but viewed against the backdrop of history
they do not look good (despite the recent small rises, which, it should be
remembered, have taken place partly because of the failings of the private
pensions industry and the low relative value of the state pension).
Essentially, there has been a slow de-industrialisation of older workers
over the past 120 years, which has gradually spread down the age structure.
Their employment rates will remain low unless there are real efforts to
'make work pay'. This would involve not only financial support, via a
range of fiscal policies, but changes in working conditions to reduce stress
levels. If the working lifecourse really is to change, and offer more choice
and flexibility to British 'fifty-somethings', then a comprehensive package
of expensive policies will have to be introduced. So far, British governments have shown a reluctance to contemplate such policies. In the final
analysis, the litmus test of policies to enhance 'choice' and 'flexibility' is
whether they make a real difference in those high-unemployment, economically blighted parts of Britain in which de-industrialised older male workers are concentrated. Unless they do, they will remain at the level of
middle-class sloganising.

A long section of this book examines the historical debate on retirement,
health status and work-disability. This is an important (and under-
researched) topic. Beginning with the quest for longevity, the debate
took a more pessimistic turn in the late nineteenth century with the emerging concerns over the 'worn-out' older worker. Social commentators began
to notice that work-disability was profoundly affected by a variety of
work-related factors, notably sectoral labour market demand. However,
for the first half of the twentieth century there was relatively little research
into working capacity at later ages: the 1930s recession led to a shake-out
of older workers (and, accordingly, little interest in their labour market
problems), geriatric medicine was undeveloped, and there was only very
slight improvement in life expectancy in old age. However, all of this

changed in the 1950s, when in both Britain and America there took place a complex and well-informed debate on whether the working lifespan could be extended: there was discussion of such 'modern' issues as flexible retirement, varying retirement ages and age discrimination. Despite the intensive research, no magic formula was discovered to re-enlist older workers in significant numbers. From the 1960s onwards, however, there were slow falls in mortality at later ages, plus empirical evidence of apparently worsening health and disability: accordingly, there arose a complex and intriguing debate over whether health status at later ages was actually improving. This debate took on new significance in the 1990s, when it began to be argued that extending the working life was imperative: if older people were healthier than any previous generation, could they not delay retirement?

What is clear from this long debate on health status is that labour market demand is one of the most important of several factors that shape subjective perceptions of health and working capacity. On the one occasion in the twentieth century when there existed a tight labour market for older workers – the Second World War – self-defined working capacity improved, and older workers' employment rates rose dramatically in both Britain and the USA. Intuitively, therefore, we may believe that today's older workers 'could' work later in life, but ultimately this verdict is dependent upon whether there are jobs for them. Whether they 'should' work later in life is becoming a major political and ethical question. But forcing older citizens to 'work till they drop' may be the ultimate form of ageism.

Finally, the example of the USA needs to be considered. Curiously – for a nation which in other respects is such a 'welfare laggard' – the USA has experienced a lively debate on age discrimination in employment since at least the 1930s. By the 1950s and 1960s, the 'social justice' and 'labour supply' motives that are so evident in today's British debate were being strongly articulated, and the political urgency of dealing with the wider issue of civil rights was a vital factor in delivering legislation in 1967. There was, however, some confusion about precisely what the Age Discrimination in Employment Act was trying to achieve. A theme suggested in this book – perhaps a rather risky meta-narrative – is that the USA's path to economic modernisation in the 1960s was based upon an attempted abandonment of age proxies and their replacement by more individualised performance appraisal. However, the workforce downsizings of the 1980s were conducted largely by 'traditional' age-based criteria; and the 1967 Act did not (as far as we can tell) significantly arrest the decline in older men's economic activity, which the USA experienced along with other industrialised nations. The 1967 Act has engendered a considerable amount of fascinating legal controversy. But its 'success' or 'failure' cannot easily be demonstrated in relation to its original aims.

The current British revival of interest in age discrimination in employment can be seen as belatedly raising issues about older workers that have been on the policy agenda since the 1930s. Yet it is also a massive distraction from the real challenge – that we now have a large, unwaged dependent population in late middle age who need better state support. Disturbingly, the age discrimination debate may also be the harbinger of a new Social Darwinist era in which – legitimised by the appealing slogans of 'agelessness' – older people will be forcibly re-enlisted into paid work at the bottom end of the labour market. Combating age discrimination in employment may lead on to a wider, and much-needed, onslaught upon ageism in social relations and attitudes. On the other hand, it may be the Trojan horse of an attack upon the welfare rights of older people.

Bibliography

'139 MPs Oppose Blair Stand Against Ageism Law', *Guardian*, 3 Feb. 1998.

Aaron, H. J. (ed.), *Behavioral Dimensions of Retirement Economics* (Washington, DC, 1999).

Aarts, L. J. M., Burkhauser, R. V. and de Jong, P. R. 'Introduction and Overview', in L. J. M. Aarts, R. V. Burkhauser and P. R. de Jong (eds.), *Curing the Dutch Disease. An International Perspective on Disability Policy Reform* (Aldershot, 1996).

Abel-Smith, B. and Townsend, P. *New Pensions for the Old* (London, 1955).

Abrams, A. J. 'Barriers to the Employment of Older Workers', *Annals of the American Academy of Political and Social Science*, vol. 279, Jan. 1952, pp. 62–71.

'Discrimination Against Older Workers in Various Countries', in *Old Age in the Modern World. Report of the Third Congress of the International Association of Gerontology, London 1954* (Edinburgh, 1955).

Achenbaum, W. A. *Social Security: Visions and Revisions* (Cambridge, 1986).

'Putting ADEA Into Historical Context', *Research on Aging*, vol. 13, no. 4, Dec. 1991, pp. 463–9.

Crossing Frontiers. Gerontology Emerges as a Science (Cambridge, 1995).

Ackerman, B. A. *Social Justice in the Liberal State* (London, 1980).

Acton Society Trust, *Retirement. A Study of Current Attitudes and Practices* (London, 1960).

'Age-analysis of Employed Persons', *Ministry of Labour Gazette*, vol. LIX, no. 6, June 1951, pp. 224–6.

Age and Sex Discrimination in Employment and Review of Federal Response to Employment Needs of the Elderly. Hearing Before the Subcommittee on Retirement Income and Employment of the Select Committee on Aging, House of Representatives, Dec. 10 1975 (Washington, DC, 1976).

'Age Code Fails to Satisfy Campaigners', *Guardian*, 17 Nov. 1998.

Age Concern, *Age Discrimination Affecting Older People* (London, 1989).

Reflecting Our Age: Images, Language and Older People (London, 1993).

Age Discrimination. Make It a Thing of the Past (London, 1998).

Equal Access to Cardiac Rehabilitation (London, 1998).

Health and Care. Interim Report (London, 1998).

Turning Your Back on Us. Older People and the NHS (London, 1999).

'Age Discrimination Barred in Public Employment in New Jersey', *Monthly Labor Review*, vol. 30, no. 6, June 1930, p. 106.

Age Discrimination in Employment. Hearings Before the General Subcommittee on Labor of the Committee on Education and Labor. House of Representatives, August 1, 2, 3, 15, 16 and 17 1967 (Washington, DC, 1967).

The Age Discrimination in Employment Act of 1967.

Age Discrimination in Employment Amendments of 1995: Hearing of the Committee on Labor and Human Resources. United States Senate, March 8 1996 (Washington, DC, 1996).

Age Discrimination in the Workplace: a Continuing Problem for Older Workers. Hearing Before the Select Committee on Aging. House of Representatives, September 24 1991 (Washington, DC, 1992).

'Age of Compulsory Retirement from Work', *Ministry of Labour Gazette*, vol. LVII, no. 4, April 1949, pp. 121–2.

'Age positive' website: www.agepositive.gov.org.

The Aged and the Aging in the United States. Hearings Before the Subcommittee on Problems of the Aged and Aging of the Committee on Labor and Public Welfare, United States Senate, June 16, 17 and 18 1959 (Washington, DC, 1959).

'Ageism', *Oxford English Dictionary* (Oxford, 1989 edn).

'The Aging Population', *Fortune*, vol. XXXIV, no. 6, Dec. 1946, pp. 250–4.

Agulnik, P. 'Pension Reform in the UK: Evaluating Retirement Income Policy' (University of London (LSE) Ph.D. thesis, 2001).

Alcock, P., Beatty, C., Fothergill, S., Macmillan, R. and Yeandle, S. 'New Roles, New Deal', in P. Alcock, C. Beatty, S. Fothergill, R. Macmillan and S. Yeandle, *Work to Welfare. How Men Become Detached from the Labour Market* (Cambridge, 2003).

American Association of Retired Persons (AARP), *Employment Discrimination Against Midlife and Older Women. Volume II: An Analysis of Discrimination Charges Filed With the EEOC* (Washington, DC, 1997).

Annual Report 1998 (Washington, DC, 1998).

Annual Report 1999 (Washington, DC, 1999).

The Public Policy Agenda 1999 (Washington, DC, 1999).

American Bar Association. The Commission on Legal Problems of the Elderly, *Downsizing in an Aging Work Force* (Washington, DC, 1992).

'Analysis: Disability', *Guardian*, 24 Nov. 1998.

Anderson, W. F. and Cowan, N. R. 'A Consultative Health Centre for Older People. The Rutherglen Experiment', *The Lancet*, vol. CCLXIX, 30 July 1955, pp. 239–40.

'Work and Retirement. Influences on the Health of Older Men', *The Lancet*, vol. CCLXXI, 29 Dec. 1956, pp. 1344–7.

Andrews, M. 'The Seductiveness of Agelessness', *Ageing and Society*, vol. 19, pt. 3, May 1999, pp. 302–3.

'Ageful and Proud', *Ageing and Society*, vol. 20, pt. 6, Nov. 2000, pp. 791–5.

Anon. memo, 'Treatment of Redundancy' (1971), PRO LAB 108/3.

Appleby, J. *Financing Health Care in the 1990s* (Buckingham, 1992).

Arber, S. and Ginn, J. (eds.), *Connecting Gender and Ageing. A Sociological Approach* (Buckingham, 1995).

Armitage, R. and Scott, M. 'British Labour Force Projections: 1998–2011', *Labour Market Trends*, vol. 106, no. 6, June 1998, pp. 281–9.

Axel, R. 'Sociological Factors in Old Age Dependency', *Social Forces*, vol. 13, no. 4, May 1935, pp. 580–7.

Bailey, J. B. *Modern Methuselahs* (London, 1888).

Bailey, T. *Records of Longevity: with an Introductory Discourse on Vital Statistics* (London, 1857).

Baily, M. N. 'Aging and the Ability to Work: Policy Issues and Recent Trends', in G. Burtless (ed.), *Work, Health, and Income Among the Elderly* (Washington, DC, 1987).

Ball, R. M. 'Old Age Retirement: Social and Economic Implications', *Social Security Bulletin*, vol. 13, no. 9, Sept. 1950, pp. 4–8.

Bancroft, G. 'Older Persons in the Labor Force', *Annals of the American Academy of Political and Social Science*, vol. 279, Jan. 1952, pp. 52–61.

Barham, C. 'Economic Inactivity and the Labour Market', *Labour Market Trends*, vol. 110, no. 2, Feb. 2002, pp. 69–77.

'Patterns of Economic Inactivity Among Older Men', *Labour Market Trends*, vol. 110, no. 6, June 2002, pp. 301–10.

Barker, D. J. P. *Mothers, Babies and Health in Later Life* (Edinburgh, 1994).

Barkin, S. *The Older Worker in Industry: a Study of New York State Manufacturing Industries* (Albany, NY, 1933).

'Should There Be a Fixed Retirement Age? Organised Labor Says No', *Annals of the American Academy of Political and Social Science*, vol. 279, Jan. 1952, pp. 77–80.

Beard, G. M. *Legal Responsibility in Old Age, Based on Researches into the Relation of Age to Work* (1874), reprinted in G. J. Gruman, *The 'Fixed Period' Controversy. Prelude to Ageism* (New York, NY, 1979).

Bearon, L. B. 'Famous Aged', in E. B. Palmore (ed.), *Handbook on the Aged in the United States* (Westport, CT, 1984).

Beatty, C. and Fothergill, S. *The Detached Male Workforce* (Sheffield, 1999).

Incapacity Benefit and Unemployment (Sheffield, 1999).

'Moving People Into Jobs. Jobcentre Plus, New Deal and the Job Shortfall for the Over 50s' (unpublished paper, Centre for Regional Economic and Social Research, Sheffield Hallam University, Sheffield, 2004).

Bebbington, A. C. 'The Expectation of Life Without Disability in England and Wales', *Population Trends*, no. 66, Winter 1991, pp. 26–9.

Becker, G. S. *The Economics of Discrimination* (Chicago, 1957).

'Discrimination, Economic', in D. L. Sills (ed.), *International Encyclopedia of the Social Sciences Vol. 4* (New York, NY, 1968).

Being Positive About Age Diversity at Work. A Practical Guide for Business (2002), www.agepositive.gov.uk.

Belbin, R. M. 'Difficulties of Older People in Industry', *Occupational Psychology*, vol. 27, no. 4, Oct. 1953, pp. 177–90.

Bell, Lady G. *At the Works* (London, 1907).

Bengtson, V. 'Will "Generational Accounting" Doom the Welfare State?' *The Gerontologist*, vol. 33, no. 16, 1993, pp. 812–16.

Bennett, G. and Ebrahim, S. *The Essentials of Health Care of the Elderly* (London, 1992).

Benson, J. *Prime Time. A History of the Middle Aged in Twentieth-century Britain* (London, 1997).

Berkowitz, E. D. and Burkhauser, R. V. 'A United States Perspective on Disability Programmes', in L. J. M. Aarts, R. V. Burkhauser and P. R. de Jong (eds.), *Curing the Dutch Disease. An International Perspective on Disability Policy Reform* (Aldershot, 1996).

Berkowitz, M. 'Functioning Ability and Job Performance as Workers Age', in M. E. Borus, H. S. Parnes, S. H. Sandell and B. Seidman (eds.), *The Older Worker* (Madison, WI, 1988).

Berthoud, R. *Disability Benefits. A Review of the Issues and Options for Reform* (York, 1998).

Bessey, B. L. and Ananda, S. M. 'Age Discrimination in Employment. An Interdisciplinary Review of the ADEA', *Research on Aging*, vol. 13, no. 4, Dec. 1991, pp. 413–57.

Beveridge, W. H. *Unemployment, a Problem of Industry* (London, 1909; 1912 edn). 'Pensions Finance', 16 July 1942, Beveridge Papers VIII 33.

Bevin, E. *My Plan for 2,000,000 Workless* (London, 1933).

Binstock, R. H. 'The Politics of Aging Interest Groups', in R. B. Hudson (ed.), *The Aging in Politics. Process and Policy* (Springfield, IL, 1981).

Blaikie, A. 'The Emerging Political Power of the Elderly in Britain 1908–1948', *Ageing and Society*, vol. 10, pt. 1, Mar. 1990, pp. 17–39.
   Ageing and Popular Culture (Cambridge, 1999).

Blaikie, A. and Macnicol, J. 'Towards an Anatomy of Ageism: Society, Social Policy and the Elderly, 1918–48', in C. Phillipson, M. Bernard and P. Strang (eds.), *Dependency and Interdependency in Old Age: Theoretical Perspectives and Policy Alternatives* (Beckenham, 1986).
   'Ageing and Social Policy: a Twentieth Century Dilemma', in A. M. Warnes (ed.), *Human Ageing and Later Life: Multidisciplinary Perspectives* (London, 1989).

Blair, T. and Schroder, G. 'Europe: the Third Way/Die Neue Mitte', appendix in B. Hombach, *The Politics of the New Centre* (Cambridge, 2000).

Blakemore, K. and Boneham, M. *Age, Race and Ethnicity. A Comparative Approach* (Buckingham, 1994).

'Blunkett Aide in Row Over Race', *Guardian*, 20 Mar. 2004.

Bone, J. and Mercer, S. *Flexible Retirement* (London, 2000).

Bone, M., Bebbington, A. C., Jagger, C., Morgan, K. and Nicolas, G. *Health Expectancy and Its Uses* (London, 1995).

Boskin, M. J. 'Social Security and Retirement Decisions', *Economic Inquiry*, vol. XV, no. 1, Jan. 1977, pp. 1–25.

Bowling, A. 'Ageism in Cardiology', *British Medical Journal*, vol. 319, 20 Nov. 1999, pp. 1353–5.

Bridgen, P. 'The State, Redundancy Pay, and Economic Policy-Making in the Early 1960s', *Twentieth Century British History*, vol. 11, no. 3, 2000, pp. 233–58.

Brooks, R. G. *Health Status Measurement: a Perspective on Change* (Basingstoke, 1995).

Brown, K. 'How Long Have You Got?', *Scientific American*, vol. 11, no. 2, Summer 2000, pp. 8–15.

Brown, R. A. 'Age and "Paced" Work', *Occupational Psychology*, vol. 31, no. 1, Jan. 1957, pp. 11–20.

Brown, R. G., McKeown, T. and Whitfield, A. G. W. 'Observations on the Medical Condition of Men in the Seventh Decade', *British Medical Journal*, 8 Mar. 1958, pp. 555–62.

Bugeja, G., Kumar, A. and Banerjee, A. K. 'Exclusion of Elderly People from Clinical Research: a Descriptive Study of Published Reports', *British Medical Journal*, vol. 315, 25 Oct. 1997, p. 1059.

Burchardt, T. 'The Dynamics of Being Disabled', *Journal of Social Policy*, vol. 29, pt. 4, Oct. 2000, pp. 645–68.

Enduring Economic Exclusion. Disabled People, Income and Work (York, 2000).

Bureau of National Affairs, *Employment Discrimination Reports*: vol. 10, no. 1, 7 Jan. 1998; vol. 10, no. 3, 21 Jan. 1998; vol. 10, no. 6, 11 Feb. 1998; vol. 10, no. 14, 8 April 1998; vol. 15, no. 11, 20 Sept. 2000; vol. 15, no. 18, 8 Nov. 2000.

Burkhauser, R. V. 'US Policy Toward Workers With Handicaps', in O. S. Mitchell (ed.), *As the Workforce Ages. Costs, Benefits and Policy Challenges* (Ithaca, NY, 1993).

Burkhauser, R. V., Glenn, A. J. and Wittenburg, D. C. 'The Disabled Worker Tax Credit', in V. P. Reno, J. L. Mashaw and B. Gradison (eds.), *Disability: Challenges for Social Insurance, Health Care Financing, and Labor Market Policy* (Washington, DC, 1997).

Burstein, P. *Discrimination, Jobs and Politics. The Struggle for Equal Opportunity in the United States Since the New Deal* (Chicago, 1985).

Burtless, G. 'Introduction and Summary', in G. Burtless (ed.), *Work, Health, and Income Among the Elderly* (Washington, DC, 1987).

'Occupational Effects on the Health and Work Capacity of Older Men', in G. Burtless (ed.), *Work, Health, and Income Among the Elderly* (Washington, DC, 1987).

Burtless, G. and Moffitt, R. A. 'The Effect of Social Security Benefits on the Labor Supply of the Aged', in H. J. Aaron and G. Burtless (eds.), *Retirement and Economic Behavior* (Washington, DC, 1984).

Bury, M. *Health and Illness in a Changing Society* (London, 1997).

'Business – Redundancy', www.agepositive.gov.org.

Butler, J. *The Ethics of Health Care Rationing* (London, 1999).

Butler, R. N. 'Age-Ism: Another Form of Bigotry', *The Gerontologist*, vol. 9, no. 4, pt. 1, Winter 1969, pp. 243–6.

Why Survive? Being Old in America (Baltimore, MD, 1975).

'The Relation of Extended Life to Extended Employment since the Passage of Social Security in 1935', *Milbank Memorial Fund Quarterly*, vol. 61, no. 3, 1983, pp. 420–9.

'Dispelling Ageism: the Cross-Cutting Intervention', *Annals of the American Academy of Political and Social Science*, vol. 503, May 1989, pp. 142–51.

'Ageism' in G. L. Maddox (ed.), *The Encyclopedia of Aging* (New York, NY, 1995 edn).

Bytheway, B. *Ageism* (Buckingham, 1995).

'Youthfulness and Agelessness: a Comment', *Ageing and Society*, vol. 20, pt. 6, Nov. 2000, pp. 781–9.

Cabinet Office. Performance and Innovation Unit, *Winning the Generation Game. Improving Opportunities for People Aged 50–65 in Work and Community Activity* (London, 2000).

Campbell, H. 'The Treatment of Chronic Bronchitis in the Elderly and Aged', *British Medical Journal*, 12 Oct. 1901, pp. 1063–4.

Campbell, N. *The Decline of Employment Among Older People in Britain* (London, 1999).

Cardarelli, R., Sefton, J. and Kotlikoff, L. J. 'Generational Accounting in the UK', *Economic Journal*, vol. 110, no. 467, Nov. 2000, pp. F547–74.

'Care of Ageing Tissues', *British Medical Journal*, 2 May 1942, p. 554.

Caselli, G. and Lopez, A. D. 'Health and Mortality Among the Elderly: Issues for Assessment', in G. Caselli and A. D. Lopez (eds.), *Health and Mortality Among Elderly Populations* (Oxford, 1996).

Casey, B., Metcalf, H. and Lakey, J. 'Human Resource Strategies and the Third Age: Policies and Practices in the UK', in Institute of Personnel Management, *Age and Employment. Policies, Attitudes and Practices* (London, 1993).

'Causes of Discrimination Against Older Workers', *Monthly Labor Review*, vol. 46, no. 5, May 1938, pp. 1138–43.

Central Statistical Office, *Social Trends No. 1 1970* (London, 1970).

Social Trends No. 26 1996 Edition (London, 1996).

'Characteristics of Extra Workers in the Labor Force, April 1944', *Monthly Labor Review*, vol. 59, no. 2, Aug. 1944, pp. 270–8.

Chartered Institute of Personnel and Development, *Age Discrimination at Work* (London, 2001).

Age, Pensions and Retirement (London, 2003).

'Children Will Die Before Their Parents', *Guardian*, 27 May 2004.

Chirikos, T. N. 'Accounting for the Historical Rise in Work-disability Prevalence', *Milbank Quarterly*, vol. 64, no. 2, 1986, pp. 271–301.

Clague, E. 'The Aging Population and Programs of Security', *Milbank Memorial Fund Quarterly*, vol. 18, no. 4, 1940, pp. 345–58.

'The Working Life Span of American Workers', *Journal of Gerontology*, vol. 4, no. 4, Oct. 1949, pp. 285–9.

'Labor Force Trends in the United States', *Journal of Gerontology*, vol. 7, no. 1, Jan. 1952, pp. 92–9.

'Do American Workers Save for Retirement?', in G. B. Hurff (ed.), *Economic Problems of Retirement: a Report on the Fourth Annual Southern Conference on Gerontology held at the University of Florida, 27–28 January 1954* (Gainesville, FL, 1954).

Clark, F. le Gros *The Later Working Life in the Building Industry. A Study of 320 Ageing Maintenance Workers* (London, 1954).

Ageing Men in the Labour Force. The Problems of Organising Older Workers in the Building Industry (London, 1955).

The Working Fitness of Older Men. A Study of Men Over Sixty in the Building Industry (London, n.d., c. 1955).

Bus Workers in Their Later Lives (London, 1957).

Age and the Working Lives of Men (London, 1959).

Woman, Work and Age (London, 1962).

Work, Age and Leisure. Causes and Consequences of the Shortened Working Life (London, 1966).

Clark, F. le Gros and Dunne, A. C. *Ageing in Industry* (London, 1955).

Clarke, J. S. *The Assistance Board* (London, 1941).

'Code to Counter Ageism at Work', *Guardian*, 14 Aug. 1998.

Cohen, W. J. 'Economics, Employment and Welfare', in N. W. Shock (ed.), *Problems of Aging* (New York, NY, 1951).

'Income Maintenance for the Aged', *Annals of the American Academy of Political and Social Science*, vol. 279, Jan. 1952, pp. 154–63.

'Government Policy Concerning Private and Public Retirement Plans', in G. B. Hurff (ed.), *Economic Problems of Retirement: a Report on the Fourth Annual Southern Conference on Gerontology held at the University of Florida, 27–28 January 1954* (Gainesville, FL, 1954).

Cole, D. with Utting, J. *The Economic Circumstances of Old People* (Welwyn, 1962).

Cole, T. R. *The Journey of Life: a Cultural History of Aging in America* (Cambridge, 1992).

Coleman, P. 'Psychological Ageing', in J. Bond, P. Coleman and S. Peace (eds.), *Ageing in Society. An Introduction to Social Gerontology* (London, 1993).

Collis, C. and Mallier, T. 'Third Age Male Activity Rates in Britain and its Regions', *Regional Studies*, vol. 3, no. 8, Dec. 1996, pp. 803–9.

Colvez, A. and Blanchet, M. 'Disability Trends in the United States Population 1966–76: Analysis of Reported Causes', *American Journal of Public Health*, vol. 71, no. 5, May 1981, pp. 464–71.

Comfort, A. *A Good Age* (New York, 1976).

Commission of the European Communities, *Age and Attitudes. Main Results from a Eurobarometer Survey* (Brussels, 1993).

Conyngton, M. 'Extent and Distribution of Old-Age Dependency in the United States', *Monthly Labor Review*, vol. 38, no. 1, Jan. 1934, pp. 1–10.

Costa, D. L. *The Evolution of Retirement. An American Economic History, 1880–1990* (Chicago, 1998).

'Understanding the Twentieth-Century Decline in Chronic Conditions Among Older Men', *Demography*, vol. 37, no. 1, Feb. 2000, pp. 53–72.

'Changing Chronic Disease Rates and Long-Term Declines in Functional Limitation Among Older Men', *Demography*, vol. 39, no. 1, Feb. 2002, pp. 119–37.

Cox, B. D. *et al. The Health and Lifestyle Survey* (London, 1987).

Cox, B. D., Huppert, F. A. and Whichelow, M. J. (eds.), *The Health and Lifestyle Survey: Seven Years On* (Aldershot, 1993).

Cribier, F. 'Changes in Life Course and Retirement in Recent Years: the Example of Two Cohorts of Parisians', in P. Johnson, C. Conrad and D. Thomson (eds.), *Workers Versus Pensioners. Intergenerational Justice in an Ageing World* (Manchester, 1989).

Crichton-Browne, Sir J. 'Old Age', *British Medical Journal*, 3 Oct. 1891, pp. 727–36.

Crimmins, E. M. 'Mixed Trends in Population Health Among Older Adults', *Journal of Gerontology: Social Sciences*, vol. 51B, no. 5, 1996, S223–5.

Crimmins, E. M. and Saito, Y. 'Getting Better and Getting Worse. Transitions in Functional Status Among Older Americans', *Journal of Aging and Health*, vol. 5, no. 1, Feb. 1993, pp. 3–36.

Crimmins, E. M., Hayward, M. D. and Saito, Y. 'Changing Mortality and Morbidity Rates and the Health Status and Life Expectancy of the Older Population', *Demography*, vol. 31, no. 1, Feb. 1994, pp. 159–75.

'Differentials in Active Life Expectancy in the Older Population of the United States', *Journal of Gerontology: Social Sciences*, vol. 51B, no. 3, 1996, pp. S111–20.

Crimmins, E. M., Saito, Y. and Ingegneri, D. 'Trends in Disability-Free Life Expectancy in the United States, 1970–90', *Population and Development Review*, vol. 23, no. 3, September 1997, pp. 555–72.

Crimmins, E. M., Saito, Y. and Reynolds, S. 'Further Evidence on Recent Trends in the Prevalence and Incidence of Disability Among Older Americans from Two Sources: the LSOA and the NHIS', *Journal of Gerontology: Social Sciences*, vol. 52B, no. 2, 1997, pp. S59–71.

Crook, G. H. and Heinstein, M. *The Older Worker in Industry. A Study of the Attitudes of Industrial Workers Toward Aging and Retirement* (Berkeley, CA, 1958).

Crouch, K. A. 'Late Life Job Displacement', *The Gerontologist*, vol. 38, no. 1, 1998, pp. 7–17.

Cuddy, A. J. C. and Fiske, S. T. 'Doddering But Dear: Process, Content, and Function in Stereotyping of Older Persons', in T. D. Nelson (ed.), *Ageism. Stereotyping and Prejudice Against Older Persons* (Cambridge, MA, 2002).

Cumming, E. and Henry, W. E. *Growing Old. The Process of Disengagement* (New York, NY, 1961).

Daniels, N. 'Justice Between Age Groups: Am I My Parents' Keeper?', *Milbank Memorial Fund Quarterly/Health and Society*, vol. 61, no. 3, 1983, pp. 489–522.

Just Health Care (Cambridge, 1985).

Am I My Parents' Keeper? An Essay on Justice between the Young and the Old (New York, NY, 1988).

'Justice and Transfers Between Generations', in P. Johnson, C. Conrad and D. Thomson (eds.), *Workers Versus Pensioners. Intergenerational Justice in an Ageing World* (Manchester, 1989).

'Darling's New Dictum: Grey is Good', *Daily Telegraph*, 13 May 2000.

de Beauvoir, S. *Old Age* (translated by P. O'Brien, London, 1972).

de la Mare, G. C. and Shepherd, R. D. 'Ageing: Changes in Speed and Quality of Work Among Leather Cutters', *Occupational Psychology*, vol. 32, no. 3, July 1958, pp. 204–9.

Department for Education and Employment, *Action on Age: Report of the Consultation on Age Discrimination in Employment* (London, 1998).

Advantage – Consultation on a Code of Practice for Age Diversity in Employment (London, 1998).

Age Diversity in Employment: a Code of Practice (London, 1999).

Age Diversity in Employment. Guidance and Case Studies (London, 1999).

DfEE press releases: 23 Feb. 1999; 9 Mar. 1999; 14 June 1999; 6 Sept. 1999.

Department for Work and Pensions, *Work and Pensions Statistics 2002* (London, 2002).

Older Workers: Statistical Information Booklet. Spring 2003 (Sheffield, 2003).

Department of Health, *National Service Framework for Older People* (London, 2001).

Health and Personal Social Services Statistics. England. As at 1st June 2002 (London, 2002).

Department of Social Security, *Building a Better Britain for Older People* (London, 1998).

Department of Trade and Industry, *Equality and Diversity: the Way Ahead* (London, 2002).

Developments in Aging: 1996. Volume 1. Report of the Special Committee on Aging. United States Senate (Washington, DC, 1997).

Devine, E. T. *Misery and its Causes* (New York, NY, 1909).

Dewey, J. 'Introduction', in E. V. Cowdry (ed.), *Problems of Ageing: Biological and Medical Aspects* (London, 1939).

Dex, S. and Phillipson, C. 'Social Policy and the Older Worker', in C. Phillipson and A. Walker (eds.), *Ageing and Social Policy: a Critical Assessment* (Aldershot, 1986).

'The Diabetes Timebomb', Guardian, 30 May 2000.

Diamond, P. A. and Hausman, J. A. 'The Retirement and Unemployment Behavior of Older Men', in H. J. Aaron and G. Burtless (eds.), *Retirement and Economic Behavior* (Washington, DC, 1984).

'Disabled People and the Labour Market', *Labour Market Trends*, vol. 109, no. 12, Dec. 2001, pp. 541–2.

'Discriminate' and 'Discrimination', *Oxford English Dictionary* (Oxford, 1989 edn).

'Disease in Old Age', *British Medical Journal*, 31 Jan. 1903, p. 270.

Disney, R. 'Why Have Older Men Stopped Working?', in P. Gregg and J. Wadsworth (eds.), *The State of Working Britain* (Manchester, 1999).

Disney, R., Grundy, E. and Johnson, P. (eds.), *The Dynamics of Retirement: Analyses of the Retirement Surveys* (London, 1997).

Displaced Older Workers. Hearing Before the Select Committee on Aging. House of Representatives, July 24 1985 (Washington, DC, 1985).

Drake, J. T. *The Aged in American Society* (New York, NY, 1958).

Drucker, P. F. 'Population Trends and Management Policy', *Harvard Business Review*, vol. XXIX, no. 3, May 1951, pp. 73–8.

Drury, E. *Age Discrimination Against Older Workers in the European Community* (London, 1993).

Dublin, L. I. *Possibilities of Reducing Mortality at the Higher Age Groups* (New York, NY, 1913).

Health and Wealth. A Survey of the Economics of World Health (New York, NY, 1928).

Dublin, L. I. and Lotka, A. J. 'The History of Longevity in the United States', *Human Biology*, vol. VI, no. 1, Feb. 1934, pp. 43–86.

Length of Life: a Study of the Life Table (New York, NY, 1936).

Dudley, N. J. and Burns, E. 'The Influence of Age on Policies for Admission and Thrombolysis in Coronary Care Units in the United Kingdom', *Age and Ageing*, vol. 21, 1992, pp. 95–8.

Dunaway, S. 'Thirty Years Later: the ADEA, an Essential Shield for the Older Worker' (unpublished AARP paper, Washington, DC, April 1998).

Dunnell, K. 'Are We Healthier?', in J. Charlton and M. Murphy (eds.), *The Health of Adult Britain 1841–1994 Vol. 2* (London, 1997).

Ebrahim, S. 'Ethnic Elders', *British Medical Journal*, vol. 313, 7 Sept. 1996, pp. 610–13.

'Demographic Shifts and Medical Training', *British Medical Journal*, vol. 319, 20 Nov. 1999, pp. 1358–60.

'Economic Status of the Aged', *Monthly Labor Review*, vol. 46, no. 6, June 1938, pp. 1348–9.

Edgar, A., Salek, S., Shickle, D. and Cohen, D. *The Ethical QALY. Ethical Issues in Healthcare Resource Allocations* (Surrey, 1988).

EFA (Employers Forum on Age), *The Business Benefits* (1999), www.efa.org.uk.

Case Studies of the Moment (1999), www.efa.org.uk.

What Is the EFA? (1999), www.efa.org.uk.

Generation Flex. Current Attitudes to the Retirement Debate (London, 2000).

Rude Shock (2001), www.efa.org.uk.

A Summary of the Debate (2002), www.efa.org.uk.

About EFA – Useful Facts and Figures (2002), www.efa.org.uk.

Age Discrimination Legislation (2002), www.efa.org.uk.

Why Is Age Important? (2002), www.efa.org.uk.

Speak Up (2003), www.efa.org.uk.

All You Need to Know About the EFA (2004), www.efa.org.uk.

Working Age, 1, 2004, www.efa.org.uk.

*EFA Newsline*s: 12, Summer 1999; 13, Autumn 1999; 17, Autumn 2000; 20, Autumn 2001; 21, Spring 2001, www.efa.org.uk.

EFA press releases: 7 Sept. 1999; 3 April 2003; 3 Sept. 2003; 17 Oct. 2003, www.efa.org.uk.

Eglit, H. 'Old Age and the Constitution', *Chicago-Kent Law Review*, vol. 57, no. 4, 1981, pp. 859–97.

'The Age Discrimination in Employment Act at Thirty: Where It's Been, Where It is Today, Where It's Going', *University of Richmond Law Review*, vol. 31, 1997, pp. 579–756.

Ellis, N. D. and McCarthy, W. E. J. 'Part One: Introduction and Interpretation', in S. R. Parker, C. G. Thomas, N. D. Ellis and W. E. J. McCarthy, *Effects of the Redundancy Payments Act. A Survey Carried Out in 1969 for the Department of Employment* (London, 1971).

Epstein, A. *Facing Old Age: A Study of Old Age Dependency in the United States and Old Age Pensions* (New York, NY, 1922).

Epstein, L. A. and Murray, J. H. *The Aged Population of the United States. The 1963 Social Security Survey of the Aged* (Washington, DC, 1967).

Epstein, R. A. *Forbidden Grounds: the Case Against Employment Discrimination Laws* (Cambridge, MA, 1992).

Estes, C. L. *The Aging Enterprise* (San Francisco, CA, 1979).

European Union, *Council Directive 2000/78/EC of 27 November 2000*.

Evans, J. G. 'Challenge of Ageing', in R. Smith (ed.), *Health of the Nation: the BMJ View* (London, 1991).

'Human Ageing and the Differences Between Young and Old', in J. Grimley Evans *et al.*, *Health and Function in the Third Age. Papers Prepared for the Carnegie Inquiry into the Third Age* (London, 1993).

'This Patient or That Patient?', in British Medical Journal, *Rationing In Action* (London, 1993).

'The Case Against', in B. New (ed.), *Rationing: Talk and Action in Health Care* (London, 1997).

'Geriatric Medicine: a Brief History', *British Medical Journal*, vol. 315, 25 Oct. 1997, pp. 1075–7.

'A Rejoinder to Alan Williams', in B. New (ed.), *Rationing: Talk and Action in Health Care* (London, 1997).

'Age Discrimination: Implications of the Ageing Process', in S. Fredman and S. Spencer (eds.), *Age as an Equality Issue* (Oxford, 2003).

Evanson, E. 'Social and Economic Change Since the Great Depression: Studies of Census Data, 1940–1980', *Focus* (University of Wisconsin-Madison Institute for Research on Poverty), vol. 11, no. 3, Fall 1988, pp. 1–10.

'Extent, Distribution and Causes of Old-Age Dependency', *Monthly Labor Review*, vol. 30, no. 4, April 1930, pp. 9–23.

'Facts and Figures' (2002), www.agepositive.gov.uk.

Falkingham, J. 'Dependency and Ageing in Britain: a Re-Examination of the Evidence', *Journal of Social Policy*, vol. 18, pt. 2, April 1989, pp. 211–33.

'Who Are the Baby Boomers? A Demographic Profile', in M. Evandrou (ed.), *Baby Boomers. Ageing in the 21st Century* (London, 1997).

Featherstone, M. 'Post-Bodies, Aging and Virtual Reality', in M. Featherstone and A. Wernick (eds.), *Images of Aging: Cultural Representations of Later Life* (London, 1995).

Featherstone, M. and Hepworth, M. 'Images of Positive Aging: a Case Study of *Retirement Choice* Magazine', in M. Featherstone and A. Wernick (eds.), *Images of Aging: Cultural Representations of Later Life* (London, 1995).

'Ageing, the Lifecourse and the Sociology of Embodiment', in G. Scambler and P. Higgs (eds.), *Modernity, Medicine and Health: Medical Sociology Towards 2000* (London, 1998).

Feldman, J. J. 'Work Ability of the Aged Under Conditions of Improving Mortality', *Milbank Memorial Fund Quarterly/Health and Society*, vol. 61, no. 3, 1983, pp. 430–44.

Feldstein, M. 'The Social Security Explosion', *The Public Interest*, no. 81, Fall 1985, pp. 94–106.

Field, D. 'Chronic Illness and Physical Disability', in S. Taylor and D. Field (eds.), *Sociology of Health and Health Care* (Oxford, 1997 edn).

Foner, N. *Ages in Conflict: a Cross-Cultural Perspective on Inequality between Old and Young* (New York, NY, 1984).

Foresight: Ageing Population Panel, *The Age Shift* (London, 2000).

Fothergill, J. M. *The Diseases of Sedentary and Advanced Life: a Work for Medical and Lay Readers* (London, 1885).

Frank, L. K. 'Foreword', in E. V. Cowdry (ed.), *Problems of Ageing: Biological and Medical Aspects* (London, 1939).

Fredman, S. 'The Age of Equality', in S. Fredman and S. Spencer (eds.), *Age as an Equality Issue* (Oxford, 2003).

Fredman, S. and Spencer, S. (eds.), *Age as an Equality Issue* (Oxford, 2003).

Freedman, V. A. and Martin, L. G. 'Understanding Trends in Functional Limitations Among Older Americans', *American Journal of Public Health*, vol. 88, no. 10, 1998, pp. 1457–62.

'Contribution of Chronic Conditions to Aggregate Changes in Old-Age Functioning', *American Journal of Public Health*, vol. 90, no. 11, 2000, pp. 1755–60.

Friedenwald, J. S. 'The Eye', in E. V. Cowdry (ed.), *Problems of Ageing: Biological and Medical Aspects* (London, 1939).

Friedman, J. W. and Strickler, G. M. *Cases and Materials on the Law of Employment Discrimination* (New York, NY, 1987).

Friedman, L. M. *Your Time Will Come: The Law of Age Discrimination and Mandatory Retirement* (New York, NY, 1984).

'Age Discrimination Law: Some Remarks on the American Experience', in S. Fredman and S. Spencer (eds.), *Age as an Equality Issue* (Oxford, 2003).

Fries, J. F. 'Aging, Natural Death and the Compression of Morbidity', *New England Journal of Medicine*, vol. 303, no. 3, 17 July 1980, pp. 130–5.

'The Compression of Morbidity', *Milbank Memorial Fund Quarterly/Health and Society*, vol. 61, no. 3, 1983, pp. 397–419.

'The Compression of Morbidity: Near or Far?', *Milbank Quarterly*, vol. 67, no. 2, 1989, pp. 208–323.

Frogner, M. L. 'Skills Shortages', *Labour Market Trends*, vol. 110, no. 1, Jan. 2002, pp. 17–26.

Gallie, D. 'The Labour Force', in A. H. Halsey and J. Webb (eds.), *Twentieth-Century British Social Trends* (Basingstoke, 2000).

George, V. *Social Security: Beveridge and After* (London, 1968).

Ghosh, U. K. and Ghosh, K. 'The History of Geriatric Medicine in Scotland', *Scottish Medical Journal*, vol. 42, no. 5, Oct. 1997, pp. 158–9.

Gibson, H. B. 'It Keeps Us Young', *Ageing and Society*, vol. 20, pt. 6, Nov. 2000, pp. 773–9.

Giddens, A. *The Third Way: the Renewal of Social Democracy* (Oxford, 1998).

Gilford, H. 'The Nature of Old Age and of Cancer', *British Medical Journal*, 27 Dec. 1913, pp. 1617–20.

Gilroy, R. *Good Practice in Equal Opportunities* (Aldershot, 1993).

Ginn, J. and Arber, S. '"Only Connect": Gender Relations and Ageing', in S. Arber and J. Ginn (eds.), *Connecting Gender and Ageing. A Sociological Approach* (Buckingham, 1995).

Gokhale, J. and Kotlikoff, L. J. 'Generational Justice and Generational Accounting', in J. B. Williamson, D. M. Watts-Roy and E. R. Kingson (eds.), *The Generational Equity Debate* (New York, NY, 1999).

Goldacre, M. J. 'Disease in the Third Age: a Profile from Routine Statistics', in J. Grimley Evans *et al.*, *Health and Function in the Third Age. Papers Prepared for the Carnegie Inquiry into the Third Age* (London, 1993).

Gordon, M. S. 'Changing Patterns of Retirement', *Journal of Gerontology*, vol. 15, no. 3, July 1960, pp. 300–4.

'The Income Status of Older Persons', in W. Haber and W. J. Cohen (eds.), *Social Security. Programs, Problems, and Policies* (Homewood, IL, 1960).

Graebner, W. *A History of Retirement. The Meaning and Function of an American Institution, 1885–1978* (New Haven, CT, 1980).

Grattan, P. 'Age Discrimination in Employment', in Help the Aged, *Age Discrimination in Public Policy. A Review of Evidence* (London, 2002).

Work After 60 – Choice or Necessity, Burden or Benefit? (London, 2003).

Green, S. 'A Two-Faced Society', *Nursing Times*, vol. 87, no. 33, 14 Aug. 1991, pp. 26–9.

Greenberg, J., Schimel, J. and Martens, A. 'Ageism: Denying the Face of the Future', in T. D. Nelson (ed.), *Ageism. Stereotyping and Prejudice Against Older Persons* (Cambridge, MA, 2002).

Gregory, R. F. *Age Discrimination in the American Workplace: Old at a Young Age* (New Brunswick, NJ, 2001).

'Greys Attack Ageist Firms', *Guardian*, 3 Dec. 1998.

Gruenberg, E. M. 'The Failures of Success', *Milbank Memorial Fund Quarterly/ Health and Society*, vol. 55, no. 1, 1977, pp. 3–24.

Gruman, G. J. *A History of Ideas About the Prolongation of Life: the Evolution of Prolongevity Hypotheses to 1800* (Philadelphia, PA, 1966).

Grundy, E. 'The Health and Health Care of Older Adults in England and Wales, 1841–1994', in J. Charlton and M. Murphy (eds.), *The Health of Adult Britain 1841–1994 Vol. 2* (London, 1997).

Guild, S. R. 'The Ear', in E. V. Cowdry (ed.), *Problems of Ageing: Biological and Medical Aspects* (London, 1939).

Haber, C. *Beyond Sixty-Five: the Dilemma of Old Age in America's Past* (Cambridge, 1983).

Haber, C. and Gratton, B. *Old Age and the Search for Security. An American Social History* (Bloomington, IN, 1994).

Hagberg, J.-E. 'Old People, New and Old Artefacts – Technology for Later Life', in B.-M. Oberg, A.-L. Narvanen, E. Nasman and E. Olsson (eds.), *Changing Worlds and the Ageing Subject. Dimensions in the Study of Ageing and Later Life* (Aldershot, 2004).

Hall, G. S. *Senescence: the Last Half of Life* (New York, NY, 1922).

Hancock, R. 'Financial Resources in Later Life', in M. Evandrou (ed.), *Baby Boomers: Ageing in the 21st Century* (London, 1997).

Hancock, R., Jarvis, C. and Mueller, G. *The Outlook for Incomes in Retirement. Social Trends and Attitudes* (London, 1995).

Hankins, F. H. 'Social Discrimination', in E. R. A. Seligman and A. Johnson (eds.), *Encyclopaedia of the Social Sciences, Vol. 14* (New York, NY, 1934).

Hannah, L. *Inventing Retirement: the Development of Occupational Pensions in Britain* (Cambridge, 1986).

'Happiness is a Warm Friend', *Observer*, 19 May 2002.

Harper, S. 'The Emergence and Consolidation of the Retirement Tradition in Post-War Britain', in M. Bury and J. Macnicol (eds.), *Aspects of Ageing. Essays on Social Policy and Old Age* (Egham, 1990).

Harper, S. and Thane, P. 'The Consolidation of "Old Age" as a Phase of Life, 1945–1965', in M. Jefferys (ed.), *Growing Old in the Twentieth Century* (London, 1989).

Harrington, M. *The Other America* (New York, NY, 1962).

Harris, A. I. *Handicapped and Impaired in Great Britain, Pt. I* (London, 1970).

Harris, B. 'Growing Taller, Living Longer? Anthropometric History and the Future of Old Age', *Ageing and Society*, vol. 17, pt. 5, Sept. 1997, pp. 491–512.

Harris, T. 'Projections: a Look Into the Future', in Office for National Statistics, *Social Trends No. 27 1997 Edition* (London, 1997).

Hatch, D. 'Destination of Claimant Count Departures: How the Over-50s Compare', *Labour Market Trends*, vol. 107, no. 4, April 1999, pp. 169–74.

Hauser, P. M. 'Changes in the Labor-Force Participation of the Older Worker', *American Journal of Sociology*, vol. LIX, no. 4, Jan. 1954, pp. 312–23.

Hausman, J. A. and Pacquette, L. 'Involuntary Early Retirement and Consumption', in G. Burtless (ed.), *Work, Health, and Income Among the Elderly* (Washington, DC, 1987).

Havighurst, R. J. 'Old Age – an American Problem', *Journal of Gerontology*, vol. 4, no. 4, Oct. 1949, pp. 298–304.

'Health Transitions and the Compression of Morbidity', in D. M. Gilford (ed.), *The Aging Population in the Twenty-First Century. Statistics for Health Policy* (Washington, DC, 1988).

Hearing Before the Subcommittee on Employment Opportunities of the Committee on Education and Labor, House of Representatives, To Amend the Age Discrimination in Employment Act of 1967, 9 September 1982 (Washington, DC, 1982).

Heginbotham, C. 'Why Rationing is Inevitable in the NHS', in B. New (ed.), *Rationing: Talk and Action in Health Care* (London, 1997).

Hendricks, J. and Hendricks, C. D. 'Ageism and Common Stereotypes', in V. Carver and P. Liddiard (eds.), *An Ageing Population. A Reader and Sourcebook* (Sevenoaks, 1978).

Hills, J. 'Does Britain Have a Welfare Generation?', in A. Walker (ed.), *The New Generational Contract: Intergenerational Relations, Old Age and Welfare* (London, 1996).

Himes, C. L. 'Obesity, Disease and Functional Limitation in Later Life', *Demography*, vol. 37, no. 1, Feb. 2000, pp. 73–82.

Hirsch, D. *Crossroads After 50. Improving Choices in Work and Retirement* (York, 2003).

Hodkinson, M. 'Active Life Expectancy and Disability', in J. Grimley Evans *et al.*, *Health and Function in the Third Age. Papers Prepared for the Carnegie Inquiry into the Third Age* (London, 1993).

Holden, C. 'Decommodification and the Workfare State', *Political Studies Review*, vol. 1, no. 3, Sept. 2003, pp. 303–16.

Holmes, P., Lynch, M. and Molho, I. 'An Econometric Analysis of the Growth in the Numbers Claiming Invalidity Benefit: an Overview', *Journal of Social Policy*, vol. 20, no. 1, Jan. 1991, pp. 87–105.

Holtzman, A. 'Analysis of Old Age Politics in the United States', *Journal of Gerontology*, vol. 9, no. 1, Jan. 1954, pp. 56–66.

Hope, S. C. 'Should There Be a Fixed Retirement Age? Some Managers Say Yes', *Annals of the American Academy of Political and Social Science*, vol. 279, Jan. 1952, pp. 72–3.

Hornstein, Z. (ed.), *Outlawing Age Discrimination. Foreign Lessons, UK Choices* (Bristol, 2001).

House of Commons Debates, 5s and 6s.

House Report No. 805, 90th Cong. 1st Sess., 23 Oct. 1967: *Age Discrimination in Employment Act of 1967. Report from the Committee on Education and Labor*, in US Equal Employment Opportunity Commission, *Legislative History of the Age Discrimination in Employment Act* (Washington, DC, 1981).

Howell, T. H. 'Social Medicine in Old Age', *British Medical Journal*, 16 Mar. 1946, pp. 399–400.

Our Advancing Years (London, 1953).

Hudson, C. 'It Will Take More Than This to Fortify the Over Forties', *Evening Standard*, 16 Nov. 1998.

Hufeland, C. W. *The Art of Prolonging Life* (London, 1797).

Humphry, G. M. 'The Annual Oration on Old Age and the Changes Incidental to It', *British Medical Journal*, 9 May 1885, pp. 927–31.

Hushbeck, J. C. *Old and Obsolete. Age Discrimination and the American Worker, 1860–1920* (New York, NY, 1989).

'Increasing Pension Age is "Work Until You Drop"', *Guardian*, 16 June 2004.

Independent Inquiry into Inequalities in Health. Report (Chairman: Sir D. Acheson) (London, 1998).

International Labour Office, *Report of the Office on the Question of Discrimination Against Elderly Workers* (Geneva, 1938).

'Introduction', in Institute of Personnel Management, *Age and Employment. Policies, Attitudes and Practices* (London, 1993).

Issacharoff, S. and Harris, E. W. 'Is Age Discrimination Really Age Discrimination?: the ADEA's Unnatural Solution', *New York University Law Review*, vol. 72, no. 4, Oct. 1997, pp. 780–840.

Itzin, C. 'Ageism Awareness Training: a Model for Group Work', in C. Phillipson, M. Bernard and P. Strang (eds.), *Dependency and Interdependency in Old Age: Theoretical Perspectives and Policy Alternatives* (Beckenham, 1986).

Jefferys, M. 'Is There a Need for Geriatric Medicine? Does it do More Harm than Good?', in P. Kaim-Caudle, J. Keithley and A. Mullender (eds.), *Aspects of Ageing* (London, 1993).

Jerrome, D. 'Ties That Bind', in A. Walker (ed.), *The New Generational Contract: Intergenerational Relations, Old Age and Welfare* (London, 1996).

Jeune, B. and Vaupel, J. W. (eds.), *Validation of Exceptional Longevity* (Odense, 1999).

'Job to Combat an Age Old Problem', *Guardian*, 31 Jan. 1998.

Johnson, J. and Bytheway, B. 'Ageism: Concept and Definition', in J. Johnson and R. Slater (eds.), *Ageing and Later Life* (London, 1993).

Johnson, P., Conrad, C. and Thomson, D. 'Introduction' in P. Johnson, C. Conrad and D. Thomson (eds.), *Workers Versus Pensioners. Intergenerational Justice in an Ageing World* (Manchester, 1989).

Johnson, R. W. and Neumark, D. 'Age Discrimination, Job Separations, and Employment Status of Older Workers. Evidence from Self-Reports', *Journal of Human Resources*, vol. XXXII, no. 4, Fall 1997, pp. 779–811.

Jordan, B. *A Theory of Poverty and Social Exclusion* (Cambridge, 1996).

Judy, R. W. and d'Amico, C. *Workforce 2020: Work and Workers in the 21st Century* (Indianapolis, IN, 1997).

Kahn, R. L. 'Productive Behavior Through the Life Course', in The Aging Society Project, *Human Resource Implications of an Aging Work Force* (New York, NY, 1984).

Kalet, J. E. *Age Discrimination in Employment Law* (Washington, DC, 1990).

Katz, M. B. *Improving Poor People. The Welfare State, the 'Underclass' and Urban Schools as History* (Princeton, NJ, 1995).

Katz, S. 'Imagining the Life-Span: from Pre-Modern Miracles to Postmodern Fantasies', in M. Featherstone and A. Wernick (eds.), *Images of Aging: Cultural Representations of Later Life* (London, 1995).

   Disciplining Old Age. The Formation of Gerontological Knowledge (Charlottesville, VA, 1996).

Kelley, K. J. 'Massachusetts Law Against Age Discrimination in Employment', in New York State Joint Legislative Committee on Problems of the Aging, *No Time to Grow Old* (Albany, NY, 1951).

Keyworth, G. H. 'Notes on Disease in Advanced Life', *British Medical Journal*, 31 Jan. 1903, pp. 240–1.

Kirkwood, T. 'New Directions', Reith Lecture 5, 2001, www.bbc.co.uk.

Klein, R. *The New Politics of the National Health Service* (London, 1995 edn).

Klein, R., Day, P. and Redmayne, S. *Managing Scarcity. Priority Setting and Rationing in the National Health Service* (Buckingham, 1996).

Kodz, J., Kersley, B. and Bates, P. *The Fifties Revival* (Brighton, 1999).

Kohli, M., Rein, M., Guillemard, A.-M. and van Gunsteren, H. (eds.), *Time for Retirement. Comparative Studies of Early Exit from the Labour Force* (Cambridge, 1991).

Korenchevsky, V. 'The Longest Span of Life Based on the Records of Centenarians in England and Wales', *British Medical Journal*, 5 July 1947, pp. 14–16.

   'The Problem of Ageing. Basic Difficulties of Research', *British Medical Journal*, 8 Jan. 1949, pp. 66–8.

Kotlikoff, L. J. *Generational Accounting. Knowing Who Pays, and When, for What We Spend* (New York, NY, 1992).

Kramer, M. 'The Rising Pandemic of Mental Disorders and Associated Chronic Diseases and Disabilities', *Acta Psychiatrica Scandinavica*, 62, 1980 (Suppl. 283), pp. 382–97.

Kuhns, E. D. 'Employment Opportunities for Older Workers (and Others): A Labor View of Short- and Long-Term Prospects', in R. Morris and S. A. Bass (eds.), *Retirement Reconsidered. Economic and Social Roles for Older People* (New York, NY, 1988).

'Labour Market Data', *Labour Market Trends*, vol. 112, no. 1, Jan. 2004.

Labour Party, *New Labour. Because Britain Deserves Better* (London, 1997).

Laczko, F. and Phillipson, C. *Changing Work and Retirement. Social Policy and the Older Worker* (Milton Keynes, 1991).

'Great Britain: the Contradictions of Early Exit', in M. Kohli, M. Rein, A.-M. Guillemard and H. van Gunsteren (eds.), *Time for Retirement. Comparative Studies of Early Exit from the Labor Force* (Cambridge, 1991).

Landis, P. H. 'Emerging Problems of the Aged', *Social Forces*, vol. 20, no. 4, May 1942, pp. 460–70.

Laslett, P. 'Is There a Generational Contract?', in P. Laslett and J. S. Fishkin (eds.), *Justice between Age Groups and Generations* (New Haven, CT, 1992).

Laslett, P. and Fishkin, J. S. 'Introduction: Processional Justice', in P. Laslett and J. S. Fishkin (eds.), *Justice between Age Groups and Generations* (New Haven, CT, 1992).

Layard, R. *What Labour Can Do* (London, 1997).

Layard, R., Nickell, S. and Jackman, R. *The Unemployment Crisis* (Oxford, 1994).

Lazear, E. P. 'Why Is There Mandatory Retirement?', *Journal of Political Economy*, vol. 87, no. 6, Dec. 1979, pp. 1261–84.

Lebergott, S. 'Comment on "Discrimination Against Older Workers in Industry"', *American Journal of Sociology*, vol. LI, no. 4, Jan. 1946, pp. 322–4.

Lehr, R. I., Middlebrooks, D. J. and Rutledge, D. J. (eds.), *How to Avoid Charges of Age Discrimination in the Workplace* (New York, NY, 1989).

Leonesio, M. V. 'The Economics of Retirement: a Nontechnical Guide', *Social Security Bulletin*, vol. 59, no. 4, Winter 1996, pp. 29–50.

Levine, M. L. *Age Discrimination and the Mandatory Retirement Controversy* (Baltimore, MD, 1988).

Levy, B. R. and Banaji, M. R. 'Implicit Ageism', in T. D. Nelson (ed.), *Ageism. Stereotyping and Prejudice Against Older Persons* (Cambridge, MA, 2002).

Linford, A. A. *Old Age Assistance in Massachusetts* (Chicago, IL, 1949).

Lipscomb, F. M. *Diseases of Old Age* (London, 1932).

Lister, R. *Social Security: the Case for Reform* (London, 1975).

Logan, W. P. D. 'Work and Age: Statistical Considerations', *British Medical Journal*, 28 Nov. 1953, pp. 1190–3.

Longman, P. *Born to Pay. The New Politics of Aging in America* (Boston, 1987).

Lonsdale, S. and Aylward, M. 'A United Kingdom Perspective on Disability Policy', in L. J. M. Aarts, R. V. Burkhauser and P. R. de Jong (eds.), *Curing the Dutch Disease. An International Perspective on Disability Policy Reform* (Aldershot, 1996).

Lorand, A. *Old Age Deferred: the Causes of Old Age and its Postponement by Hygienic and Therapeutic Measures* (Philadelphia, PA, 1910).

Lundberg, S. 'Family Bargaining and Retirement Behavior', in H. J. Aaron (ed.), *Behavioral Dimensions of Retirement Economics* (Washington, DC, 1999).

Lusardi, A. 'Information, Expectations and Savings for Retirement', in H. J. Aaron (ed.), *Behavioral Dimensions of Retirement Economics* (Washington, DC, 1999).

Mackay, T. *Methods of Social Reform* (London, 1896).

Mackintosh, J. M. 'New Jobs for Old', *The Lancet*, vol. CCLXI, 1 Dec. 1951, pp. 1033–4.

Macmillan, R. 'Getting By', in P. Alcock, C. Beatty, S. Fothergill, R. Macmillan and S. Yeandle, *Work to Welfare. How Men Become Detached from the Labour Market* (Cambridge, 2003).

Macnicol, J. 'Ageing and Justice', *Labour History Review*, vol. 55, no. 1, Spring 1990, pp. 75–80.

'Old Age and Structured Dependency', in M. Bury and J. Macnicol (eds.), *Aspects of Ageing. Essays on Social Policy and Old Age* (Egham, 1990).

'Beveridge and Old Age', in J. Hills, J. Ditch and H. Glennerster (eds.), *Beveridge and Social Security. An International Retrospective* (Oxford, 1994).

'Is There an Underclass? The Lessons from America', in M. White (ed.), *Unemployment and Public Policy in the Changing Labour Market* (London, 1994).

The Politics of Retirement in Britain 1878–1948 (Cambridge, 1998).

'Retirement and Health Status: the Paradox', in H. Bartlett, J. Stewart and J. Andrews (eds.), *Historical and Contemporary Perspectives on Health, Illness and Health Care in Britain Since the Seventeenth Century* (Oxford, 1998).

'The New Retirement Agenda', *Work, Employment and Society*, vol. 13, no. 2, June 1999, pp. 403–5.

'Retirement', in J. Mokyr (ed.), *Oxford Encyclopedia of Economic History, Vol. 4* (Oxford, 2003).

'Alfred William Watson (1870–1936)', *New Dictionary of National Biography* (Oxford, 2004).

'Analysing Age Discrimination', in B.-M. Oberg, A.-L. Narvanen, E. Nasman and E. Olsson (eds.), *Changing Worlds and the Ageing Subject. Dimensions in the Study of Ageing and Later Life* (Aldershot, 2004).

(ed.), *Paying for the Old: Old Age and Social Welfare Provision* (Bristol, 7 vols., 2000).

Macnicol, J. and Blaikie, A. 'The Politics of Retirement, 1908–48', in M. Jefferys (ed.), *Growing Old in the Twentieth Century* (London, 1989).

Maddox, G. 'Aging Differently', *The Gerontologist*, vol. 27, no. 5, 1987, pp. 557–64.

Maddox, G. L. and Clark, D. O. 'Trajectories of Functional Impairment in Later Life', *Journal of Health and Social Behavior*, vol. 33, June 1992, pp. 114–25.

Maddox, G. L., Clark, D. O. and Steinhauser, K. 'Dynamics of Functional Impairment in Late Adulthood', *Social Science and Medicine*, vol. 38, no. 7, 1994, pp. 925–36.

Mandatory Retirement: the Social and Human Costs of Enforced Idleness. Report by the Select Committee on Aging. Ninety-Fifth Congress, August 1977 (Washington, DC, 1977).

Mann, K. *Approaching Retirement. Social Divisions, Welfare and Exclusion* (Bristol, 2001).

Mannheim, K. 'The Problem of Generations', in K. Mannheim, *Essays on the Sociology of Knowledge. Collected Works Volume Five* (edited by Paul Kecskemeti) (London, 1957 edn).

Manton, K. G. 'Changing Concepts of Morbidity and Mortality in the Elderly Population', *Milbank Memorial Fund Quarterly/Health and Society*, vol. 60, no. 2, 1982, pp. 183–244.

'Life-Style Risk Factors', *Annals of the American Academy of Political and Social Science*, vol. 503, May 1989, pp. 72–88.

'The Dynamics of Population Aging: Demography and Policy Analysis', *Milbank Quarterly*, vol. 69, no. 2, 1991, pp. 309–38.

Manton, K. G., Stallard, E. and Tolley, H. D. 'Limits to Human Life Expectancy: Evidence, Prospects, and Implications', *Population and Development Review*, vol. 17, no. 4, December 1991, pp. 603–37.

Manton, K. G. and Soldo, B. J. 'Disability and Mortality Among the Oldest Old: Implications for Current and Future Health and Long-Term Care Service Needs', in R. M. Suzman, D. P. Willis and K. Manton (eds.), *The Oldest Old* (New York, NY, 1992).

Manton, K. G., Singer, B. H. and Suzman, R. M. 'The Scientific and Policy Needs for Improved Health Forecasting Models for Elderly Populations', in K. G. Manton, B. H. Singer and R. M. Suzman (eds.), *Forecasting the Health of Elderly Populations* (New York, NY, 1993).

Manton, K. G., Stallard, E. and Corder, L. 'Changes in the Age Dependence of Mortality and Disability: Cohort and Other Determinants', *Demography*, vol. 34, no. 1, Feb. 1997, pp. 135–57.

Marshall, R., Knapp, C. B., Liggett, M. H. and Glover, R. W. *Employment Discrimination: the Impact of Legal and Administrative Remedies* (New York, NY, 1978).

Martin, J., Meltzer, H. and Eliot, D. *The Prevalence of Disability Among Adults* (London, 1988).

Martin, J. and White, A. *The Financial Circumstances of Disabled Adults Living in Private Households* (London, 1988).

Martin, R. 'Industrial Restructuring, Labour Shake-out and the Geography of Recession', in M. Danson (ed.), *Redundancy and Recession. Restructuring the Regions?* (Norwich, 1986).

Mashaw, J. L. 'Findings of the Disability Policy Panel', in V. P. Reno, J. L. Mashaw and B. Gradison (eds.), *Disability: Challenges for Social Insurance, Health Care Financing, and Labor Market Policy* (Washington, DC, 1997).

McCallum, J. 'Health and Ageing: the Last Phase of the Epidemiological Transition', in A. Borowski, S. Encel and E. Ozanne (eds.), *Ageing and Social Policy in Australia* (Cambridge, 1997).

McConnell, S. R. 'Age Discrimination in Employment', in H. S. Parnes (ed.), *Policy Issues in Work and Retirement* (Kalamazoo, MI, 1983).

McCord, C. and Freeman, H. P. 'Excess Mortality in Harlem', *New England Journal of Medicine*, vol. 322, no. 3, 18 Jan. 1990, pp. 173–7.

McFarland, R. A. 'The Older Worker in Industry', *Harvard Business Review*, vol. XXI, no. 4, Summer 1943, pp. 505–20.

McGowan, T. G. 'Ageism and Discrimination', in J. E. Birren (ed.), *Encyclopedia of Gerontology. Age, Aging, and the Aged, Vol. I* (1996).

McIntyre, A. (ed.), *Aging and Political Leadership* (Melbourne, 1988).

McKay, S. 'Older Workers in the Labour Market', *Labour Market Trends*, vol. 106, no. 7, July 1998, pp. 365–9.

McKay, S. and Middleton, S. *Characteristics of Older Workers* (London, 1998).

McKay, S. and Smeaton, D. *Research Summary. Working After State Pension Age: Quantitative Analysis* (2003), www.agepositive.gov.uk.

McKeown, T. *The Modern Rise of Population* (London, 1976).

McKerlie, D. 'Equality Between Age Groups', *Philosophy and Public Affairs*, vol. 21, no. 3, Summer 1992, pp. 275–95.

McKie, J., Richardson, J., Singer, P. and Kuhse, H. *The Allocation of Health Care Resources. An Ethical Evaluation of the 'QALY' Approach* (Aldershot, 1998).

McMurdo, M. E. T. 'Physical Activity and Health in Old Age', *Scottish Medical Journal*, vol. 42, no. 5, October 1997, pp. 154–5.

Meadows, P. *Retirement Ages in the UK: a Review of the Literature* (London, 2003).

'Memorial Edition', *Modern Maturity*, Jan. 1968.

'Men Over 50 Give Up on Jobs', *Guardian*, 11 June 1999.

Menchin, R. S. *New Work Opportunities for Older Americans* (Englewood Cliffs, NJ, 1993).

Metchnikoff, E. *The Prolongation of Life: Optimistic Studies* (London, 1907).

Middleton, R. *The British Economy Since 1945. Engaging with the Debate* (Basingstoke, 2000).

Midwinter, E. *Ageism, Discrimination and Citizenship* (London, 1991).
  The British Gas Report on Attitudes to Ageing 1991 (London, 1991).
  Citizenship: From Ageism to Participation (Dunfermline, 1992).

Miles, C. C. and Miles, W. R. 'The Correlation of Intelligence Scores and Chronological Age From Early to Late Maturity', *American Journal of Psychology*, vol. 44, no. 1, Jan. 1932, pp. 44–78.

Miles, W. R. 'Correlation of Reaction and Co-ordination Speed with Age in Adults', *American Journal of Psychology*, vol. 43, no. 3, July 1931, pp. 377–91.
  'Psychological Aspects of Ageing', in E. V. Cowdry (ed.), *Problems of Ageing: Biological and Medical Aspects* (London, 1939).

Miles, W. R. and Miles, C. C. 'Principal Mental Changes With Normal Aging', in E. J. Stieglitz (ed.), *Geriatric Medicine: Diagnosis and Management of Disease in the Aging and in the Aged* (Philadelphia, PA, 1941).

Miller, R. A. 'Extending Life: Scientific Prospects and Political Obstacles', *Milbank Quarterly*, vol. 80, no. 1, 2002, pp. 155–74.

'Minister's Message', www.agepositive.gov.org.

Ministry of Labour and National Service, *Employment of Older Men and Women* (London, 1952).

Ministry of Pensions and National Insurance, *National Insurance Retirement Pensions. Reasons Given for Retiring or Continuing at Work* (London, 1954).

Minkler, M. and Estes, C. (eds.), *Critical Gerontology. Perspectives from Political and Moral Economy* (Amityville, NY, 1999).

Moody, H. R. 'The Contradictions of an Aging Society: From Zero Sum to Productive Society', in R. Morris and S. A. Bass (eds.), *Retirement Reconsidered: Economic and Social Roles for Older People* (New York, NY, 1988).

Mosley, A. G. and Capaldi, N. *Affirmative Action. Social Justice or Unfair Preference?* (Lanham, MD, 1996).

Moynagh, M. and Worsley, R. *The Opportunity of a Lifetime: Reshaping Retirement* (King's Lynn, 2004).

Mullan, P. *The Imaginary Time Bomb. Why an Ageing Population Is Not a Social Problem* (London, 2002).

Murray, C. *Losing Ground: American Social Policy, 1950–1980* (New York, NY, 1984).

Myles, J. *Old Age in the Welfare State: the Political Economy of Public Pensions* (Boston, MA, 1984).

Nascher, I. L. *Geriatrics. The Diseases of Old Age and Their Treatment, Including Physiological Old Age, Home and Institutional Care, and Medico-Legal Relations* (London, 1914).

National Advisory Committee on the Employment of Older Men and Women. First Report, Cmd. 8963, 1953.

National Advisory Committee on the Employment of Older Men and Women. Second Report, Cmd. 9628, 1955.

National Centre for Social Research, *Health Survey for England 2000. The Health of Older People. Summary of Key Findings* (London, 2002).

National Council of Senior Citizens, *The Nation's Stake in the Employment of Middle-Aged and Older Persons* (Washington, DC, 1971).

The National Plan, Cmnd. 2764, 1965.

Nelson, T. D. 'Preface', in T. D. Nelson (ed.), *Ageism. Stereotyping and Prejudice Against Older Persons* (Cambridge, MA, 2002).

Neugarten, B. L. 'Age Distinctions and Their Social Functions', in D. A. Neugarten (ed.), *The Meanings of Age: Selected Papers of Bernice L. Neugarten* (Chicago, IL, 1996).

'The End of Gerontology?', in D. A. Neugarten (ed.), *The Meanings of Age: Selected Papers of Bernice L. Neugarten* (Chicago, IL, 1996).

(ed.), *Age or Need? Public Policies for Older People* (Beverly Hills, CA, 1982).

Neugarten, B. L., Moore, J. W. and Lowe, J. C. 'Age Norms, Age Constraints, and Adult Socialisation', in D. A. Neugarten (ed.), *The Meanings of Age: Selected Papers of Bernice L. Neugarten* (Chicago, IL, 1996).

Neumark, D. 'Age Discrimination Legislation in the US: Assessment of the Evidence', in Z. Hornstein (ed.), *Outlawing Age Discrimination. Foreign Lessons, UK Choices* (Bristol, 2001).

Neumark, D. and Stock, W. A. *Age Discrimination Laws and Labor Market Efficiency* (National Bureau of Economic Research Working Paper No. 6088, Cambridge, MA, July 1997).

New, B. (ed.), *Rationing: Talk and Action in Health Care* (London, 1997).

New, B. and Le Grand, J. *Rationing in the NHS. Principles and Pragmatism* (London, 1996).

New Ambitions for Our Country: a New Contract for Welfare, Cm. 3805, 1998.

New York State Joint Legislative Committee on Problems of the Aging, *No Time to Grow Old* (Albany, NY, 1951).

Age Is No Barrier (Albany, NY, 1952).

Newman, Sir G. *The Building of a Nation's Health* (London, 1939).

The NHS Plan. A Plan for Investment. A Plan for Reform. Cm. 4818-I, July 2000.

'NHS Says Sir Magdi is Too Old to Operate', *Evening Standard*, 20 Nov. 2001.

Nickell, S. 'Unemployment in Britain', in P. Gregg and J. Wadsworth (eds.), *The State of Working Britain* (Manchester, 1999).

Norman, A. *Aspects of Ageism: a Discussion Paper* (London, 1987).

Northrup, J. P. *Old Age, Handicapped, and Vietnam-era Antidiscrimination Legislation* (Philadelphia, PA, 1980).

Nuffield Foundation, *Old People. Report of a Survey Committee on the Problems of Ageing and the Care of Old People Under the Chairmanship of B. Seebohm Rowntree* (London, 1947).

Oakley, J. R. *God's Country: America in the Fifties* (New York, NY, 1990).

Office for National Statistics, *Social Focus on the Unemployed* (London, 1998).

Social Trends No. 28 1998 Edition (London, 1998).

Social Focus on Older People (London, 1999).

Social Trends No. 29 1999 Edition (London, 1999).

Social Focus on Men (London, 2001).

Social Trends No. 31 2001 Edition (London, 2001).

Social Trends No. 32 2002 Edition (London, 2002).

Social Trends No. 33 2003 Edition (London, 2003).

Social Trends No. 34 2004 Edition (London, 2004).

Office for National Statistics. Social Survey Division, *Living in Britain. Results from the 1998 General Household Survey* (London, 2000).

Living in Britain. Results from the 2000 General Household Survey (London, 2001).

'The Older American Worker. The US Must Make Better Use of Him', *Time*, 19 Oct. 1953, p. 100.

'Older Workers Mean Happier Customers', *Guardian*, 17 Nov. 1998.

Oliver, M. *The Politics of Disablement* (London, 1990).

Understanding Disability. From Theory to Practice (Basingstoke, 1996).

Olshansky, S. J. and Ault, A. B. 'The Fourth Stage of the Epidemiologic Transition: The Age of Delayed Degenerative Diseases', *Milbank Quarterly*, vol. 64, no. 3, 1986, pp. 355–91.

Olshansky, S. J., Carnes, B. A. and Cassel, C. 'In Search of Methuselah: Estimating the Upper Limits to Human Longevity', *Science*, vol. 250, pt. 2, 1990, pp. 634–40.

Olshansky, S. J. and Carnes, B. 'Prospect for Extended Survival: a Critical Review of the Biological Evidence', in G. Caselli and A. D. Lopez (eds.), *Health and Mortality Among Elderly Populations* (Oxford, 1996).

O'Meara, D. P. *Protecting the Growing Number of Older Workers: the Age Discrimination in Employment Act* (Philadelphia, PA, 1989).

Organisation for Economic Co-operation and Development, *Age and Employment* (Paris, 1962).

Health at a Glance 2003 (2003), www.oecd.org.

Paffenbarger, R. S., Hyde, R. T., Wing, A. L. and Hsieh, C.-C. 'Physical Activity, All-Cause Mortality and Longevity of College Alumni', *New England Journal of Medicine*, vol. 314, no. 10, 6 Mar. 1986, pp. 605–13.

Paffenbarger, R. S., Hyde, R. T., Wing, A. L., Lee, I-M., Jung, D. L. and Kampert, J. B. 'The Association of Changes in Physical-Activity Level and Other Lifestyle Characteristics with Mortality Among Men', *New England Journal of Medicine*, vol. 328, no. 8, 25 Feb. 1993, pp. 538–45.

Page, A. W. Letter in *Oddfellows Magazine*, vol. xxvi, no. 243, Mar. 1895, p. 82.

Palmer, D. L. and Brownell, J. A. 'Influence of Age on Employment Opportunities', *Monthly Labor Review*, vol. 48, no. 4, April 1939, pp. 765–80.

Palmore, E. B. 'Compulsory Versus Flexible Retirement: Issues and Facts', *The Gerontologist*, vol. 12, no. 4, Winter 1972, pp. 343–8.

'Trends in the Health of the Aged', *The Gerontologist*, vol. 26, no. 3, June 1986, pp. 298–302.

Ageism. Negative and Positive (New York, NY, 1990).

Palmore, E. B. and Manton, K. 'Ageism Compared to Racism and Sexism', *Journal of Gerontology*, vol. 28, no. 3, 1973, pp. 363–9.

Pampel, F. C. and Williamson, J. B. 'Age Patterns of Suicide and Homicide Mortality Rates in High-Income Nations', *Social Forces*, vol. 80, no. 1, Sept. 2001, pp. 251–82.

Parker, F. E. 'Experience Under State Old-Age Pension Acts in 1933', *Monthly Labor Review*, vol. 39, no. 2, August 1934, pp. 255–72.

Parker, S. R. and Thomas, C. G. 'Part Two: the Findings of the Survey', in S. R. Parker, C. G. Thomas, N. D. Ellis and W. E. J. McCarthy, *Effects of the Redundancy Payments Act. A Survey Carried Out in 1969 for the Department of Employment* (London, 1971).

Parnes, H. S. 'The Retirement Decision', in M. E. Borus, H. S. Parnes, S. H. Sandell and B. Seidman (eds.), *The Older Worker* (Madison, WI, 1988).

Parsons, D. O. 'The Decline in Male Labor Force Participation', *Journal of Political Economy*, vol. 88, no. 3, June 1980, pp. 117–34.

Patterson, J. T. *America's Struggle Against Poverty 1900–1994* (Cambridge, MA, 1994).

Pearson, M. 'The Transition from Work to Retirement (1)', *Occupational Psychology*, vol. 31, no. 2, April 1957, pp. 80–8.

'The Transition from Work to Retirement (2)', *Occupational Psychology*, vol. 31, no. 3, July 1957, pp. 139–49.

Pemberton, J. and Smith, J. C. 'The Return to Work of Elderly Male Hospital In-Patients', *British Medical Journal*, 6 Aug. 1949, pp. 306–8.

Pensions: 2000 and Beyond, Vol. I: the Report of the Retirement Income Inquiry (London, 1996).

Perlman, J. and Kumin, H. I. 'Employment and Earnings Under Old-Age and Survivors Insurance During the First Year of the War', *Social Security Bulletin*, vol. 8, no. 3, Mar. 1945, pp. 10–16.

Peterson, D. A. and Coberly, S. 'The Older Worker: Myths and Realities', in R. Morris and S. A. Bass (eds.), *Retirement Reconsidered. Economic and Social Roles for Older People* (New York, NY, 1988).

Phillipson, C. *Reconstructing Old Age: New Agendas in Social Theory and Practice* (London, 1998).

Transitions from Work to Retirement. Developing a New Social Contract (Bristol, 2002).

Piachaud, D. 'Disability, Retirement and Unemployment of Older Men', *Journal of Social Policy*, vol. 15, pt. 2, April 1986, pp. 145–62.

Pickard, J. 'Grey Areas', *People Management*, vol. 5, no. 15, 29 July 1999, pp. 31–7.

Pickering, A. *Pensions Policy. How Government Can Get Us Saving Again* (London, 2004).

Pieroni, R. E. 'Centenarians', in E. B. Palmore (ed.), *Handbook on the Aged in the United States* (Westport, CN, 1984).

Platman, K. *The Glass Precipice. Employability for a Mixed Age Workforce* (London, 1999).

Platt, L. S. and Ventrell-Monsees, C. *Age Discrimination Litigation* (Costa Mesa, CA, 2000).

Player, M. A. *Federal Law of Employment Discrimination in a Nutshell* (St Paul, MN, 1981).

Political and Economic Planning, *The Exit from Industry* (London, 1935).

Pollak, O. 'Discrimination Against Older Workers in Industry', *American Journal of Sociology*, vol. L, no. 2, Sept. 1944, pp. 99–106.

'Rejoinder', *American Journal of Sociology*, vol. LI, no. 4, Jan. 1946, pp. 324–5.

The Poor Law Report of 1834 (edited by S. G. and E. O. A. Checkland, Harmondsworth, 1973).

Porteba, J. M. and Summers, L. H. 'Public Policy Implications of Declining Old-Age Mortality', in G. Burtless (ed.), *Work, Health, and Income Among the Elderly* (Washington, DC, 1987).

Posner, R. A. *Aging and Old Age* (Chicago, 1995).

Pratt, H. J. *The Gray Lobby* (Chicago, 1976).

Gray Agendas: Interest Groups and Public Pensions in Canada, Britain and the United States (Ann Arbor, MI, 1993).

Priestley, M. 'Adults Only: Disability, Social Policy and the Life Course', *Journal of Social Policy*, vol. 29, pt. 3, July 2000, pp. 421–39.

'Private Lives', *Guardian*, 23 Nov. 1998.

Public Record Office (National Archives): PRO AST 7/317; CAB 129/121; CAB 129/122; LAB 8/3290; LAB 108/3; LAB 108/11.

Putnam, J. K. *Old-Age Politics in California. From Richardson to Reagan* (Stanford, CA, 1970).

Quadagno, J. *The Transformation of Old Age Security. Class and Politics in the American Welfare State* (Chicago, 1988).

Quadagno, J. S. and Hardy, M. 'Regulating Retirement Through the Age Discrimination in Employment Act', *Research on Aging*, vol. 13, no. 4, Dec. 1991, pp. 470–5.

Quinn, J. F. 'Retirement Patterns and Bridge Jobs in the 1990s', *Employee Benefit Research Institute Issue Brief*, no. 206, Feb. 1999, pp. 1–22.

Ransome, R. L. and Sutch, R. 'The Labor of Older Americans: Retirement of Men On and Off the Job, 1870–1937', *Journal of Economic History*, vol. 46, no. 1, Mar. 1986, pp. 1–30.

'The Impact of Aging on the Employment of Men in American Working-Class Communities at the End of the Nineteenth Century', in D. Kertzer and P. Laslett (eds.), *Aging in the Past: Demography, Society, and Old Age* (Berkeley, CA, 1995).

Rappoport, S. S. *Age Discrimination: a Legal and Practical Guide for Employers* (Washington, DC, 1989).

Rawls, J. *A Theory of Justice* (Cambridge, MA, 1999 edn).

Reisine, S. and Fifield, J. 'Expanding the Definition of Disability: Implications for Planning, Policy and Research', *Milbank Quarterly*, vol. 70, no. 3, 1992, pp. 491–508.

Remenyi, A. *Safeguarding the Employability of Older Workers: Issues and Perspectives* (Melbourne, 1994).

Report of the Commissioner for the Special Areas in England and Wales for the Year Ended 30th September 1937, Cmd. 5595.

Report of the Commissioner for the Special Areas in England and Wales for the Year Ended 30th September 1938, Cmd. 5896.

Report of the Committee on the Economic and Financial Problems of the Provision for Old Age, Cmd. 9333, 1954.

Report of the Royal Commission on Population, Cmd. 7695, 1949.

Report of the Royal Commission on the National Health Service, Cmnd. 7615, 1979.

Report of the Secretary of Labor, *Labor Market Problems of Older Workers* (Washington, DC, 1989).

Report of the Unemployment Assistance Board for the Year Ended 31st December 1937, Cmd. 5752.

Report of the Unemployment Assistance Board for the Year Ended 31st December 1938, Cmd. 6021.

'Return of the Wrinklies', *Economist*, 16 January 2004.

Richardson, I. M. *Age and Need. A Study of Older People in North-East Scotland* (Edinburgh, 1964).

Rickard, S. *A Profits Warning. Macroeconomic Costs of Ageism* (London, n.d., c. 2000).

Rix, S. E. 'Public Policy and the Older Worker: Fifty Years of More or Less Benign Neglect' (paper to the 48th Annual Scientific Meeting of the Gerontological Society of America, Los Angeles, November 1995).

Roberts, A. 'British Trade Union Attitudes to the Employment of Older Men and Women', in *Old Age in the Modern World. Report of the Third Congress of the International Association of Gerontology, London 1954* (Edinburgh, 1955).

Roberts, E. 'Age Discrimination in Health', in Help the Aged, *Age Discrimination in Public Policy. A Review of Evidence* (London, 2002).

Roberts, E., Robinson, J. and Seymour, L. *Old Habits Die Hard. Tackling Age Discrimination in Health and Social Care* (London, 2002).

Roberts, N. *Our Future Selves* (London, 1970).

Robine, J.-M. and Ritchie, K. 'Healthy Life Expectancy: Evaluation of a New Global Indicator for Change in Population Health', *British Medical Journal*, vol. 302, 23 Feb. 1991, pp. 457–60.

Robine, J.-M., Mathers, C. and Brouard, N. 'Trends and Differentials in Disability-Free Life Expectancy', in G. Caselli and A. D. Lopez (eds.), *Health and Mortality Among Elderly Populations* (Oxford, 1996).

Robinson, J. 'Age Equality in Health and Social Care', in S. Fredman and S. Spencer (eds.), *Age as an Equality Issue* (Oxford, 2003).

Rolleston, Sir H. *Medical Aspects of Old Age* (London, 1922; 1932 edn).

Rosenblum, M. *The Next Steps in Combating Age Discrimination in Employment: With Special Reference to Mandatory Retirement Policy. A Working Paper Prepared for Use by the Special Committee on Aging, United States Senate* (Washington, DC, August 1977).

Rothstein, F. R. 'Older Worker Employment Opportunities in the Private Sector', in R. Morris and S. A. Bass (eds.), *Retirement Reconsidered. Economic and Social Roles for Older People* (New York, NY, 1988).

Rowe, E. K. and Paine, T. H. 'Pension Plans Under Collective Bargaining, Part I', *Monthly Labor Review*, vol. 76, no. 3, Mar. 1953, pp. 237–48.

'Pension Plans Under Collective Bargaining, Part II', *Monthly Labor Review*, vol. 76, no. 5, May 1953, pp. 484–9.

Royal Commission on the Aged Poor, 1895, C-7684-II, Vol. III, *Minutes of Evidence*.

Rubinow, I. M. *Social Insurance* (New York, NY, 1913).

Samuelson, P. *Economics. An Introductory Analysis* (New York, NY, 1958 edn).

Sandell, S. H. 'The Labor Force by the Year 2000 and Employment Policy for Older Workers', in R. Morris and S. A. Bass (eds.), *Retirement Reconsidered. Economic and Social Roles for Older People* (New York, NY, 1988).

Sandell, S. H. (ed.), *The Problem Isn't Age. Work and Older Americans* (New York, NY, 1987).

Sargeant, M. *Age Discrimination in Employment* (London, 1999).

Saving Lives: Our Healthier Nation, Cm. 4386, July 1999.

Schneider, E. L. and Brody, J. A. 'Aging, Natural Death and the Compression of Morbidity: Another View', *New England Journal of Medicine*, vol. 309, no. 14, 6 Oct. 1983, pp. 854–6.

Schuck, P. H. 'The Graying of Civil Rights Law', *The Public Interest*, no. 60, Summer 1980, pp. 69–93.

'Age Discrimination Revisited', *Chicago-Kent Law Review*, vol. 57, no. 4, 1981, pp. 1029–47.

Schuster, M., Kaspin, J. A. and Miller, C. S. *The Age Discrimination in Employment Act: an Evaluation of Federal and State Enforcement, Legal Processes and Employer Compliance. A Final Report to the AARP Andrus Foundation* (Syracuse, NY, 1989).

Scientific American, vol. 11, no. 2, Summer 2000.

Scrutton, S. 'Ageism: the Foundations of Age Discrimination', in E. McEwen (ed.), *Age: the Unrecognised Discrimination* (London, 1990).

Seligman, D. 'The Case for Ageism', *Fortune*, 20 Sept. 1982, p. 47.

Sennett, R. *The Corrosion of Character: The Personal Consequences of Work in the New Capitalism* (New York, NY, 1998).

Shapiro, D. and Sandell, S. H. 'The Reduced Pay of Older Job Losers: Age Discrimination and Other Explanations', in S. H. Sandell (ed.), *The Problem Isn't Age. Work and Older Americans* (New York, NY, 1987).

Shaw, L. B. 'Special Problems of Older Women Workers', in M. E. Borus, H. S. Parnes, S. H. Sandell and B. Seidman (eds.), *The Older Worker* (Madison, WI, 1988).

Sheldon, J. H. *The Social Medicine of Old Age. Report of an Inquiry in Wolverhampton* (London, 1948).

'The Role of the Aged in Modern Society', *British Medical Journal*, 11 Feb. 1950, pp. 319–23.

'The Social Philosophy of Old Age', in *Old Age in the Modern World. Report of the Third Congress of the International Association of Gerontology, London 1954* (Edinburgh, 1955).

Sheldon, T. A. and Maynard, A. 'Is Rationing Inevitable?', in British Medical Journal, *Rationing In Action* (London, 1993).

Shenfield, B. E. *Social Policies for Old Age. A Review of Social Provision for Old Age in Great Britain* (London, 1957).

Sheppard, H. 'Work and Retirement', in R. H. Binstock and E. Shanas (eds.), *Handbook of Aging and the Social Sciences* (New York, NY, 1976).

Sher, G. 'Ancient Wrongs and Modern Rights', in P. Laslett and J. S. Fishkin (eds.), *Justice between Age Groups and Generations* (New Haven, CT, 1992).

Shock, N. W. 'Older People and Their Potentialities for Gainful Employment', *Journal of Gerontology*, vol. 2, no. 2, April 1947, pp. 93–102.

A Classified Bibliography of Gerontology and Geriatrics (Stanford, CA, 1951).

Trends in Gerontology (Stanford, CA, 1951).

Siegel, J. S. *A Generation of Change. A Profile of America's Older Population* (New York, NY, 1993).

Simplicity, Security and Choice: Working and Saving for Retirement, Cm. 5677, Dec. 2002.

Slater, R. 'Age Discrimination', *New Society*, 10 May 1973, pp. 301–2.

Social Insurance and Allied Services, Cmd. 6404, 1942.

'Social Security in Review', *Social Security Bulletin*, vol. 8, no. 2, Feb. 1945, pp. 1–2.

Sontag, S. 'The Double Standard of Aging', in V. Carver and P. Liddiard (eds.), *An Ageing Population. A Reader and Sourcebook* (Sevenoaks, 1978).

Sowell, T. *Markets and Minorities* (Oxford, 1981).

Spencer, S. and Fredman, S. *Age Equality Comes of Age. Delivering Change for Older People* (London, 2003).

Squirer, L. W. *Old Age Dependency in the United States: a Complete Survey of the Pension Movement* (New York, NY, 1912).

Stahl, S. M. and Feller, J. R. 'Old Equals Sick: an Ontogenetic Fallacy', in S. M. Stahl (ed.), *The Legacy of Longevity. Health and Health Care in Later Life* (Newbury Park, CA, 1990).

State of California, Department of Employment and Citizens' Advisory Committee on Aging, *A Survey of the Employment of Older Workers – 1964. A Report to the California Legislature, 1965 Session* (Sacramento, CA, 1965).

'Staying Power', *Guardian*, 13 April 1999.

Stead, W. H. 'Trends of Employment in Relation to the Problem of Aging', *Journal of Gerontology*, vol. 4, no. 4, Oct. 1949, pp. 290–7.

Stecker, M. L. 'Beneficiaries Prefer to Work', *Social Security Bulletin*, vol. 14, no. 1, Jan. 1951, pp. 15–17.

Steiner, P. O. and Dorfman, R. *The Economic Status of the Aged* (Berkeley, CA, 1957).

Stieglitz, E. J. 'Orientation', in E. J. Stieglitz (ed.), *Geriatric Medicine: Diagnosis and Management of Disease in the Aging and in the Aged* (Philadelphia, PA, 1941).

Stockman, D. A. *The Triumph of Politics* (London, 1986).

'The Story of AARP', *Modern Maturity*, Aug.–Sept. 1974, pp. 55–62.

Straka, J. W. *The Demand for Older Workers: the Neglected Side of a Labor Market* (Washington, DC, 1991).

'Supplement', *British Medical Journal*, 11 Dec. 1886.

Sutton, G. C. 'Will You Still Need Me, Will You Still Screen Me, When I'm Past 64?', *British Medical Journal*, vol. 315, 25 October 1997, pp. 1032–3.

Suzman, R. M., Manton, K. G. and Willis, D. P. 'Introducing the Oldest Old', in R. M. Suzman, D. P. Willis and K. G. Manton (eds.), *The Oldest Old* (New York, NY, 1992).

Szafran, J. and Welford, A. T. 'On the Problem of Generalised Occupational Transfer Effects in Relation to Studies of Ageing', *Quarterly Journal of Experimental Psychology*, vol. 1, pt. 4, Oct. 1949, pp. 160–6.

Taylor, P. and Walker, A. *Too Old at 50? Age Discrimination in the Labour Market* (London, 1991).

'The Employment of Older Workers in Five European Countries', in Institute of Personnel Management, *Age and Employment. Policies, Attitudes and Practices* (London, 1993).

'Intergenerational Relations in the Labour Market: the Attitudes of Employers and Older Workers', in A. Walker (ed.), *The New Generational Contract: Intergenerational Relations, Old Age and Welfare* (London, 1996).

'Teen Drivers Face Half Pint Limit', *Guardian*, 2 Jan. 2001.

Thane, P. *Old Age in English History. Past Experiences, Present Issues* (Oxford, 2000).

Thatcher, R. 'Trends and Prospects at Very High Ages', in J. Charlton and M. Murphy (eds.), *The Health of Adult Britain 1841–1994 Vol. 2* (London, 1997).

Thewlis, M. W. *Geriatrics: a Treatise on Senile Conditions, Diseases of Advanced Life, and Care of the Aged* (St Louis, IL, 1919).

Thomas, G. *The Employment of Older Persons* (UK Social Survey Report, London, 1947).

Thomas, G. and Osborne, B. *Older People and Their Employment* (UK Social Survey Report, London, 1951).

Thompson, W. E., Streib, G. F. and Kosa, J. 'The Effect of Retirement on Personal Adjustment', *Journal of Gerontology*, vol. 15, no. 2, April 1960, pp. 165–9.

Thoms, W. E. and Dooley, F. J. *Airline Labor Law: The Railway Labor Act and Aviation After Deregulation* (Westport, CN, 1990).

Thoms, W. J. *Human Longevity. Its Facts and Its Fictions* (London, 1873).

Thomson, A. P. 'Problems of Ageing and Chronic Sickness', *British Medical Journal*, 30 July 1949, pp. 243–50.

'Problems of Ageing and Chronic Sickness', *British Medical Journal*, 6 Aug. 1949, pp. 300–5.

Thomson, D. *Selfish Generations? How Welfare States Grow Old* (Cambridge, 1991).

Thurow, L. C. 'Generational Equity and the Birth of a Revolutionary Class', in J. B. Williamson, D. M. Watts-Roy and E. R. Kingson (eds.), *The Generational Equity Debate* (New York, NY, 1999).

Tibbitts, C. 'Retirement Problems in American Society', *American Journal of Sociology*, vol. LIX, no. 4, Jan. 1954, pp. 301–8.

Titley, J. *Health Care Rights for Older People. The Ageism Issue* (London, 1997).

Titmuss, R. M. 'Pension Systems and Population Change', in R. M. Titmuss, *Essays on 'The Welfare State'* (London, 1958).

'Social Administration in a Changing Society', in R. M. Titmuss, *Essays on 'The Welfare State'* (London, 1958).

Toossi, M. 'A Century of Change: the US Labor Force, 1950–2050', *Monthly Labor Review*, vol. 125, no. 5, May 2002, pp. 15–28.

Townsend, P. *The Family Life of Old People. An Inquiry in East London* (London, 1957; 1963 edn).

Townsend, P. and Wedderburn, D. *The Aged in the Welfare State* (London, 1965).

Tuckman, J. and Lorge, I. 'Attitudes Toward Old People', *Journal of Social Psychology*, vol. 37, May 1953, pp. 249–60.

Turner, B. S. 'Aging and Identity: Some Reflections on the Somatization of the Self', in M. Featherstone and A. Wernick (eds.), *Images of Aging: Cultural Representations of Later Life* (London, 1995).

Twenty Years of the Age Discrimination in Employment Act: Success or Failure? Hearings Before the Special Committee on Aging, United States Senate, September 10 1987 (Washington, DC, 1988).

Twomey, B. 'Disability and the Labour Market: Results from the Summer 2000 LFS', *Labour Market Trends*, vol. 109, no. 5, May 2001, pp. 241–51.

Uchitelle, L. and Kleinfield, N. R. 'The Price of Jobs Lost', in The New York Times, *The Downsizing of America* (New York, NY, 1996).

US Bureau of the Census, *Statistical Abstract of the United States: 1976* (Washington, DC, 1976).

US Census Bureau, *Statistical Abstract of the United States: 1999* (Washington, DC, 2001).

Statistical Abstract of the United States: 2001 (Washington, DC, 2001).

US Commission on Civil Rights, *The Age Discrimination Study* (Washington, DC, 1977).

US Department of Commerce and US Bureau of the Census, *Historical Statistics of the United States. Colonial Times to 1970, Part 1* (Washington, DC, 1975).

US Department of Labor, *The Older American Worker. Age Discrimination in Employment. Report of the Secretary of Labor to the Congress Under Section 715 of the Civil Rights Act of 1964* (Washington, DC, 1965).

US Equal Employment Opportunity Commission, *Legislative History of the Age Discrimination in Employment Act* (Washington, DC, 1981).

Annual Report 1995 (Washington, DC, 1995).

US Equal Employment Opportunity Commission. Technical Assistance Program, *Age Discrimination* (Washington, DC, 1995).

Theories of Discrimination. Intentional and Unintentional Employment Discrimination (Washington, DC, 1995).

Van Atta, D. *Trust Betrayed: Inside the AARP* (Washington, DC, 1998).

Ventrell-Monsees, C. 'How Useful Are Legislative Remedies: America's Experience with the ADEA', *Aging International*, vol. XX, no. 3, Sept. 1993, pp. 41–5.

Verbrugge, L. M. 'Longer Life But Worsening Health? Trends in Health and Mortality of Middle-aged and Older Persons', *Milbank Memorial Fund Quarterly/Health and Society*, vol. 62, no. 3, 1984, pp. 475–519.

'Recent, Present and Future Health of American Adults', in L. Breslow, J. E. Fielding and L. B. Lave (eds.), *Annual Review of Public Health*, vol. 10, 1989, pp. 333–61.

'The Iceberg of Disability', in S. M. Stahl (ed.), *The Legacy of Longevity. Health and Health Care in Later Life* (Newbery Park, CA, 1990).

Victor, C. R. *Health and Health Care in Later Life* (Milton Keynes, 1991).

Vincent, J. *Inequality and Old Age* (London, 1995).

Waggaman, M. T. 'Improved Employment Situation of Older Workers', *Monthly Labor Review*, vol. 54, no. 1, Jan. 1942, pp. 59–69.

'Older Workers in Wartime', *Monthly Labor Review*, vol. 59, no. 1, July 1944, pp. 24–38.

Waidmann, T., Bound, J. and Schoenbaum, M. 'The Illusion of Failure: Trends in the Self-Reported Health of the US Elderly', *Milbank Quarterly*, vol. 73, no. 2, 1995, pp. 253–87.

Walker, A. 'The Benefits of Old Age? Age Discrimination and Social Security', in E. McEwen (ed.), *Age: the Unrecognised Discrimination* (London, 1990).

'Intergenerational Relations and the Provision of Welfare', in A. Walker (ed.), *The New Generational Contract: Intergenerational Relations, Old Age and Welfare* (London, 1996).

'Older People and Health Services. The Challenge of Empowerment', in M. Purdy and D. Banks (eds.), *Health and Exclusion. Policy and Practice in Health Provision* (London, 1999).

Walker, A. and Maltby, T. *Ageing Europe* (Buckingham, 1997).

Wall, R. 'Intergenerational Relationships Past and Present', in A. Walker (ed.), *The New Generational Contract: Intergenerational Relations, Old Age and Welfare* (London, 1996).

Walters, W. 'The "Active Society": New Designs for Social Policy', *Policy and Politics*, vol. 25, no. 3, July 1997, pp. 221–34.

'Warning! Ageism at Work', *Guardian*, 2 Mar. 1996.

Warr, P. and Pennington, J. 'Views About Age Discrimination and Older Workers', in Institute of Personnel Management, *Age and Employment. Policies, Attitudes and Practices* (London, 1993).

Warren, M. 'Activity in Advancing Years', *British Medical Journal*, 21 Oct. 1950, pp. 921–4.

Warthin, A. S. *Old Age, the Major Involution: the Physiology and Pathology of the Aging Process* (New York, NY, 1929).

Watson, A. W. *An Account of an Investigation of the Sickness and Mortality Experience of the I.O.O.F. Manchester Unity During the Five Years 1893–1897* (Manchester, 1903).

Weaver, C. L. *The Crisis in Social Security. Economic and Political Origins* (Durham, NC, 1982).

Webster, C. *The Health Services Since the War, Vol. I. Problems of Health Care. The National Health Service Before 1957* (London, 1988).

'The Elderly and the Early National Health Service', in M. Pelling and R. M. Smith (eds.), *Life, Death and the Elderly* (London, 1991).

Weir, N. U. and Dennis, M. S. 'Meeting the Challenge of Stroke', *Scottish Medical Journal*, vol. 42, no. 5, October 1997, pp. 145–7.

Welford, A. T. *Skill and Age. An Experimental Approach* (London, 1951).

'Extending the Employment of Older People', *British Medical Journal*, 28 Nov. 1953, pp. 1193–7.

Wentworth, E. C. 'Why Beneficiaries Retire', *Social Security Bulletin*, vol. 8, no. 1, Jan. 1945, pp. 16–20.

Wermel, M. T. and Gelbaum, S. 'Work and Retirement in Old Age', *American Journal of Sociology*, vol. LI, no. 1, July 1945, pp. 16–21.

Wilkinson, R. G. *Unhealthy Societies. The Afflictions of Inequality* (London, 1996).

Willetts, D. *The Age of Entitlement* (London, 1993).

Williams, A. 'Intergenerational Equity: an Exploration of the "Fair Innings" Argument', *Health Economics*, vol. 6, no. 2, Mar.–Apr. 1997, pp. 117–32.

'Rationing Health Care by Age: the Case For', in B. New (ed.), *Rationing: Talk and Action in Health Care* (London, 1997).

'Economics, QALYs and Medical Ethics: a Health Economist's Perspective', in S. Dracopoulou (ed.), *Ethics and Values in Health Care Management* (New York, NY, 1998).

Williamson, J. B. and Watts-Roy, D. M. 'Framing the Generational Equity Debate', in J. B. Williamson, D. M. Watts-Roy and E. R. Kingson (eds.), *The Generational Equity Debate* (New York, NY, 1999).

Wilmoth, J. R. and Horiuchi, S. 'Rectangularisation Revisited: Variability of Age at Death Within Human Populations', *Demography*, vol. 36, no. 4, Nov. 1999, pp. 475–95.

Wilson, H. *Purpose in Politics* (London, 1964).

Wilson, W. J. *The Truly Disadvantaged: the Inner City, the Underclass and Public Policy* (Chicago, 1987).

Wise, D. A. 'Retirement Against the Demographic Trend: More Older People Living Longer, Working Less, and Saving Less', *Demography*, vol. 34, no. 1, Feb. 1997, pp. 83–95.

Wolfe, B. L. and Haveman, R. 'Trends in the Prevalence of Work Disability from 1962 to 1984, and Their Correlates', *Milbank Quarterly*, vol. 68, no. 1, 1990, pp. 53–80.

Worcester, A. *The Care of the Aged, the Dying and the Dead* (Springfield, IL, 1935).

Worsley, R. *Age and Employment. Why Employers Should Think Again About Older Workers* (London, 1996).

'Left Out of Things for Ages', *Guardian*, 2 Mar. 1996.

'The Generation Game', *The Bookseller*, 8 Mar. 1996, pp. 36–7.

Yeandle, S. *Personal Histories: the Context for Joblessness, Disability and Retirement* (Sheffield, 1999).

Yelin, E. H. 'The Recent History and Immediate Future of Employment Among Persons with Disabilities', *Milbank Quarterly*, vol. 69, supplements 1/2, 1991, pp. 129–49.

Yelin, E. H. and Katz, P. P. 'Making Work More Central to Work Disability Policy', *Milbank Quarterly*, vol. 72, no. 4, 1994, pp. 593–619.

Young, M. and Schuller, T. *Life After Work. The Arrival of the Ageless Society* (London, 1991).

Index

Page numbers in italics refer to tables and figures.